CONTEMPORARY INFLUENCES IN EARLY CHILDHOOD EDUCATION

CONTEMPORARY INFLUENCES IN EARLY CHILDHOOD EDUCATION

ELLIS D. EVANS
University of Washington

With an introduction to the Early Childhood Education Series
by Celia Lavatelli, University of Illinois

HOLT, RINEHART AND WINSTON, INC.
New York   Chicago   San Francisco   Atlanta
Dallas   Montreal   Toronto   London   Sydney

372.21
E 92

Copyright © 1971 by Holt, Rinehart and Winston, Inc.
Library of Congress Catalog Card Number 77–135131
SBN: 03–081410–3
Printed in the United States of America
2 3 4 5 6 7 8 9 22 1

For my daughters,
JENNIFER and ALICIA,
who were the inspiration
for this book and who
continue to bring to life
the beauty of early childhood

Introduction

Early Childhood Education Series

More than any other decade in American history, the sixties might be called the Decade of Early Childhood Education. Interest in and activity concerning the young child were sparked by the exciting idea that early human development is plastic and can be altered in significant ways. In particular, the notion that mental growth is cumulative and that later development of intelligence depends in part upon early intellectual stimulation led to the emergence of a cognitive emphasis in early education, an emphasis that attracted educational psychologists to the scene. The educational psychologists attacked the "child-development"–based type of nursery-school program with its strong emphasis on social–emotional development through play and the creative arts, and argued instead for a systematic, structural approach to cognitive development. The child-development school drew upon the newer theoretical framework to defend its programs; its advocates pointed out the value of play and the creative arts for cognitive growth. They also began to search for ways to use play more explicitly for development of concepts of number, space, time, matter, and causality, in line with development as described by Piaget.

The controversy is still far from being resolved, but it is safe to predict for the seventies that some of the very extreme, even bizarre programs on both sides of the continuum will disappear. Educational psychologists will discover that "learning is child's play," as one writer has phrased it, and child developmentalists will recognize the need for some structuring for maximum cognitive effectiveness. Hopefully, both schools will recognize the affective and social determinants of learning, often lost sight of while controversy between different schools of thought raged. Hopefully, too, the tight, rigidly scheduled programs of the traditional kindergarten and primary grades with their emphasis upon workbooks, seat-work, show-and-tell, and other teacher-dominated activities will also be modified.

If progress is made in this decade, it will be due in large part to the extraordinary amount of recent research to determine which environmental correlates, including special educational programs, accelerate or retard development. Teachers and teachers-in-training need to be aware of the antecedent conditions of a given state of development. One still hears all too often the argument in justification of a program, "But the children love it," as if children instinctively like that which is good for them and dislike that which is bad. Only as teachers can evaluate the theory and research findings in early childhood education will they be able to protect children against inevitable faddists.

The Holt, Rinehart and Winston Series in Early Childhood Education is designed to present in readable fashion what the state of the art is with respect to some of the continuing problems in early childhood education.

The treatments will be scholarly and practical. Each book will review pertinent research findings and present practices and describe promising trends in the field. In my opinion, it should make a uniquely positive contribution to early childhood education for years to come.

Urbana, Illinois   Celia Lavatelli
October 1970

Preface

The subject of *Contemporary Influences in Early Childhood Education* is preprimary educational programs; the focus is upon broad educational strategies variously applicable to children ages three to six. My main purpose for writing this book is to communicate to readers the great variety in educational and psychological thinking about young children as we enter the 1970s. Therefore, I have generally attempted to distill the conceptual bases of early education strategies in order to clarify their unique and common features. Inevitably, there are risks involved in any individual author's treatment of such strategies. For example, there is the risk that some very important programs and influences may inadvertently be excluded from the discussion. Space limitations also represent a frustrating obstacle for an author. Failure to mention a given program should not be taken to indicate a personal disregard for it. Discussion is limited also to comparatively formal educational programs not ordinarily considered under the rubric of *day care* for young children. It is true, however, that in practice there is often very little to distinguish comprehensive day-care programs from many nursery schools in this country.

In addition to a distillation of early education program components, I have attempted to maintain a consistent research perspective. The frame of reference for discussion has been empirical wherever possible. My decision to draw heavily upon empirical investigations in early childhood education was made with full recognition that some readers may not be familiar with the style and technical details of research activity. It is conceivable that some readers may wish to skip the segments of the book that concern research reviews. If so, I trust that such readers will not disregard the importance of children's measured behavior changes as a criterion for program validity.

Although it is likely that I have overlooked useful research reports, the data introduced in this book are representative and current as of early 1970. Important new research findings are certain to be reported in the early childhood literature before this book is published. Accordingly, persons interested in the accumulation of documentative evidence for various educational programs are encouraged to update the research discussed herein.

Finally, I have attempted to couch much of my commentary in terms of issues that are basic to strategies for early childhood education, both individually and collectively. Many of these issues are particularly acute in relation to compensatory education. None is easily resolved. As the reader will see, these variously complex issues are largely grounded in educational philosophy, psychological theory, and sociocultural values and ethics.

I wish to express my gratitude to several persons who have made substantial and unique contributions to this writing project. Any success for this book will also be their success; however, the author takes sole responsibility for any of the book's deficiencies. First, my wife Cindy has been a faithful and patient helper; it is with much love that I acknowledge her encouragement and emotional support. Boyd R. McCandless has provided me with innumerable suggestions, constructive criticisms, and major insights. Celia Lavatelli has helped me to sharpen the precision and accuracy of my writing in important ways. Valuable feedback on individual chapters has been supplied by several friends and colleagues, including Margo Fitzgerald, Mary Ann Hauck, Norris Haring, and Margaret Johnston. In addition I very much appreciate the assistance of J. Myron Atkin, Roland Barth, Helen Bee, Margaret Bland, David Boynton, Bettye Caldwell, Jessica Daniel, Marie Hughes, Constance Kamii, Harold Kunzelmann, Glen Nimnicht, Halbert Robinson, Bruce Rusk, David Weikart, Aline Wolf, and students of early childhood education at the University of Washington.

Seattle, Washington   Ellis D. Evans
October 1970

Contents

7

The British Infant School Movement and Miscellaneous Programs

8

Major Issues Revisited

CONTEMPORARY
INFLUENCES
IN EARLY CHILDHOOD
EDUCATION

1
Psychology and Early Childhood Education: A Brief Perspective

INTRODUCTION

The 1960s will undoubtedly be marked by historians-at-large as a decade of Vietnam conflict, political assassinations, urban crises, student dissent, and moon walks. Less sensational, but perhaps as significant in its own way, has been a psychological and educational renaissance with respect to infant and early childhood development. To be sure, many of the seeds of this renaissance have been sown for years. They have lain fallow, however, until a mixture of ingredients (political, social, economic, behavioral science research, and the like) seemingly jelled during the past several years to regenerate their growth potential. There is no dearth of descriptive analyses of this jelling process (for

1

example, Senn, 1969; Shane, 1969; Gordon, 1968). In fact, the literature on early childhood learning, development, and education is growing at an unparalleled rate. Fortunately, this growth has not been totally haphazard. Certain patterns have developed, most of which can now be identified as having made more viable society's thinking about early childhood. These patterns include new conceptions of the nature of psychological development during infancy (Kessen, 1963), an overhaul of concepts of human motivation (White, 1959), creative insights into the thought processes of children and the variables that affect them (Piaget, 1961), greater understanding of learning patterns (especially language) associated with social class variation (Bernstein, 1961), the effects of early stimulation on brain structure and chemistry (Kresh, 1969), an apparent shift in child-rearing practices to include a greater emphasis upon children's achievement training (Bronfenbrenner, 1961), and data from the study of intelligence (Scott and Ball, 1965). These and other factors have combined to create an unprecedented concern for children's *cognition,* or the ways in which children acquire and utilize knowledge and thinking skills.

Illustrative of the chain of psychological developments which has extended into the realm of cognitive enrichment and education for young children is the work of psychologist William Fowler. Fowler's first major treatment of early childhood was an analytic review (Fowler, 1962) of the gaps in our understanding of early cognitive learning and the reason for these gaps. Data synthesized in this review led Fowler to several important conclusions. Among them was that the potential of the preschool years for cognitive education, based upon what evidence can be gleaned from the literature, may be employed much more advantageously than it has in the past. (Whether the preschool years *should be* used for this purpose is, of course, a philosophical issue.) A second conclusion was addressed to the possibility that the early years, as compared to later in the development cycle, are better for the establishment of conceptual learning sets, interests, and habit patterns; early learning is assumed to facilitate positively that which occurs later.[1]

Fowler's elaborate review has since been followed by a general proposal to promote early conceptual learning based upon reality structures and learning sequences appropriate to the cognitive abilities of preschoolers (Fowler, 1965). This proposal is strongly addressed to the task of devising sequential levels of complexity which lead from perception to classification (conceptual) activities. Fowler's general teaching strategy requires the establishment of an atmosphere of "play-game activi-

[1] A concrete manifestation of Fowler's orientation is his study of process variables relevant to a two-year-old learning to read (Fowler, 1962b).

ties" coordinated with the problem-solving capacity of children. A further elaboration of this cognitive-stimulation model is a developmental curriculum for disadvantaged children (Fowler, 1966). The main features of this model include psychocognitive diagnosis procedures and the precise programming and pacing of stimulation sequences.

Fowler's work is cited primarily as an example of a growing commitment to the value of promoting early cognitive development in systematic ways. This commitment represents a shift away from more traditional emphasis in nursery school (and in kindergarten to some extent) upon social-emotional development. Such a shift is indicated in many ways, including statements from high-level professional organizations. Consider, for example, the following excerpt from the introductory statement of the influential Educational Policies Commission (1966) in a document entitled, *Universal Opportunity for Early Childhood Education:*

> The development of intellectual ability and of intellectual interest is fundamental to the achievement of all the goals of American education. Yet these qualities are greatly affected by what happens to children before they reach school. A growing body of research and experience demonstrates that by the age of six most children have already developed a considerable part of the intellectual ability they will possess as adults. Six is now generally accepted as the normal age of entrance to school. We believe this practice is obsolete. All children should have the opportunity to go to school at public expense beginning at the age of four. [p. 1]

While the recent EPC recommendations have not by any means delegated emotional development to a subsidiary role, a concern for children's intellectual life is clear. The above quotation is based upon the assumption that earlier school experience will result in greater intellectual gain than is otherwise likely; support for this assumption has been induced largely from data supplied by developmental psychology research. Examples of such data are those synthesized by Hunt (1961) and Bloom (1964). The former has integrated classical and new data from the study of intellectual development and its measurement in ways that permit a reinterpretation of the concept of intelligence. Basically, Hunt's thesis is a challenge to the notion that intelligence is fixed or predetermined by genetic forces. Rather, Hunt views intelligence as a network of central neural processes and information processing strategies, the quality of which is affected significantly by the kinds of encounters a child has with his environment. Bloom's (1964) summary and analysis of longitudinal data concerning intelligence has led to the inference that the *rate* of intellectual development is at its point of highest acceleration during the early years. Bloom couples this inference with the general idea that growth variables are most affected by environmental intrusions during their period of most rapid acceleration. Therefore, it is argued that the greatest payoff from environmental stimulation, in terms of intellectual growth, will come through experiences for children in the first four to six years of life. This thinking is, of course, fraught with problems and issues, descriptions of which lurk in the chapters to follow. Further, not all authorities are convinced of the evidence upon which these inferences and implications are based (Foster, 1967).

As social change, psychological and educational controversies, and new insights into child development continue to affect our thinking, children also continue to grow, to be socialized, and to be educated for better or worse. The influences which are currently being applied and tested within early childhood education variously imply dissatisfactions among "experts" with the ways in which society, particularly educators, has been operating in the past. Consider, for example, the spectre of challenge created by authorities who are convinced that kindergarten is "too late" for children to achieve their maximum potential (Edwards, 1968).

For a broader perspective within which to examine issues and problems associated with the design of early educational environments, consider next a brief overview of kindergarten-nursery education in the United States. This overview is followed by a summary of major educational and psychological issues. An explication of these issues hopefully will assist the reader toward a frame of reference relevant to the entire book.

KINDERGARTEN

History

The tap roots of contemporary early childhood education extend clearly to European thinkers such as J. A. Comenius (1592–1670), J. J. Rousseau (1712–1778), and J. H. Pestalozzi (1746–1827), all of whom championed the rights of children. But it was out of the chaotic life of Frederick Froebel (1782–1852) that came perhaps the first solidified approach to the education of young children. Froebel's attention to the "preschool child" and the training of young, single women to teach young children mark his contributions of lasting importance.

Having derived his educational principals from the observation of children, Froebel formulated a philosophy built upon the spontaneous, self-sustaining nature of children. Play and the cultivations of children's spiritual feelings were considered to be paramount. Then-unfamiliar educational materials, such as geometric blocks used to teach form and number concepts, musical activities, and games systematized through play, constituted the core of Froebel's kindergarten.[2] What Froebel contended to be the child's "natural tendency" to play and dance in circles with other children was capitalized upon for the purpose of cultivating the child's imagination.

Froebel's child-centered orientation has persisted among his successors and provides, at least in theory, the backbone of modern nursery and kindergarten practices. It was not, however, until several years after Froebel's death that the concept of kindergarten as a matter of regular public school experience was formalized.

A primary agent in this formalization was Susan Blow (1843–1916), whose early educational experiments at the kindergarten level took place in St. Louis, Missouri, shortly after the Civil War. Susan Blow's ideas were tailored directly from the Froebellian approach—most particularly the elements of spontaneous self-activity and specific curricular activities advocated by Froebel. Shortly after the Missouri experiments, a department of kindergarten was established by the National Education Association (1874).[3] This move was followed by a significant NEA recommendation that kindergarten programs be included as a regular part of the public school enterprise. As the thinking of John Dewey (1859–1952) gathered support around the turn of the century, philosophical and pedagogical controversy over the purpose and content of kindergarten programs became strikingly apparent. Among the major figures involved were Dewey himself, Patty Smith Hall (a translator of Dewey's ideas into kindergarten-primary grade experiences), Susan Blow, a scattering of Montessori followers (see Chapter 2), and others. In retrospect, this early controversy seems to have anticipated that which currently flourishes in this country with respect to the content and nature of early childhood education.

Contemporary Status, Objectives, and Curriculum Patterns

In the United States a kindergarten program is generally restricted to five-year-old children who spend eight to ten months in activities which precede formal academic work (first grade). Most are set up for half-

---

[2] Kindergarten is the German word for "garden of children" and thus portrays the original analogy of children as garden plants to be carefully nurtured.

[3] Earlier programs were evident in the United States, although they were essentially private operations. An exception was a brief experience with public school kindergarten in Boston (1870).

day sessions. Not all school systems in this country support kindergartens, however, and severe restrictions on kindergarten offerings exist in others. Despite this, survey data illustrate a remarkable increase in the number of eligible children enrolled in public kindergartens during the past several decades. In 1949, for example, 960,000 children were official kindergarten participants. By 1966, over 2.4 million kindergarten enrollees were reported (Ream, 1968). In 1968, this figure had reached 3.1 million (Nehrt and Hurd, 1969). This massive increase must be considered in relation to the number of children found in any given classroom, for overloading is generally considered detrimental to program quality.[4] Large (over thirty) classes of children are directly antithetical to the principle of individual differentiation so basic to general kindergarten philosophy. That the enrollment fort is being held reasonably well is indicated by an average of twenty-six children per class in the kindergartens of some 1100 school systems (Ream, 1969).

Objectives of the kindergarten vary in their specific terminology but generally converge upon broad dimensions of growth including sociability, aesthetics, sensory-motor development, and achievement motivation. Headley (1965), for example, suggests that the function of the kindergarten is to assist the child toward the following objectives:

> Friendliness and helpfulness in relationships with other children
> Greater power to solve problems based in individual activities and
>   group relationships
> Respect for the rights, property, and contributions of other children
> Responsiveness to intellectual challenge
> Achievement of good sensory-motor coordination
> Understanding of concepts necessary for the continued pursuit
>   of learning
> Responsiveness to beauty in all forms
> Realization of individuality and creative propensities

The breadth and abstractness of these goals permit countless programmatic variations.[5] Thus, perhaps the most unifying aspect of kindergarten programs is the commitment among the personnel who man them to the positive and total growth of children. This includes a firm belief in the need for a benevolent and responsive learning environ-

[4] Most authorities agree that a reasonable class limit is around twenty-five children. This writer has witnessed classes as large as forty, however, and even larger classes may occasionally be observed. Teacher shortage and financial handicaps are usually the contributing factors.

[5] Variation in content and quality, if nothing else, may be implied by statistics relevant to per pupil expenditures in kindergarten. In 1967–1968, the average cost per pupil ranged from $150 to $800 per academic year (Ream, 1969).

ment. Another broadly unifying feature is that, unlike nursery school operations in many states, certification standards apply to kindergarten teaching. These requirements include special course work related to child development and practice teaching under supervision. Certification is believed to increase the probability that minimum technical skills are developed by teachers prior to actual kindergarten service. Society has no guarantee, however, that all kindergarten teachers will be personally suited to work effectively with young children. The most obviously maladjusted prospective teachers are usually prevented from entering the classroom, but screening procedures in teacher education generally are woefully inadequate. This issue, is, of course, made manifestly complicated by (1) slow strides among educators toward a definition of the "effective" teacher and (2) a dearth of valid measurement devices to detect unsuitable candidates.

The general activities prescribed by kindergarten curricula, while remarkably similar from one school district to another, seem to vary in the degree of emphasis placed upon pre-academic training (specific academic "readiness" building) and the degree to which evaluation procedures are implemented. According to Headley (1965), roughly 40 to 50 percent of a typical kindergarten day is usually devoted to specific creative activities (art work, model building, and so on), music (singing, listening, and rhythmic activities), and language-based activities (story listening and telling, poetry, "group discussion" such as show and tell, and question-answer activities). The remaining time is distributed among self-care, free play, and rest periods. The flexibility of a kindergarten curriculum, however, enables a good teacher to infuse daily activities with ample doses of basic language, mathematical, science, and social studies concepts if she so desires. In fact, both the nursery school and kindergarten settings provide an extensive opportunity for a teacher to "do her own thing," at least by comparison to most upper grades, where parameters are typically firmer. This freedom could simultaneously represent a boon and a hazard to young children. Nevertheless, the development of a positive attitude toward learning which will serve as a foundation for future school learning is seen as a central concern. Curriculum flexibility would seem to enhance progress toward this goal.[6]

Close examination of any kindergarten curriculum usually will reveal a potpourri of materials and techniques that can best be described as *eclectic;* that is, combinations of activities that may transcend a given philosophy or theory of educational psychology. In other words, unlike

[6] See Mager (1969) for a specific treatment of this objective.

most approaches to early childhood education to be examined in this book, the kindergarten concept as it is applied in the public schools does not necessarily imply an articulated psychology or philosophy of growth. And substantial use is made of commercial materials prepared for widespread consumption which still reflect, among others, the influence of Froebel and Montessori.[7]

This apparent eclecticism prevents one from making neat categorizations of programs although some writers (for example, Davis, 1963) maintain that broad differences in kindergarten-primary curriculum patterns may be identified. One such pattern, according to Davis, is based upon the *socialization* theory of instruction. The socialization pattern invests its energies primarily in the child's social behavior and development. Responsible group interaction, activities built from the interests of children, a permissive learning environment, social adjustment, and free play are among the basic guidelines for this approach. A second theme, the *developmental pattern,* is based upon "levels of experiences that permit growth to proceed at its normal rate and direction." (Davis, 1963, p. 35). Maturational readiness is duly considered within this pattern, with education primarily geared to assist the child toward an understanding of himself and his world. A recognition of children's self-regulatory mechanisms of learning and growth leads developmental educators to encourage self-selection and self-pacing for children's educational activities. It is from within this pattern that the now-familiar plea for "education of the whole child" is strongly heard. A third blueprint for curriculum organization is based upon the *instructional pattern.* It is this pattern which emphasizes the selection and sequencing of subject matter content. Language and sensory-motor skills are singled out for major attention, although this does not exclude a concern for the child's socio-emotional life. Mainly it is a matter of viewing content (ideas and skill-building activities) as the best nutrient for total growth.

As Davis suggests, most kindergarten programs probably represent a fusion of all patterns. Variation is most likely a function of individual teachers' philosophies and competencies. Kindergarten curriculum development has been plagued, however, with a persistent problem,

---

[7] No attempt will be made to itemize and classify these materials, although it should be kept in mind that the quality of learning outcomes in kindergarten is usually directly related to the quality and sequencing of materials used. Examples of the newer materials which are receiving close attention are the Science Research Associates (SRA) Mathematics Program, the AAAS Science Program, the Initial Teaching Alphabet Program (an augmented Roman alphabet program known as i/t/a, used for beginning reading), Words-in-Color, and others. Most are still being researched. See Williams (1965) and Leiderman (1965).

namely, the problem of intellectual content (Robison and Spodek, 1965). Childhood educators who are content-oriented seem to have been viewed with suspicion by those who feel such an emphasis implies a priority higher than children themselves. It is a shift to content consideration that signifies part of the current revolution in early childhood education. This will become increasingly clear in the succeeding pages of this book.

Perhaps anticipating the pressures for substantive reorientation of kindergarten curricula, Robison and Spodek (1965)[8] have recommended a format for kindergarten practice under the flag of "new directions." Basically, these authorities attempt to demonstrate, by specific attention to content and organizational variables, how the substance of a curriculum can be made more commensurate with the needs and cultural backgrounds of today's children. For Robison and Spodek, the selection of content comes from a structural analysis of major disciplines — geography, history, economics, social science, science, and mathematics — whereby pivotal concepts in each are identified and interrelated in the service of economical and permanent learning for children. Only the "big ideas" are brought to kindergarten children. These ideas are translated through concrete, manipulative experiences, dramatic play, and developmental language activities. From this base of "big ideas" children go on to confront hierarchically more complex concepts, generalizations, and principles. This requires of the teacher organizational and long-range planning skills, adeptness in the conducting of guided discovery learning activities, motivational power, and a concept of herself as a resource person — a clarifier of ideas and experience — rather than as one whose function it is to pontificate. As such, this redefined teaching role is technically complex and requires a sound insight into the structure of knowledge and the psychology of learning. The implications of this conceptualization of the teacher have been specified elsewhere (Spodek, 1969).

The impact of positions such as the one above and others (for example, Leeper and others, 1968) on actual kindergarten practice is not easily determined. Printed material such as statements of curriculum theory, program recommendations and innovative ideas abound in the literature. One cannot readily assume that practices "on the firing line" are a direct outgrowth of practices advocated in the literature. We may observe no quarrel with the idea and the general characteristics of good programs for young children. Yet we observe great variations in educators' concepts of specifically what is "good" for children and their skills

[8] These writers have been strongly influenced by Jerome Bruner's *The Process of Education.*

of implementation for early school programs. An exploration of these variations is, of course, a major purpose of this book.

Some of the most current insights into contemporary kindergarten practice are to be found in the extensive survey data of Ream (1969). Ream was provided with information concerning enrollment, administrative policy, financing, and curriculum by some 110 public school districts. Ream reports that where formalized procedures are found in a kindergarten curriculum they are most likely to be associated with number concepts and reading readiness activities. The "exposure to experience" technique, rather than structured methods, is more often preferred for science and social studies. Curriculum areas least frequently included in the kindergartens of these districts were estimated to be language arts, music, and direct reading instruction. Health, physical education, and art activities, in contrast, were reported with great frequency. Over all, Ream's data suggest that most districts lean toward informal learning experiences, a leaning consistent with most traditional views on the functions of kindergarten. One question which immediately looms concerns whether the predominantly informal kindergarten experience makes a real difference in the subsequent academic and motivational development of the child.

Certainly the data above are not inconsistent with the viewpoint of Pratcher (1968), who looks to the kindergarten teacher for a development of "creative patterns of readiness" among children. This would involve, for example, a unification of number readiness, reading readiness, and mature study in the kindergarten setting, where experiences are arranged to allow each child to exercise initiative and originality— *at his own pace.*

Other manifestations of this view are found in materials circulated by the Association for Childhood Education International (Law and others, 1966). Included is a warning of the danger that programs designed with a future orientation may too easily neglect children *as children.* Recommended for kindergarten curricula, therefore, are episodes of integrated experiences—social, aesthetic, emotional, and intellectual—which allow children to follow their natural growth patterns. These sentiments are also endorsed by Leeper and her associates (1968), who view preparatory academics as subservient to the objective of helping children live "fully and richly" *as five-year-olds.* Such an objective would demand of a teacher great skill and knowledge with respect to children's processes of growth and learning. A "full and rich" existence at any one point in time seemingly would require that the child's needs are well met. At least two things are therefore required: (1) valid means for the identification of children's specific needs, including teacher skill in applying these means; and (2) teacher skill in planning and executing activities which in fact meet children's needs. The extent to which practicing kindergarten teachers generally are skillful in these areas is not clearly known, although it is likely that a wide range of individual difference in these skills could be observed.

Evaluative Research

The most typical strategy for kindergarten evaluative research has involved broad comparisons on selected criteria of children who have participated in a kindergarten with children who have not. Outcomes immediately subsequent to the kindergarten experience have most often been assessed, although one occasionally uncovers a study concerned with long-range results. Many reviews of such comparative research have appeared in the literature. Bricker and Lovell (1965), for example, have reviewed the academic and social effects of kindergarten training. A majority of the studies summarized by these writers have dealt with very global behavioral patterns, such as "social adjustment." Several, however, indicate specific favorable outcomes for kindergarten in longer-term reading skills such as improved word recognition, word comprehension, and reading rate. Such data indicate that favorable outcomes can and do occur, but they do not mean that such outcomes necessarily will occur in a given kindergarten setting.

Bricker and Lovell believe that sufficient evidence exists to document with confidence the academic and social advantages of kindergarten education.[9] This confidence is apparently shared by society. No longer does the educational defense of the kindergarten seem to be a serious problem. Yet the absence of kindergarten programs in many school systems and the relatively low priority they apparently carry in others are testimonial to the light regard in which kindergarten is held among some segments of the general public. This light regard may be due, in part, to a general lack of understanding of kindergarten and its important function in a total school curriculum. Further, school programs not clearly subject-matter based, as is often the case with kindergartens, fail to qualify in some quarters as "education." This problem again anticipates a theme which appears in various forms throughout this volume.

[9] These authorities have exercised selectivity in the choice of studies which appear in their review, namely, a showcasing of research which demonstrates the capabilities of well-designed kindergartens for promoting behavior change. Not all comparative studies reveal advantages for kindergarten children, nor do these children all respond favorably to a given program. The issue is not whether kindergarten can make a difference, rather whether kindergarten will.

While general evaluations have treated the kindergarten concept kindly, several tormenting issues are associated with kindergarten practices. One of these has already been mentioned — the issue of intellectual content and its bedmate, academic acceleration. A second involves the search for the most appropriate combination of techniques and materials to accomplish the goals professed by kindergarten educators. This, we shall see, is still another major theme which haunts most early childhood educators. Other psychologically based issues include age of entry to kindergarten (McCandless, 1957), the full-day kindergarten (Gorton and Robinson, 1969), continuous admission plans (Jones, 1969), grouping for individual differences (Harris and Fisher, 1969), the early reader (Durkin, 1966), screening practices (Rogolsky, 1969), readiness for reading (de Hirsch, Jansky, and Langford, 1966), and general school readiness (Ames and Ilg, 1965). Finally, the compartmentalization phenomenon is a persistent problem for which adequate solutions have been slow in coming (Headley, 1965). Compartmentalization refers to a tendency among teachers and curriculum developers to segment or isolate learning experiences both within the kindergarten proper and in relation to the vertical progression of the primary grade curriculum. This problem may be created by a failure or reluctance among some school administrators to consider the kindergarten as an integral part of a total school curriculum.

Greater detail with respect to kindergarten practices, issues, and philosophy is supplied by a prolific kindergarten literature. (See, for example, Pratcher, 1968; Foster and Headley, 1966; Leeper and others, 1968; and Fuller, 1961.)

NURSERY SCHOOLS

History

Nursery school education in the United States has a much more recent history than does the kindergarten. Public nursery schools were first established in 1919 (Mayer, 1960), yet only a handful of nursery schools existed in the early 1920s. The first parent-cooperative nursery of record was that formed by Cambridge, Massachusetts, parents in 1923. With the gathering momentum of the child guidance movement in the late 1920s, nursery schools began to flourish. Several important centers for child study operated model programs, including the Gesell Child Guidance Nursery at Yale University, the Merrill-Palmer Institute in Detroit, Teachers College (Columbia University), and the Iowa Child

Welfare Research Station at the University of Iowa. Emergency legislation during the great depression, subsumed under Franklin Roosevelt's WPA program, created a federal nursery school sponsorship. Further federal subsidization for nursery school education occurred during World War II by way of the famous Lanham Act.[10]

By the mid-1960s close to 700,000 children three to five years of age were officially enrolled in public and private nurseries (excluding day care and Head Start programs) (Schloss, 1967). More recently, Nehrt and Hurd (1969) have placed this figure at 816,000. Although the enrollment continues to rise, it is clear that children's nursery school experiences are not coextensive. Regardless of how one dissects his pie, a piece which clearly symbolizes "the nursery school" cannot be cut. Nursery schools exist on the campuses of colleges and universities, in churches, homes, shopping centers, and civic buildings. Some are commercial; others are nonprofit. Some require professional credentials; others do not. Some are exclusively parent-cooperative ventures, while others may exercise no apparent commitment to parental involvement. Some accommodate three-, four-, and five-year-olds, others accept four-years-olds only. Some are limited to half-day programs, others include a full day. Some schools convene two or three days a week, others utilize the full five-day week. In short, variation is the rule rather than the exception. Exceptional, however, is the sponsorship of nursery school programs by public school systems. During the 1966–1967 school year nursery programs were manned by only 148 public school systems as compared to nearly 9,800 which regularly mount kindergarten programs (Ream, 1968).

Objectives and Contemporary Status

In theory, the objectives of the many thousands of nursery programs now in operation are not grossly dissimilar. Actual procedures, however, are perhaps less uniformly articulated. The generality of the nursery school concept is perhaps best illustrated by the following schedule of activities typical of American programs for four-year-olds (Green and Woods, 1965; Pitcher and Ames, 1964; Farwell, 1958).

Arrival and health inspection	
Outdoor and/or indoor play	20–30 minutes
Toilet and clean-up	10 minutes

---

[10] See Frank (1962) for a succinct historical overview of the emergence of child study and family life education in the United States.

Music	10–20 minutes
Snack time	10–15 minutes
Rest (may include listening to records, looking at books, etc.)	15 minutes
Indoor free play	20–30 minutes
Story time; toilet and clean-up	15–30 minutes
Outdoor play and departure	

✓ The above schedule reflects several emphases commonly found in nursery schools. One is an accent upon basic socialization and the child's physical health needs. A second is the emphasis upon fantasy play to promote sensory-motor and emotional development. Nursery school educators have long reasoned that it is through organized and free play that a child learns to know himself, his capabilities, and the realities of his social existence. Play is also thought to provide a medium through which aesthetics and self-expressional activities may be elaborated. Traditionally, most nursery school programs have not dealt in specific ways with the matter of academic readiness, although some attention is usually paid to the grooming of general sensory discrimination skills and to social responses necessary for group learning activities.

✓ The binding force for most nursery programs is considered to be the rapport between the teacher and each child—a rapport capable of fostering self-confidence, security, and spontaneity within the child. Hence, the teacher-child ratio, as in the kindergarten, is by consensus viewed as a critical factor in nursery schools (Farwell, 1958).[11] A goodly portion of nursery school philosophy is conveyed by the belief that young children should enjoy a learning environment as free as possible from restraint and direction. Consequently, children are provided with a supportive latitude as regards their specific activities. Respect for and accommodation to individuality are essential. Teachers usually assume responsibility for guiding music activities and informal discussion periods, but in many cases the most apparent evidence of planning and organization is represented by a teacher's selection of play equipment and the creation of art activity centers. Parent relations, including family life education activities, also receive systematic attention in the more comprehensive nursery programs.

Representative of an influential approach to preschool programs (and

[11] It is advised that nursery groups should not exceed twenty children in schools for four-year-olds (three or four less where two- and three-year-olds are involved). This assumes further that at least two teachers are available for constant supervision within such groups.

early childhood education generally) which has encompassed many of the above features is that supported by The Bank Street College of Education (New York City). Over the years Bank Street personnel have maintained that the primary objective for education during early childhood should be for every child to achieve a positive image of himself as a learner. A learning context conducive to social-emotional development therefore has top priority. Cognitive skills, including language, are thought best to develop within a context of "total life experience." For Bank Street followers, attempts to teach cognitive skills separately from such total life experiences constitute an unnatural instructional policy.

Teaching is conceived at Bank Street in terms of a "disciplined practice of differentiation and particularization" (Gilkeson, 1969). This means that a teacher, fully grounded in child development theory and subject matter, adapts her behavior to the needs of individual children. Such adaptation is said to occur through a combination of teacher assessments, mutual planning with parents, and hypothesis testing. Active discovery within a "well-defined" physical and social environment is encouraged. Play and freedom to experiment provide the media through which skills such as categorizing, information gathering, and problem solving are thought to accumulate. It is through play that cooperative group projects are also conceived and developed.

Other Bank Street techniques include (1) conventional language stimulation activities (reading to children, discussing books and pictures, and various individual teacher-child contacts); and (2) the organization of springboard activities around central themes beginning with personal, concrete experiences (for example, pet and plant care) and extending to broader aspects of the community (for example, food marketing and traffic control). Transition from nondirective to directive teaching behavior may occur frequently, depending upon a teacher's evaluation of a child's current needs and interests; the approach in general, however, is unstructured.

No one set or type of learning materials is advocated apart from minimum resource requirements. As Gilkeson (1969) states, successful implementation of Bank Street techniques assumes (depends upon) a "high level of autonomous professional judgment" among those involved in the education of children. Perhaps most crucial is an appropriate application of the principle of differentiating in specific ways the needs, motivations, and learning styles of children. Once such differentiation has been accomplished, the creative deployment of varied resources is required to nurture the total educational growth of the child. Thus, Bank Street technique is not prescriptive in the sense that specific sequences of teacher behavior are programmed in advance to produce "narrowly defined intellectual skills." Yet the teacher consistent with the Bank Street approach encourages children, introduces new materials and activities at strategic moments, and instructs systematically for mastery as the individual situation dictates.

Overall outcomes claimed by the Bank Street approach include an expansion of every child's world, a sensitization to and differentiation of sensory experiences, the expression of fantasy and an understanding of reality, and improved ability to deal with social crises, felt problems, and frustrations (Minuchin and Biber, 1968). Bank Street philosophy and goals are considered appropriate for all children. No marked departures are advised for compensatory purposes, an issue which will be discussed further in Chapter 3 of this book.

Evaluative Research

Concern for the influence of nursery school on children has most commonly been expressed in terms of global behaviors such as "improved" social skills, "greater" intellectual competence, or "increased" emotional adjustment. This concern automatically awakens a sleeping giant which psychologists have called the *criterion problem,* that is, determining specifically what defines a given behavior change and how it can be measured. An incisive review of nursery school research has resulted in several inferences germane to this problem (Swift, 1964). First, Swift believes that, while studies of the global affects of nursery experiences are at times encouraging, they are frequently inconclusive. This inconclusiveness, Swift charges, is due to the failure of researchers to relate expected changes (sensory-motor, social, or intellectual) to specific program features thought to be relevant antecedents.[12] Secondly, most nursery studies suggest that effects, if any, depend largely upon the extent to which a program supplements (versus duplicates) the experiences the children in question receive elsewhere. Third, Swift concludes that nursery programs per se depend for their effectiveness upon the skill of the individual teacher and the socio-emotional climate in which activities are pursued. Swift implies that diffuse programs leave a substantial degree of potential effectiveness to chance. An overriding philosophical question, of course, is whether nursery school programs must justify their existence in terms of measurable outcomes. One might satisfy himself with the notion that children's lives are being enriched and made more enjoyable (assuming a sound

[12] See Thompson (1944) for a respectable early effort to counter this failure.

physical, psychological, and social environment). Yet as long as programs purport to accomplish growth objectives the question of their validity is legitimate.

Swift's (1964) remarks are echoed in an independent review of nursery research by Sears and Dowley (1963), as the following quotation will demonstrate:

> It is clear that attendance at nursery school, in and of itself, does not radically alter personalities of children. The evidence suggests, but not strongly, that certain social participation skills are enhanced by a good ✓ nursery school experience and that in certain cases these effects can be observed several years later. Language and intellectual development may be influenced, apparently, particularly if the home or out-of-school environment of the child is meager in stimulating qualities. [p. 850]

As for the difficulties faced in interpreting such research these authorities further maintain that:

> . . . firm knowledge of the effect of teaching methods or roles cannot be gained without taking into account characteristics of the children toward whom the methods are directed. It is clear by now that a "method" cannot be abstracted from the interpersonal setting, methods are employed by teachers having certain characteristics and they are directed toward children with certain characteristics. Shorn of these factors statements about a method (and its effects) must necessarily be stated in such tentative terms that they are of little value. [p. 859]

Thus is pinpointed another issue whose identity will appear under various guises in succeeding chapters: the degree of matching or interrelationship between a method, the children involved, the teacher's skill, and the emotional climate in which learning takes place. It is precisely this issue, among others, which has incited continuous research into educational strategies for young children.

A preoccupation among authorities with the behavioral outcomes of nursery school may result in a failure to acknowledge less obvious contributions. Consider, for example, the opportunity provided by nursery school contact for specialists to identify childhood problems at an early age. Or, as Westman and others (1967) have put it, the nursery school represents a "strategic outpost" for mental health screening and intervention. Westman's follow-up research on 130 nursery schoolers disclosed that the early adjustment problem of these children tend to persist in later life. The most valuable data obtainable at the nursery level for predicting subsequent need for mental health service were

found to be teachers' judgments of the children's social relations, behavior eccentricities, and family relationships. This assumes nursery
school personnel sufficiently trained to discriminate valid adjustment
problems, but it also indicates the potential of a nursery school setting
for preventive mental health programs and early detection of emotional
problems.[13]

Some Current Issues

The notion of trained personnel and the significance attached to
individual teacher skill introduces a major issue in nursery school education, namely, the quality of school personnel. Only minimal professional qualifications may be required in many settings. State certification standards rarely reach into pre-kindergarten undertakings.
In-service training facilities within nursery school operations themselves are often limited. This leaves a great deal to the sense of moral
responsibility toward children held by those who conduct nursery programs. A persistent shortage of persons qualified for instructional
positions has been heightened by the demands of Project Head Start.
This issue is not being overlooked, as the work of organizations such
as the National Association for the Education of Young Children indicates. That training programs are gearing up to the current challenges
is also evidenced in a recent report by the World Organization for Early
Childhood Education (OMEP, 1966) on the preparation opportunities
and status of preschool teachers.

A second issue, one which has grown in proportion during the past
decade, involves the content of nursery school programs. Specifically
challenged has been the validity of assumptions which underly such a
heavy investment by nursery schools in free play activities. Deutsch
(1964), for example, has been critical of the fantasy play orientation
and maternal protectiveness of conventional nursery programs. A major
question is whether this orientation is suitable for children ill-equipped
to profit from this sort of learning environment due to language and
conceptual deficits. It would seem inappropriate to this writer for the
issue to reduce to polar extremes—play versus no play. More significant is the function of types of play in relation to the child's total
growth—cognitive, affective, and sensory-motor—and to what degree
a given program depends upon play for its effectiveness. With respect
to play functions, Almy (1966) has expressed serious concern over a

---

[13] The potential of nursery schools for human relations training is further examined by
Read (1966).

sharp swing of the pendulum away from spontaneous play activities in many of the newer cognitive-based preschool programs. Almy's position exemplifies a long-standing conviction of nursery school authorities, namely, that self-initiated play is an indispensable stimulus to children's total development. A similar conviction is implied by Sigel (1965) who contends that a child's interaction with a physical world properly "adjusted to his size and relative fragility" will aid his growing sense of competence and mastery.

These thoughts about play are perhaps most explicitly supported at the theoretical level by Erik Erikson, an internationally recognized psychoanalyst. For Erikson (1963), personality development during the first six years of life involves the achievement of a basic sense of trust, autonomy, and initiative. The latter two "senses" are accomplished largely through volitional motor and social play, including fantasy role enactments, in a responsive environment. Erikson would perhaps agree with the *autotelic* principle of Moore and Anderson (1969) which states that the best learning takes place in an environment of safety, that is, an environment conducive to free exploration without adverse physical or social consequences. At the ideal level this principle is at least implicit in general nursery school approaches. The assumption that its application and augmentation is constant among nursery schools, however, is less tenable.

At a more empirical level, Sutton-Smith (1967) has examined research which suggests, tentatively, a functional relationship between play (especially children's game activity) and cognitive development. The value of sociodramatic play, a special stage of play behavior including imitation and make-believe, for socio-emotional and conceptual development has been stressed by Smilansky (1968). Still other studies (for example, Humphrey, 1966) support the academic benefits of active games approaches to classroom learning. All of these data prompt one to consider carefully the importance of types of play that extend beyond a random, nonpurposive level. Thus, the way in which a learning environment is arranged for the occurrence of play activities is perhaps more critical than some might believe. This notion finds indirect support in a perceptive review of cognitive-developmental theories (Dewey, Piaget, Vygotsky, among others) and their implications for preschool education and intellectual stimulation strategies (Kohlberg, 1968). Kohlberg concludes that for cognitive growth, the matter of specific forms of stimulation or content (for example, preacademic and language training) is subordinate to a *systematic formulation* of activities traditionally associated with the nursery school, including play, aesthetics, and social activities. Thus may be identified a criterion for

the evaluation of early education programs: the extent to which activities beyond the dimension of specific academic preparations are
systematically incorporated into a child-centered curriculum.

SUMMARY OF MAJOR ISSUES

A discussion of early childhood published several decades ago identified three interrelated issues faced by those who assume responsibility
for children's education: what, when, and how (Anderson, 1947). As
the reader already may have surmised, these issues are no less critical
today than they were in the 1940s. The issue of *what,* as mentioned
earlier, concerns the content of a program. As will become more apparent in the chapters to follow, a wide range among programs may be
observed. This range involves several dimensions, including type of
content and degree to which content is structured by adults for children's learning encounters.

The *when* issue in early childhood education concerns timing, or the
sequential management of experiences appropriate to the developmental process. This issue cannot be separated from the problem of
content, for it involves a determination of what experiences are most
appropriate at what points in time. Both issues raise the broad philosophical question of long-range goals for early education. Other problems related to timing concern the stability of early learning and
possible hazards of beginning "too early" or "too late" (Robinson and
Robinson, 1968) and the extent to which behavior, particularly intellectual and school achievement behavior, can be "boosted" by early intervention programs (Jensen, 1969). The latter idea will be examined more
specifically later in the book, particularly within the context of compensatory education.

Fused to the issues of content and timing is the issue of *how.* This
involves a set of questions concerning methodology valid for early childhood education, whatever the purposes of such education might be.
Teaching methods suitable at one stage of development may not be suitable at earlier or later stages. Methods which contribute to early mastery
may not be appropriate for longer-term objectives (Robinson and
Robinson, 1968). The variety of methods applied to early childhood
education is remarkable. Varied also is the quality of research performed to assess the validity of such methods.

To the above triad may be added a fourth issue, one that concerns
who will prosecute programs of early childhood education. This issue
has at lease two facets. First, there is the problem of what qualifications

(standards) an individual should (must) demonstrate prior to actual involvement with children where educational purposes are professed. (This subsumes a number of other problems, including the nature of pre-service training and teacher selection procedures.) A second major facet of the "who" problem concerns the assessment of in-service teaching effectiveness and reliable measures for the removal of individuals who may be judged unsuitable in relation to established objectives of early childhood education. Related to this notion is the type of teaching role prescribed by a given program.

A fifth issue or problem involves *where* a program for early childhood education is conducted. In American education it has rather been taken for granted that formal education best takes place in a special setting away from the home where groups of children homogeneous in chronological age are established. Sub-issues related to the *where* problem include the age at which group instruction is begun, the degree to which homogeneity in grouping is practiced, group size, and the nature of the physical facilities provided for children.

Programs for young children currently in existence all attempt to solve the problems of what, when, how, who, and where in one way or another. Decisions related to these problems inevitably reflect variations in philosophy, psychological conceptions of child development and learning, availability of personnel, and the formulation of day-to-day practices. But perhaps the one most overriding question relevant to the five issues above is the *why* question. For example, as a given program is reviewed one may ask, Why this content as opposed to something else? Why is a set of experiences provided at a given point in time? Why is this method of execution or technique preferred over other possible methods or techniques? Why are certain teaching skills established as more imperative than others?

The why question serves to point up several traditional and emerging conflicts in early childhood education theory. A conflict of long standing involves two diverse views of education. One holds that education should be preparation for the future; the momentary needs and interests of children may receive secondary consideration. In contrast is a view of education based upon the immediate needs and interests of children, where concern for subsequent responsibilities and societal demands is de-emphasized (Anderson, 1947). The first view most clearly underlies a curriculum based upon an analysis of what society requires generally in order for one to operate "successfully" according to broadly defined adult roles. The second view is based upon the assumption that a full and complete daily existence during childhood is actually the best insurance for successful adulthood. The writer does not mean to establish a false dichotomy by virtue of this distinction. Educators now generally agree that the issue is not an either-or matter and that discussions of the issue frequently involve the risk of oversimplification. It is apparent, however, that such a distinction generates a great deal of controversy among adults who think that they know best what kind of experiences children should have. As we shall see, this controversy frequently centers around a *product-oriented* versus a *process-oriented* concept of education.

Within the discipline of developmental psychology there exists a conflict parallel to that in early childhood education. This parallel can be described as a schism between inheritors of "naturalistic, indigenous growth" theories of development and those who hold the "cultural competence" or "environmental determination" point of view. Supporters of the "natural growth" viewpoint believe that maximum socialization benefits can be reaped by providing children with an enriched, benign, accepting, permissive, informal educational environment. The highest value is placed upon the need for children to express their creative growth forces. It is through such expression that children's self-development can be nurtured, and developmental-maturational sequences provide whatever cues may be important for self-actualization. Innate factors (maturational processes that unfold in a predetermined manner) provide the basis for cultivating complete and integrated growth patterns, including the child's mental structure. In contrast, supporters of the "cultural competence" school place a greater emphasis upon the shaping power of experience; collective teaching forces are therefore assumed to play a stronger role. Skill development and mastery of the environment are seen as the means to achieve positive growth; children need to be helped in systematic ways by trained pedagogues if children are to develop their maximum potentials. Response pattern development in children is primarily determined by the structure and association of events in their environment (Kohlberg, 1968). Again, the difference in these two conceptions is more a matter of degree than of a "clear" dichotomy. And whether one is more correct than the other is largely a matter of conjecture — if, in fact, either of them is (McCandless, 1967). As broad orientations, however, they are the basis of many issues which pervade the current scene in early childhood education, including the degree to which specific content and teaching techniques are stressed.

It seems fair to say that most traditional early childhood education practices in America, at least nursery-kindergarten practices, have mirrored the "natural development" position, while many new programs now being tested are clearly in the direction of the systematic achievement of cultural competence. Some may evolve as a constructive blend of traditional and experimental programs. Theoretical foundations for interactionism-based (cognitive-developmental) approaches now exist and will be discussed later in this book, most specifically in Chapter 7.

To summarize, the strong commitment by many educators to early childhood education has for many years been based in the belief that children will more likely realize their developmental potential with nursery and kindergarten experience than without it. But it is only recently that the search for a better yield from early educational programs has involved a careful examination of cognitive behavior. As Kohlberg (1968) suggests, a principal contribution to this search has been a growing awareness among educators that differences in early academic achievement among children are due less to formal schooling functions than to children's general background of preschool experience and the personal characteristics they develop during the early years of life. Yet basic schisms in educational and psychological thought have continued to affect program development, particularly at the preprimary level (Elkind, 1969). Hopefully these theoretical conflicts among adults do not occur at the expense of children. One could argue that the most important issue now concerns what specific experiences are best for individual children rather than what one approach or set of experiences is best for all children.

References

Almy, Millie. "Spontaneous Play: An Avenue for Intellectual Development." *Bulletin of the Institute for Child Study,* 1966, 28, No. 2.

Ames, Louise, and Frances Ilg. *School Readiness.* New York: Harper & Row, 1965.

Anderson, John E. "The Theory of Early Childhood Education." In Nelson B. Henry (Ed.), *Early Childhood Education.* 46th Yearbook of the National Society for the Study of Education. Chicago: University of Chicago Press, 1947, 70–100.

Bernstein, Basil. "Social Structure, Language, and Learning." *Educational Research,* 1961, 3, 163–176.

Bloom, Benjamin. *Stability and Change in Human Characteristics.* New York: Wiley, 1964.

Blow, Susan E. *Educational Issues in the Kindergarten.* New York: Appleton, 1904.

Bricker, W., and L. Lovell. "What Research Says About the Advantages of the Kindergarten." Eugene, Ore.: Eugene Committee for Preschool Education, 1965.

Bronfenbrenner, Urie. "The Changing American Child: A Speculative Analysis." *Journal of Social Issues,* 1961, 17, 6–18.

Cole, Louella. *A History of Education: Socrates to Montessori.* New York: Holt, Rinehart and Winston, 1950.

Davis, David C. *Patterns of Primary Education.* New York: Harper & Row, 1963.

de Hirsch, Katrina, Jeannette Jansky, and William S. Langford. *Predicting Reading Failure.* New York: Harper & Row, 1966.

Deutsch, Martin. "Facilitating Development in the Pre-school Child: Social and Psychological Perspectives." *Merrill-Palmer Quarterly,* 1964, 10, 249–264.

Durkin, Delores, *Children Who Read Early.* New York: Teachers College, 1966.

Edwards, Esther P. "Kindergarten Is Too Late." *Saturday Review,* 1968 (June 15), 68–704.

Elkind, David. "Preschool Education: Enrichment or Instruction?" *Childhood Education,* 1969, 46, 321–328.

Erikson, Erik. *Childhood and Society* (2d ed.). New York: Norton, 1963.

Farwell, Denise. "The Nursery School Program." In Jerome Leavitt (Ed.), *Nursery-Kindergarten Education.* New York: McGraw-Hill, 1958, 51–94.

Foster, Clifford D. "Changing Patterns of Education: Early Childhood." *The College of Education Record.* Seattle: University of Washington Press, 1967, 33, 55–61.

Foster, Josephine, and Neith E. Headley. *Education in the Kindergarten.* (4th ed.). New York: American Book, 1966.

Fowler, William. "Cognitive Learning in Infancy and Early Childhood." *Psychological Bulletin,* 1962a, 59, 116–152.

Fowler, William. "Teaching a Two-year-old to Read: An Experiment in Early Childhood Learning." *Genetic Psychology Monographs,* 1962b, 66, 181–283.

Fowler, William. "A Study of Process and Method in Three-year-old Twins and Triplets Learning To Read." *Genetic Psychology Monographs,* 1965, 72, 3–89.

Fowler, William. "The Design of Early Developmental Learning Programs for Disadvantaged Young Children." *IRCD Bulletin,* 1966, 1A, 1–4.

Frank, Lawrence. "The Beginnings of Child Development and Family Life Education in the 20th Century." *Merrill-Palmer Quarterly,* 1962, 8, 207–227.

Fuller, Elizabeth. *What Research Says to the Teacher about the Kindergarten.* Washington, D.C.: National Education Association, 1961.

Gilkeson, Elizabeth C. *Bank Street Approach to Follow Through.* New York: Bank Street College of Education, 1969.

Goodykoontz, Bess, Mary D. Davis, and Hazel F. Gabbard. "Recent History and Present Status of Education for Young Children." In Nelson B. Henry (Ed.), *Early Childhood Education.* 46th Yearbook of the National Society for the Study of Education. Chicago: University of Chicago Press, 1947, 44–69.

Gordon, Ira. "The Young Child: A New Look." In Joe L. Frost (Ed.), *Early Childhood Education Rediscovered.* New York: Holt, Rinehart and Winston, 1968, 11–20.

Gorton, Harry B., and Richard L. Robinson. "For Better Results—A Full Day Kindergarten." *Education,* 1969, 89, 217–221.

Green, Marjorie M., and Elizabeth Woods. *A Nursery School Handbook for Teachers and Parents.* Sierra Madre, Calif.: Sierra Madre Community Nursery School Association, 1965.

Hammond, Sarah L., and others. *Good Schools for Young Children.* New York: Macmillan, 1963.

Harris, B. H., and R. J. Fischer. "Distortions in the Kindergarten." *Young Children,* 1969, 24, 279–284.

Headley, Neith. *The Kindergarten: Its Place in the Program of Education.* New York: Center for Applied Research in Education, 1965.

Huey, J. Frances. "The Kindergarten Program." In Jerome Leavitt (Ed.), *Nursery-Kindergarten Education.* New York: McGraw-Hill, 1958, 94–117.

Humphrey, James H. "An Exploratory Study of Active Games in Learning of Number Concepts by First Grade Boys and Girls." *Perceptual Motor Skills,* 1966, 23, 341–342.

Hunt, J. McV. *Intelligence and Experience.* New York: Ronald, 1961.

Jensen, Arthur R. "How Much Can We Boost IQ and Scholastic Achievement?" *Harvard Educational Review,* 1969, 39, 1–123.

Jones, Daisy M. "A Feasible Plan for Continuous Admission." *Education,* 1969, 89, 195–202.

Kessen, William. "Research in the Psychological Development of Infants: An Overview." *Merrill-Palmer Quarterly,* 1963, 9, 83–94.

Kohlberg, Lawrence A. "Early Education: A Cognitive-developmental View." *Child Development,* 1968, 39, 1013–1062.

Kresh, David. "Psychoneurobiochemeducation." *Phi Delta Kappan,* 1969, 50, 370–375.

Lambert, Hazel M. *Early Childhood Education.* Boston: Allyn and Bacon, 1960.

Law, Norma, and others. *Basic Propositions for Early Childhood Education.* Washington, D.C.: Association for Childhood Education International, 1966.

Leavitt, Jerome E. *Nursery-Kindergarten Education.* New York: McGraw-Hill, 1958.

Leeper, Sarah H., Ruth J. Dales, Dora S. Skipper, and Ralph J. Witherspoon. *Good Schools for Young Children* (2d ed.). New York: Macmillan, 1968.

Leiderman, Gloria F. "Mathematics and Science Programs for the Elementary School Years." *Review of Educational Research,* 1965, 35, 154–162.

McCandless, Boyd R. "Should a Bright Child Start to School before He's Five?" *Education,* 1957, 77, 1–6.

McCandless, Boyd R. *Children: Behavior and Development* (2d ed.). New York: Holt, Rinehart and Winston, 1967.

Mager, Robert. *Developing a Positive Attitude toward Learning.* Palo Alto: Fearon Press, 1969.

Mayer, Frederick. *A History of Educational Thought.* Columbus: Merrill, 1960.

Minuchin, Patricia, and Barbara Biber. "A Child Development Approach to Language in the Preschool Disadvantaged Child." *Monographs of the Society for Research in Child Development,* 1968, 33, Serial No. 124, 10–18.

Moore, O. K., and A. R. Anderson. "Some Principles for the Design of Clarifying Educational Environments." In D. A. Goslin (Ed.), *Handbook of Socialization Theory and Research.* Skokie, Ill.: Rand McNally, 1969, 571–613.

Nehrt, R. C. and G. E. Hurd. *Preprimary Enrollment of Children under Six: October, 1968.* Washington, D.C.: U.S. Office of Education, 1969.

OMEP. *The Preparation and Status of Preschool Teachers.* Oslo: 1966.

Piaget, Jean. "The Genetic Approach to the Psychology of Thought." *Journal of Educational Psychology,* 1961, 52, 275–281.

Pines, Maya. *Revolution in Learning.* New York: Harper & Row, 1966.

Pitcher, Evelyn G., and Louise B. Ames. *The Guidance Nursery School.* New York: Harper & Row, 1964.

Pratcher, Mary. *Teaching in the Kindergarten.* New York: Exposition Press, 1968.

Read, Katherine H. *The Nursery School.* Philadelphia: Saunders, 1966.

Ream, Marsha A. *Nursery School Education, 1966–67.* Washington, D.C.: *Research Division—National Education Association,* 1968.

Ream, Marsha A. *Kindergarten Education in Public Schools, 1967–68.* Washington, D.C.: *Research Division—National Education Association,* 1969.

Robinson, Halbert B., and Nancy M. Robinson. "The Problem of Timing in Pre-school Education." In Robert Hess and Roberta Bear (Eds.), *Early Education.* Chicago: Aldine, 1968, 37–51.

Robison, Helen, and Bernard Spodek. *New Directions in the Kindergarten.* New York: Teachers College Press, 1965.

Rogolsky, Maryrose M. "Screening Kindergarten Children: A Review and Recommendation." *Journal of School Psychology,* 1969, 7, No. 2, 18–27.

Rusk, Robert R. *A History of Infant Education.* London: University of London Press, 1933.

Schloss, Samuel. *Nursery-Kindergarten Enrollment of Children under Six: October, 1966.* Washington, D.C.: U.S. Dept. of Health, Education, and Welfare, 1967.

Sears, Pauline S., and Dowley, Edith M. "Research on Teaching in the Nursery School." In N. L. Gage (Ed.), *Handbook of Research on Teaching.* Skokie, Ill.: Rand McNally, 1963, 814–864.

Senn, Milton J. E. "Early Childhood Education: For What Goals?" *Children,* 1969, 16, 8–13.

Shane, Harold G. "The Renaissance of Early Childhood Education." *Phi Delta Kappan,* 1969, 50, 369ff.

Sigel, Irving E. "Developmental Considerations of the Nursery School Experience." In Peter B. Neubauer (Ed.), *Concepts of Development in Early Childhood Education.* Springfield, Ill.: Charles C Thomas, 1965, 84–111.

Spodek, Bernard. "Constructing a Model for a Teacher Education Program in Early Childhood Education." *Contemporary Education,* 1969, 40, 145–149.

Stott, Leland H., and Rachel S. Ball. "Infant and Preschool Mental Tests: Review and Evaluation." *Monographs of the Society for Research in Child Development,* 1965, 30, Serial No. 101.

Sutton, Marjorie Hunt. "Children Who Learned to Read in Kindergarten: A Longitudinal Study." *Reading Teacher,* 1969, 22, 595–602.

Sutton-Smith, Brian. "The Role of Play in Cognitive Development." In W. W. Hartup and Nancy L. Smothergill (Eds.), *The Young Child.* Washington, D.C.: National Association for the Education of Young Children, 1967, 96–108.

Swift, Joan. "Effects of Early Group Experience: The Nursery School and Day Nursery." In Martin L. Hoffman and Lois Hoffman (Eds.), *Review of Child Development Research,* Vol. I. New York: Russell Sage, 1964, 249–288.

Thompson, George G. "The Social and Emotional Development of Preschool Children under Two Types of Educational Programs." *Psychological Monograph,* 1944, Whole No. 528.

Westman, J., D. Rice, and E. Bermann. "Nursery School Behavior and Later School Adjustment." *American Journal of Orthopsychiatry,* 1967, 37, 725–731.

White, Robert W. "Motivation Reconsidered: The Concept of Competence." *Psychological Review,* 1959, 66, 297–323.

Williams, Joanna P. "Reading Research and Instruction." *Review of Educational Research,* 1965, 35, 147–153.

2
The Montessori Method

INTRODUCTION

Parallel to the growing federal commitment to early childhood education has been a dramatic rebirth of interest in the Montessori Method, perhaps the first truly systematic attempt to educate children under six years of age. Widely acclaimed in Europe shortly after its inception around the turn of the century, initial enthusiasm in America for the Montessori Method was short-lived. Not only did Montessori education receive a cool reception among distinguished members of the professional educational establishment (for example, Kilpatrick, 1914) but the onset of World War I apparently did much to prevent Montessorian education from gaining widespread acceptance in America. A sufficient number of early devotees were successful, however, in establishing a handful of Montessori schools in America (Martin, 1965), and since 1958 the number of such schools has increased markedly.

Paradoxically, Montessorian education has been the province of highly privileged children in this country rather than that of underprivileged children, for whom the method was initially designed. Probably the greatest single reason for this is that Montessori schools have been private operations, thus requiring tuition unaffordable by low income families.[1] To this writer's knowledge bonafide Montessori schools have never been affiliated with nor supported by public school systems in America, although, as we shall see, many Montessorian concepts have been incorporated into public school practice.

Several factors have apparently combined to rekindle the sparks of Montessorian education in America. One has involved the search for appropriate methods for educating disadvantaged children. Another has been the linking of Jean Piaget's influential developmental psychology with the pedagogical principles of Montessori by perceptive psychologists (Hunt, 1964; Elkind, 1966). Still another may be the appeal of learning by discovery, a style so well articulated by authorities such as Jerome Bruner (1961). The highly popular book, *Learning How to Learn* (Rambusch, 1962) undoubtedly has done much to alert the lay public to features of the Montessori Method. This chapter includes a brief description of the Montessori Method and its originator, a general critique, and a sampling of research performed on this Method.

THE PERSON

Maria Montessori (1870–1952) became interested in problems of learning through her contact with mentally retarded and disturbed children while working toward a medical degree at the University of

---

[1] In 1965, the national average cost per child for a year of Montessori education was $500 (Miller, 1965).

Rome. Her search for more adequate techniques of instruction for these children led her to study the earlier work of O. Edouard Seguin (1812–1880), a French psychiatrist whose pioneer efforts to treat the problems of the mentally ill were exemplary. Seguin developed a set of ingenious didactic materials to facilitate the learning of basic discrimination skills among retarded children. Montessori, duly impressed, drew heavily upon the principles underlying the Seguin materials and became totally proficient in their application.

After earning her medical degree, the first woman in Italy ever to do so, Montessori served as a faculty member at the University of Rome and simultaneously did postgraduate work in psychiatry. In 1898 she accepted an appointment as directress of Rome's Orthophrenic School, a tax-supported institution for "subnormal" or retarded children. Her phenomenal success with these children, attributed largely to her materials and methods, gained Montessori wide visibility. This success also prompted her to question the effectiveness of regular public school educational practices then performed with normal children. She reasoned that if retarded children could progress to an academic level comparable to that of normal children in conventional educational settings then much more could be done with normal children given a properly designed educational environment.

An opportunity to test this thesis presented itself around 1907 when Dr. Montessori accepted responsibility for the education of slum children in Rome, a population of children which had created considerable concern among officials of the Italian government. Involved were the now famous *case dei bambini* (houses of children) which brought to life Montessori's ideas about the learning environment she thought essential for the self-realization of children's potentials. It was through the medium of such houses that the Montessori Method matured and attracted worldwide attention. Montessori, firmly convinced that the most critical period in a child's development was the first six years of life, devoted the remainder of her life to the service of young children. Accordingly, her efforts were coordinated to capitalize on the spontaneity and "natural energy" of children during these early years.

THE METHOD

The Prepared Environment

Ultimately important to the Montessori Method is the *prepared environment,* an organized and coordinated set of materials and equipment the use of which will promote in the child significant learnings. The arrangement of the prepared environment is predicated upon the child's need to order and attach meaning to his world. Among other things, this means that the environment must be scaled both physically and conceptually to children, not adults. For example, child-sized furniture and utensils are viewed as prerequisites for meaningful learning.

The original Montessori house consisted of a set of rooms (a central room for intellectual work in which the children spent two hours a day, shelters for individual play or sleep, a club room for games and music, a dining room, a dressing room) and a garden. Today's Montessori schools are rarely so elaborate. Most, however, still subscribe to the fundamental objective involved, namely, the development of children's skills for the care of self and property. Foremost among procedures designed to achieve this objective are the exercises of practical life. These exercises in the care and management of self and property are instrumental for one of three primary components of the Montessori Method: motor education. The other two components, sensory education and education for language, will be treated subsequently.

Motor Education   For Montessori, freedom of movement is the keystone for motor education. Such education is effected by developing self-management skills in children. Imperative is the provision of *order* to motility; all motor activities are goal-oriented and functional for the child in managing his environment. Basic motor acts such as walking, sitting, and carrying objects are given precise attention. Various exercises in the opening and shutting of drawers, pouring water from pitcher to basin, folding and packing of linens, scissor work, buttoning, and lacing are considered fundamental and preparatory for the development of practical life skills. Occupational skills such as sweeping, washing, brushing, and the care of plants and animals are also emphasized. Integrated into such motor education are such things as responsibility training (based upon the concept that plants and animals are dependent upon the children for their survival) and training to develop patience (the children must wait to observe natural growth).

While play-like activities pervade a Montessorian classroom, Montessori herself did not consider fantasy play to have a place in children's education; all activities have a purpose and are geared toward the building of self-discipline and a work-orientation. For example, even gymnastic exercises and rhythmic movement exercises are provided, but not just for exercise or to promote social interaction. Rather, they are provided systematically to facilitate the child's developing sense of equilibrium; the age period of three to six years was thought by Montessori to be critical for the development of this sense.

In sum, motor education is executed by way of activities many people take for granted. They are, for the most part, activities which children do "naturally," playing in water, for example. Montessori believed that such common activities were of supreme importance for the development of work habits necessary to accomplish more complex learnings. In effect, all learning is thought to have a sensory-motor base; the acquisition of knowledge rests upon the development and refinement of motor and perceptual skills. Freedom for the child to move and involve himself actively with concrete materials is necessary in order for him to create his own learning situations. For Montessori, practice in the coordination of the musculature with the sense organs contributes to "readiness" for later academic learning.

Most motor activities are taught initially by precise demonstration. Isolated verbal instructions are rare. Subtle cues from the teacher substitute for explanations, for example, a touch, a hint or two—just enough to get the child started. A Montessori classroom depends heavily upon the learning that children do by observing and interacting with one another. Even with the practical life exercises a regular sequence of actions is stressed. One such activity, table scrubbing, involves a sequence of pouring water into a basin, wetting and soaping a brush, scrubbing, rinsing, drying, and clean-up. This routine may encompass a period of 15 to 20 minutes. It is one of several which purport to assist a child to lengthen his attention span. In a sense, the practical life exercises are prototypic for all subsequent exercises in that a fixed sequence of actions is involved. There exists only one right way to deal with the materials in the prepared environment.

Sensory Education   Once a child has mastered the practical life exercises, he is considered ready to sample the main course of the Montessori pre-academic menu: sensorial exercises. Education of the senses is made possible through involvement with elaborate didactic materials. These varied materials are designed to promote sensory discrimination skills and concepts of form, size, color, weight, temperature, and texture. It is significant that the sensory materials are coordinated so that a child's activities are not in any way haphazard. Insurance that the proper sequence of activities is followed and that appropriate materials are studied simultaneously is provided by the teacher.

Most of the sensorial materials are designed to foster in the child techniques of observation and decision-making abilities. An example is the popular *cylinder block*. This apparatus consists of a block of wood into which are bored sockets of graded size. Cylinders sized to correspond to the sockets may then be placed into the block. The cylinders are identical in form and color and thus vary on one dimension only: size. The experience of placing the cylinders in correct order into their respective sockets helps the child to sharpen his discrimination of different sized objects. As such, the target behavior is the child's visual sense. This exercise has a still further feature of significance. Each cylinder has a small knob at its top which the child must grasp with the three fingers he will subsequently use to hold a pencil. Hence the exercise is designed to provide practice in sensory-motor coordinations and establish control over the small finger muscles necessary for cursive writing.

Other materials important to the education of the child's visual sense are the *pink tower* (blocks of the same color, shape, and texture but which differ in size; the child's task being to construct a tower with the largest block as its base and build upward with successively smaller blocks), the *brown stair* (blocks of the same length but which differ in width and height; these blocks are graded in stair fashion to highlight the concepts of thickness and thinness), and the *color tablets* (tablets of the same size, shape and texture which vary according to color; exercises in color matching and chromatic grading are provided; eventually the child tackles the task of ordering graduated shades of one color, for example, from darkest to lightest blue; and ultimately the pairing of colors from memory is achieved). While the ability to discriminate form and color is important in its own right, Montessori saw it fundamental to the growth of a child's aesthetic appreciation.

The child's *tactile* sense is educated by way of materials which dramatize texture and form. Touchboards with surfaces ranging from rough to smooth are introduced followed by experiences with feeling various cloth materials such as wool, silk, velvet, linen, satin, and cotton. Delicacy of fondling is stressed after children have washed their hands thoroughly. Form tracing is encouraged by still another set of materials, namely, wooden tablets upon which are nested plane geometric inserts. Form identity is sought by tracing outlines of squares, circles, triangles, and the like. This tracing experience again anticipates motor movements involved in writing. Eventually the child is required to match the geometric figures with their respective *outline drawings,* a strategy which purports to bridge the gap between concrete reality and abstract representation. Geometric solids are also provided, and the names of all forms are taught.

Other exercises oriented to the child's sense of feeling include the thermic bottles which involve matching and grading by temperature. This "thermic sense" is reinforced by having the children dip their hands into water of varying temperatures.

Aural sense education is initiated by introducing cylindrically shaped sound boxes in which are housed objects of various kinds. Consistent with the principle of graduation, these cylinders are graduated according to sound intensity. The sound cylinder exercises are analogous to those discussed earlier regarding color. Specifically, children engage themselves in the process of (1) matching cylinder pairs of equal intensity, and (2) sequencing the sound cylinders in gradations of softness to loudness. Montessori's original strategy involved blindfolding the children while they worked with auditory materials thereby permitting the child to concentrate his full attention on sounds. Similar matching and grading exercises are performed on musical bells, resonant metal tubes, and wooden bars. As the reader probably suspects, these exercises are all viewed as essential preparation for the cultivation of musical skill.

Montessori's appreciation for things delicate and subtle is reflected in a unique activity related to *aural sense* education, namely, the *lesson of silence.* This lesson first seeks to establish immobility among the children so as to permit auditory training in a quiet atmosphere. It ends with the directress (or another child) whispering each child's name. The child whose name is called must make his way, blindfolded and as quietly as possible, to his caller. The immediate purpose of such an activity is to familiarize children with silence and sharpen their sound perceptions. Montessori also intended that this would help children to savor and prefer an unraucous environment. The longer-range objective of this and similar lessons is much more philosophical in nature: the development of self-inhibitory powers and cooperativeness within one's social community. Such self-control and cooperation were seen by Montessori to be imperative if social groups are successfully to achieve a common purpose.

Up to this point we have considered examples of *visual, tactile,* and *auditory* sense education. Other senses educated via didactic materials are the *baric* sense, the *olfactory* sense, and the sense of *taste.* The first of these, the baric sense, refers directly to the ability to discern weight. Thus, kinesthesia is involved. Basic tablets of the same size, yet differing in weight, may be manipulated with the initial objective being to distinguish heavy and light. Smelling activities such as matching spices and identifying foodstuffs by type and quality while blindfolded are arranged to cultivate the olfactory sense. Similar procedures are employed for tasting exercises, for example, matching sweet, sour, salty, and bitter substances.

To summarize, three objectives are sought through sensory education procedures: the ability to recognize and match identities; the ability to recognize contrasts and extremes in a series of objects; and the ability to discriminate among items quite similar in shape, color, texture, weight, and the like.

Language Education   Of the preparatory sensory material exercises, auditory training is most closely related to language development in a Montessori classroom. The sounds of articulate language are thought to require powerful discrimination skills. It must be noted that language education occurs in conjunction with, not subsequent to, sensory education. At no time, however, does language training *precede* discrimination learning.

An inviolable principle in Montessori language education is the use of precise pronunciation by the children's principal model—the directress. Equally important is the three-period sequence applied to vocabulary development. Period one, *naming,* is initiated by the directress, usually during a demonstration period. For example, a child manipulating the blocks of the "brown stair" will be shown (by pointing) which ones are thick ("This is thick.") or thin ("This is thin."). In period two, the *recognition* phase, the child is required to respond to identity statements which take the form of a request. The teacher says, for example, "Give me the thick" or "Give me the thin." Eventually, the child enters period three, the *pronunciation* phase, and is able to respond appropriately to such questions as "What is this?"

It is intended that children achieve a high degree of accuracy in their use of words to describe their environment. For example, when only one dimension is varied in sensory materials such as the color tablets, objects are identified as dark and light. If the target dimension is length, the correct identification is in terms of long and short. If the defining criterion is height, the descriptions tall and short apply, and so on. An interesting example of the concern for precise language apparently shown in authentic Montessori classrooms is provided in the original handbook (Montessori, 1914). After the directress had ruled a blackboard with extremely fine lines a child exclaimed spontaneously, "What small lines!" "They are not small," reminded a second child, "they are thin!" The example serves also to illustrate a basic objective of language education, namely, the crystallization of basic ideas by way of exacting terminology.

Academic Learning

The experiences heretofore described are deemed preparatory; in the current educational jargon they would be considered pre-academic in nature. Normally the child who has reached this point in the program, now four years of age, is ready to commence activities of the "essential culture": writing, reading, and arithmetic. Such activities are thought to represent a natural extension of all that has come before. Presumably the child has mastered his fundamentals and possesses an appropriate sense of responsibility, cooperation, and initiative. His movements in space are satisfactorily coordinated, and he is predisposed to make ordered observations in his environment.

Writing and Reading   Readers will recall that prior activities, form tracing for example, represented indirect preparation for writing. Hand movement exercises are now pursued which constitute more direct training. Direct training procedures initiated at this time are based upon Montessori's analysis of the writing act. Critical are exercises which enable the child to manage the instruments of writing. Again, a pre-scribed sequence of activities is applied. The sequence is initiated by having the child trace geometric figures on paper with color pencils. A series of ten double outline figures is used. Next, the double outline tracings are filled in by the child using line markers. Great care is exercised to stay within the traced form. Subsequently, prepared designs of varied shapes and sizes are introduced to the child for more practice. The child then graduates to the next series of exercises, which involves the famous sandpaper letters.

Montessorian alphabetical signs involve a series of smooth-surface cards to which are attached (1) the letters of the alphabet cut from sandpaper and (2) combinations of letters grouped on the basis of form analogy (1, b, f, for example). Typically, vowels appear on red cards, consonants on blue ones. Letters and letter groupings are traced, using the index and middle fingers, in movements which correspond to actual writing. During this tracing process, the teacher pronounces letter sounds (vowels are named, consonants are sounded out). In this way the child simultaneously sees a letter, feels its shape, and hears its sound. Having learned the sandpaper letters and their sounds, the child is ready to construct words composed of letters from a large movable alphabet. Ordinarily, experience with large letter vowels precedes that with smaller letters and consonants.

As words are constructed, usually small words with a personal reference, the child learns to read them. Typically, three letter words with a short vowel sound are encouraged and the child sounds out the letter sounds as he combines the letters. In effect, this represents a single letter method of reading and word construction as opposed to word methods found in many conventional schools. The process is generally quite gradual, and children are said to engage in word building for some time before they realize that reading responses are now possible. Such a revelation is observed to be associated with great excitement, an excitement magnified still further when a child discovers that he is also now capable of writing entire words.[2]

Notable is the combination of didactic materials and exercises which culminate in beginning skills of writing and reading. Still more elaborate materials are introduced for advanced work in sounding out vowel-consonant combinations, learning the parts of speech, grammar, word and picture matching, and responding to command words. For the latter activity, cards upon which appear action words such as "jump," "sit," and "run" may be provided. As each card is presented, the children execute the correct activity. Such procedures are extended to more complex directions, such as "Place the pencil on the chair," or "Close the lid on the blue box."

Arithmetic The reader will recall that inherent in many of the sensorial materials are certain concepts basic to mathematical learning: quantity, identity, and difference. Formal introduction to numbers comes with the presentation of the red and blue rods, a set based upon the decimal system. These sets are carefully scaled so that the smallest rod represents a model unit of measurement, that is, the next smallest rod is twice the size of the first, the next largest is thrice the size of the first, and so on. Thus, these rods may be graded in succession from one through ten, during which time the number names and their corresponding symbols are taught in the customary sequence.

Greater levels of complexity follow the rod exercise, including exercises which teach the meaning of zero, odd and even numbers, and the decimal system. To accomplish the latter objective, Montessori designed an ingenious device known as the Golden Bead Material in which a single bead represents a unit. The quantity ten is represented by a vertical row of ten beads, a square composed of ten vertical rows of ten beads each represents 100 and a cube comprised of ten one-hundred squares indicates a thousand. Activities which require the child to count large quantities of beads dramatize the need for a more economical strategy than the counting of single units. Substitutions may be made by the child when necessary (exchanging a ten bar for ten units, for

---

[2] The incorporation of reading and writing by Montessori is unique. Elliot (1967), for example, comments favorably upon the ability of this technique to facilitate reading skill acquisition, particularly during the "sensitive period" for reading thought by Montessori to occur during the late preschool period.

example), thus illustrating concretely a basic principle of the decimal system.

The Golden Beads may also be used for games which are designed to teach the basic mathematical operations. However, still further didactic materials are inserted at this stage in order that the child may teach himself the teen numbers, fractions, and the processes of squaring and cubing. Basic to all such materials is the coordination of movement with symbolic activity. At this time activities of science education may also be interposed, including exercises in botany and geography. The child has now completed his preparatory program and, according to Montessori, is ready to encounter higher levels of cultural experience. Through intense exercise the child's mind has been made healthy, thus capable of receiving newer and more complex materials. For this purpose, an advanced program for children ages six to twelve was designed and first published in 1917 (Montessori, 1965a).

FUNDAMENTALS OF THE METHOD

The Montessori Method is a provocative combination of philosophy, psychological concepts, and pedagogical techniques. It is fueled, in principle, by love for the child and respect for his natural capabilities. It is the child in whom Montessori placed her hopes for a world based upon fundamental values such as cooperation, self-control, order, responsibility, patience, and the common good. In fact, the Golden Rule is perhaps the foremost operational principle of the Montessori Method. For Montessori, such kindness requires the sensitive interpretation of other's needs and a willingness to sacrifice, if necessary, one's own desires in deference to those of others.

Philosophically, Montessori was linked quite early to the Rousseau-Pestalozzi-Froebel group (Kilpatrick, 1914) although she reflects disagreements with each of these at various places in her original writings. Essentially, this group emphasizes the inherent goodness of children, the spontaneous nature of development, and the importance of deriving educational practices from children's natural interests. The Montessori Method is clearly predicated upon a belief in liberty of the spirit; such liberty is thought to develop best in an environment organized around sensory experiences. This emphasis upon individual freedom of action must not be misconstrued, however, for its limit is the collective interest. Montessori clearly subscribed to policies which discourage children from acting in ways libertine or otherwise offensive to others. Out of the chaotic world of the small child must be generated order.

Order, a condition requisite for security, is combined with the objective of self-discipline. This master objective literally transcends any particular academic or social one.

Role of the Teacher

A child-centered philosophy of behavior and education has as its natural extension the building and maintenance of positive interpersonal relations. Yet social games and dramatic play are not a part of the authentic Montessori Method. Rather, a climate of emotional support, helpfulness, and consideration is to be established by the teacher. To be successful, the teacher must relinquish a pontifical or pedantic role and serve more as a resource person, a catalyst for progress. Hence, deductive teaching is rare; inductive learning prevails. Also imperative is the abandonment of evaluative tactics, especially those based upon a comparison of a child to his peers. The teacher does, however, serve a demonstration role. Above all, she must be a highly skilled observer, capable of determining when and under what circumstances a child is ready successfully to encounter advanced exercises. Ideally, observational data taken by the teacher enables her to collaborate with the child in the construction of his individual learning activities. In this way may be achieved what Montessorians term "functional independence." Appropriately, scientific techniques of child study are stressed in Montessori teacher training which, incidentally, is controlled entirely by organizations such as the Association Montessori Internationale.

Montessori seemed convinced that poorly arranged learning materials and insensitive, authoritarian teachers presented obstacles to children, thus producing such negative consequences as rebellion, failure, and aggression. Condemned also are such teacher behaviors as verbally imposed rules (the "don'ts" so frequently encountered by children many of which are arbitrary), moralizing, and the interruption or rushing of children's work. Experimentation on the part of the teacher is encouraged, but primarily in order to observe children's reactions to various materials so that poorly received ones may be discarded. It should be apparent that the Montessori directress must be a sound model for her children, temperamentally, linguistically, and organizationally.

Preeminent qualities for an effective teacher are, in Montessori's view, imagination and faith in the child's ability to realize himself through purposive work activities. In theory, teacher efforts incorporate a tripartite function. The first function is essentially custodial. Meticulous order, clean apparatus in good repair, and a generally attractive environment must be maintained. This stress upon attractiveness and dignity includes the teacher's own person as she is the most significant part of the child's environment. The second function involves the exercise of the teacher's motivating power. Prior to the achievement of full concentration, children will need to be enticed, charmed, and stimulated within the context of developmentally appropriate activities. During this stage the teacher may intervene in the interests of classroom socialization. The third and final function is served when the children begin to manifest genuine concentration. At this point, the teacher must not interfere in any way. Praise, assistance, or attention of any sort will have the effect of interrupting the child. Thus, once a captivated child initiates independent task behavior the teacher must behave as if he no longer exists (Montessori, 1967, p. 280). A teacher's normal affections for the child must be subordinated to an advanced level of love, a level based upon a love for the spirit of men. Once this level has been achieved, the teacher will find that children will proceed to organize an orderly society unaided by adults. If disorder and negativism develop *after* children have once established concentration, they are evidence of teacher failure.

Concerning teacher preparation, Montessorians offer no substitute for direct, practical experience. A first objective entails learning to distinguish between the "purely impulsive" behavior of children and their spontaneous expressions of energy which may be harnessed for educational purposes. Categories of responses identified by Montessori to indicate a lack of inner discipline include: (1) disordered voluntary movements (ill-coordinated motor movements), (2) distractibility and low levels of objective concentration, and (3) an affinity for imitating the inappropriate behavior of others, to be "seduced" into undesirable acts. General principles of human interaction and development must guide a teacher in the management of discipline problems. Yet, the ultimate authority in such matters is the teacher's own judgment based upon an assessment of the particulars of a given situation. Practical life exercises for the child are thought to serve an important preventative function. The reality contacts inherent in these exercises are purported to strengthen the child's capacities for free choice, persistence, and order, all of which are basic to self-discipline. Self-discipline is equally important for the teacher who must refrain from creating dependency relationships with her children. This points up one of the most basic differences between conventional nursery-kindergarten practices and the Montessori Method. The former stresses the creation of an emotional bond between teacher and child; a strong teacher-pupil relationship is frequently viewed as the key to the child's success-ful learning. For Montessori, however, the critical relationship is that between the child and his learning materials.

Principles of Learning and Instruction

A number of instructional and learning principles pervade the Montessori Method, some of which apply to the didactic materials, others to the management of the children. These include: heterogeneous grouping by age, active involvement, self-selection and pacing in the use of materials, the self-correctional nature of the materials, graduated sequence, sensory attribute isolation, the provision of extraneous cues to facilitate subtle discriminations, practice, and the principle of contiguity.

Heterogeneous Grouping by Age   In the preparatory Montessori program, around thirty children ranging in age from three to six or seven are gathered together in the same classroom. This practice is markedly different from American public school education which traditionally has been age-graded. The rationale for such grouping contains several ingredients. For one thing, it is thought to provide a sound precondition for social development. Since all of the children will not be working at similar levels, they will neither need nor want the same materials at the same time. Thus, conflict among children is avoided.

Heterogeneous grouping also provides the variety in companionship thought desirable by Montessori for young children. Related is the notion that the older children may serve as models for their younger counterparts. Three points may be made in connection with this "modeling hypothesis." First, a child of five, for example, may be a better teacher of some things to a three-year-old than an adult. Second, the act of teaching another is among the most effective learning experiences possible. And third, the excitement conveyed by older children learning to write and read may be very contagious for the younger ones. Thus, a motivational advantage may be gained.[3]

Finally, heterogeneous grouping is thought to make possible (within the parameters of the Montessori Classroom) the operation of peer-based social controls which are both more natural and more effective for maintaining order than are adult-imposed controls.

---

[3] Psychologists have recently initiated the study of young children's teaching styles. See Feshbach and Devor (1969), for example.

Active Involvement Unquestionably, Montessori was committed to action and movement as the basis for learning. Virtually all of the didactic materials are based upon Montessori's concept of the relationship between physical and mental development and require the performance of some response(s) by the child in order that an effect be observed. Particularly notable is the accentuation of hand movements. Such a performance orientation is not dissimilar to the Deweyian motion of "learning by doing." Few would argue with the soundness of this principle, especially as far as children are concerned.

Self-Selection and Pacing A concrete manifestation of freedom-within-structure in Montessori education is the child's prerogative of selecting, from among designed alternatives, the didactic materials which suit him at the moment. Technically, a child may spend as long as he wishes with any set of materials. Also important is the flexibility which allows the child to proceed through a sequence of materials at his self-imposed rate. In this sense, Montessori education is individualized education; unblocked time periods prevail. This feature has led Millar (1965), per example, to envision a Montessorian classroom as the original nongraded learning environment. All children must, however, engage themselves with the same materials, in proper sequence, at some time. Such vital issues as when and how rapidly this occurs are determined largely by the child. The reader will perhaps recognize these concepts as fundamental to contemporary techniques of programmed learning (Glaser and others, 1966).

Self-Correctional Materials Montessorian didactic materials are carefully designed so that errors (and successes) are for the most part self-evident. In other words, the child may correct his own mistakes by modifying his actions upon the materials. This amounts to a sort of trial-and-success process where the probability of error is low. Children do not depend heavily upon the teacher for evaluative feedback. Auto-educative materials are used either correctly or incorrectly. For example, the cylinder blocks fit only one way; the Golden Beads work only one way; the brown stair can be built in one way only. Hence, the child's task is to converge upon the correct combination of actions; he knows immediately how successful he has been. Teacher intervention may occur on occasion, although intervention is more likely to prevent materials from being misused than to indicate "answers" to the child. It should be noted that Montessori viewed the commission of errors to be a natural and important aspect of learning by the auto-educative method. Reinforcement or reward is said to emanate primarily from the child's sense of pleasure through accomplishment.

Graduated Sequence   As we have seen, the major components of the Montessori program are carefully sequenced in graduated steps from simple to complex. Sensory motor movements are perfected first, followed by discrimination skill and vocabulary training. All sensory discrimination tasks follow the pattern *gross-to-fine*. A fixed order with regard to particular sense presentation is not demanded. However, for each sense there is the same order in presentation method: contrasts, identity matching, and qualitative gradations for purposes of finer discrimination. Didactic materials are integrated such that the activities of writing and reading flow naturally from preceding sensorial tasks. Montessori strove for complete consistency in her approach to pedagogy. While one might question the necessity of all the steps children must take, there can be little argument that a coordinated matrix of stimulus elements characterizes the Method.

Isolation of Sensory Attributes   To promote concentration and sharpen discriminations, Montessori arranged for children generally to deal with one sensory modality at a time. Thus, children are frequently blindfolded when working with auditory and tactile materials. Further, a single sensory (conceptual) dimension of a given set of materials is highlighted at one time. For example, while color is varied for a given exercise, size, form, and texture are held constant. Likewise, while size is varied, other dimensions such as form, texture, and color are held constant.

Provision of Extraneous Cues To Facilitate Fine Discriminations
Noteworthy is Montessori's strategy for introducing cues, especially color cues, in stimuli which pose initial discrimination difficulties. These cues have the effect of drawing the child's attention to the critical or defining attribute of a stimulus and enriching the meaning of it. For example, in the grammar exercises each part of speech has its peculiar color. (Nouns are black for without a verb they "lack life.")

A legitimate procedural question may be raised in reference to the strategy of extraneous cues, namely, whether children may be trained to be dependent upon artificial prompts. As an initial training strategy, however, there is evidence that the principle of cue provision is efficacious (Meyer, 1964; Deese and Hulse, 1967).

Practice   Montessorian materials lend themselves to highly repetitive use. Freedom to practice making discriminations, manipulating objects, tracing, counting, and the like is thought to facilitate a high degree of proficiency in these skills. As indicated in the psychological literature on learning, such practice is directly related to rates of retention (Rock, 1958). That is, while learning may be accomplished in one trial, the retention of what is learned may depend heavily upon a repetition of experiences.

The Contiguity Principle Contiguity refers to the position or occurrence of objects or events close together in place or time. Although the basic idea of association by contiguity may be traced to Aristotle, a generalized law of learning based upon contiguity has been formalized (Guthrie, 1935). This law concerns the strength of an association between a stimulus pattern and a response. Full associative strength develops, according to this view, on the first pairing of a stimulus pattern and a response. When a stimulus pattern which has been accompanied by a movement recurs, it will tend to be followed by that same movement, thus conditioning is involved. When one considers the nature of the Montessorian didactic materials it appears that an application of Guthrie's principle anticipated its eventual formalization. By the simultaneous or contiguous association of the sensorial materials and motor responses, in this case the association of symbol and sound, learning is achieved. As Craig (1966) suggests, application of the contiguity principle provokes concern for cues which will simultaneously direct a learner's attention and prompt an appropriate response. It is precisely this concern which is reflected in the design of most Montessori materials.

CRITIQUE

Many commentaries on the Montessori Method are sprinkled throughout the literature of the past sixty years. Notable among the early responses to the method were those of Morgan (1912) and Kilpatrick (1914). These reports are representative of those published on the North American continent, most of which had the effect of dampening initial enthusiasm for Montessori, and only their criticisms will be discussed. The reader should keep in mind the social context and times in which these reports appeared.

Morgan (1912) addressed his criticisms primarily to Montessorian philosophy and contentions about learning. A nearly exclusive emphasis placed upon the child's mastery of the physical environment, contended Morgan, blunts the social character of learning. The cultivation and analysis of higher thought processes and feeling, he charged, were crucial elements missing from Montessorian education. Morgan further maintained that to attempt sensory education independently of the acquisition of knowledge about self and real life phenomena was to flirt with total educational failure. Finally, he maintained that Montessori was guilty of a logical conflict in her proposals regarding liberty and discipline. For example, while espousing the "law of liberty," Montessori observes that a teacher must exercise authority sufficient to distinguish between individual freedom and the good of others. Admittedly this requires the drawing of a very fine line. Critics of Montessori have seemingly never felt comfortable with this facet of Montessorian doctrine. Self-expression, usually considered to be the essence of freedom, finds little encouragement from the didactic materials.

While Morgan's critique was among the first to appear in this country, Kilpatrick's essay (1914) is generally considered to be the most tarnishing exposition. Kilpatrick acknowledged the attitude he sensed to accompany Montessorian education, namely, a feeling that the chains of repressive educational practices were being broken. However, this revolutionary ideal was felt by Kilpatrick to be presumptuous in light of the stirrings of American progressive education. In fact, the concepts and philosophy of progressive education, as articulated by Kilpatrick's colleague, John Dewey, were believed to be much more consistent with then-contemporary theories of learning and child development. Kilpatrick questioned seriously Montessori's implicit assumptions about the transfer of learning. He perceived the Method's success to be based upon excessive practice of highly specific skills which in no way could be shown to generalize to broader classes of behavior. Further criticized was the restriction of children's individuality. In sum, Kilpatrick maintained that Montessori's personal contribution to education and psychology was minor, particularly in view of her heavy reliance upon concepts earlier advanced by Seguin and Pestalozzi.

As one of the most respected members of the educational elite in America, Kilpatrick had a deadly impact on Montessorian education at that time. It is perhaps one basic reason for the relative isolation of Montessorians from professional educators which seems to have persisted over the years. Additional events, such as the trend toward progressivism in American education and the exciting influence of theoreticians such as Sigmund Freud (psychoanalytic concepts of child development), Edward Thorndike (learning theory applied to education), and the Gestalt psychologists courted in various ways the attention of American educators. Montessori is, however, credited with having stimulated innovations in equipment and materials for kindergarten practice in this country. Further, the fact that her child-centered orientation was firmly consistent with the tenets of progressive education probably added momentum to the forces for change which were pressing educators at that time.

Recent Analysis

The passage of time has now permitted the luxury of placing Montessori in a broader, more elaborate context. Emergent social conditions have apparently done much to provoke a revisitation of Montessori by many psychologists and educators. This "second wave" of interest is somewhat paradoxical, since Montessori schools have, after all, been operating all over the world for more than fifty years. Nevertheless, professional journals in psychology and education have reflected during the past five years a noticeable increase in the number of articles pertinent to Montessorian concepts.

One eminently influential statement is that of Hunt (1964), who suggests that the relative neglect of Montessori is due, in part, to dissonance created by a comparison of her educational psychology to the more popular conceptions of her day. For example, implicit in American psychology, Hunt reasons, were such things as the belief that (1) early cognitive experience is unimportant, (2) the development of intelligence is essentially fixed by genetic phenomena (hence, environmental influences are of minor importance), and (3) motivation is essentially a homeostatic process based upon drive reduction. Montessorian educational strategies were, therefore, perceived as basically irrelevant, if not to be rejected as inaccurate. As the discipline of psychology has matured, these beliefs have been altered (Hunt, 1964). Consequently a more favorable orientation toward Montessori is "possible."

As a point of further analysis, Hunt has argued that a significant obstacle has long impeded the process of achieving one's maximum intellectual potential. This obstacle, termed "the problem of the match," concerns a motivational mechanism critical to the success of an individual's transactions with his environment and the pleasure one derives from such transactions. According to this notion, success and pleasure are dependent upon the degree of incongruity one encounters in new situations. Incongruity, as used by Hunt, refers to the gap between one's expectations and abilities and the circumstances (tasks required) with which one must deal in a given situation. If the gap is too large, an individual may withdraw, become fearful, or become apathetic. If no gap exists, one is not motivated to respond in ways which would result in learning. Somewhere between complete congruity and excessive incongruity is a point which represents a situation sufficiently challenging and appealing to prompt constructive responses with concomitant positive affect. This point, called optimum incongruity, represents a solution of the "problem of the match." This becomes the motivational basis for continuous cognitive growth, the basis for what Montessori interpreted as spontaneous energy and interest in learning.

Hunt believes that Montessorian materials, provided within an atmosphere of personal freedom, represent a long step toward a practical solution for the "problem of the match." Further, since psychologists and educators do not currently know how to solve these match problems for children from without, it is reasonable to allow children to solve these for themselves through the self-selection of appropriate activities and materials. This assumes, of course, a careful arrangement of well-sequenced events, the acme of which may not be the Montessori method. What Hunt has revealed is an important psychological basis for strategies such as Montessori's.

While the favorable relationships between Montessori practice and current psychological evidence are highlighted, so also is the caution customary of the scientist. Foremost among these cautions is the notion that the didactic materials should not be considered so sacred that innovation and scrupulous evaluation are restrained; whether all the didactic materials designed for retarded and poverty-stricken Italian children some seventy years ago are relevant for American children, impoverished or otherwise, is not absolutely clear. Nor should rigidity prevail, Hunt warns, in the use of the materials. A greater variety of experiences, particularly those aesthetic in nature, may be necessary to provide a more balanced program. Finally, Hunt is not enamored of Montessori's theory on the grounds that it lacks heuristic power. In other words, it is deficient as a provoquer of research desirable to help resolve issues borne of the Method itself.

Dr. Riley Gardner of Topeka's Menninger Foundation has also noted the relevance of Montessorian contributions to our current priorities in early cognitive enrichment for children. Focal in this commentary on Montessori's genius are the provision of sensory-motor underpinnings for subsequent conceptual growth and the sophistication of Montessorian observational techniques.[4] Gardner further likens Montessori's concept of autonomy to that basic to successful psychotherapy. While Montessori was concerned with cognitive growth and psychotherapists concern themselves with emotional growth, both are dependent for

---

[4] It is a fact that with few exceptions, notably the developmental psychology of Jean Piaget, theory-building in child development has not involved extensive child-observing. Rats and monkeys have been carefully observed, emotionally-disturbed adults have been carefully observed, but too infrequently have children themselves been carefully observed.

their success upon self-instigated change. Such change is likely only within a context free from negative evaluation and where personal responsibility for change is encouraged. This context, combined with the meaningful activity characteristic of a Montessori child's interactions with reality, is further thought positively to influence *cognitive style* development.[5] Riley thus generates an empirical question which conceivably may be answered with controlled research. Perhaps the most telling issue raised by Gardner's analysis is whether the Montessori Method truly accommodates individual differences among children. Is the same sequence of activities, for example, ideal for all children? Does the prescriptive format blunt individual differences in creative expression? Is the Montessori Method in actuality a means to "individualize" conformity? In point of fact, the didactic materials are quick to impose on a child intellectual distinctions made in advance by adults, but whether this feature of the Method is viewed as an asset or a liability probably depends on one's personal philosophy of education.

Both Hunt (1964) and Gardner (1966) have performed some theoretical splices with the concepts of Montessori and Jean Piaget. (Piaget, whose impact on developmental psychology has been most profound, will be examined in more detail in a later chapter; it is perhaps significant that such splicing has not been done by Piaget himself.) The grounds for a theoretical linkage have been most explicitly clarified by Elkind (1966). Elkind extracts three original ideas concerning children's cognitive development conceived independently by Piaget and Montessori.

According to Elkind's analysis, both authorities conceive a dual character for nature-nurture interaction; for mental capacities, nature is directive and nurture is subordinate—the reverse is true for the *content* of thought. Secondly, both Piaget and Montessori believe that capacity determines learning; at any given developmental level, the child's existing mental structures set the limits for learning. In other words, the quantity of knowledge acquired does not change the child's capacity for problem solving. Third, Elkind sees Piaget and Montessori as sharing a conceptual relationship between cognitive need and repetitive behavior; a child's repetitive behavior frequently signals the emergence of new cognitive ability and the need to develop such ability through activity.

A sophisticated content analysis of Montessori's writings has led Travers (1969) to suggest that Montessori's singular contributions,

---

[5] Cognitive style refers to the characteristic way in which an individual perceives, decodes, and encodes environmental stimuli.

while important, have in actuality been few. One involves the pedagogical principle that if children are to create their own learning situation, then activity and freedom of movement are requisite conditions. A second is the insight that motor behavior and expression are a function of a child's idosyncratic physical proportions. The theme that sensory learning facilitates the later learning of more complex perceptual skills (proactive facilitation) anticipated contemporary psychological thought on this topic as did Montessori's (Seguin's) techniques of elementary discrimination learning. Also anticipatory were Montessori's views on the critical effect of early experiences upon mental development and the concept of intrinsic motivation upon which the didactic materials were grounded. On the other hand, Travers (1969) correctly reveals features of Montessori unacceptable to most psychologists today. Among these include the recapitulationism implicit in her concept of development, that is, that children in the course of their development recapitulate the cultural evolution of man.[6] Another involves the untestable assumptions Montessori made about human nature; these assumptions were apparently a function of her highly religious commitment. One does not, however, have to accept Montessori's philosophical assumptions in order to make constructive use of her pedagogical insights.

The motivational power of the Montessori method emerges as the distinctive feature in other analyses (for example, Morra, 1967). Current motivational theory maintains that children do, in fact, act upon their environment to effect changes rather than simply to maintain a state of psychological equilibrium; such theory also suggests that a variety of stimuli presented across varying sensory modalities will have the effect of maintaining optimal arousal. Optimal arousal, a precondition for effective learning, is generated in theory by the Montessori apparatus. Thus, the aggregate of opportunities for an aroused learner to act and effect changes upon his environment may represent the most fertile component of the Method. Furthermore, the child's activity appears to be self-maintaining and essentially independent of artificial rewards.

Less enthusiastic views of Montessori, however, are dispersed liberally in the psycho-educational literature (for example, Beyer, 1962; Edmondson, 1963; Pitcher, 1966). Generally, the criticisms of Montessorian theory and practice conveyed by these views are similar. At

---

[6] Montessori was in good company at the time for recapitulationism was basic to the theory of G. Stanley Hall (1916), generally viewed as the father of modern child psychology.

the top of most lists is skepticism. This is usually in response to the many claims made by Montessorians concerning the dramatic success of the Method in changing children's behavior. As a point of fact, most "evaluative reports" of Montessori programs are anecdotal and subjective in nature. Therefore, cautious skepticism is not unwarranted. Lack of attention to the value of social and emotional play among Montessorians is frequently mentioned. So is the failure of the Method to provide for "creative" problem solving. The former issue, play, is usually perceived as a serious weakness from two viewpoints: emotional development through motor play and social development through small group planning and cooperative activity. Finally, the relative lack of emphasis upon verbal interaction and language development is occasionally questioned, particularly in light of contemporary developmental psycholinguistics. Of the various criticisms, those involving social and language development are perhaps most worthy of additional comment. Consider first the issues related to social development.

Social Development   Montessori defined social life as a continual process of solving social problems, during which one must behave in concert with other people and cooperate in striving toward goals desired by the social collective (Montessori, 1967). With such a philosophy it strikes this writer as odd that the Method is often considered to be at variance with the concept of group adjustment so pervasive in American society. The pathway to genuine social consciousness is first marked by an identification with one's peer group. This makes possible cohesive action. Such a phenomenon is said to be a natural occurrence when children are placed in a social embryo characterized by purposive activities. Later will come the child's intellectual concern for customs and laws, leaderships, and organized government.

So intertwined are Montessori's ideas on child growth and political philosophy that it is her discussion on social group development that possibly marks her ideological zenith. Montessori's commitment to the achievement of harmony and mutual cooperation among people cannot be questioned. According to Montessori, this objective requires, among other things, respect for the work of others. The rationale for certain techniques applied in the classroom is clarified by this premise. For example, if an item wanted by one child is being used by another, the first child must wait until his peer has finished.

Relevant to the development of social consciousness are Montessori's views on the function of obedience. This characteristic is seen to unfold naturally in a series of three levels. At level one, obedience is sporadic due to the child's lack of ability to obey an order save when it may correlate with a "vital urge." In short, the child's capacity to obey is limited until around the age of three. A consolidation of powers occurs during the next three years. This allows the child to absorb the wishes of another person and manifest them in behavior (conformity). Montessori charged that most public school teachers are satisfied if children achieve stage two, hence may often fail to stimulate further development.

Under appropriate circumstances, stage two is succeeded by a yet higher form of obedience. A child who has reached this third stage says to a significant other, in effect, "I submit my will to you. I want to obey for I enjoy the feeling it gives me." (This is roughly parallel to the notion of psychological identification discussed so widely in the behavioral sciences literature.) The power to obey and experience positive affect as a consequence purportedly is the apex in the growth of the child's *will*. Thus Montessori saw true sociality to require a combination of self-imposed controls, initiative, and the will to subordinate oneself in the interests of others. The validity of her pedagogy to achieve such goals of socialization remains to be clearly established. Further, Montessori's views with respect to the development of social behavior are pitched at a highly theoretical level.

Language Development   There can be little argument that Montessori did not assume verbal behavior to be of much significance in early education. Clearly, the Method depends very little upon verbal interchange to accomplish learning. Equally clear, however, is her professed appreciation for the complexity and ultimate importance of language. This apparent contradiction may be resolved, in part, by noting Montessori's belief about language. First, she did not believe that language was taught to the child by others. Rather, language occurs as a spontaneous creation (she spoke of an "absorption process" which occurs at an unconscious level in the mind), although subject to certain laws which hold for all children (Montessori, 1967, p. 111). A "border line" in the formation of the child's mentality, thought Montessori, was reached about age two and a half. This was believed to mark a new period, encompassing ages two and a half to six, during which language is organized. The perfection of syntax and vocabulary development are the child's major tasks during this stage. Consequently the Montessorian emphasis was upon vocabulary building. Apparently, Montessori felt that syntax refinement comes naturally through the child's interaction with appropriate language models (teacher and older children).[7]

---

[7] It may be noted here that vocabulary building per se is not currently viewed as the most relevant technique for language system development. See Blank and Solomon (1968), for example.

What Montessori termed as the tremendous "explosiveness" of children's language development in natural settings reinforced her general belief in the spontaneity of human behavior. Her writings refer frequently to phenomena now usually interpreted in terms of inductive language learning and concept formation. While environmental circumstances were paid their due, Montessori invested heavily in a genetic psychology. This investment was buttressed by her correct observation that a capacity for language is unique to the species. Therefore, she reasoned that genetic factors must govern language development to a large extent. Among other things, this means a predictable, orderly sequence of development. Taken as evidence for this principle are data which indicate a fixed progression from sounds to syllables to words to sentences.

It should be noted that the notion of a genetically controlled mechanism for language development is a popular hypothesis in contemporary psycholinguistic thought and will be examined in a later chapter. This should not preclude a search for the conditions which influence the rate and quality of language development, apart from emphasizing the importance of a model and a permissive environment. Apart from emphasizing the importance of a model and a strategy for vocabulary training, Montessori has little in the way of specifics to offer the educator concerned with developmental psycholinguistics.

In sum, Montessori's position on language development is not sufficiently comprehensive to satisfy today's criteria for a theory of language development. In view of the complex relationships of language to thought and the research literature on language learning, it seems legitimate to question the Montessori Method (at least in its original form) for its relative lack of stimulating language activities.

RESEARCH ON THE METHOD

Basic to the scientific method is a continual investigation into the effects of manipulations performed with phenomena, be they chemical substances or educational methods. Assessment and evaluation procedures are supremely important in education, dealing as it does with the lives of young children. Eventually, the issue of objective and systematic evaluation must be raised, regardless of theoretical or doctrinaire claims. Where methods of education are involved, this issue hopefully stimulates educators to perform a continual inquiry into the validity of their procedures (Coladarci, 1956). This means that one seeks reliable evidence, through objective means, to verify the extent to which his procedures are valid for their designed purposes. In short, given objectives X, Y, and Z, is method A an effective way to reach them? If so, how effective? Is method A necessarily the best way?

The preceding questions are prototypes for researchers in early childhood education. Generally speaking, however, most of the important answers remain to be found. This is patently true with respect to the Montessori Method. While it is possible that European journals reflect scientific research efforts, American journals (with very few exceptions) do not. On the other hand, there is no paucity of subjective testimonials and enthusiastic anecdotal reports, especially by protagonists of the Method such as Standing (1966), Rambusch (1962), and contributors to *Children's House,* an official organ of the American Montessori Society.

What little Montessori-based research has appeared in print represents several types of investigations. One type has involved the longitudinal measurement of changes in the behavior of Montessori children, where growth is presumed to reflect the total impact of the Method. An example is Naumann's (1967) study which documents substantive reading and spelling gains for children ages three to five who spent a full year in a Montessori classroom. These data were interpreted to suggest that such gains, as measured by the Wide Range Achievement Test, are greater for slow learners than for bright children. Neither slow nor fast learners demonstrated much improvement in arithmetic skills. The absence of a non-Montessori group of children for comparative purposes (control group) makes it impossible to say how much better (or worse) a Montessori experience was for these children in terms of academic gains. It should also be noted that the subjects of this study were all volunteers and mostly children of college personnel. One might ask whether such children are more or less disposed to respond favorably to a Montessorian classroom experience or will be stimulated at home to the point that any formal type of preschool experience would show benefits. At best, the Naumann study indicates that young children can develop academic skills, presumably within an atmosphere which encourages self-teaching.

Another example of the "one-group design" type of study has dealt with a heterogeneous group of mildly retarded and normal children (Naumann and Parsons, 1965). A basic purpose of this short-term project (seven weeks) was to demonstrate the efficacy of teaching a nonsegregated group of preschoolers who vary substantially in their measured ability. (The reader will note that much more typical in American education is the strategy of special classes for retardates.) Selected test and observational data were collected which indicated to the researchers that moderately retarded and normal children can learn together "effectively" in the Montessorian setting. That is, progress in the acquisition of skills such as self-care, autonomous selection and utilization of materials, courteousness, counting, and object naming was observed. Certain modifications were reported to have been made in the Montessori Method for this group of children, however, including more group-based experiences than the classical Method would provide.

A more prevalent investigative design for Montessori education (and early childhood education generally) is the standard "group comparison" design. This approach involves a comparison on selected criteria of children from a Montessori classroom with children from one or more "non-Montessorian" classrooms. Results of several recent studies of this type have been reported. For example, Banta's (1967) ongoing Sands School project is addressed to a wide range of effects attributable to Montessori experience in comparison with nongraded primary classroom and "conventional" graded kindergarten-primary experiences. (Also built into this project is the evaluation of the cumulative effects of preschool education, since three of the four groups of children involved have attended "preschool.") Preliminary data indicate a pattern of test results (for example, impulse control, analytic thinking, innovative behavior, and curiosity) that are clearly in favor of children whose preschool *and* primary education was Montessorian. Banta points out, however, that children from a non-Montessorian preschool followed by a nongraded primary program scored almost as high. Lowest test performances were noted among children who had no preschool and went on to a conventional graded primary class. A fourth group, representing preschool experience in combination with graded primary, performed at a level intermediate between the nongraded classes and the no-preschool group. For the most part, differences between the two highest groups and the two lower groups were significant. Although supportive of Montessori education, Banta's data perhaps speak more broadly to the apparent advantage of *continuity* from pre-kindergarten to nongraded primary education.[8]

The apparent influence of the Montessorian curriculum on children's cognition has been explored recently by Dreyer and Rigler (1969). Montessori children were matched on age, sex, social class, and measured intelligence with children from a "traditional" nursery school.

---

[8] This finding is relevant to the concept of open education as discussed in Chapter 7; the reader is advised to make a mental note of Banta's findings.

Significant differences in behavior were observed, with Montessori children being less socially-oriented and creative, although more task-oriented than their nursery school counterparts. An analysis of these children's creative drawings revealed less use of people and greater use of geometric forms by the Montessori children. Further, while Montessori children tended to employ physical characteristics to describe commonplace objects, the nursery children utilized functional terms more frequently in their verbalizations. These data seemingly illustrate a function of the Montessori materials whereby children are sensitized to particular features of the physical environment. The Dreyer and Rigler study, more than any other, appears to bear out certain criticisms which have long been made of Montessori education, namely a relative de-emphasis of social and creative development. It must be remembered, however, that techniques for the measurement of such development during early childhood are far from perfect; some, including the test of creativity used by Dreyer and Rigler, are hotly disputed.[9]

A set of data reported by Kohlberg (1968) involves the responses to a year-long Montessori program for socially disadvantaged black children (not dissimilar in background from the deprived children in Rome for whom the Method was originally conceived). Significant increases in intelligence test performance (Stanford-Binet) and decreases in personal distractibility were observed for these children. A positive correlation between IQ increase and attention increase (.65) revealed by this study led Kohlberg to suggest that perhaps the most valuable contribution of a Montessori program is its potential to promote the development of attentional responses basic to cognitive task learning. This, of course, speaks to the concentration factor emphasized by Dr. Montessori.

Related to the Kohlberg data are the results of two independent longitudinal comparisons involving Afro-American and Puerto Rican children (Berger, 1969). Several groups of three- and four-year-old children were assigned to one of two treatment programs. One treatment was Montessorian, and executed by certified Montessori teachers. The other was a conventional pre-kindergarten program prescribed by the New York City Board of Education and implemented by certified early childhood teachers. Data collected from all children at the end

---

[9] Dreyer and Rigler utilized one segment of the figural portion of Torrance's Tests of Creative Thinking (1966). This battery, including both verbal and figural sections, has been published as a research edition.

of one year's treatment indicated an advantage in autonomous problem solving and perceptual discrimination skills for Montessori children. As in the Naumann study mentioned earlier, this advantage was salient chiefly among children whose initial status was below average. Measures of motor impulse control, field independence, and task persistence also were indicative of a trend favoring Montessori children. All three of these characteristics would seem to foster efficiency in structured problem-solving situations.

With respect to curiosity—exploratory responses, verbal and memory skills, and unstructured problem-solving tasks—Berger noted no reliable differences between groups. However, where differences in these phenomena among children were observed, Berger suggests that teaching style, rather than program variables per se, is the key factor. Teaching style (tightly prescribed-mechanistic versus permissive-fluid) was not clearly associated with either the Montessori or conventional programs. This suggests that teaching style may vary considerably from classroom to classroom even when all may be identified as Montessori, conventional, or whatever. Support for this suggestion comes from Banta (1966), who has observed a substantial range of differences between Montessori schools on several counts, including the degree to which activities are structured by Montessori teachers, the percentage of didactic activities initiated by teachers, and the actual amount of time spent by children on the didactically correct use of materials.[10]

The variations mentioned above highlight a major difficulty of research strategies that compare one method to another. Without knowing precisely what features within a program are operating to produce change, one is left with a prodigious speculative task. This is clearly the case with the Montessori Method. As Kohlberg (1968) correctly observes, Montessorian education is simultaneously a philosophy with ideological overtones, an aggregate of concepts of development, learning, and teaching, and a package of specific, concrete materials. Add to this the important component of the individual teacher's skill and personality. What orchestration of these dimensions is the most productive in terms of objectives sought by the Method?

In summary, research data on record tend to reinforce the hypothesis that Montessorian experience may benefit the child chiefly in terms of

---

[10] Banta's (1966) study illustrates a third type of Montessori research, namely, that designed to describe through systematic observation the activities of the Montessori classroom, including the behavior of children and teachers, and their interactions. Still another example is Naumann's (1966) behavioral interaction analysis technique.

learning style development. Specifically, this involves the development of appropriate attentional responses, persistence, and discrimination sets. Gains vary according to the initial status of the children. The Montessori experience may be much more potentially valuable for children with specific deficits than for those whose developmental status is average or above.

Many questions about Montessori deserve further study. For example, in precisely what ways and for whom is the Montessori Method superior as compared to other approaches? Does a Montessori "preschool" experience make a real achievement and motivational difference in terms of children's subsequent schooling? What are the effects on children who make a transition from a Montessori school to a regular public school classroom? In what way are parents who elect to send their children to a Montessori school different from those who do not, and would parental characteristics condition the effectiveness of the Method?[11] How much variation in Montessori children's behavior is due to the teacher's skill, the didactic materials and their sequencing, and the influence of other children? The investigation of these questions will require carefully executed research within authentic Montessori classrooms. Merely the label *Montessori* obviously does not make a Montessori classroom. As Pitcher (1966) remarks, Montessori schools in America range from the ultra-orthodox to those modified to incorporate other materials and methods. No one knows what the appropriate "mix" should be with respect to children with varying needs.

SUMMARY

For Montessori, a spontaneous, natural process of education is primarily a function of learners acting upon their environment—it is not something a teacher does to a child. Individual activity is the source of nourishment for all educational growth. A teacher's principal task is to prepare and order a sequence of activities which capitalize upon children's innate motive structures. Therefore, the best of all possible

---

[11] Only one study relevant to this question is known to the present writer. Dreyer and Rigler (1969) found no differences between the parents of Montessori and non-Montessori nursery school children on various measures of social and parental attitudes, but the small number of parents involved severely limits the generalizability of this finding.

educational environments is one which allows the child to develop those powers with which he has been endowed by nature.

The Montessori program for children ages three to six consists of three broad phases: exercises for practical life, sensory education, and language activities (writing and reading). This Method strives to develop proficiency with the basic tool subjects and the basic concepts of geography and science earlier than is customary in conventional American schools. Fundamental is the concept that mental development is related to physical movement or, more specifically, is dependent upon such movement. Therefore, the coordination of motor with mental activity is a guiding Montessorian principle.

For the most part, the principles of learning reflected in Montessorian didactic materials are supported by contemporary psychological evidence. In contrast, apart from testimonials, most of the claims associated with Montessorian education have yet to be verified independently by controlled scientific research. With published literature of the past fifty years as evidence, one can, however, observe the considerable amount of emotionalism that surrounds the Method. Responses range from a complete acceptance, on faith, of the entire Montessori complex to cautious objective scrutiny to total rejection on philosophical and methodological grounds. This controversy, as we shall see, is by no means limited to Montessorian early childhood education. Controversy notwithstanding, American educators should be able to profit from many features of the Method, including its stress upon the careful observation of children and the utilization of children's behavior as the criterion for determining the validity of educational procedures.

With control of Montessori teacher training maintained by private societies it remains to be seen how extensively Montessori education may be extended to young children in America. State Departments of Public Instruction are unlikely to negotiate for tax-supported Montessori schools. Nevertheless, Montessorian techniques of sensory education and concepts of freedom and order have found their way variously into many nursery schools and kindergartens in this country. There can be little argument over Montessori's lasting influence on early childhood education. As Banta (1966) has observed, at least four Montessorian orientations are relevant for early childhood educators in general to consider. One is the child-centeredness of the Method. A second is a concern for learning style development based upon freedom. A third is the contribution of structure as an assist to this freedom. And a fourth is a commitment to the child's moral development so as to promote "responsible" freedom, that is, freedom without license.

References

Banta, Thomas J. "Is There Really a Montessori Method?" Paper read at joint meeting of the Ohio Psychological Association and the Ohio Psychiatric Association, Cincinnati, 1966 (February).

Banta, Thomas J. "The Sands School Project: First Year Results." Department of Psychology, University of Cincinnati, 1967.

Berger, Barbara. "An Investigation of Montessori vs. Conventional Pre-Kindergarten Training with Inner City Children: An Assessment of Learning Outcomes." Paper delivered at American Educational Research Association meeting, Los Angeles, 1969 (February).

Beyer, Evelyn. "Let's Look at Montessori." *Journal of Nursery Education,* 1962, 18, 4–9.

Blank, Marion, and Frances Solomon. "A Tutorial Language Program to Develop Abstract Thinking in Socially Disadvantaged Preschool Children." *Child Development,* 1968, 39, 379–389.

Bruner, Jerome. "The Act of Discovery." *Harvard Educational Review,* 1961, 31, 21–32.

Coladarci, Arthur. "The Relevancy of Educational Psychology." *Educational Leadership,* 1956, 13, 489–492.

Craig, Robert C. *The Psychology of Learning in the Classroom.* New York: Macmillan, 1966.

Deese, James, and Stewart H. Hulse. *The Psychology of Learning.* (3d ed.). New York: McGraw-Hill, 1967.

Dreyer, Albert S., and David Rigler. "Cognitive Performance in Montessori and Nursery School Children." *Journal of Educational Research,* 1969, 62, 411–416.

Edmondson, Barbara. "Let's Do More Than Look—Let's Research Montessori." *Journal of Nursery Education,* 1963, 18, 20–25.

Elkind, David. "Piaget and Montessori." *Harvard Educational Review,* 1966, Fall, 535–545.

Elkind, David. "Piaget and Montessori." *Harvard Educational Review,* 1967, 37, 535–545.

Elliot, L. "Montessori's Reading Principles Involving Sensitive Period Method Compared to Reading Principles of Contemporary Reading Specialists." *Reading Teacher,* 1967, 21, 163–168.

Feshbach, Norma D., and Geraldine Devor. "Teaching Styles in Four-year-olds." *Child Development,* 1969, 40, 183–190.

Gardner, Riley W. "A Psychologist Looks at Montessori." *Elementary School Journal,* 1966, 67, 72–83.

Glaser, Robert, James H. Reynolds, and Margaret G. Fullick. "Studies of the Use of Programmed Instruction in the Intact Classroom." *Psychology in the Schools,* 1966, 3, 318–333.

Guthrie, E.R. *The Psychology of Learning.* New York: Harper & Row, 1935.

Hall, G. Stanley. *Adolescence.* 2 vols. New York: Appleton, 1916.

Hunt, J. McV. "Revisiting Montessori." Introduction to *The Montessori Method.* New York: Schocken Books, 1964.

Kilpatrick, William H. *The Montessori System Examined.* Boston: Houghton Mifflin, 1914.

Kohlberg, Lawrence. "Montessori with the Culturally Disadvantaged: A Cognitive-developmental Interpretation and Some Research Findings." In Robert Hess and Roberta Bear (Eds.), *Early Education.* Chicago: Aldine, 1968, 105–118.

Martin, John Henry. "Montessori After 50 Years." *Teachers College Record,* 1965, 67, 552–554.

Meyer, William J. *Developmental Psychology.* New York: Center for Applied Research in Education, 1964.

Miller, Bruce. "Montessori: The Model for Pre-school Education?" *Grade Teacher,* 1965, 82, 36–39, 112–117.

Montessori, Maria. *Dr. Montessori's Own Handbook.* New York: Frederick A. Stokes Company, 1914.

Montessori, Maria. *The Montessori Elementary Material.* Cambridge: Robert Bentley, 1965a.

Montessori, Maria. *Spontaneous Activity in Education.* Cambridge: Robert Bentley, 1965b.

Montessori, Maria. *The Absorbent Mind.* New York: Holt, Rinehart and Winston, 1967.

Morgan, S.A. *The Montessori Method: An Exposition and Criticism.* Ontario Dept. of Education, Bulletin No. 1, 1912.

Morra, Mike. "The Montessori Method in Light of Contemporary Views of Learning and Motivation." *Psychology in the Schools,* 1967, 4, 48–53.

Naumann, Theodore F., and Bobbie Parsons. "A Creative Learning Environment for Normal and Handicapped Pupils." *American Montessori Society Bulletin,* 1965, Spring, 31–35.

Naumann, Theodore F. "Behavioral Interaction Analysis: A New Approach in Child Study." Department of Psychology, Central Washington State College, Ellensburg, Wash., 1966.

Naumann, Theodore F. "Academic Learning of Young Children in a Montessori Class." Paper read at Mental Health Research Meeting, University of Washington, Seattle, 1967 (November).

Perryman, Lucile, Evelyn Beyer, Mary Moffitt, and Eveline Omwake (Eds.). *Montessori in Perspective.* Washington, D.C.: National Association for the Education of Young Children. 1966.

Pitcher, Evelyn G. "An Evaluation of the Montessori Method in Schools for Young Children." *Childhood Education,* 1966, 42, 489–492.

Plank, Emma. "Reflection on the Revival of the Montessori Method." *Journal of Nursery Education,* 1962, 17, 131–136.

Rambusch, Nancy. *Learning How to Learn: An American Approach to Montessori.* Baltimore: Helicon Press, 1962.

Rock, Irvin. "Repetition and Learning". *Scientific American,* 1958, 199, 68–72.

Smith, T.L. *The Montessori System in Theory and Practice.* New York: Harper and Bros., 1912.

Standing, E.M. *The Montessori Revolution in Education.* New York: Schocken Books, 1966.

Torrance, E. Paul. *Torrance Tests of Creative Thinking.* Princeton: Personnel Press, 1966.

Travers, Robert. "Analysis of the Characteristics of Children Implicit in the Montessori Method." In Joe L. Frost (Ed.), *Early Childhood Education Rediscovered.* New York: Holt, Rinehart and Winston, 1968, 96–101.

Willcott, P. "Initial American Reception of the Montessori Method." *School Review,* 1968, 76, 147–65.

3

Project Head Start
and Follow Through

PROJECT HEAD START

Introduction

Educators have long observed that conventional school practices have not been successful for many children who are the product of economically handicapping conditions. Until recently, however, few tangible efforts have been made to attempt to rectify this problem. Without question the most comprehensive recent attempt is Operation

Head Start. The result of a groundswell of federal legislative support which began in the early 1960s, Head Start also represents a significant and concrete deployment of resources to wage the war on poverty. Since its inception in 1964—extending preschool services to over a half a million children from impoverished circumstances—Head Start has grown to represent an educational enterprise of immense proportions.[1]

At the outset, Project Head Start authorized the establishment of organized summer programs for children whose socioeconomic status predicted marginal success or failure for them in the elementary grades. This authorization reflected a basic faith in the idea that relevant pre-kindergarten or pre-first grade experience would facilitate the adjustment of these children to the regular school setting. Its broader conceptual foundation, however, rests upon the notion that the quality of children's intellectual development depends upon their early experience, that the achievement of intellectual potential is often impeded by an impoverished environment. Thus, it has been maintained that the earlier the intellectual enrichment the less likely it is that the debilitating effects of such an environment will be sustained (Goldberg, 1966).

Under the auspices of the Office of Economic Opportunity, Head Start programs were initiated on a national scale in the summer of 1965. This was accomplished through federal grants to local community agencies capable of meeting basic standards and implementing procedures to foster the health and learning of four- and five-year-old children. Apart from a uniform guarantee that child, family, and community welfare would be maintained, experimentation and variety in program design and program emphases were encouraged. This encouragement resulted in a broad spectrum of programs staffed by personnel with widely diverse talents. While a concern for childhood education was at the forefront of Project Head Start from the outset, it was not the sole concern. Project Head Start has been broadly conceived as a seven-component multi-disciplinary enterprise including education, medical-dental care, nutrition, social services, psychological services, parent education, and the involvement of community volunteers.

Subsequent to the first summer's operation, Head Start programs have been extended to encompass the full academic year prior to formal school entrance. Gradually, greater levels of program specificity have been achieved, although the original variety characteristic of Head

---

[1] See the March 1968, National Educational Association (NEA) Research Bulletin for data on public school system involvement and a sampling of financial expenditures associated with this movement.

Start programs is still apparent. This chapter will be devoted to a discussion of Head Start objectives, types of Head Start Programs, preliminary findings with regard to Head Start influences and contributions, variables which seemingly contribute to variations in Head Start effectiveness, and Project Follow Through, a recent extension of Project Head Start.

Guiding Objectives and Principles of Head Start

Seven broad objectives have guided the national Head Start Program, including the many research and demonstration projects which have been conducted under federal auspices since 1965 (Grotberg, 1969). These guidelines are

1. Improving the child's physical health and physical abilities
2. Helping the emotional and social development of the child by encouraging self-confidence, spontaneity, curiosity, and self-discipline
3. Improving the child's mental processes and skills with particular attention to conceptual and verbal skills
4. Establishing patterns and expectations of success for the child which will create a climate of confidence for his future learning efforts
5. Increasing the child's capacity to relate positively to family members and others while at the same time strengthening the family's ability to relate positively to the child and his problems
6. Developing in the child and his family a responsible attitude toward society, and fostering constructive opportunities for society to work together with the poor in solving their problems
7. Increasing the sense of dignity and self-worth within the child and his family.

These objectives were prepared by a panel of child development authorities and are not dissimilar to those established for conventional nursery and kindergarten programs. The breadth of such objectives, however, does allow for latitude in interpreting what specific activities will be undertaken in a given program. The similarity of Head Start to traditional preschool programs of long standing is also apparent in the following format recommended for a Head Start Center program (Project Head Start, Pamphlet No. 11).

Arrival, Independent Activity Period, (Breakfast in
Some Centers)   8:00–8:45
Work-Play Activity Period, including Self-Directed
Activities   8:45–10:00
   Dramatic Play
   Block-Building
   Creative Experiences with Unstructured Media
      (e.g., painting, clay modeling, and waterplay)
   Activities with Structured Media
      (e.g., games, puzzles, alphabet sets)
   Informal Experiences in Language, Literature, Music
Transition (clean-up, snack)   10:00–10:15
Outdoor Work–Play   10:15–11:15
Clean-Up   11:15–11:30
Lunch   11:30–12:30
Departure
P.M. Program (in All-day Centers)
   A typical afternoon program includes a nap, outdoor play, and
miscellaneous activities such as a cooking project, experiments
with various classroom materials, book browsing, record listening,
and game playing.

Head Start guidelines call for a limit of fifteen children per class and
require a one-to-five adult-child ratio; one teacher, one paid aide, and
at least one volunteer are necessary to achieve this ratio. Variations
exist, but these guidelines comprise the accepted standard generally
imposed. Most programs operate 3 to 4 hours a day (for example, from
9:00 to 1:00 P.M.) with full-day programs being the exception. Head
Start guidelines require that each child attend his program for a minimum of 15 hours a week. On the surface, there is little to distinguish the
above format from the routines long followed in most nursery schools
and kindergartens—thus may be introduced the question of whether
programs of a general traditional type are necessarily the most suitable
for compensatory purposes.

   A recognition that many things could occur within such a general
format has led some to account more specifically for the Head Start
effort from the standpoint of principles to which Head Start classes
subscribe. One of the few such accounts has been provided by the Educational Testing Service (Dobbin, 1966). Out of a morass of observational data gathered from some 1300 classes has been formulated a
seven-point conceptual pattern:

1. For young children the teaching-learning process must be intimately woven into the fabric of human social interaction.
2. Parents and the community at large should share with teachers the teaching process.
3. The probability that meaningful learning experiences can be arranged cooperatively by adults is vastly increased if planners are aware of the intellectual and emotional patterns of development characteristic of the early years.
4. Children learn best by doing, not just by being told.
5. Methods of known validity for reinforcing and encouraging children's total development are available and should be used.
6. A commonly overlooked but remarkably rich material for instruction is food.
7. The real test of Project Head Start is what happens to its children in the early grades immediately following Head Start.

As the reader can see, the above guidelines represent a scrambling of philosophical and psychological principles. While these are possibly helpful to researchers, a careful analysis of the activities in an individual Head Start classroom, including teacher behavior, would be required to determine the extent to which these and additional principles are operational (Katz, 1969).

Types of Head Start Programs

Despite general agreement among educational strategists on the psycho-educational rationale for compensatory education, uniform paper objectives, and selected common principles, a classification of Head Start programs poses many difficulties. Program variation, for example, may be expected on the basis of beliefs about the needs of disadvantaged children (Getzels, 1966; Hechinger, 1966). The creators of some programs have maintained that the observed deficiencies of disadvantaged children are primarily social in nature. Thus, activities with a predominantly social base have been prescribed. Close attention is therefore given to such matters as helping children to (1) adjust to the rules necessary for successful group activity, (2) develop responsiveness to new authority figures, and (3) achieve constructive social interaction through organized and free play. Another sort of program has assumed that the disadvantaged child's major deficiency is a lack of familiarity with preparatory academic activities and school-related objects (Hechinger, 1966). Hence, organized pre-academic activities under the close supervision of adults prevail. Training children to become skilled in following directions, using materials appropriately (pencils, crayons, books, and the like), and other general "readiness building" activities are pursued. Still another approach is based on the assumption that, because of powerful environmental influences, disadvantaged children are often basically different in values, language, and conceptual equipment. Programs which are built upon this view become highly specialized in function and detailed strategies are devised to counteract the depressing effects of the child's early environment. Within Project Head Start the latter, more intensive type of program has perhaps been the most rare. Recently, however, an increase in support for direct instruction has been noted. (Chapter 4 deals specifically with an example of this type of program although its employment in Head Start programs per se has not been widespread.)

It would be unwise to suggest that the three broad types of programs mentioned above are necessarily mutually exclusive; academic straw men are easily created. It does seem valid, however, to maintain that program emphases and structure vary in important ways. In this connection, a germane analogy has been drawn comparing intervention programs to firearms (Gray and Miller, 1967): the rifle technique (precise; a single target and a single bullet); the shotgun approach (expected to form a broad, more diffuse pattern on the target); and the blunderbuss approach (shooting a short distance with a wide scattering of ammunition). This analogy, incidentally, is not limited to compensatory programs and can be applied generally to early childhood education strategies.

Head Start Research

An analysis of Project Head Start which subscribes as closely as possible to empirical observations gives rise to several related issues.[2] One already mentioned concerns the goals of Head Start. Another concerns the relevance of conventional methods for the achievement of these goals. With respect to the first issue, there is some evidence to indicate conflict among Head Start personnel. Omwake (1968), for example, suggests that the broad objective of Head Start has gradually undergone a metamorphosis. Originally, it was intended that Head Start children would be helped to enter school with greater pleasure,

---

[2] The issues selected for discussion here are illustrative only and do not begin to tap the many philosophical issues associated with the education of "economically disadvantaged" children. For a thorough exploration of these issues see Kaplan (1963) and Elam (1965).

self-confidence, and positive expectation. In other words, a variety of new experiences to facilitate the transition from home to school would be considered a sufficient criterion for success. It is increasingly apparent, however, that more concrete evidence of success is being sought for Head Start programs, particularly in the domain of primary grade achievement. The mounting concern for childrens' cognitive development and preparatory academics is acutely disturbing to many childhood educators (Omwake, 1968). The reader is again reminded of the either-or fallacy implicit in some treatments of this issue, namely, that either one strives for cognitive growth or one concentrates upon education for emotional (affective) growth. Philosophical differences associated with Head Start goals are perhaps most clearly reflected in the various approaches to Project Follow Through which will be discussed later.

The second issue, namely, the general relevance of conventional methods for the educational development of disadvantaged children, may be examined empirically. The most basic question (regardless of stated objectives), is whether subsequent and reliable differences can be observed in children who attend Head Start programs as compared to those who do not. A meaningful answer to this question assumes, among other things, that comparisons are made with children of similar ethnic and socioeconomic backgrounds. This assumption is not always met in practice. In many cases, children in one Head Start program may be compared to those in another or to children not in a program. Group composition may be influenced by race, ethnicity, and other variables. As Wattenberg (1966) suggests, research based on gross categorizations is not unlike comparing baskets of oranges, pears, and grapefruit to baskets of pineapples, strawberries, and peaches. The fruit is grown in different areas and nurtured by different elements. Thus only rough, tentative statements may legitimately be made concerning the effects of this nurturance. This situation is further complicated by the frequently unproven validity of evaluation instruments and the frequently tacit assumption that something universal defines a Head Start program.

With the above limitations in mind, a brief and selective excursion through the modest Head Start research literature follows. Two types of research efforts have been predominant: descriptive and evaluative. The former type has involved the search for general behavioral characteristics which may (1) differentiate Head Start children (or more broadly, socially or economically disadvantaged children) from their more advantaged or privileged age-mates and (2) suggest implications for curriculum development. The second, or evaluative type of research, has attempted to identify the results of Head Start intervention.

Descriptive Studies   Great masses of data that describe the characteristics of socially or economically disadvantaged children have been
published.[3] Most generally, this descriptive research has been oriented
toward the discovery of response "deficits" rather than strengths. It is
further based on the study of large groups of children from differing
social classes and ethnic groups. While generalizations thus derived
may apply to many such children, they do not apply to all. Commonly
found among disadvantaged children, however, are comparative deficiencies in (1) developmental language response patterns (such as
vocabulary size, sentence length, and syntax), (2) logical reasoning
skills (such as the ability to categorize concepts, deal with causal relations, and exercise sequential thought), (3) auditory discrimination
skills, (4) attentional responses (such as high rates of attentional shifts,
lowered persistence, and high motor impulsivity), and (5) selected
social-emotional behaviors (such as greater dependency conflicts,
lessened intellectual achievement responsibility, and less consistency
in relationships with adults) (Grotberg, 1969).

On the other hand, there is little evidence to indicate that memory
skills or basic aquisitional skills of disadvantaged children are markedly
different (Bereiter and Engelmann, 1966). Thus many authorities are
convinced that a learning capacity deficit is not the primary issue. It
is rather a matter of deficits in the conceptual tools which facilitate
learning (Jensen, 1968). Conventional public school encounters generally serve successively to magnify this problem in a fashion akin to a
"vicious cycle." That is, the initial gap between a "disadvantaged" child's
developmental status and the language-based tasks faced in school
frequently increases due to incomplete learning. This phenomenon is
frequently interpreted within the framework of the *cumulative deficit*
hypothesis (Ausubel, 1964; Deutsch, 1964; Jensen, 1966). In brief, this
hypothesis suggests that experiential deficiencies induce growth deficits
which interfere progressively with subsequent growth processes, learning, and motivational development. Implicit is the notion of a hierarchical arrangement of developmental phenomena that affects future
cognitive growth in a cumulative fashion. Data pertinent to this hypothesis include school failure rates among children from low socioeconomic backgrounds and research on the effects of environmental
deprivation and enrichment on measured intelligence and language
development (Ausubel, 1964).

At best, comparative descriptive data may assist toward more rea-

---

[3] Elaborate reviews are available elsewhere (Havighurst, 1964; Gordon 1968; Cazden,
1966; Stodolsky and Lesser, 1967; Hellmuth, 1967; Grotberg, 1969), and a detailed accounting of these characteristics will not be offered here.

soned decisions about program planning, but there always remains the dual risk of overgeneralization and stereotyped perceptions among those who deal with the socially disadvantaged. A timely call for new and better ways to measure various classes of young children's behavior has also been issued (Grotberg, 1969). Meanwhile, it seems apparent that the influence of this type of research has not as yet been fully realized within Head Start. Mounting pressures on Head Start personnel to deal more forcefully with cognitive "deficits" may result in the overhaul of many programs. A serious problem with respect to this kind of educational planning, however, is the possible failure of deficit-oriented teaching to capitalize upon the positive attributes, such as spontaneity and game skills, which many disadvantaged children bring to the classroom.

Evaluative Studies Easily the most encompassing evaluative research project to date has been a joint effort by the Westinghouse Learning Corporation and Ohio University to assess the general impact of Head Start. The principle focus of this study was the intellectual and personal-social development of primary grade children with Head Start backgrounds. Children from a sample of 104 Head Start Centers were chosen, all of whom were attending first, second, or third grade at the time of the study. This sample included both children whose Head Start experience was limited to one summer and those who attended full-year programs. These children were then compared to a sample of "matched controls," that is, children equal of the same age, grade, socioeconomic status, and so on, who had not attended Head Start classes. Psychometric instruments were administered to all children to obtain data on language development, reading readiness, and academic achievement.[4] Projective techniques and teacher ratings were employed to describe such affective characteristics as positive self-concept, desire for achievement, and attitudes toward school, home, peers, and society.

Comparative analyses of the Westinghouse-Ohio data have led to several tentative conclusions. First, no persistent gains in either cognitive or affective development were associated with summer Head Start programs. Second, while full-year programs appeared to result in selected cognitive advantages (improved reading readiness), affective measures did not indicate any advantage to Head Start children. This latter finding is somewhat qualified by a subanalysis based upon variables such as geographic location. For example, more favorable patterns

---

[4] Utilized were the Illinois Test of Psycholinguistic Abilities, the Metropolitan Readiness Test, and the Stanford Achievement Test (see Appendix 1).

of affective development were detected among Head Start children from predominantly black population centers in the Southeastern United States and among children from ghetto areas in large cities. Taken as a whole, the Westinghouse-Ohio data, limited as they may be, at best permit only moderate optimism regarding longer-term Head Start influences. Encouraging, however, was the subsidiary finding that parents of Head Start strongly approve of the program and have been motivated to participate in many of its activities.

It should be noted that the Westinghouse-Ohio report has not escaped serious criticism, particularly in terms of the procedures used for sampling Head Start centers and the statistical analyses of test scores obtained from the children involved. For example, Smith and Bissell's (1970) detailed statement on this national evaluation study involves both a methodological critique and a reanalysis of the test data. These critics conclude that, in contrast to the pessimistic tone of the Westinghouse-Ohio report, "educationally significant" gains were made by many children, particularly black children in urban Head Start centers. In rebuttal, still other authorities have challenged the validity of the Smith and Bissell (1970) critique, suggesting that the original Westinghouse-Ohio findings are basically accurate (Cicirelli, Evans, and Schiller, 1970).

While debate over the Westinghouse-Ohio data is sure to continue, the report should not be interpreted as an attempt to discredit the Head Start concept. In fact, such evaluations are necessary steps toward the improvement of Head Start practices and a better understanding of the complexities involved.

Meanwhile, it is important to consider the various recommendations that have emanated from the Westinghouse-Ohio data. Included is the recommendation that summer programs be abandoned in favor of more extended programs. Extended programs, it is recommended, should include younger children, more varied teaching strategies, remedial teaching techniques to combat specific language deficiencies, and parental training. These recommendations all pertain to the flow of cognitive and affective development. They are not directly addressed to other possible outcomes of Head Start, such as medical or nutritional benefits and the improved quality of children's existence while enrolled in Head Start.

The general Westinghouse-Ohio finding of no differences in affective characteristics cannot be interpreted to suggest that changes did not occur among children in this behavioral domain. In any intervention there is the possibility that certain changes go unmeasured. It is also difficult to determine in broad, general evaluations the extent to which observed changes in any domain are a direct outcome of Head Start treatment. For example, Caliguri and Robertson (1968) have inferred positive changes in social behavior from teachers ratings of children before and after Head Start to be a direct function of the intervention program.[5] Grotberg's (1969) comprehensive review of Head Start research also contains some evidence that measured changes in affective (attitudes, motivation) and social behavior generally tend to surpass those in cognition or measured intelligence. This is not surprising if a majority of Head Start programs are, in fact, based on traditional practices.

A second representative Head Start study is the Social Change Evaluation Project (Brink, Ellis, and Sarason, 1968), in which two stages of assessment were planned. During the first stage differences between children eligible for Head Start and more economically privileged children of the same age were explored. Among nine behavioral characteristics selected for a study, Head Start children were comparatively deficient on six; all of these involved cognitive skills and motivational phenomena. For example, Head Start children were determined through observation and testing to be less adept at motor control, less persistent, less imitative of adults, and less proficient with problem solving strategies. (These differences were established prior to the time the children eligible for Head Start actually entered a preschool program.) The second stage of this project was completed seven months later when the Head Start sample was compared to an equal group of children also eligible for Head Start but who did not attend. Similar data had been obtained on this non-Head Start group in stage one. Thus the question became that of determining the extent to which Head Start experience produced immediate change on any of the six previously identified behavioral deficits. While general improvement was noted over the seven month period, only two of the six characteristics were demonstrated to have been influenced differentially by the Head Start experience: increased control of cognitive impulsivity and increased tendencies to imitate the behavior of others.

The Social Change Evaluation Project results may be taken as support for a basic hypothesis which appears frequently in the literature on disadvantaged children: that the observed academic and intellectual difficulties of lower-class children are outgrowths of deficits in basic underlying cognitive and motivational processes. To the extent that these are amenable to change by formal educational procedures, efforts

---

[5] These researchers failed to provide a control group for comparison, however, which renders difficult any interpretation of their data.

in this direction within the context of Head Start have been urged. In addition, to the extent that current educational procedures for this purpose are ineffective, research is needed to develop better ones.

In smaller scale studies, findings similar to those reported above have appeared. Ramsey (1968), for example, compared similar numbers of children with and without Head Start summer experience in terms of their progress in a conventional first grade reading instruction program. No real differences in end-of-first-grade reading achievement were found for these two groups, although the Head Start sample had a slightly higher percentage of deficient readers at that checkpoint. Ramsey maintains that, despite the latter tendency, Head Start helps many children whose reading achievement would ordinarily be much lower in the first grade. This interpretation is buttressed by the fact that the Head Start sample was, by comparison, initially lower in socioeconomic status and measured intelligence. Both of these attributes are associated with variation in reading achievement. A further observation by Ramsey suggests that Head Start was of little apparent help to a certain hard core of potentially poor readers.

Ramsey has joined other Head Start researchers in recommending that compensatory programs of longer duration will be necessary for significant achievement gains to be realized. He also has advised that for Head Start children conventional reading materials should be abandoned in favor of material written in their own dialect. This he feels is necessary to facilitate mastery of the basic reading process. Once children have learned to speak standard English, a better transition may then be made to reading materials written in standard English. Research related to Ramsey's hypothesis is only beginning to appear (for example, Nolan, 1970) and will require careful scrutiny.

Still another approach to the assessment of Head Start effects was pursued by Lessler and Fox (1968). This involved a combination psychometrics-structured interview technique developed by a team of specialists to sample behaviors basic to successful first grade achievement.[6] A random sample of twenty subjects (ten white, ten black) was then taken from a large number of children who had attended the 1965 eight-week Head Start program. Assessment data for these children were then compared to those obtained on a random sample of youngsters eligible for Head Start but who did not attend. Test data and teacher ratings based upon interview material revealed few differences between the two groups. The few differences observed were conspicuously in the

---

[6] Domains sampled were: school expectation, visual-motor coordination, auditory understanding and memory, vocabulary, motor coordination, picture interpretation, paragraph interpretation, informal communication, and psychological comfort.

area of increased language receptivity (verbal understanding) and verbal fluency, particularly among the Afro-American Head Start children. This, coupled with an observably more positive attitude toward school among Head Starters, speaks favorably toward such a brief intervention program. Whether the control children achieved similar levels in these domains subsequent to school entry cannot be determined by this singular comparison.

A less rigorous evaluation, yet one based upon the same general design as Lessler and Fox (1968), is the "six months later" study of Wolff and Stein (1967).[7] Involved were kindergarteners with Head Start backgrounds, whose social and educational readiness for first grade was compared to non-Head Start peers. Global teacher rankings of such characteristics as "adjustment to class routines," "interpersonal behavior," language, and work habits were combined with data from the Caldwell *Preschool Inventory.*

Three broad conclusions were drawn from Wolff and Stein's comparison. First, that greater numbers of Head Start children received high rankings within all Afro-American or predominately Puerto Rican kindergarten classes. In a school comprised of children with mixed racial and ethnic backgrounds this phenomenon was not observed. Second, teachers generally rated Head Start children as superior in initial school adjustment, although this advantage had apparently dissipated after several months in kindergarten. Third, the educational attainment of these children, as measured by the *Preschool Inventory,* did not differ significantly as a function of pre-kindergarten experience. There was some indication that the quality of kindergarten teaching exerted some influence in this regard. Head Starters in classes manned by "good teachers" consistently outperformed their non-Head Start peers on this instrument. The reverse held for classes handled by "poor teachers." These interactions and the lack of specificity of Wolff and Stein's data complicate the formulation of sound generalizations. It does appear that effects, when observed, vary according to the nature of the experiences which follow Head Start and as yet undefined factors involving ethnicity, race, and general cultural background. Given such ambiguity, the need for sophisticated follow-up procedures is extremely important.

The effects of Head Start preschool experience upon children's measured intelligence and vocabulary development was investigated by Smith (1968). A group of fifty-five poverty-area children was examined at the completion of a full-year Head Start program in reference to

[7] This study dealt exclusively with the New York City Head Start Program.

comparable children (N = 47) who had no preschool experience. Head Starters scored significantly higher on both measures; however, this superiority was accounted for primarily by the girls in the preschool sample.[8] This sex difference was further magnified by the fact that the Head Start boys performed only slightly better than boys with no preschool experiences and at roughly the same level as girls who did not attend Head Start. Thus, the Smith data indicate salutary Head Start effects for girls only.

Even significant gains by girls on intelligence measures may be deceiving. Zigler and Butterfield (1968), for example, claim that spurts in intelligence test performance often are attributable largely to motivational factors and refinements of test-taking skills rather than real changes in underlying intellectual ability. Changes in the vicinity of 15 IQ points have been "explained" by this hypothesis. If the Zigler and Butterfield data are valid (and there is some question about their interpretation), it could be that pre-test measures for disadvantaged children frequently underestimate true ability. Credence for this hypothesis is added by the general observation among Head Start researchers that stunning initial gains in intelligence test scores typically level off or decelerate after a lapse of one or two years (Weikart, 1967). Frequently this results in a failure of psychometric measures to distinguish between groups of children who have taken Head Start and those who have not. In cases where initial gains are not sustained, it is possible that adverse problems of transition from Head Start classes to regular school programs occur. This may be especially true among Head Start classes which have provided copious amounts of individualized attention to children.

While not affiliated officially with Project Head Start, the Perry Preschool Project for disadvantaged children (Weikart, 1967) merits discussion at this point for its attempt to meet the major criticisms of Head Start experience: insufficient time allotted for preschool education and lack of specific focus in terms of critical educational activities. The Perry Preschool Project has involved, since 1962, successive "waves" of disadvantaged preschoolers in a two-year cognitively-oriented compensatory program. "Verbal-bombardment" techniques, dramatic play, field trips, and structured cognitive tasks have been packaged in an effort to influence positively early school achievement. Integrated with this collage of activities has been a system of home visits by trained staff to encourage the involvement of mothers in the instructional process. Longitudinal data have been collected over the past several

[8] Stanford-Binet Intelligence Scale and Peabody Picture Vocabulary Test.

years on such variables as intellectual growth, classroom behavior, and school achievement.[9] Successive groups of Perry Project children have been compared to equal groups without preschool stimulation (control groups).

Several insights may be gleaned from the Perry Preschool longitudinal data. One is that a superiority in measured intelligence for the preschool groups at the end of the first compensatory year is no longer apparent by the end of the second grade. This finding reinforces the "temporary spurt" phenomenon, or lack of early gain stability characteristic of so many Head Start programs (Hyman and Kliman, 1967).[10]

A second major trend in the Perry Preschool data is that, despite a lack of measured differential intellectual ability, children who have experienced the compensatory preschool program demonstrate reliably stronger patterns of academic achievement in the primary grades as compared to controls. Weikart interprets this finding to mean that, while compensatory programs are not likely to produce major changes in measured intelligence, they may nourish many processes which underly academic development. Therefore, planned intervention may assist a child to utilize his intellectual ability more effectively in the school setting. Third, data concerning social behavior, school conduct, emotional adjustment, and academic motivation, while not totally convincing, reveal differences in favor of the compensatory group. These differences, detected by teacher ratings, are more apparent later in the primary grades. Weikart infers this to indicate that changes in behavior and motivational patterns are *preceded* by academic success. If this finding is replicated convincingly elsewhere it could conceivably become a substantial weapon in the arsenal of those who advocate that cognitive competence is the critical target for compensatory education. In other words, desirable affective characteristics may spring from, rather than always be a necessary precondition for sound academic achievement.

Certainly the Perry Project data are moderately encouraging. They also strike a solemn note in that distinctive achievement gains associated with educational therapy occurred primarily among roughly 50 percent of the preschool group. That is, the advantage maintained by the experimental sample was a function of gains by about one-half of that sample. The remainder of the sample is reminiscent of Ramsey's

[9] Instruments used for assessment have been the Stanford-Binet, California Achievement Tests, Pupil Behavior Inventory, and the Ypsilanti Rating Scale.

[10] It must be noted, however, that there is not universal agreement regarding this interpretation of Head Start data. Some authorities believe it is more a matter of non-Head Start children "catching up" later. A major factor may be the type of public school experience which succeeds Head Start.

"hard core" unresponsives described earlier. It remains to be seen why the Perry intervention curriculum is effective with only a portion of the children and whether this phenomenon is discovered in similar programs elsewhere.

It is entirely likely that children uninfluenced by compensatory education will need early placement in more specialized classroom situations if efforts to increase their educability are to pay off. Some support for this policy is suggested by McNamara's (1968) work with children who manifested limited progress in regular Head Start classrooms. Nine slow-learning children were consigned to a "learning disorders" class staffed by a master teacher and several hand-picked teacher aides. Educational consultants and a social worker also assisted in this seven-month project. A majority of this small group of children is reported to have achieved greater increments of educational growth than matched controls who continued in the regular Head Start program. Particularly notable were positive changes in cognitive functioning in such task areas as concept labelling and matching (color, size, and shape). Promising results have also been observed by Allen (1969) from implementing a special program for Head Start "drop-outs." Widespread application of the policy illustrated by the above will, of course, require sophisticated techniques of diagnosis and remediation currently beyond the capabilities of many Head Start teachers. It also suggests the necessity of a still more favorable teacher-pupil ratio and of procedures for grooming children for eventual regular classroom assignment.

With regard to teacher characteristics there is some evidence to indicate that resourcefulness, flexibility, and supportiveness are particularly important characteristics for Head Start operations (Grotberg, 1969). Other points stressed by research on Head Start teacher behavior are that (1) personal biases interfere with teachers' assessments of children and (2) variations in instructional objectives and teaching strengths apparently do make a difference in children's learning. Taken together, these findings carry a number of implications for Head Start teacher training programs including criteria for the selection of teaching personnel, how best to achieve objective viewpoints on the developmental learning process and its assessment, how to determine the parameters within which teachers should operate regarding Head Start objectives, and how best to capitalize on individual teacher competencies.

Parental Involvement

While researchers ponder the complexities of behavioral change and teacher training, several sparkling cues for the improvement of compensatory education programs may be observed in the Head Start literature. One of the brightest of these cues is the concept of parental involvement. Other things being equal, indications are that program success is enhanced in all respects when intervention strategies include efforts actively to involve and educate parents. (Klaus and Gray, 1968; Gordon, 1968; Weikart and Lambie, 1968; McCarthy, 1969; Willmon, 1969). Involvement of parents with the process of their children's learning in ways consistent with a given compensatory program is advantageous in several ways. First, such involvement often bridges a continuity gap which may exist between home and school. Secondly, use of inexpensive educational materials and parental-applied techniques can encourage the practice of important cognitive skills sorely lacking in many disadvantaged children. Third, the indirect effects of parental self-worth and respect engendered by a meaningful contribution to their children's development may go a long way toward improving affectional relationships in the home.

A major wellspring for the emphasis upon parent education techniques has been research into the teaching styles of mothers from middle and lower socioeconomic backgrounds. In fact, some have argued that a portion of the economically disadvantaged child's behavioral deficits is related to austere and stereotyped maternal teaching styles. A classic portrayal of social class differences in maternal teaching behavior is the work of Hess and Shipman (1965). From various socioeconomic levels (ranging from college-educated professional to the category of unskilled occupations) Hess and Shipman selected 160 Negro mothers with four-year-old children. To extensive interview data were added the results of situational testing of these mothers and children. This "testing" involved the careful observation of mothers who were taught three sorting and copying tasks and then requested to teach these same tasks to their children.

The teaching behavior of the mothers was then charted and related to the response patterns of the children being taught. Marked differences in maternal-child cognitive transactions were observed, as were social class differences in the children's ability to profit from their mothers' "teaching." Variations in the extent to which children successfully performed the required tasks were associated with both the amount and quality of verbal interchange between mother and child. Middle-class mothers tended to encourage "active-search" learning behavior among their children in contrast to lower-class mothers, who reinforced docility. Reduced levels of conceptualization were found among the directions and clues provided to children by lower-class mothers. All in all, Hess and Shipman argue that the linguistic codes and cognitive interchanges that ensue early in the socialization of children exert a profound influence on the development of learning style.

Maternal teaching patterns and language codes have also been investigated by Bee and others (1969). These data strengthen the contentions of Hess and Shipman; distinct social class differences were found on several fronts. In contrived "waiting room" and "problem-solving" situations, maternal responses directed toward their children (aged four to five) varied in terms of the (1) amount of disapproval and behavioral control techniques utilized, (2) specificity of suggestions and extent of nonverbal help, and (3) complexity and objectivity of expressive language. These findings are taken to infer a generally less adequate environment for early language development and systematic problem solving strategy development in the case of many lower-class children.

While it is tempting to conclude a cause-effect relationship between parental teaching style and children's learning style, the jury is still out.[11] What we have is an accumulation of rich hypotheses upon which to base further inquiry. A deeply serious issue also pervades this network of hypotheses, however, an issue based in cultural values. It is possible that in some cases middle-class value holders evaluate negatively teaching styles which are appropriate for the goals of a different social class or "co-culture." This accentuates the problem of the extent to which universal values and goals must be applied across subcultures, thus establishing some homogeneity among children for their mutual benefit. Or, to phrase it differently, to what extent can differential values and behavioral styles be encouraged and maintained without affecting negatively a child's success in dealing with a complex social system?

Serious issues notwithstanding, the above data and related analyses (Strodtbeck, 1964; Hertzig and others, 1968) suggest that one of the more promising methods of early intervention involves assisting parents to become better teachers in day-to-day transactions with their children. That parents generally are receptive to this policy is conveyed by the Westinghouse-Ohio report mentioned earlier and by the work of Weikart and Lambie (1968).

A prototype for the coordination of parent education with compensatory education is the Florida Model (Gordon, 1968). This Model has a twofold purpose: (1) to develop nonprofessionals (mothers) to serve as parent educators and teacher aides, and (2) to devise workable, effective educational techniques for home use and procedures for the study

---

[11] The reader is encouraged to consult Freeburg and Payne (1967) for a critical overview of research in this area.

of individual and classroom behavior. The major parent education activity consists of periodic home visits (once per week preferred) in which tasks designed to foster children's cognitive and affective development are demonstrated. During the course of demonstration, mothers are shown the purposes behind each task, helped to perform it themselves, and provided with guidelines to estimate a child's readiness for each task. Parent educators also serve as liaison agents for medical and social service referrals. Hence information concerning community services and those in need of such services may be more effectively catalogued.

Ordinarily, one or two mothers per pre-kindergarten or kindergarten-primary grade classroom are trained as parent educators in the Florida program. Carefully planned activities to promote positive changes in the mothers of school children, classroom teachers, and children reflect the influence of the literature on self-concept development and Piagetian theory (Chapters 6 and 7). As such, language and cognition, attitudes toward self, and interpersonal relations receive high priority. Monthly reports of all activities are monitored at a central location (University of Florida) from which consultant visits are scheduled periodically. Although published research data on the effects of this complex system are not likely to appear for several years, there is no reason to believe that this vehicle for change will only be spinning its wheels. Less elaborate programs have shown promise even in the absence of concurrent organized classroom experience for children (Karnes and others, 1968).

In summary, the evaluative data on Head Start and related programs for disadvantaged children carry a bittersweet taste. Clearly, short term crash programs are unlikely to have much lasting influence, at least in terms of school-related behavior. For reasons still uncertain, some children respond more obviously to Head Start than others; reported effects of intervention are neither consensual nor uniform in relation to the general population of Head Start children. It is entirely plausible that effects will vary according to certain major dimensions relevant to any educational strategy, namely, the skill level of teachers involved, the objective components of a curriculum, and home-school relations. There is the possibility, however, that Head Start programs are ill-timed, that is, programmed too late for any genuine changes in pre-academic response patterns. In fact, this thesis is implicit in the work of Painter (1968) and others who are studying procedures for education (linguistic-conceptual and sensory-motor) of infants aged eight months to two years (see Chapter 7).

Where positive longer-term effects on classroom achievement behavior are revealed, it is most probably a function of programs which (1) clearly identify the cognitive responses to be developed among the children and (2) proceed systematically with a sequence of activities and parental assistance to reach these objectives. Taken as a whole, the measured effects of Head Start to date suggest most obviously a need for constructive program improvement. One can easily become narrow in his concept of effectiveness, however, and surely measured academic achievement is not the sole applicable criterion.

Broader Contributions of Head Start

Evaluation studies have almost universally taken changes in children's behavior as the ultimate standard for Head Start success. This is both logical and legitimate, particularly when one considers the great volume of resources which has been invested in this venture. It would be unfortunate, however, for this standard completely to overshadow other, less direct contributions of the Head Start undertaking. For example, it seems clear that Head Start has virtually forced American educators to take a long, hard look at the learning patterns and instructional problems of many children who have in the past been viewed as bad risks or incapable of success in academic programs. Evidence for this long overdue scrutiny is the explosion in the professional literature of data on disadvantaged children. The ideal of equal educational opportunity may be realized sooner, now that educators have assumed a greater responsibility for these children.

Related to the above point is that Head Start has spurred the revolution currently underway with respect to the design of learning materials most suitable for children from varied social backgrounds. While new materials are not by definition more effective, there is reason to believe that action research will validate the increased value of many of these materials. A third indirect contribution of Head Start is the brainpower this enterprise has attracted for solving problems of program evaluation. Among other things, new techniques and broader concepts of evaluation are gradually evolving. The utilization of these is bound to assist us toward a greater understanding of the educational process (Goldberg, 1966; Goths and Jones, 1968; Zimiles, 1968).

Still another significant contribution is that Head Start has facilitated the earlier identification of children whose problems of mental and physical health might otherwise have gone unnoticed or been inadvertently overlooked. In a large scale Boston Head Start program, for example, previously unknown defects identified among participating children outweighed already known defects by a three-to-one margin;

three-fourths of the children examined required a further referral, thus indicating the existence of more than just routine problems (Mico, 1966). In other quarters, a high incidence of neurological handicaps and emotional disturbances has been found among disadvantaged children referred because of serious learning disorders (Kappelman, 1969).

Generally, the earlier the identification of such problems the more probable it is that remediation efforts will succeed. This marks as extremely salient the functions of community health services. As unmet health needs of great numbers of children have been revealed to medical personnel, the improvement of health services has been stimulated in many areas (North, 1968).

Neither should the salubrious influence of Head Start in creating new careers for professional and paraprofessional personnel be overlooked. While it would be difficult to justify this on purely economic grounds, opportunities for Head Start involvement have been extended to many people, including those who are themselves economically disadvantaged. The problem is, of course, that this involvement must not occur at the expense of children's psychological development, a point which introduces the issue of training procedures that guarantee quality staffing within various programs. It is entirely possible that many of the disappointing early returns from Head Start research are in part a function of "faculties" unprepared to deal with the complexities of compensatory education problems. Formally, three types of training programs have persisted within Head Start: in-service or on-the-job training, summer orientation training (ordinarily one week in duration), and eight-week training (Benoit, 1968). The latter two types have typically been executed in conjunction with colleges or universities. Short-term training programs cannot be expected to produce highly skilled personnel, although desirable changes in the verbalized preferences of personnel regarding the needs of children have been reported (Lane and others, 1967). Undoubtedly the quality of the training programs themselves have also varied substantially. The burden remains on in-service training methods; yet high turnovers of parent volunteers and teacher aides intensify this burden greatly. Recently, a Supplementary Training Program has been initiated to involve Head Start, community action agencies, and institutions of higher learning. Its intent is to provide longer-term training and greater employment security for Head Start workers.

Finally, in many communities Project Head Start has stirred early and enthusiastic support from many parents who themselves may have been alienated from formal education and otherwise may never have identified with it. As Weikart and Lambie (1968) suggest, the most fruitful outcomes of compensatory programs could be in terms of changes in parental behavior and the total home environment of disadvantaged children.

Some Critical Head Start Issues

Perhaps the most basic of all psychological issues raised to date in reference to Head Start and other compensatory programs concerns a reincarnation of the nature-nurture controversy which has appeared in various guises in theology, political thought, and behavioral science research for many years.[12] Applied to Head Start, this controversy concerns the question of how extensively general compensatory education timed to involve the late preschool years can influence behavioral development thought to be controlled heavily by genetic mechanisms. In other words, is too much being expected from Head Start? Or, as Jensen (1968) implies, have authorities failed sufficiently to recognize the "biological basis" of educability? In short, just how modifiable is the human intellect?

These and other questions have recently formed the basis for an explosive exchange of scholarly views on heredity, environment, and educational strategies. (Caspari, 1968; Hunt, 1969; Jensen, 1969a; Jensen, 1969b; Kagan, 1969; Voyat, 1969). Among the contentions mentioned in this exchange are that (1) individual differences in measured intelligence are predominantly a function of genes, with experience playing a minor role; (2) genetic factors are "strongly implicated" in patterns of intellectual differences among social classes and races; and (3) compensatory education (as presently conceived) is generally a failure because it has produced little real improvement in the measured intelligence or academic achievement among children for whom this intervention was conceived (Jensen, 1969a).

These contentions have been challenged variously on empirical, logical, and, to some extent, ideological grounds. A full exposition of such challenges, counter-arguments, and supporting data is far beyond the scope of this chapter. However, the reader is advised that a critical element in this literature involves semantic confusion over terms such as "intelligence" and "mental ability." This writer agrees with Schweiker's (1968) interpretation of conventional IQ tests as measures of both *learning* and *opportunity to learn*. For preschool children, both the learning of specific content related to test performance and general

---

[12] See Anastasi (1958) for an overview of this controversy as it has occurred in psychological research.

opportunities to learn vary widely; and variation in opportunities for learning IQ test material is immense, especially among children with lower socioeconomic backgrounds. Hence, to the extent that IQ tests measure "opportunity to learn background material useful in school" we would normally expect social class or cultural differences in test performance. General acculturation experiences in Head Start classes are not likely in one summer or one year to equalize social class-based learning opportunities so as to make the standard IQ test a suitable measure of educability, much less an indication of genetically determined potential.

The third contention above relative to compensatory education failure also requires additional comment. As Hunt (1969) has stated, Head Start and compensatory education are not always synonymous. Head Start programs have been patterned largely after the only model for early childhood education available until recently, namely, the free-play socialization approach of traditional nursery school practice. As many smaller scale experiments suggest, more precise, cognitively-oriented programs for compensatory education argue against "failure," particularly in terms of academic objectives (Van De Reit, Van De Reit, and Sprigle, 1969; DiLorenzo and Salter, 1968; Clasen, Spear, and Tomara, 1969). These and other data should serve to clarify the objectives of Head Start, that is, forsaking general cultural indoctrination for the teaching of processes and information more intimately associated with future school success (Schweiker, 1968). This proposal would be based upon several assumptions, however, including that present public school curricula continue as the standard for all children.

In retrospect, it should be noted that compensatory education generally is under fire for reasons other than ambiguous research and conflict over goals. Shanker (1969), for example, charges that a tendency has developed in some parts of the country for compensatory education to serve as a substitute for school integration. He also maintains that our society has yet to demonstrate a genuine financial commitment to compensatory education, Head Start included. More frequently than not, Head Start and related programs have involved inordinately large classes, inadequately trained teachers, and weak curricula. Shanker (1969) believes that commitment should be defined by small classes of six to eight children with one fully trained teacher and an aide so that tutorial methods may become more reality than myth. Whether this approach will solve present Head Start problems is conjecture, although in theory the closer educators can come to the ideal of individualized instruction the better. Regardless, one could hope that energetic, creative teachers who respect children are not shackled by administrative rigidities and the attitudes of school personnel conditioned to authoritarian, lock-step approaches to education.

A final issue to receive consideration here concerns an implication of much compensatory education literature, namely that a most basic source of problems is the make-up of children rather than a problem of schools, teachers, and our society's structure of values (Shanker, 1969; Sroufe, 1970). Few would argue that major improvements in school practices are needed or that prejudicial behavior throughout our society has contributed to many social problems. The fact remains, however, that such values as competency in basic communication skills, independence of judgment, and positive self-esteem seem to be desired for all children irrespective of social class or racial status.

Nevertheless, the implication that compensatory education is based upon a social pathology model, thus necessitating the assumption that lower-class children are basically inferior, requires thoughtful consideration. Perhaps the most powerful discussion of this issue to date has been offered by Baratz and Baratz (1970). These critics maintain that compensatory education generally has been devised to prevent cognitive deficiencies that in fact do not exist. Rather, the problems encountered by ghetto children (especially black children) are thought to derive from a different, nonetheless distinctly well-developed and "functionally adequate" cultural and linguistic system. Baratz and Baratz (1970) maintain further that the appropriate course for educators to follow is respectfully to adapt instructional procedures and curricula to children whose cultural identification differs from white, middle-class American children. This recommendation does not, however, preclude the need for economically disadvantaged children to learn standard English, as Baratz (1970) herself has clearly indicated. Issues related to the social pathology model will appear in later sections of this book, but every reader is encouraged to consult the Baratz' paper for detailed study.

PROJECT FOLLOW THROUGH

Introduction

While issues related to the timing and efficacy of educational intervention are being debated, Project Follow Through has been implemented in various parts of the country. A fundamental assumption of this Project is that further environmental planning can provide a more sustained pattern of early gains by Head Start (or at least further increase the probability of long-term benefits).[13] Authorized full-scale in 1968 under the Economic Opportunity Act of 1964, Follow Through programs have been established throughout the nation to include, during the school year 1968–1969, over 16,000 children.[14] In addition, a philosophy supporting the development of educational alternatives has been created. This philosophy is reflected in the subsidization of nineteen "program models," each of which emphasizes somewhat different intervention strategies with respect to disadvantaged children of primary school age. By no means mutually exclusive, these "planned variations" do range along continua such as structure, parental involvement, and cognitive activities. All are devoted to continuous and objective inquiry in the quest for meritorious practices. And, in each case, the "program model" is couched within a context of broad community social and health service involvement.

Available space considerations delimit a review of all nineteen Follow Through programs. Several of the models involved, however, are alternatives whose bases appear in separate chapters in this book. Specifically, these include the Behavior Analysis Project at the University of Kansas (see Chapter 5), the Educational Development Center program inspired by the English primary school revolution (see Chapter 7), and the Bereiter-Engelmann program (Champaign, Illinois) for language remediation (see Chapter 4).

For purposes of illustration only two of the remaining sixteen Follow Through programs will be discussed in any detail: the New Nursery School (Nimnicht, 1968) and the Tucson Early Education Model (Hughes, 1969).[15]

Examples of Project Follow Through Models

The New Nursery School Armed with concepts from research in educational and developmental psychology, Meier, Nimnicht, and

[13] Formulated primarily to service Head Start "graduates," Project Follow Through is available to children who come from other preschool programs for the disadvantaged. Eligibility is limited, however, to children from low-income homes as defined by the poverty-line index of the OEO.

[14] Follow Through was initiated on a pilot basis in 1967. Funds allocated for the fiscal year totaled 15 million dollars. This sum was doubled to finance the 1969 fiscal year operation.

[15] The exclusion of other Follow Through program models in no way is intended as a comment on their quality or their potential contributions. Interested readers may obtain information on these programs by writing The Division of Compensatory Education, Follow Through Branch, Bureau of Elementary and Secondary Education, 400 Maryland Avenue S.W., Washington, D.C. 20202.

McAfee (1968) have operationalized a New Nursery School program, so named because its approach deviates in significant ways from the conventional nursery school pattern. Developed originally for environmentally deprived three- and four-year-olds, this program has now been extended to service the kindergarten-primary grade span. The model consists principally of a systematically arranged physical environment, selected conceptual materials, and organized "learning episodes," which seek in combination to achieve two major goals for children: increased positive self-esteem and increased intellectual abilities. Both objectives have been proposed on the basis of research and theory regarding developmental processes and behavioral patterning of young children, particularly disadvantaged children. The former objective, positive self-esteem, is viewed simultaneously as a determinant and an outcome of successful learning experiences. Intellectual development is essentially an umbrella term which covers sensory development and perceptual activity, language skills, concept formation ability (including the ability to classify hierarchical concepts), and problem-solving skills.

The New Nursery School is committed to the notion of providing children with exploratory freedom in a controlled learning environment where exploration culminates in the discovery of physical and social reality. Thus children are allowed to proceed at their own pace — encouraged at all times to interact with their environment in a self-directing fashion. Didactic activities are carefully avoided. Teachers are advised to cast away a teaching role in deference to a responsive role. This "responsiveness" function is defined by several guidelines. First, teacher initiated conversation is de-emphasized in order to dwell extensively upon conversation initiated by the child. Secondly, children are always read to at their request, but are not asked by a teacher if they would like to have a story read. Third, children are not asked to terminate an ongoing activity in order to participate in another, different activity. And fourth, children are not forced to become involved in group activities. Rather, group activities are made attractive so that children will elect to participate (only 15 minutes per day are reserved for group activities). All four of these guidelines represent attempts to reduce teacher direction and permit the child to make his own decisions about learning. Once these decisions are made, the teacher and the materials operate to make the chosen activity rewarding and constructive. In this regard, materials (the correct use of which requires little teacher intervention) are preferred. So are activities inherently appealing to children. Thus, in theory, artificial rewards and coercive measures are not required in order to maintain pupil involvement. Nor does the responsive environment depend upon pupil competition for motivational purposes. Children's names are used in all adult-child transactions, and each child has his own cubicle in which to keep personal possessions and art work. Such techniques are considered to contribute to a child's sense of selfhood.

To facilitate perceptual-motor coordinations and discriminations, manipulative toys are utilized extensively (for example, nesting cups, puzzles, pegboards, and color lotto). Providing experience with these toys is considered insufficient, however. Hence, these activities are accompanied by vocabulary training and are sprinkled liberally with encouragement and personal recognition of the child by a teacher. Likewise, auditory discrimination activities are provided. For example, listening games are included which require children to identify familiar objects (coins, pencils, books) by the sound they make when they are dropped to the floor and common activities (clapping, sweeping, ball bouncing) by their sounds when executed. Discrimination activities are extended into the language development phase of the program, where it is believed that the children need (1) ample opportunities for self-expression; (2) clear, unambiguous verbal cues used consistently throughout teacher-child interchanges where concrete referents for words used are present, and (3) specific assistance for the purpose of developing listening skills.

Interesting applications of educational technology in the New Nursery School are represented by the *Language Master* and the *Tutoring Booth.* The *Language Master* is a sound recording machine, operable by a child working independently, which utilizes magnetic tape cards of various sizes. Sounds may be recorded and played back on cards, each of which is equipped with two channels of magnetic type across its bottom. Space at the top of each card permits a graphic recording to correspond with a sound recording, thus enabling a child to see and hear something simultaneously. For example, the word "blue" may be recorded on a card upon which has also been placed a spot of blue paint. Or, a sentence such as "The elephant has a long trunk," may be printed and sound recorded on the same card. Children are free to play with the Language Master, and extensive use is made of it in the "reading readiness" component of the program.

Another major feature of this responsive environment is the *Tutoring Booth,* within which an individual child may explore in the company of a teacher (once a day for as long as 20 minutes if he so desires) the use of items like an electric typewriter.

Activities built around the typewriter include the matching of letter symbols and sounds, word constructions, and story writing. For the latter activity, words that a child has learned to type are used to write a story. As the child tells his story with these words, the teacher records it. Subsequently, the complete story is typed and a copy provided to the child who then sees his own creation in print.

Concept formation and problem-solving abilities are fostered through an organization of integrated learning episodes. For instance, episodes have been devised for specific concepts such as "same" and "not the same," and for concepts of relative size such as "wider-widest" and "bigger-biggest." Concrete materials, including unit blocks, dowel rods, and clay serve useful functions in this regard. Pattern building exercises, ordered on a simple-to-complex progression, are also included. This provides still another purpose for the manipulative toys. Children are encouraged both to copy patterns from memory and to formulate their own.

The acme of success for the New Nursery School is the emancipation of a child from a self-defeating attitude and academic failure. While originally designed for children from impoverished homes, particularly those with Spanish surnames, the principles and content of the program have wide generalizability and are thus not restricted to this group of children. Attesting to this is the recent commercial publication of the Nursery School program by the Early Learning Division of the General Learning Corporation.

Nimnicht and his colleagues freely acknowledge the eclectic base of their program. It represents most clearly a combination of Montessorian principles, concepts of compensatory education suggested by Martin Deutsch (Institute for Developmental Studies, New York City), and O. K. Moore's *Autotelic Responsive Environment* (Moore, 1964; Moore and Anderson, 1968). Moore, perhaps best known for the development of the "talking-typewriter," has provided a thoroughly articulate theoretical foundation from which technological advances for preschool and early school learning have emerged. Moore's central concern has been language acquisition. Preschoolers of widely ranging backgrounds and measured abilities have been studied within his autotelic environment. In this context, Moore has produced accelerated patterns of language learning and reading skill development. Faster rates of progress have been noted, however, among children whose speaking-listening abilities and measured intelligence are advanced to begin with. This makes doubly interesting the incorporation of Moore's instructional system into the New Nursery School program inasmuch as the target children are from a population whose cognitive skills are generally below average.

During the 1968–1969 academic year the New Nursery School "model" was being applied in nine school districts across the country.

In addition to these field test centers, teacher training program development and instructional materials development are being carried out in the Berkeley (California) Public Schools and in Tacoma, Washington. Research into the effects of the New Nursery School program has consisted mainly of assessing changes over time on selected psychological tests and inventories. Comparisons have been made between the New Nursery School (NNS) children from disadvantaged circumstances and environmentally privileged children from middle-class homes who participate in a similar program called the Responsive Environment Nursery (REN). These comparisons have been limited to the preschool portion of the program since its Follow Through counterpart has not been operational long enough for its success to be reviewed. Preliminary data, however, serve to establish this model as one with good potential for promoting children's cognitive development and self-esteem (Nimnicht, McAfee, and Meier, 1969). Children whose initial educational prognosis was extremely poor prior to their New Nursery School experience have demonstrated impressive gains in several key areas. These include reading readiness and performance on instruments such as the Preschool Inventory and the Cincinnati Autonomy Test Battery (see Appendix 1). Further, as of 1969, no New Nursery School children had been retained to repeat kindergarten or first grade. This is a substantive achievement, because a number of NNS children upon entry to the program could not even be evaluated by the Stanford-Binet Scale and others scored at levels that would classify them as mentally retarded.

The Tucson Early Education Model The Tucson Early Education Model (TEEM) is similar to the New Nursery School in that it was designed to serve as an innovative educational experience for impoverished Spanish-American children (Hughes, Wetzel, and Henderson, 1969). This population of children was chosen for study specifically for two related reasons. First, the dropout rate in the Tucson school system has traditionally been highest among these children. Secondly, the longitudinal study of achievement patterns revealed that, as successive grade levels were encountered, a progressively larger gap between the academic performance of these children and their Anglo-American counterparts occurred. This "lagging" pattern was notable in the areas of reading and social studies (Paulsen, Morrow, Hughes, and Taylor, 1968). Incidental data indicated also an association between retention-in-grade and social skill deficits among many Spanish-American children. TEEM is basically a strategy to solve the problems implicit in the above findings. Its major objectives are subsumed under four categories: language competence, an intellectual base, a motivational base, and societal arts and skills.

Language competence is considered to be a "major technical skill" which is essential for successful cultural adaptation. Selected linguistic labels, language forms, and language functions are emphasized. For TEEM personnel, the achievement of language competence requires for children the opportunity to interact with adults whose speech demonstrates a wide variety of syntactical elements. Also necessary are adult-child interactions which have the effect of extending children's language and reinforcing children's attempts to express new linguistic patterns. Thus every attempt is made by TEEM personnel to systematize and accelerate a child's "natural method" of language learning.

Intellectual base skills, most of which are complex and involve higher-order mental processes, include strategies for organizing sensory data, reproductive thought, planning for specific goal attainment, and skills for modeling the significant behavior of others. The latter involves both discriminatory and evaluative power. Attitudes and values which dispose children toward productive social involvement define TEEM's motivational base. Also included in this category are persistence and success expectancies. The traditional academic skills (reading, writing, and arithmetic) and skills for democratic living comprise the final category, societal arts and skills.

As TEEM's objectives are classified, so are its principal ingredients. These include process-oriented ingredients and organizational components. Of the process variables, the *individualization of teaching* is foremost. The puissant influence of imitation learning is saddled methodically, especially with respect to social skills and language acquisition. Information-seeking responses such as question asking and "thinking-out-loud" are modelled verbally by means of teacher demonstration and in the course of verbal teacher-child interchange. *Gratification through learning* is still another process variable instrumental to TEEM. To provide children with gratifying experiences, frequent social recognition is dispensed, materials are selected for their intrinsic value to children, and failure-frustration is eliminated. Activities are also sorted on the basis of how well they facilitate the *generalization of learned skills* across classroom content areas and from the formal classroom to the child's natural environment. Finally, the *orchestration process* ensures that the four major objectives do not result in independent or isolated activities. The intention here is, wherever possible, to provide singular contexts for the development of skills embraced by the four principle objectives of TEEM. This intent is well stipulated in the following excerpt:

> When skills are acquired in real and meaningful settings, it is possible to develop more than one skill simultaneously. A teacher organizing a small group of children in the activity of ice cream making; for example, will be teaching new words, the processes of proper order and sequence of events, new concepts, and new technical and social skills. In addition; the manner of her interaction with children plus the eating of the product will significantly influence the child's attitude towards the activity and the learning experience. [Hughes, Wetzel, and Henderson, 1969, p. 5]

The organizational components of TEEM involve a cavalcade of guidelines. The *room arrangement* includes a variety of interest centers to meet individual differences in children's preferences and developmental levels. Seating strategies support independent study and small group instruction. A teacher-pupil ratio of roughly one to five triggers higher rates of *interaction* than is found in traditional classrooms. Self-selection and structured activities are coordinated, as closely as possible, with the cultural background, attitudes, and values of the children. This *local adaption strategy* is an attempt to reduce the typical discontinuities engendered when non–middle-class children encounter a stereotyped middle-class curriculum.

An indispensable feature of TEEM is the *change agent*. The role of change agent is served by a technical consultant who introduces innovative practices and assists teachers in their implementation: In the early stages of implementation, a ratio of one change agent to every five teachers is recommended. Change agents receive continuous training at the Arizona Center for Early Childhood Education. These agents, together with teachers and teacher aides, are encouraged to exercise originality and ingenuity within the latitude provided by TEEM for this purpose. As functional practices are developed they may then be shared by other cooperating TEEM classrooms.

While the above principles and components serve broadly to define the Tucson Early Education Model, its viability is provided most specifically by the language training emphasis. Curriculum experiences such as cooking, walking trips, and bus trips, are organized to develop sensory perception and provoke verbalization among children. Verbatim records of children's spontaneous remarks, and stories including errors, are recorded, analyzed, and used as cues to program subsequent strategies which lead children to higher levels of language sophistication.[16]

Heavy use is made of an expansion feedback technique whereby a

---

[16] TEEM language analyses currently are based upon Carroll's (1965) system of grammatical analysis.

teacher attends to the grammatical structure of a child's verbalizations and responds with a full, grammatically correct version of the child's idea. For example, during a cooking experience a child, Louis, may remark, "Water hot." This telegraphic response and other remarks about the experience may then be recorded on Louis' individual language card. Later, cards are read back to Louis (and other children) verbatim prefaced by phrases such as, "Louis said," or "Louis exclaimed." Immediately after the verbatim remark is read a teacher will model the correct structure for Louis (depending, of course, upon specific circumstances). In this example it might be, "I saw the water get hot, too!" or, "The water got hotter!" Once correct structure has been modeled, a teacher will usually proceed, by way of questioning techniques, to elicit correct usage from the child and reinforce positively his attempts to do so.

Additional techniques are employed to provoke verbalization of recall among children who have shared planned experiences. Reminiscing with children about past activities is performed to highlight certain forms of speech (such as past tense) and adjectival phrases. Systematic remembering practice may also involve skills such as sequencing (the recall of events in chronological order) and categorizing (attributes such as size, shape, and color). Comparing and associating skills also receive systematic attention. Together, the aforementioned skills are considered by TEEM personnel as important background competencies for learning to read, making predictions, and thinking discriminatively. Verbatim records in these and other areas serve as a cumulative indication of progress in language and conceptual development.

In summary, TEEM represents a systematic plan for the acceleration of language learning and the control of language for intellectual and social purposes. Teachers and aides work together in order to provide a language-rich learning environment, especially activities which encourage children to develop higher rates and refinements of expressive language. Data from which individual and group language training activities are created come from the recorded verbalizations of children and a generalized structural analysis of the English language.

TEEM has been extended during 1969 into sixty-eight primary grade classrooms. Underway is the development of a fourth-grade program which carries the follow-through philosophy even farther. All classrooms are located in metropolitan Tucson; however, evaluation data are not available at the time of this writing. Like the New Nursery School program, TEEM's unique attribute may well be its deliberate eclecticism and breadth of scope. Further, the incorporation of a change agent has the potential of providing for continual dissemination of new techniques and materials and in-service training. This is a feature unfortunately lacking in many approaches to early childhood education.

Optimistic supporters of Follow Through trust that the empirical outcomes of these various alternatives will provide documentation for practices which can be expanded into a comprehensive national service program for disadvantaged kindergarten and primary grade children. This outgrowth of Head Start is, then, a developmental research project, the results of which will probably begin to appear gradually during 1970 and beyond. One cannot help being impressed with the vast amounts of manpower and financial support that are being injected into this project. Also impressive are the staffing needs for these programs, the care required for program development if continuity with Head Start programs is to be maintained, and the scope of the evaluation to be conducted as these programs are consummated. Early anecdotal reports of this project are optimistic (Runke, 1969), but only time and the behavior of Follow Through children will permit an objective assessment of this ambitious plan.

SUMMARY

Operation Head Start has been conceived to compensate for disadvantages which have long plagued many children within the confines of public school education. As Lessler and Fox (1968) have remarked, this social experiment must rank among the most significant educational efforts of the past several decades. Pressing social needs and modest encouragement from experimental preschool programs for disadvantaged children have stimulated the near lightning-fast growth of this compensatory strategy. This growth has been accompanied by growing pains including staffing, curriculum, assessment problems, and philosophical issues.

To the question, "Is Head Start effective?" must be given a qualified answer, namely, "It depends." On the basis of research findings to date general programs within Head Start have been apparently ineffective or only moderately beneficial in facilitating cognitive and affective changes of the magnitude necessary to insure academic success. Where increased success has been observed, programs are of full-year duration and have elicited productive parental involvement. A number of indirect contributions can be identified, however, which may override for the time being the somewhat ambiguous empirical effects of Head Start. Thus, an assessment of Head Start influence depends upon the criteria one applies to this operation. Further, there have perhaps existed unrealistic expectations for this comparatively short-term modification procedure. Head Start is still basically an experiment, and it would be premature to expect clear, immediate answers to basic questions which in various forms have faced psychologists for decades (Grotberg, 1969).

Project Follow Through has been launched to reinforce the modest gains demonstrated by children from Head Start and other compensatory programs as these children proceed through the primary grades. As additional data have accumulated relative to the instructional and other needs of disadvantaged children, a number of relevant, yet varied programs have been implemented under Follow Through auspices. The future of our society is in no small way dependent upon the results produced by this creative and complex program.

References

Allen, K. Eileen. "Head Start Drop-Outs: A Progress Report." Personal correspondence, University of Washington, Seattle, 1969.

Alpern, Gerald. "The Failure of a Nursery School Enrichment Program for Culturally Disadvantaged Children." *American Journal of Orthopsychiatry,* 1966, 36, 244–245.

Anastasi, Anne. *Differential Psychology* (3d ed.). New York: Macmillan, 1958.

Anastasiow, Nicholas. "Educational Relevance and Jensen's Conclusions." *Phi Delta Kappan,* 1969, 51, 32–35.

Ausubel, David P. "A Teaching Strategy for Culturally Deprived Pupils: Cognitive and Motivational Considerations." *School Review,* 1963, Winter, 454–463.

Ausubel, David P. "How Reversible Are The Cognitive and Motivational Effects of Cultural Deprivation?" *Urban Education,* 1964, Summer, 16–37.

Baratz, S. S., and Joan C. Baratz. "Early Childhood Intervention: The Social Science Base of Institutional Racism." *Harvard Educational Review,* 1970, 40, 29–50.

Bee, Helen, and others. "Social Class Differences in Maternal Teaching Strategies and Speech Patterns." *Developmental Psychology,* 1969, 1, 726–734.

Benoit, William J. "New Careers in Head Start." In Jerome Hellmuth (Ed.), *Disadvantaged Child,* Vol. II. Seattle: Special Child Publications, 1968, 563–569.

Bereiter, Carl, and Seigfried Engelmann. *Teaching the Disadvantaged Child in the Preschool.* Englewood Cliffs, N.J.: Prentice-Hall, 1966(a).

Brazziel, William F. "Two Years of Head Start." *Phi Delta Kappan,* 1967, 48, 345–348.

Brink, Charles, Jack Ellis, and Irwin G. Sarason, and others. *Social Change, Evaluation Project: Final Report.* Seattle: University of Washington Press, 1968.

Bronfenbrenner, Urie. "The Psychological Costs of Creativity and Equality in Education." *Child Development,* 1967, 38, 909–926.

Caliguri, Joseph, and Emery Robertson. "Preschool Children's Comparative Performance on the Headstart Social Behavior Inventory." *Journal of Negro Education,* 1968, 37, 75–78.

Capabianco, R. J. "A Pilot Project for Culturally Disadvantaged Preschool Children." *Journal of Special Education,* 1967, 1, 191–195.

Carroll, John B. *Language and Thought.* Englewood Cliffs: Prentice-Hall, 1965.

Caspari, Ernest. "Genetic Endowment and Environment in the Determination of Human Behavior: Biological Viewpoint." *American Educational Research Journal,* 1968, 5, 43–55.

Cazden, Courtney B. "Subcultural Differences in Child Language: An Interdisciplinary Review." *Merrill-Palmer Quarterly,* 1966, 12, 185–219.

Cicirelli, V. G., J. W. Evans, and J. S. Schiller. "The Impact of Head Start: A Reply to the Report Analysis." *Harvard Educational Review,* 1970, 40, 105–129.

Clasen, Robert E., Jo Ellen Spear, and Michael P. Tomara. "A Comparison of the Relative Effectiveness of Two Types of Preschool Compensatory Programming." *Journal of Educational Research,* 1969, 62, 401–405.

Deutsch, Martin. "Facilitating Development in the Pre-school Child: Social and Psychological Perspectives." *Merrill-Palmer Quarterly,* 1964, 10, 249–263.

DiLorenzo, Louis T., and Ruth Salter. "An Evaluative Study of Prekindergarten Programs for Educationally Disadvantaged Children." *Exceptional Children,* 1968, 35, 111–119.

Dobbin, John E. "Strategies and Innovations Demonstrated in Project Head Start." *Journal of School Psychology,* 1966, 4, 9–14.

Egbert, Robert L. "Follow Through: Fulfilling the Promise of Head Start." In Jerome Hellmuth (Ed.), *Disadvantaged Child,* Vol. II. Seattle: Special Child Publications, 1968, 573–580.

Eisenberg, Leon. "Strengths of the Inner City Child." *Baltimore Bulletin of Education,* 1963–64, 41, 10–16.

Elam, Stanley M. (Ed.). "Compensatory Education." *Phi Delta Kappan,* 1965, 47, 65–95.

Formanek, Ruth. "Head Start Follow Up: 1965–1968: Validation of an Observational Instrument for Prediction Regarding School Success." Paper read at meeting of American Educational Research Association, Los Angeles, 1969 (February).

Freeburg, Norman E., and Donald T. Payne. "Parental Influence on Cognitive Development in Early Childhood: A Review." *Child Development,* 1967, 38, 65–87.

Getzels, Jacob W. "Preschool Education." *Teachers College Record,* 1966, 68, 219–228.

Goldberg, Miriam L. "Problems in the Evaluation of Compensatory Programs for Disadvantaged Children." *Journal of School Psychology,* 1966, 4, 26–36.

Goodman, Yetta T. "The Culturally-deprived Child: A Study In Stereotyping." *Integrated Education,* 1969, 7, 58–63.

Gordon, I. "The Young Child: A New Look." In Joe L. Frost (Ed.), *Early Childhood Education Rediscovered.* New York: Holt, Rinehart and Winston, 1968, 11–20.

Goth, Edward E., and John Pierce-Jones. "Evaluating Head Start Inputs and Outcomes." In Joe L. Frost (Ed.), *Early Childhood Education Rediscovered.* New York: Holt, Rinehart and Winston, 1968, 305–314.

Gray, Susan, and James Miller. "Early Experience in Relation to Cognitive Development." *Review of Educational Research,* 1967, 37, 475–493.

Grotberg, Edith H. *Review of Research 1965 to 1969.* Washington, D.C.: Project Head Start, Office of Economic Opportunity, 1969.

Harrington, Gordon M. "Genetics and Education: Comments on the Jensen and Casperi Addresses." *American Educational Research Journal,* 1968, 5, 712–716.

Havighurst, Robert J. "Who Are the Socially Disadvantaged?" *Journal of Negro Education,* 1964, Summer, 31–38.

"Head Start in the Public Schools, 1966–67: Summary." *NEA Research Bulletin,* 1968 (March), 46, 3–8.

Hechinger, Fred (Ed.). *Preschool Education Today.* Garden City, N.Y.: Doubleday, 1966.

Hellmuth, Jerome (Ed.). *The Disadvantaged Child,* Vol. I. Seattle: Special Child Publications, 1967.

Hertzig, Margaret E., Herbert G. Birch, Alexander Thomas, and Olga A. Mendez. "Class and Ethnic Differences in the Responsiveness of Preschool Children to Cognitive Demands." *Monographs of the Society for Research in Child Development,* 1968, 33, Serial No. 117, 69 pp.

Hess, Robert D., and Virginia C. Shipman. "Early Experience and the Socialization of Cognitive Modes in Children." *Child Development,* 1965, 36, 869–886.

Hughes, Marie M., Ralph J. Wetzel and Ronald W. Henderson, *The Tucson Early Education Model.* Tucson: University of Arizona College of Education, 1969 (Mimeographed).

Hunt, J. McV. "Has Compensatory Education Failed? Has It Been Attempted?" *Harvard Educational Review,* 1969, 39, 278–300.

Hyman, I. A. and D. S. Kliman. "First Grade Readiness of Children Who Have Had Head Start Programs." *Training School Bulletin,* 1967 (February), 63, 163–167.

Jensen, Arthur R. "Cumulative Deficit in Compensatory Education." *Journal of School Psychology,* 1966, 4, 37–47.

Jensen, Arthur R. "The Culturally Disadvantaged: Psychological and Educational Aspects." *Educational Research,* 1967, 10, 4–20.

Jensen, Arthur R. "Social Class, Race, and Genetics: Implications for Education." *American Educational Research Journal,* 1968, 5, 1–42.

Jensen, Arthur R. "How Much Can We Boost IQ and Scholastic Achievement?" *Harvard Educational Review,* 1969a, 39, 1–123.

Jensen, Arthur R. "Intelligence, Learning Ability and Socioeconomic Status." Journal of Special Education, 1969b, 3, 23–35.

Kagan, Jerome S. "Inadequate Evidence and Illogical Conclusions." *Harvard Educational Review,* 1969, 39, 274–277.

Kamii, Constance K., and Norma L. Radin. "The Retardation of Disadvantaged Negro Preschoolers: Some Characteristics Found from an Item Analysis of the Stanford-Binet Test." *Psychology in the Schools,* 1969, 6, 283–288.

Kaplan, Bernard G. "Issues in Educating the Culturally Disadvantaged." *Phi Delta Kappan,* 1963, 43, 70–76.

Kappelman, Murray M. "A Study of Learning Disorders among Disadvantaged Children." *Journal of Learning Disabilities,* 1969, 2, 262–268.

Karnes, Merle B., William M. Studley, Willis R. Wright, and Audrey S. Hodgins. "An Approach for Working with Mothers of Disadvantaged Preschool Children." *Merrill-Palmer Quarterly,* 1968, 14, 174–184.

Karnes, Merle B., and others. "Effects of a Highly Structured Program of Language Development on Intellectual Functioning and Psycholinguistic Development of Culturally Disadvantaged Three-year-olds." *Journal of Special Education,* 1967, 2, 405–412.

Katz, Lillian C. "Children and Teachers in Two Types of Head Start Classes." *Young Children,* 1969, 24, 342–349.

Klaus, Rupert A., and Susan W. Gray. "The Early Training Project for Disadvantaged Children: A Report After Five Years." *Monographs of the Society for Research in Child Development,* 1968, 53, Serial No. 120.

Lane, Mary B., Freeman F. Elzey, and Mildred Sabath. "Evaluation of the Head Start Orientation Training Program." *California Journal of Educational Research,* 1967, 18, 32–9.

Lehew, Charmon. "The Performance of Four- and Five-year-old Children in Operation Head Start on Selected Arithmetic Abilities." *Arithmetic Teacher,* 1968 (January), 53-59.

Lessler, Ken, and Ronald E. Fox. "An Evaluation of a Head Start Program in a Low Population Area." *Journal of Negro Education,* 1968, 37, 444–446.

McCarthy, Janet. "Changing Parent Attitudes and Improving Language and Intellectual Abilities of Culturally Disadvantaged Four-Year-Old Children through Parent Involvement." *Contemporary Education,* 1969, 40, 166–168.

McCreary, Eugene. "Some Positive Characteristics of Disadvantaged Learners and Their Implications for Education." In Staten W. Webster (Ed.), *The Disadvantaged Learner.* San Francisco: Chandler Publishing Co., 1966, 47–52.

McNamara, J. R. "Pilot Program for Preschool Culturally Deprived Children with Learning Disabilities." *Journal of Negro Education,* 1968 (Fall), 37, 444-446.

Meier, John H., Glen Nimnicht, and Oralie McAfee. "An Autotelic Responsive Environment Nursery School for Deprived Children." In Jerome Hellmuth, (Ed.), *The Disadvantaged Child,* Vol. II. Seattle: Special Child Publications, 1968, 301-398.

Mico, Paul R. "A Look at the Health of Boston's Project Head Start Children." *Journal of School Health,* 1966, 36, 241-244.

Moore, O. K. "Autotelic Responsive Environments for Learning." In Ronald Gross and Judith Murphy (Eds.), *The Revolution in the Schools.* New York: Harcourt, Brace and World, 1964, 184-219.

Moore, O. K., and A. R. Anderson. "The Responsive Environments Project." In R. D. Hess and R. M. Bear (Eds.), *Early Education.* Chicago: Aldine, 1968, 171-189.

Neale, Daniel C., and John M. Proshek. "School-related Attitudes of Culturally Disadvantaged Elementary School Children." *Journal of Educational Psychology,* 1967, 58, 238-244.

Nimnicht, Glen, Oralie McAfee, and John Meier. *The New Nursery School.* New York: General Learning Corporation, 1969.

Nolan, Patricia. "A Study of Black Dialect in Reading." Doctoral Dissertation, University of Washington College of Education, Seattle, Wash., 1970.

North, A. Frederick, Jr. "Pediatric Care in Project Head Start." In Jerome Hellmuth (Ed.), *Disadvantaged Child: Head Start and Early Intervention.* Seattle: Special Child Publications, 1968, 95-124.

Omwake, Eveline. "Head Start—Measurable and Immeasurable." In Jerome Hellmuth (Ed.), *Disadvantaged Child,* Vol. II. Seattle: Special Child Publications, 1968, 533-544.

Painter, Genevieve. *Infant Education.* San Rafael, Calif.: Dimensions Publishing Company, 1968.

Paulsen, F. Robert, Robert D. Morrow, Marie M. Hughes, and Jewell C. Taylor. "A Project Designed to Afford Optimal Conditions to Promote Intellectual and Personality Growth of Selected Six-Year-Olds." Cooperative Research Project, Arizona Research and Development Center, University of Arizona, 1968.

Ramsey, Wallace. "Head Start and First Grade Reading." In Jerome Hellmuth (Ed.), *The Disadvantaged Child,* Vol. II. Seattle: Special Child Publications, 1968, 291-298.

Raph, Jane B. "Language and Speech Deficits in Culturally Disadvantaged Children: Implications for the Speech Clinician." *Journal of Speech and Hearing Disorders,* 1967, 32, 203-214.

Runke, Ruth. "A Pilot Follow Through Program." *Contemporary Education,* 1969, 40, 154-158.

Schweiker, Robert. "Discard the Semantic Confusion Related to Intelligence." *American Educational Research Journal,* 1968, 5, 717-721.

Scott, Ralph. "Head Start before Home Start?" *Merrill-Palmer Quarterly,* 1967, 13, 317–321.

Shanker, Albert. "What's Wrong with Compensatory Education." *Saturday Review,* 1969 (Jan. 11), 56–61.

Shaw, Robert, Carol J. Eagle, and Franklin N. Goldberg. "A Retrospective Look at the Experiences of a Community Child Guidance Center with Project Head Start." In Jerome Hellmuth (Ed.), *Disadvantaged Child,* Vol. II. Seattle: Special Child Publications, 1968, 503–530.

Smith, Marshall P. "Intellectual Differences in Five-year-old Underprivileged Girls and Boys with and without Pre-Kindergarten School Experience. *Journal of Educational Research,* 1968, 61, 348–350.

Smith, M. S., and Joan S. Bissell. "Report Analysis: The Impact of Head Start." *Harvard Educational Review,* 1970, 40, 51–104.

Sontag, Marvin. "The Effect of Head Start Training on the Cognitive Growth of Disadvantaged Children." *Journal of Educational Research,* 1969, 62, 387–389.

Sroufe, D. "A Methodological and Philosophical Critique of Intervention-Oriented Research." *Developmental Psychology* (In press, 1970).

Stodolsky, Susan S., and Gerald Lesser. "Learning Patterns in the Disadvantaged." *Harvard Educational Review,* 1967, 37, 546–593.

Strodbeck, Fred L. "The Hidden Curriculum of the Middle-class Home." In C. W. Hunnicutt (Ed.), *Urban Education and Cultural Deprivation.* Syracuse: Syracuse University Press, 1964, 15–31.

Van De Reit, Vernon. "The Effectiveness of a New Sequential Learning Program with Culturally Disadvantaged Preschool Children." *Journal of School Psychology,* 1969, 7, 5–14.

Van De Reit, Vernon, Hani Van De Reit, and Herbert Sprigle. "The Effectiveness of a New Sequential Learning Program with Culturally Disadvantaged Preschool Children." *Journal of School Psychology,* 1969, 7, 5–14.

Voyat, Gilbert. "IQ: God-given or Man-made?" *Saturday Review,* 1969, May 17, 734.

Wattenberg, William W. "Review of Trends." In W. W. Wattenberg (Ed.), *Social Deviancy Among Youth.* Chicago: University of Chicago Press, 1966, 4–27.

Weikart, David P. "Preschool Programs: Preliminary Findings." *Journal of Special Education,* 1967, 1, 163–181.

Weikart, David P., and Dolores Z. Lambie. "Preschool Intervention through a Home Teaching Program." In Jerome Hellmuth (Ed.), *Disadvantaged Child,* Vol. II. Seattle: Special Child Publications, 1968, 437–500.

Weiner, Paul S. "The Cognitive Functioning of Language Deficient Children." *Journal of Speech and Hearing Research,* 1969, 12, 53–64.

Westinghouse Learning Corporation (in conjunction with Ohio University). "The Impact of Head Start: An Evaluation of the Effects of Head Start Experience on Children's Cognitive and Affective Development." *Preliminary Report,* 1969 (April), 8 pp.

Willmon, Betty. "Parent Participation as a Factor in the Effectiveness of Head Start Programs." *Journal of Educational Research,* 1969, 62, 406–410.

Wolff, Max, and Annie Stein. "Head Start Six Months Later." *Phi Delta Kappan,* 1967, 48, 349–350.

Wolman, Marianne. "Evaluating Language Development in Two Head Start Groups." *Elementary English,* 1969, 46, No. 4, 500–504.

Zigler, Edward, and Earl C. Butterfield. "Motivational Aspects of Changes in IQ Test Performance of Culturally Deprived Nursery School Children." *Child Development,* 1968, 39, 1–14.

Zimiles, Herbert. "An Analysis of Current Issues in the Evaluation of Educational Programs." In Jerome Hellmuth (Ed.), *Disadvantaged Child,* Vol. II. Seattle: Special Child Publications, 1968, 547–554.

4
Structural Pedagogy
for Language Development

INTRODUCTION

Among the most marked departures from the free-play, socialization model for early childhood education is a structural pedagogy conceived by Carl Bereiter and Seigfried Engelmann (1966). This pedagogy is based upon an articulate rationale derived from observations of children similar to those for whom Project Head Start was designed. According to Bereiter and Engelmann, many underprivileged children enter into the process of formal schooling already a year or more behind their more privileged peers in areas such as language and reasoning skills. If at the starting line (kindergarten or first grade) children are handicapped due to cognitive limitations, Bereiter and Engelmann argue that under normal circumstances only successively decelerated academic progress can be expected for these children. (Recall the cumulative deficit hypothesis described in Chapter 3.) Warranted therefore is an intervention strategy designed to accelerate children's rate of development (particularly language) and for Bereiter and Engelmann, time is the most precious commodity in the intervention process.

That time is a premium factor is indicated by Bereiter and Engelmann's analysis of developmental rate. These authorities argue that if a child is a year or more retarded in language and conceptual development at age four he needs to develop at twice the normal rate in order to compare favorably to his peers when they all reach age five. A decision to double the learning rate requires that priorities be established; available time will not allow the luxury of attending to all desirable educational goals. Since Bereiter and Engelmann believe that the fundamental problem for these children is an academic one, they award highest priority to academic skill development. Similarly, they argue that since the heartbeat for academic achievement is supplied by language skills, a preschool program must eliminate language handicaps for the academic pulse to be strengthened. There can be no other conclusion. Once this conclusion is reached, two basic tasks emerge: first, the identification of conceptual skills that any child must have in his repertoire in order to cope adequately with the elementary school curriculum; second, the arrangement of instructional materials and conditions in such a way that the refinement of these skills is possible in a compressed time period. In other words, given "X" amount of time, how can the child's rate of language and thought development be accelerated so that he meets the conceptual criteria implicitly demanded for satisfactory school entry?

To focus a preschool laser beam on a single target, language development, is rank heresy to the prevailing nursery school establishment, which has long subscribed to a "whole child" philosophy (see Chapter 1). Yet Bereiter and Engelmann argue cogently the "futility" of alternatives such as shotgun enrichment strategies and permissive nursery school practices. In anticipation of criticism of their approach, Bereiter and Engelmann have included in their rationale a currently popular view in developmental psychology. This view states that the most important role to be served in a child's development is the active role served by the child himself (White, 1959). In order to fulfill this role, however, a child needs certain equipment which will stimulate the successful pursuit of self-development. Children who lack such equipment must be helped to acquire it. Necessary cognitive equipment, it is contended, may be acquired most efficiently in a structured educational environment programmed for this specific purpose. Cognitive competence, in turn, provides the basis for such important affective characteristics as positive self-esteem and self-confidence.

Cultural Deprivation as Language Deprivation

The Bereiter-Engelmann rationale, briefly summarized above, culminates in a definition of cultural deprivation as language deprivation. This specific definition avoids many of the semantic difficulties that have been associated with the term *cultural deprivation*. One major problem of the latter term involves the implication that certain children are deprived of culturalization when in fact it is the middle-class white culture which they have not experienced.

Also disassociated from the Bereiter-Engelmann[1] definition of cultural deprivation is what they term the "sensory deprivation fad." The sensory deprivation view has been built upon research and theory in biochemistry, neurology, and sensory-motor development. Extrapolations have been made from this avenue of study which suggest that the basis of disadvantaged children's difficulties is lack of basic sensory stimulation (visual, auditory, tactile) during infancy. B-E believe that sensory stimulation per se is not lacking in the early environments of deprived children. Rather, certain *qualitative* aspects of stimulation such as variety, intensity, and patterning may be lacking. For example, while a child may confront ample sensory experiences, quantitatively speaking, the variety and patterning may be insufficient or inappropriate, especially with respect to elaborated verbal interchanges. In

[1] For the remainder of this chapter the abbreviation "B-E" will replace Bereiter-Engelmann.

many cases, a child may also be unable to moderate the intensity of stimulation (noise level emanating from a large number of children playing in the home, blaring television, and discomforting experiences with adults). Finally, the unpredictable and sometimes chaotic existence of some deprived children could have the effect of providing disorganized patterns of stimulation to them. All of this may result in two outcomes for a "deprived child: (1) a refinement of his perceptual powers rather than his auditory discrimination skills (a "tuning out" of noise), and (2) the development of language behavior limited in function.

While these conclusions are variously speculative, it is likely that verbal learning experiences, not sensory experiences, are those most apparently lacking in the homes of disadvantaged children. Therefore, if verbal skills are to be developed, direct verbal experience is necessary. Certainly this is more relevant to the development of academic aptitude than would be a program of concrete sensory experiences. Social class differences in the latter are not striking and are certainly less significant if one places in perspective the function of language in learning and the relationships of language to thought.[2] Readers will recall that this point of view rather distinctly contrasts with the Montessorian position described in Chapter 2.

To equate cultural deprivation with language deprivation, specifically verbal learning deficits which interfere subsequently with normal school progress, one must indicate the particular features of language behavior necessary to intelligent communication. Available psycholinguistic and speech development data combined with their own clinical observations (which, incidently, have been limited to a fairly small number of children) led B-E to several conclusions concerning the language and speech characteristics of many disadvantaged children. First, that the sentences or thought phrases expressed by these children are elliptical and poorly enunciated, a problem interpreted as an *inability* to encode and communicate thoughts as a "sequence of meaningful parts" (p. 35). For example, suppose a child has been asked to pick up a book, place it in a container, and put the box in the closet. He then asks, "Whaadoodat?" This "giant word," B-E would contend, represents a primitive representation of the phrase, "What do I do on that?" Whether the "giant word" in fact is evidence of a thought coding problem is highly questionable; it may simply reflect a learned speech habit. Yet B-E have attached great importance to this phenomenon.

A second developmental deficiency in the language of many dis-

---

[2] For the empirical bases established to support this argument one should consult the references reported in Chapter Two of *Teaching The Disadvantaged Child in the Preschool,* Prentice-Hall, 1966.

advantaged children is that concerning the use of words and inflections to communicate effectively their needs, observations, and understanding of logical relationships. They do not, it is argued, process sensory input linguistically and synthesize their observations through the use of verbal symbols. Nonverbal or restricted forms of verbal communication are apparently preferred, although the *social* function of language may not be impeded (for example, ordering another to do something, to facilitate social play, and so on). It is rather the function served by language in learning and reasoning that seems to be shortchanged.

A natural conclusion follows from the aforementioned twin deficiencies. If these deficiencies are shown to be responsible for academic difficulties, they must be overcome. Thus emerges the necessity for language experiences which are conducive to the (1) accelerated development of vocabulary and functional syntactical structures, (2) technical mastery of linguistic responses which allow for the symbolic manipulations inherent in reasoning, (3) use of language to control one's own behavior (such as planning actions before acting, anticipating consequences, deducing conclusions), and (4) communications of thoughts in their complete, sequential form so as to be clearly understood by others.

The final point of justification for B-E structural pedagogy involves a refutation of the argument that the problems of disadvantaged children emanate from social and emotional sources rather than cognitive ones. Crucial to this contention is the apparent lack of data which associate socio-emotional disorders with disadvantaged status in any reliable way. Although the incidence of social and emotional disturbances may be greater among disadvantaged children of school age it is probably due in large part to the negative effects of school failure which, of course, have not yet been experienced by preschoolers.[3] Further, it is suggested that inappropriate social behavior, such as aggressiveness learned quite normally in a lower-class setting, is often mistaken for deep-seated emotional disturbance. In most cases, the problem calls for the application of better socialization practices rather than psychotherapeutic procedures. Finally, disadvantaged children, inappropriately managed in preschool situations or for whom experiences are ill-designed, may react in ways to prompt a naive diagnosis of emotional disorder when, in fact, another environment may lead to quite different outcomes.

[3] Carpenter and Busse (1969) provide recent data relevant to this point. The self-concepts of white and black welfare children of elementary school age were studied: First-grade children reported more positive self-concepts than did fifth-grade children, but no race differences were observed. Soares and Soares (1969) also report data which indicate that disadvantaged children do not necessarily show lower self-esteem than advantaged children.

THE CLASSICAL PROGRAM

Objectives

Based on the above rationale, B-E have established a set of minimum objectives, the attainment of which they believe is necessary if children are to enter first grade with a successful prognosis:

Minimum Goals

1. Ability to use both affirmative and *not* statements in reply to the question "What is this?" "This is a ball. This is not a book."
2. Ability to use both affirmative and *not* statements in response to the command "Tell me about this _____ [ball, pencil, etc.]." "This pencil is red. This pencil is not blue."
3. Ability to handle polar opposites ("If it is not _____, it must be _____.") for at least four concept pairs, e.g., big-little, up-down, long-short, fat-skinny.
4. Ability to use the following prepositions correctly in statements describing arrangements of objects: on, in, under, over, between. "Where is the pencil?" "The pencil is under the book."
5. Ability to name positive and negative instances for at least four classes, such as tools, weapons, pieces of furniture, wild animals, farm animals, and vehicles. "Tell me something that is a weapon." "A gun is a weapon." "Tell me something that is not a weapon." "A cow is not a weapon." The child should also be able to apply these class concepts correctly to nouns with which he is familiar, e.g., "Is a crayon a piece of furniture?" "No, a crayon is not a piece of furniture. A crayon is something to write with."
6. Ability to perform simple *if-then* deductions. The child is presented a diagram containing big squares and little squares. All the big squares are red, but the little squares are of various other colors. "If the square is big, what do you know about it?" "It's red."
7. Ability to use *not* in deductions. "If the square is little, what else do you know about it?" "It is not red."
8. Ability to use *or* in simple deductions. "If the square is little, then it is not red. What else do you know about it?" "It's blue *or* yellow."
9. Ability to name the basic colors, plus white, black, and brown.
10. Ability to count aloud to 20 without help and to 100 with help at decade points (30, 40, etc.).
11. Ability to count objects correctly up to ten.
12. Ability to recognize and name the vowels and at least 15 consonants.
13. Ability to distinguish printed words from pictures.
14. Ability to rhyme in some fashion to produce a word that rhymes with a given word, to tell whether two words do or do not rhyme, or to

complete unfamiliar rhyming jingles like "I had a dog, and his name is Abel; I found him hiding under the _____."
15. A sight-reading vocabulary of at least four words in addition to proper names, with evidence that the printed word has the same meaning for them as the corresponding spoken word. "What word is this?" "Cat." "Is this a thing that goes 'Woof-woof'?" "No, it goes 'Meow.'" [Carl Bereiter and Siegfried Engelmann, *Teaching Disadvantaged Children in the Preschool,* © 1966, pp. 48–49. By permission of Prentice-Hall, Inc., Englewood Cliffs, New Jersey.]

B-E carefully point out that while skills such as these are taken for granted by kindergarten and primary grade teachers, they represent learnings that do not develop quickly and effectively in the child's natural environment. Culturally privileged children do generally develop and practice many of these skills in the context of a verbally stimulating atmosphere. Even so, these goals may strongly challenge children's inductive powers. In a linguistically impoverished environment this sort of skill development is less likely. Further, apart from specific instruction the goals numbered 10–15 above will rarely be reached by children, regardless of cultural background. Yet these are unquestionably relevant to basic academic development.

General Management Procedures

The prototypic B-E curriculum involves administrative and instructional procedures to accommodate about fifteen four-year-olds for two hours a day, five days a week, over a period of nine months. (The total preschool program encompasses two years, although additional material has recently been prepared to extend the program into the primary grades.) Many variations are possible, however. At least three teachers are required, each of whom is responsible for a subject— language, arithmetic, or reading. Children are divided into three groups of five members each. Assessed achievement level usually serves as the criterion for determining group membership. Thus children of comparable learning rates and developmental status are grouped together. Each teacher deals successively with all three groups in her subject matter specialty. Academic activities are conducted for periods of 20 minutes and interspersed with nonacademic activities such as music, juice and cracker time, and social play. Hence, only one-half (60 minutes) of the two-hour "school day" is spent in intensive small group work. The recommended time allotments may require slight modification in a given situation, particularly in the initial stages of the program. Modifications, however, are limited strictly to amount of time spent in instruction, *not* a reduction of the pace of instruction. Of the constellation of instructional variables which defines the B-E program, brisk pacing is one of the most sacred.

Language Curriculum

The B-E language curriculum is composed of an integrated set of basic concepts, sentence forms, and presentation strategies. For valid enactment of this curriculum, the functions of language as a "teaching instrument" must be understood. From this core understanding spring both the beginning and advanced phases of language training. B-E begin by establishing the criteria and parameters for satisfactory language communication in a learning situation involving both teacher and child. First, the organizing concept that language is a symbolic substitution for physical reality must be totally understood by the child. For example, he must learn that the expression, "Three oranges are in the brown sack," has a concrete referent which may be observed or created. The second requirement directly involves the feedback condition of learning, namely, that through language the child is provided with an independent check on the accuracy of his observations. For this reason, statements of fact represent the key element of the B-E teaching language. Statements of fact may be processed according to a correct-incorrect dichotomy. Thus, unambiguous feedback to the child by the teacher is possible. For example, a teacher may clap her hands and submit the idea, "This is an example of clapping." Such an idea can be monitored according to a true-false categorization.

B-E have developed a model for presentation strategies in the beginning language program which has as its components the *identity statement* and the *second-order* statement, which modifies and expands the identity statement. These two statement forms are empowered with the ability to teach the basic concepts of the program. As such, they fulfill the instrumental requirement of a teaching language. The identity statement is based upon a standard format and provides for the accurate symbolic representation of an object: "This is a(n) _____" (For example, "This is a bicycle," "This is an apple.") Plurals (for instance, "These are bicycles.") and identity negation statements ("This is not a bicycle," "These are not apples.") are also provided for within this format.

The second-order statement form permits the further expansion and specification of concept attributes: "This _____ is _____". (For example, "This bicycle is blue," "This apple is green.") Plurals and negations are similarly handled. ("These bicycles are blue," "These apples are not green.") Further variations are presented once the basic forms are mastered, for example, variations which allow for differential subject-predicate placement. Central are *polar concepts* (such as hard-soft and long-short), *nonpolar concepts* which pertain only to certain members of an identity class (such as "This cup is white," where the attribute color is nonpolar and other members of the class concept "cup" may differ in color), and nonpolar concepts that represent a property shared by all members of a concept class (such as "This cup is a drinking utensil.").

Throughout the language program, an emphasis is placed upon the derivation of rules to guide the child's observations, analyses, inferences, and generalizations. Teaching all concepts in the same fashion provides a consistency and an opportunity for practice which makes this sort of rule derivation feasible. For children these basic language tasks are deceptively simple. According to B-E, they learn how to identify, label correctly, and classify common objects in the environment. Children are purportedly assisted toward an understanding of the basis for object classification in terms of the sensory attributes of objects and their placement in a hierarchy of successive abstractions. Equally important, B-E maintain, is the capacity of the language program to develop the child's ability logically to formulate meaningful questions about the basic properties of concepts (concrete, functional, and abstract) and relationships among concepts.

Bereiter and Engelmann have selected for their teaching strategy a technique known as *pattern drill*. Teacher-pupil interchanges in the form of verbal presentation-demonstration followed by question-answer strategies conform to the statement models discussed above. A definitive sequence beginning with simple identity statements (singular) is programmed. Eventually the tricky concept of "opposites" is introduced through second-order statements that highlight polar attributes. Polar discriminations of key concepts such as *long* (short), *big* (small), *fat* (thin), *tall* (short), *fast* (slow), *dark* (light), and *straight* (wavy), all of which rely upon the sense of vision, are introduced, and standard questions applied to them. Other basic polar concepts involving different sensory modalities are also included. Examples are *heavy* (light), the discrimination of which is based upon one's proprioceptive sense, and *soft* (hard), one which involves the tactile sense. Singular polar discriminations are followed by multiple discriminations, polar deductions ("If this is loud it is not soft"), nonpolar concepts such as color, and preposition-linked concepts (next to, on, over, under). The remaining core content of the beginning language program is comprised of class concepts which may be broken down into sub-classes to reinforce the rule of deduction implicit in second-order statements. These class concepts include animals, plants, buildings, furniture, vehicles, toys, weapons, food, and clothing. The form and content of the beginning language program stimulate the development of verbal inquiry skills and provide the conceptual basis for elementary hypothesis-making and testing. These goals are supposedly reached through strictly patterned vocabulary and discrimination training activities. This phase of the language program is then succeeded by the advanced phase, which seeks to expand and refine these skills.

Advanced Language Program   Concept formation tasks require that the learner categorize stimuli on the basis of a property or properties shared in common by the stimuli. For example, consider the objects *gun, cannon, sword, bomb,* and *machete.* Not only do these items share concrete properties such as metal, but they have a common function, namely, to serve as instruments of offensive or defensive combat. The verbal abstraction *weapon* is used to categorize the items according to function. Activities in the advanced language program are designed to clarify the various bases for categorization. Unlike Montessori training, concrete objects themselves are not used extensively. Symbolic models, however, play an important role. A high degree of skill in the use of chalkboard illustrations is required by the teacher. Graphic representations of geometric forms (squares and triangles of two different sizes and colors) are used to teach concepts such as *and, only, all, some,* and *if-then.* Systematic procedures are employed to teach that an object can have more than one criterial attribute at a time, for example, a square can be big and white simultaneously. Learners are led from simple statements such as this to more complex forms such as "This square is not little and not black." The formula for this sort of teaching includes the use of teacher cueing procedures to encourage question-asking by the children. Predominant, however, is a pattern whereby a teacher asks a question, answers her own question, then asks it again later, this time to be answered by the children. For example, "What can I say about this triangle?" "This triangle is what? This triangle is big!" "What else can I say about this triangle? This triangle is big and black! Now you say it!"

Verb expansions are also introduced in the advanced program, intransitive verbs appearing first due to their relative simplicity. A picture of a crying baby may be shown. Children are told, "This is a baby. This baby is crying. What is this baby doing? This baby is crying! Say it!" (Children respond: "This baby is crying.") Still other forms of questions are introduced including those which deal with the *where* and *why* of observable phenomena. The sense verbs *sound, smell, taste* and *feel* are programmed in this segment, as are transitive verbs with *is* and past-tense statements and their plurals. Pronouns receive attention although these are considered less critical than exercises involving verbs and tenses.

Another integral series of tasks concerns the expansion of polar concepts along their appropriate continua. For example, consider an expansion of the polar opposite *big-small* to *smallest, bigger, biggest.* This emphasis upon gradations is similar to that inherent in the Montessori sensorial materials. Direct sensory experiences of the Montessori type are rare, however, in the B-E program.

Polar change problems comprise the final stage of the advanced language program. A unique set of exercises are utilized to help children refine their reasoning processes by constructing statements to cover the possible causes and outcomes involved in changes observed to occur in the physical environment. In all instances teaching procedures are methodically spelled out. A careful examination of the original text is required to appreciate the precision and specificity involved in the development and integration of these language activities.

Arithmetic

The format for the B-E arithmetic program as conducted at the time of this writing is not identical to that originally published (Bereiter and Engelmann, 1966). A more accurate statement of arithmetic instruction as currently practiced is the Science Research Associates publication, *DISTAR Arithmetic I* (Engelmann and Carnine, 1969). Changes notwithstanding, the rationale of the present program is much the same as that originally conceived. The DISTAR version is based upon the assumption that arithmetic is a special form of language which involves different types of questions that may be answered correctly or incorrectly depending upon one's store of conventional knowledge. Through DISTAR, the attempt is made to provide children with an understanding of arithmetic statements (statements of quantity) and the means for dealing correctly with these statements. This has led to the development of a carefully sequenced set of arithmetic exercises based upon the most basic of all arithmetic operations—the counting operation. Therefore, the first step for children in the arithmetic phase of structural pedagogy is concerned with the acquisition and practice of counting techniques.

DISTAR counting techniques are based upon the extrapolation of basic rules which, for most adults, seem "natural" or self-evident. Such rules, however, may not be at all obvious among inexperienced children. Examples of "counting rules" include (1) when objects are counted, one can start with any given item and end with any item so long as each object is counted once and only once; and (2) when one has finished counting, the last number cited tells one about both the item last counted and the entire collection of items. In the DISTAR version of basic arithmetic the important distinction is made between object-counting and event-counting. Whereas objects may be counted in any order, event-counting must be based upon the order in which events occur. For example, a successful counting of the number of doughnuts in a sack does not depend upon which doughnut is selected for a beginning point. However, correct one-by-one counting of the number of doughnuts removed from a sack must begin with the first doughnut removed. Once the doughnuts have been removed they may again be counted as objects; counting can again be done in any direction as long as the fundamental counting rules are applied. In this manner, the relationship of objects and events may be demonstrated.

Once basic counting techniques have been mastered, children are introduced to the meaning of plus, or the act of adding to a group (counting forward). This is further related to the concept of *more* and the logic involved in the addition operation. The plus sign is treated as a statement which must be translated into the addition operation. The authors of the Direct Instruction Arithmetic Program (DISTAR) are careful to point out that understanding the meaning of the plussing operation is the requisite goal. Only after children have achieved this understanding do they learn how the symbols in arithmetic statements dictate an operation.

The DISTAR Arithmetic Program continues with an emphasis upon still further symbol-operation relationships, including the equal sign—equivalent value relationship—and the minus sign—subtraction operation. A considerable amount of work is devoted to equal sign functions, which are apparently based on the analogy of a fulcrum or balance point. In other words, that a value on one end (side) of the equal sign must always be "balanced" by the value on the other end. Another basic DISTAR rule is introduced in this regard: "As many as you count to on one side of the equal sign, you have to count to on the other side." This rule is demonstrated by using objects. Gradually, children are moved from conventional arithmetic statement notations (such as $3 + 1 = ?$ and $6 + 3 = 3 + ?$) to simple word problems ("A boy has four marbles and he plusses two more. How many does he end up with?") to more complex story problems based upon general rules ("A boy has five kittens and then he gets some more. I will not tell you how many he plusses, but he ends up with eight kittens. How many did he plus?"). Story problems are translated into algebra statements in order that the relationship of operation to notation may be clarified. In the afore-mentioned kitten problem the correct notation is $5 + \square = 8$.

In summary, DISTAR Arithmetic I involves a set of strategies which are systematically arranged to teach arithmetical symbols, conventions, and operations. Basic rules which are purported to assist children to remember and classify facts are stressed. Strongly patterned arithmetic problem-asking strategies are practiced under tightly subscribed con-ditions. The principal objective involves the mastery of precision skills in basic arithmetic.

Reading

In its original form, the B-E reading program was based largely upon the linguistic reading series of Fries, Fries, and Wilson (1965). As in the case of the arithmetic program, modifications in the B-E approach to reading instruction have been made since 1966. The first major varia-tion in this phase of the curriculum was based upon certain features of the Initial Teaching Alphabet (i/t/a). This variation has since been abandoned in favor of the Direct Instruction Reading Program (DIS-TAR, Parts I and II) which has recently been made available com-mercially (Science Research Associates, Inc., Chicago, Illinois).[4]

The DISTAR Reading Program is based upon the belief that the best way to teach reading is to concentrate upon the operations that are in-volved in the reading act. Thus, this program begins with verbal and sequencing operations that are required to perform reading responses appropriate for simple words (such as mat, fan, nap). For this purpose children must know at least four things. First, they must recognize letter-sound correspondence. Second, children must know that sounds are sequenced in an order indicated by the spacial arrangement of letters which are formed into words. Third, they must understand that any spoken word can be spelled by holding each sound in that word (for example, r-a-n). Finally, children must realize that any word said slowly (as in m—a—p) can be "said fast" and identified at a normal rate of speech. These four requisites thus comprise the order in which initial reading instruction is carried out. Sounds are learned prior to letter names and simple action sequences are learned prior to sound sequenc-ing.

In DISTAR Reading I, word attack skills are groomed through the

---

[4] A recent reference pertinent to revised structural pedagogy is Engelmann's new book titled *Preventing Failure in the Primary Grades* (1969) also available through Science Research Associates, Inc.

use of convergent rhyming techniques. In other words, a sequence of exercises is practiced in which children identify words which rhyme with words presented by the teacher. For example, the teacher says, "We're going to rhyme with *cat*. What are we going to rhyme with? *Cat*. Listen carefully: rhymes with *cat*—bbb—." The children's task is to identify the word, which in this case is *bat*. Other exercises include sound sliding for purposes of word blending and sound reading skill development. Sound sliding involves the slow pronunciation of each sound in a series without pausing between sounds as is normally the case in conventional spelling drill ("fffaaannn," instead of "F-a-n"). Nine basic sounds comprise the initial series: m, a, s, e, f, d, r, i, and th. Subsequently, word reading is begun. Gradually, all the symbols of traditional orthography are introduced, as are daily worksheets to help children become skilled in translating pictures into verbal statements and in reproducing events in their proper sequence.

In later phases of the DISTAR Reading Program (Part II is designed for use during the second year of instruction) the overall workload is increased, with more time devoted to reading activities, vocabulary training, and workbook exercises that involve "sight and spell" and reading comprehension activities. DISTAR II includes learning the alphabet (forward and backward), over 200 irregular words (versus 30 irregulars in DISTAR I), and the concept of capital letters. It is claimed that children who have successfully accomplished DISTAR I and II will demonstrate fundamental word-attack skills, a comparatively large reading vocabulary, skill in following instructions, and a general comprehension of what they read.

Music

Correlated with successive steps in the language and reading programs are music activities. These activities serve generally to reinforce language principles. Specifically, singing and clapping exercises have the effect of providing (1) practice of language responses in a more playful context and (2) strategic breaks between one formal instructional period and the next. Usually no more than 15 or 20 minutes per day are spent with music, although fast pacing prevails. An important criterion for song selection is variety. However, all songs must meet the requirement of having language development potential. Consequently, not just any nursery rhyme song will do. B-E quite accurately point to the stilted and trifling nature of many songs which are unsuitable for children deficient in linguistic concepts. (Consider, for example, the language form in "Pussy Cat, Pussy Cat, What did you there?")

Children are also encouraged to generate their own lyrics to familiar tunes where the lyrics are compatible with the basic statement forms of the B-E program.

In summary, language (involving both receptive and expressive response modes), arithmetic, reading, and music activities are the four major components of the B-E program. All are programmed concurrently, and all are based upon linguistic phenomena which are thought to be related to thinking processes, especially reasoning. Pattern drill is the pervasive pedagogical technique, and everything is geared to accelerate the normal learning rate of the participants. Apart from direct observation of an ongoing program over an extended period of time, it is impossible to appreciate fully the systematic integration of activities that has been accomplished by Bereiter and Engelmann.

OTHER RECENT DEVELOPMENTS

Easily the most dramatic changes in the original B-E structural pedagogy have been in reading, and to some extent arithmetic. Only minor modifications have occurred in the basic language program. The latter has been expanded somewhat and certain changes in sequencing have been effected. For example, polar concepts are now frequently preceded by action statements, and color concepts are introduced subsequent to experiences with class concepts. In addition, further materials have been prepared to facilitate children's comprehension of part-whole relationships (Engelmann, Osborn, and Lundeen, 1968a). Concepts such as "break-fix," "win-lose," "visit-stay," and action stories built around concepts like "grow" and "give" provide the substance for still another handbook (Engelmann, Osborn, and Lundeen, 1968b). Finally, a special edition of songs designed to accompany the B-E program has been published for commercial use (McCormick and Osborn, 1969).

Aside from content modification and extensions, a "Follow Through" program has been developed which specifies resources and facilities necessary to maintain the basic features of the B-E approach up through grade three. This includes maintenance of the low teacher-pupil ratio and continued focus upon language, reading, and arithmetic. Parent training procedures are a prime feature of the follow-through plan. It is reasoned that children will need to encounter activities and reinforcements at home similar to those encountered at school if an accelerated learning rate is to be sustained. At the time of this writing, the effectiveness of the Bereiter-Engelmann method is being tested at

13 Project Follow Through sites involving some 3000 children (Ahlfield 1969).

This Follow Through plan also provides for a transition to Individually Prescribed Instruction (IPI) when B-E children reach approximately a second-grade reading level. IPI differs from the B-E approach to the extent that programmed materials and tests can be prescribed for a child by a teacher *as needed*. Thus, a shift from small group instruction to independent study is provided. IPI is still undergoing systematic development. As of 1969, its principal features include a continuum of behavioral objectives in mathematic and language arts, instructional material and aids appropriate for self-directed study, procedures for the assessment of continuous progress, and guidelines for teachers in reference to learning activity prescriptions for individual children. IPI was conceived at the University of Pittsburgh's Learning Research and Development Center, and academic continua are available for the entire kindergarten–sixth-grade span (IPI, 1967, 1968). In its "pure" form IPI is also one of the nineteen Project Follow Through programs (see Chapter 3).

BASIC TEACHING STRATEGIES AND ROLE OF THE TEACHER

The B-E program is perhaps without peer in terms of the directive, even obtrusive functions served by the teacher. This intensive academic orientation requires individuals who are highly skilled in the execution of language, reading, and arithmetic activities. Virtually nothing in the B-E program is left to chance, guesswork, or intuition, although some latitude may be permissible depending upon moment-to-moment circumstances. Goals are concrete, teacher actions are deliberate, and sequencing is predetermined. B-E take the position that the "natural teacher" is a myth with respect to intensive preschool work; teaching skills must be learned and polished. Engelmann particularly has been critical of the generalities and irrelevancies he believes to exist in many teacher education programs. He has therefore been guided by the principle that teachers must be told and shown *exactly* what to do and how to do it. Raw material from which skilled teaching may be derived includes determination, reasonable intelligence, and a lack of dogmatism.

The mix of teaching techniques used to bring the B-E curriculum to life has been conceived specifically with small group instruction in mind. These techniques range from the mechanics of presentation to feedback strategies. Some are rather conventional; others are less so. For instance, rules involving such things as ample use of examples, the encouragement of thinking behavior, and presenting material so as to reduce the probability of children's errors underlie many conventional programs. Rules regarding pacing and difficulty level are less explicitly apparent in conventional programs. Teachers are advised that while group activity is underway, an individual child should never be worked with for more than 30 seconds at a time. This policy is relevant to motivation—keeping all children actively involved—and the encouragement of total concentration as children take turns rapidly in the course of responding to teacher questions. Similarly, teachers are urged to use short explanations, geared at all times to the child's current stock of information. Rhythmic phrasing of verbal statements is urged, as is clapping to dramatize basic language patterns. No hedging in the provision of feedback is allowed. Rather, the teacher must inform a child very clearly when he has or has not made a correct response.

While the teacher works at a brisk and steady rate of speed, children are not pressured to hurry or speak unnaturally fast. A violation of this principle defeats a main purpose of training, namely, to expand and standardize expressive language. Children are, however, encouraged to speak loudly and distinctly at all times. A liberal sprinkling of teacher questions is essential to maintain the interaction characteristic of B-E instruction. Yet, teachers are cautioned to avoid communicating subtle cues which may tip off to a child the response that is expected. An example of a "tip-off" cue would involve a teacher forming the beginning of a word on her lips. Children may very quickly learn to depend upon such cues which, of course, are inappropriate under the circumstances.

Finally a most significant teaching strategy is that which calls for the presentation of tasks at varying levels of difficulty at varying times in the instructional period. Level one (least difficult) requires only that a child point to an example of a concept under study (for example, "Show me which box is smaller"). Level two requires a yes-no answer to questions ("Is this box smaller?"). The third level of difficulty requires a child to repeat basic statements (Teacher: "Is this box smaller than this box?" Child: "Yes, this box is smaller than this box.") Level four (most difficult) requires that a child identify criterial attributes or conceptual relationships by appropriate statements in the absence of direct questions (Teacher: "Tell me about this box."). Difficulty level is varied according to children's skill and fatigue level, although level four is preferred whenever possible. The reader interested in a further specification of small group teaching techniques applicable to the B-E philosophy is advised to consult Osborn (1968).

In summary, the B-E program is highly teacher-centered. Heavy stress is placed upon techniques and incentives which encourage children to work rapidly and steadily with a prescribed set of activities. According to Engelmann (1969) the most persistent difficulties faced by teachers in this system include pacing problems and the appropriate use of reinforcement. It is likely that the former is in part a function of idiosyncratic factors among teachers, for example, a tendency to interject anecdotal material and examine children's feelings in a maternal fashion. Pacing, however, depends in final analysis upon a complete mastery of the program content and presentation strategies. The second problem, that involving reinforcement strategies, is receiving increased attention now that Professor Wesley Becker has succeeded Bereiter at the University of Illinois. Becker's area of specialization is the development and scheduling of reinforcement contingencies (see Chapter 5). The explicit integration of reinforcement schedules is not readily apparent in the original B-E program. Recently, however, Engelmann himself has begun to write on the application of reinforcement techniques to teaching (Engelmann, 1968). Such techniques will be discussed more fully in the chapter on behavioral analysis (Chapter 5).

Finally, little mention is made of teacher characteristics apart from those basic to high-level skill development, such as intelligence and adaptability. The effective teacher is one who performs correctly the responses necessary to assist children toward academic mastery. There is no such thing as a natural teaching style. The manifestation of a warm benevolence toward children, so strongly championed by the protagonists of traditional programs, is not an explicit feature of B-E's structural pedagogy.

PRINCIPLES OF LEARNING AND INSTRUCTION

As in the case of Montessori, several distinct principles apply to the B-E program. They involve both the content and presentation dimensions. Few assumptions are made about the nature of childhood and motivation. It is recognized, however, that all children have a capacity to learn and that, in the case of disadvantaged children, learning problems are essentially environmentally induced, that is, an outgrowth of faulty learning experiences. Therefore, learning problems can be overcome under the right environmental circumstances. Implicit in the design of the learning activities is a belief that a child will seek to master his environment, to demonstrate competence. For motivational purposes the selection of words, songs, and phrases which appeal to young children is apparent, as is the use of games and subtle forms of competition.[5] Activities involving these techniques are for the most part highly abstract, quite unlike Montessori education. Following are classified the foremost B-E principles of learning and instruction.

Behavioral Objectives

An instructional package claiming to be systematic must clearly indicate the terminal behaviors it attempts to produce. In this respect, the B-E curriculum is unsurpassed. Nowhere are found ambiguous statements of objectives such as "improving the child's language skills," or "promoting the child's understanding of the world around him." Strictly speaking, objectives of the latter type are of little, if any, value for purposes of instructional planning. Frequently the stated objectives of school programs tell what a teacher will attempt to do, not what a child will be doing. Secondly, they fail to specify precisely what pupil behavior is involved. For example, what does an objective such as "understanding the world around us" actually mean? To have any functional value, the term "understanding" must be reduced to observable behavioral characteristics. That is, if one designs a program in an attempt to promote "understanding," a specification of what constitutes "understanding" is necessary in order to assess program effectiveness. B-E have handled this problem by a detailed accounting of the skills they believe are required of children for academic success in the primary grades. The skills are broken down into responses which may be directly observed. A child can either perform a task or he cannot. The reader is encouraged to study again the minimum goals listed earlier in this chapter. All are stated in terms of observable behavior. They have the further quality of providing functional cues for the planning of instructional activities. But perhaps the most commanding characteristic of behavioralized objectives is that they clearly indicate to the learner what it is he is supposed to be learning.[6]

Homogeneous Grouping

B-E children, theoretically all four years of age when they first enter the program, are distributed into small groups of roughly five members each according to demonstrated ability. Thus, in a typical class of fifteen children three groups, ranging from high ability to low, would be found. The rationale is similar to that followed for years by educators who

---

[5] Game-like teasing and the setting up of children with statements are liberally employed. For example, "Here's a tough one. I bet no one gets this!"

[6] Further issues related to the function of behavioralized objectives in instructional planning are examined by Bereiter (1967) and Deno and Jenkins (1969).

support the practice of ability grouping. By reducing heterogeneity with respect to such variables as learning rate and conceptual repertoire, instruction may be streamlined, pacing geared appropriately, and frustration levels reduced. The specific, convergent tasks imposed upon children by the B-E curriculum make this a reasonable procedure, although ability grouping is not without its disadvantages, including the danger of typecasting a child with lower ability.

Active Involvement

Children who participate in a B-E program are continually making active responses with a substantial emphasis upon repetitive verbalizations. Within a small group context, both unison responses and frequent individual responses are elicited. A random-order recitation strategy (versus fixed order, where children know in advance when they will be called upon) is preferred, the motivational value of which has empirical support (Hudgins and Gore, 1966). On paper, the B-E program clearly requires a greater frequency of verbal responses from teacher and children than many alternatives for early education. The question of whether a high rate of verbal interaction per se is the most significant variable in an early education environment has yet to be answered (Seifart, 1969).

Immediate Feedback

A recitation mode of instruction establishes one of the most important conditions of learning: immediate feedback (Gagné, 1965). Thus, children continuously receive knowledge of the results of their actions, a type of reinforcement which has two primary values (Jones, 1967). One value is motivational, that is, by responding to material structured to reduce error rate, children may experience the success so crucial to the development of achievement motivation. A second value is informational in the sense that when errors are made specific, unambiguous feedback from the teacher may indicate why a response was incorrect.

Graduated Sequence

Language, arithmetic, and reading activities are combined into a sequentially programmed curriculum which takes the general direction of simple-to-complex. While the sequential features of the program are obvious, however, that all steps are uniformly spaced is not. The sequence is essentially logical, based on the structure of knowledge (conceptual hierarchies) and linguistic structure. Many of the activities reflect deductive, as opposed to inductive, teaching, a format variable that increases economy of instruction (Jones, 1967).

Transfer

The ultimate objective of the B-E program is summarized by the concept, *transfer of learning.* In this sense, transfer refers to the influence that learning which occurs at one point in time will have on subsequent learning or performance. In theory the entire B-E package is designed to facilitate *positive* transfer, that is, increase the probability that mastery of its basic concepts will make future school learning more efficient and effective.[7] It should be pointed out that the transfer effects of the program are not totally clear as yet. There remains the possibility of negative transfer in some segments of the program. In other words, during the course of instruction children may be learning things which actually interfere with subsequent learning. For example, does the strong emphasis on pattern drill condition children to a teaching or learning style that may later serve them disadvantageously? Only careful follow-up research will shed light on this and other possibilities. Finally, it is important to note that the primary B-E emphasis is upon *vertical* transfer, namely, the learning of skills which will facilitate the learning of successively more complex material within conceptual systems (Gagné, 1965).

Other Principles

Several additional principles are applied in the B-E program. At least two of these merit identification. One is the principle of *contiguity* so apparent in the arrangement of learning activities (see the earlier discussion of this principle in Chapter 2). The second is *criterion reference* testing (Glaser, 1963). This form of assessment attempts to evaluate instruction where the intent is to create a specific level of skill proficiency among children. In other words, if instruction is administered for the purpose of promoting among all children the achievement of particular goals, it follows that assessment procedures should provide evidence of the validity of instructional procedures. Either a child has attained the objective or he has not. If he has, mastery has occurred. If he has not, procedures must be redesigned. Children are not ranked

[7] Efficiency as used here refers to economy in learning, that is, learning not impeded by a high error rate; effectiveness refers to the retention of what is learned.

or compared to each other. Rather their point of reference is the criterion established by a given instructional objective. In short, absolute standards prevail and testing procedures are arranged in reference to these standards, not how well or poorly children compare to one another. The philosophy and practice of criterion reference testing is exemplified by Engelmann's *Basic Concept Inventory* (see Appendix A).

RESEARCH ON THE METHOD

The recency of the B-E program means, among other things, that data relative to its effects on children are limited. What data have been published do, however, merit close examination. Since the B-E program's emphasis is on language behavior, it follows that the instruments used to assess its effects are essentially cognitive in nature. Selection of appropriate assessment tools has been a problem, for few achievement tests are currently available for use with younger children. As Bereiter (1967) indicates, a basic reason for this comparative void is that achievement objectives have not been in great favor among nursery school personnel. This virtual psychometric vacuum concerning preschool achievement tests is one factor that prompted the creation of the *Basic Concept Inventory* (Engelmann, 1967a) mentioned above. Aside from this instrument, assessment devices used to date in B-E program research include the Stanford-Binet Intelligence Scale, the Illinois Test of Psycholinguistic Abilities (ITPA), the Preschool Inventory, and the Wide Range Achievement Test (see Appendix A).

In their original pilot program, B-E enrolled fifteen black children, between four and five years old, from homes described as educationally disadvantaged. Assessments of their entering behavior revealed these children to be operating at approximately the three-year-old level on the ITPA. Subsequently, the Stanford-Binet was administered indicating a mean IQ of 93 for these children. Periodic ITPA assessments were made over a nine-month period to measure progress; the *Wide Range* was administered at the end of this period. Among the data reported were a seven point increase in IQ, average to above-average performance on the ITPA (equivalent to eighteen month's development in only nine), and reading and arithmetic performances comparable to first- or beginning second-grade level. Although spelling had not yet been taught, the average of the class was equivalent to mid-year kindergarten performance. The broadest conclusion was that this remedial curriculum was capable of accelerating learning rate to the point where school readiness had been achieved in about half the time one might expect under normal circumstances. It was on the strength of these data that the B-E program was published. Children who "graduated" from the two-year program in 1966 (original group) were in the second grade during 1968 and reported as "doing well" in basic academic subjects.

As a technical report of program validation, the original book has certain weaknesses. For example, no control group of children against which to compare the "B-E children" is reported. Other features, such as sampling design and lack of control for the effects of repeated testing represent weaknesses which would not go unchallenged by any thoughtful reader. Nevertheless, the empirical fact of changed behavior was observed. The second wave of B-E children (1967 "graduates") were studied in relation to a matched comparison group (traditional preschool one year followed by kindergarten the next), however, and the average IQ of this latter group was 21 points lower than the experimental (B-E) group at the end of the two-year program. Coupled with various anecdotal reports, these facts have attracted no small amount of attention and interest.[8]

Among the few published data concerning longer-term performance of B-E children are these of Karnes, Teska, and Hodgins (1969). These researchers examined the first-grade performance of children who previously had encountered a two-year B-E program (as a substitute for conventional nursery school and kindergarten experiences). Prior to intervention, the measured IQ's of these children (Stanford-Binet; $N = 10$) averaged 96.6; at the end of the first grade these children averaged 109.7, a net gain of 13.1 IQ points. In contrast a larger ($N = 25$) group of disadvantaged children whose nursery and kindergarten experience was "traditional," gained an average of 5.6 IQ points over the three years.

These differences were not statistically significant according to the Karnes, Teska, and Hodgins analysis.[9] While a marked superiority for B-E children in language test performance (ITPA) was noted during the two-year compensatory program, a puzzling deceleration of these language gains occurred during the first grade. These first-grade children

---

[8] Children who "graduated" fresh from the B-E kindergarten in 1967, having experienced two years of intensive instruction, are reported to have gained an average of 24 IQ points. Eleven points of this gain, however, were "lost" after a year in the first grade. More loss after grade two has apparently occurred, although the data are unreported at the time of this writing.

[9] Statistical significance refers to the probability that a performance differential could be due to chance rather than, in this case, intervention strategy; a statistically significant difference rules out any strong possibility that chance factors are responsible for change.

were, however, performing generally at a level appropriate for their chronological age. (More regressive were the patterns demonstrated by the traditional group, a phenomenon interpreted by the researchers as a discouraging language prognosis.) Finally, comparisons were made on a school readiness measure (Metropolitan Readiness Tests) and on first-grade achievement (California Achievement Tests). Significant advantages were observed for the direct instruction group in reading readiness, number readiness, and, eventually, academic achievement in the first grade. As a whole, these data support systematic academic preschool instruction insofar as immediate advantages are concerned. The researchers indicated that learning deficits initially characteristic of many disadvantaged children were, in effect, overcome by intervention procedures. This result may be less likely when traditional procedures are followed.

Undoubtedly, more definitive data will be forthcoming. Several longitudinal projects are in progress (for example, Miller, 1970; Evans, 1970) and an elaborate field-test program is underway in Toronto, Canada (Rusk, 1969). Hopefully, results will involve larger samples of children so as to bolster the generalizability of findings. Meanwhile, data emanating from shorter-term investigations will have to suffice.

An example of a short-term intervention is Rusk's (1969) recent field test. The B-E curriculum was applied to eight six-week summer Head Start classes. Eight more classes, matched with respect to socioeconomic status and designated as conventional Head Start groups were used for comparison purposes. Pre- and post-measures of cognitive behavior were taken on children in all sixteen classes, including the *Preschool Inventory* and the *Basic Concept Inventory*. Resultant data indicated a significant advantage in cognitive skills for the summer academic program children. If proficiency with the concepts measured by these two instruments facilitates school success, the children who participated in the less structured Head Start classes would therefore command a less favorable academic prognosis.

Of limited value are data scattered elsewhere in the literature. For example, Reidford and Berzonsky (1967) studied the effects of the B-E preschool curriculum over a period of eight months. An average gain of 6.4 Stanford-Binet IQ points is their most illustrative finding. These gains could easily be explained by motivational and practice effects. ITPA data were gathered at the end of the program, but failure to measure psycholinguistic characteristics prior to intervention makes these data impossible to interpret. Further, no control group was utilized. These same researchers later compared forty-six children in a B-E based short term (eight-week) Head Start program to eighteen children who received no formal pre-kindergarten training. Language test data collected several weeks after regular kindergarten enrollment revealed no significant differences between the two groups (ITPA and PPVT).[10] The training of the B-E teachers was acknowledged to be inadequate, a point which must be considered carefully in evaluating this study. Further, the gross behaviors measured by the ITPA and PPVT are not as likely to reflect short-term influences as in the case of the Rusk data mentioned earlier.

A large-scale study by DiLorenzo and Salter (1968) permits more decisive comment. The B-E program was one of several curriculum models implemented among compensatory preschools in New York State. As compared to traditional nursery school programs, the B-E approach resulted in the most striking and significant Binet IQ changes. DiLorenzo concluded that the most effective compensatory strategies are those which translate into specific, structured cognitive activities.

Still larger numbers of children were involved in a study by Day (1968) whose focus was upon the relative effects of two language programs. In this case the B-E program (N = 49) was compared to a unit of work approach (N = 38) which stressed receptive-expressive language. Assessments of total language production, use of conceptual category words, noun usage, and attributive adjective use revealed no significant differences between the two groups. B-E children did demonstrate greater use of color and form words on descriptive language tasks and used conceptual attributes more clearly and specifically. Day also reports a positive transfer effect from the instructional setting to an open-end interview situation for B-E children.

The Day (1968) study is similar to that performed by Dickie (1968) in which the B-E language program and a second structural training program were compared to an unstructured approach.[11] Results indicated significant language gains for all groups during the period of treatment.[12] Structured, or "task-oriented" methods did promote among children an advantage in verbal labelling skill; tendencies toward advantages in other areas of language performance, while not significant, were observed. The general strategy of structured experience, Dickie

[10] See Appendix A for description of these instruments.
[11] The second structured program was based upon Programmed Language Training Materials (Gotkin, 1966, 1967).
[12] This study consisted of two successive experiments, one involving a five-month period the other one month only. Certain variations in amount of time spent on language training in these experiments do not qualify them as true "tests" of the Bereiter-Engelmann program.

states, may also spill advantageously into such areas as parental attitudes, greater similarity to public school, and the promotion of children's attention to academic tasks.

Possibly the most sophisticated method-comparison study involving the B-E curriculum to date is being conducted in Louisville, Kentucky. Four basic curricula—"traditional" Head Start, Montessori, Bereiter-Engelmann, and DARCEE (see Chapter 7)—have been in operation with four-year-old economically disadvantaged children. End-of-year results on fourteen classes (two Montessori classes and four classes using each of the other curriculum approaches) have been reported in the areas of cognitive, motivational, social, and perceptual development (Miller, 1970). These data indicate a number of differences between approaches in the behavior of both teachers and children. Advantages in children's cognitive functioning, as measured by the Stanford-Binet and the Preschool Inventory, were associated most clearly with the B-E and DARCEE program. Specific gains of significance by children in the B-E program were also found in sentence production and arithmetic achievement. Verbal recitation skill increases were noted in the DARCEE program as well, an outcome that suggests that where greater emphasis is placed on verbal instruction (as in B-E and DARCEE) greater language behavior changes will likely occur among children. Interestingly, in programs where manipulation skills and role playing were stressed (Montessori and "traditional" approaches, respectively) children made commensurate gains in those areas. If nothing else, such data suggest that children learn what they are taught. The issue, therefore, remains what it is adults desire for their children. Finally, Miller (1970) reports that both Montessori and B-E children scored high in curiosity, a finding that is likely to encourage the protagonists of both programs. However, the most general impact on children's achievement motivation, persistence, resistance to distraction, and initiative was attributed to the DARCEE program. All in all, Miller (1970) concludes that, by comparison, the B-E and DARCEE programs are more valid for their own stated purposes than are the Montessori and "traditional" methods.

Taken as a whole, the research into the effects of the B-E curriculum has been conventional and gross. That is, only broad comparisons of this method have been made with one or more other methods. Little has yet been done concerning the linkage of specific curriculum components with particular content and methodological variables of the B-E program. The Day (1968) study is perhaps a step in the right direction. In general, research findings support modestly the claims of its originators. Short-term effects are more apparent than are long-term effects; unfortunately insufficient longitudinal data exist at the time of this writing. Conspicuously absent are research data pertinent to affective characteristics and generalized thinking operations of children.

CRITIQUE

Clearly, the structural pedagogy of B-E constitutes a dramatic departure from conventional early childhood education strategies. Implicitly, the program challenges the validity of intuitive teaching and the assumptions teachers frequently make about what children know or understand. While devised specifically for children with language and conceptual deficits, the causes of these deficits are of secondary importance. If a child cannot perform fundamental skills or deal adequately with basic concepts which are instrumental to school success, then these skills must be developed using the most economic remedial procedures available. The only real access to the child, it is argued, is through sensory input. This input is primarily auditory and visual and takes the form of symbolic interaction. The prevailing emphasis is upon changes in the child's behavior, not statements of what a teacher intends to do. Thus concrete steps are taken to avoid the assumption so apparent in many curricula, namely, that presentation equals learning (Rogers, 1967).

Elaborate analyses of the B-E program have not yet appeared with any frequency in the early childhood education literature. Published reactions are predictably diverse and usually elicit rebuttal (Hymes, 1967; Bereiter and Engelmann, 1967; Friedlander, 1968). More often than not, issue is taken with the philosophy which pervades the program and with the allegedly mechanistic means employed, rather than with the transcendental goal of the program, which is increased cognitive competence. The specificity and structure of the B-E program may appeal most readily to parents and teachers impatient with the generalities and ambiguities of many educational programs. Thus, protagonists heed the cry of "no nonsense," while the "pressure-cooker" nature of the program as perceived by its antagonists is condemned with equal vigor.

Objections to the program are perhaps most likely among developmental psychologists who view the rationale underlying the B-E program to be at variance with the entire school of cognitive psychology. The cognitive-developmental view (Kohlberg, 1968), for example, sees specific training (direct, contrived instruction) as an extremely limiting (if not failing) strategy, especially with regard to the establishment of basic mental structures (response organizations). Rather, it is argued that for the latter purpose there is no substitute for a mass accumulation of general age-linked experience. For cognitive-developmentalists, logical and physical knowledge is gradually derived from a basis of sensory-motor activities. Complex conceptual operations are structured and integrated in a progressive fashion, not by means of verbal material presented in a didactic form at levels which may represent too large a gap between present and past experience. Instead of viewing thinking as correct rule application, cognitive-developmentalists focus upon the process of structuring knowledge through action. Immediate, short-term gains achieved through pattern drill are considered subsidiary to the establishment of general, irreversible mental structures (Kohlberg, 1968; Kamii and Derman, 1969). This set of arguments is not without empirical support, as will be emphasized in Chapter 6 of this book. It must be noted, however, that the issue concerns fundamental cognitive operations, not the learning of specific discrimination and labeling skills, rote arithmetic knowledge, and the like.

Also stirred by the B-E program is a long-standing philosophical issue, namely, freeing the child's creative potential by refraining from structured conditions versus circumscribing the child's experience in pursuit of prescriptive, predetermined outcomes. The concern that children when forced or pushed (unduly pressured) may develop negative attitudes is hardly illegitimate. Not to be overlooked, however, are the facts that the B-E program is (1) addressed to a population of children with observed difficulties and (2) derived from a priority system affected mainly by time limitations. In other words, given "X" problems and "Y" time, what might be done to most effectively reach "Z"? In this case, "Z" is a higher probability of school success. This goal perhaps illuminates the near-compulsion our society has nurtured with respect to academic achievement. Clearly, it suggests that the B-E program is essentially *adaptive,* that is, conceived to facilitate the child's adaptation to the existing elementary school system (unlike Montessori, whose stated objectives go far beyond).

The adaptive function of the B-E program rests upon several assumptions. Among those assumptions most relevant for a critique are (1) the rationale concerning language development and use upon which the program is built, (2) the content and presentation strategies of the program, and (3) the socio-emotional climate within which instruction takes place.[13]

---

[13] In addition, since the cues for B-E program development were taken largely from deficits as revealed by the ITPA, the validity of this instrument is a core issue.

Language Rationale

The crux of the B-E language rationale may be reviewed briefly. First, it is recognized that academic success requires a functional repertoire of basic concepts and language skills. To be functional, language must be used to receive and transmit data that form the substance of classroom activity. It must also serve an "inner speech" function, that is, generate an internal guidance system for one's behavior. Most importantly, language represents the medium through which verbal reasoning is manifested. Since reasoning ability (involving a process of concept manipulation) is demanded for normal academic progress and disadvantaged children deal inadequately with language for this purpose, the remedial task is obvious: refine the linguistic processes of these children. In this way, reasoning ability can be stimulated under accelerative circumstances.

The firm B-E emphasis upon the structural features of language in achieving the above objective is reminiscent of the *linguistic-relativity* hypothesis. Basically, this hypothesis suggests that thought is shaped by the particular language through which it is processed. While this point of view has strong historical underpinnings, it has recently been championed by the late Benjamin Whorf, a widely recognized linguist. Briefly, Whorf maintained that language both shapes ideas and serves to guide one's mental behavior. In other words, both the pattern and direction of thought are functions of linguistic structure, thus making language much more than a servant of communication.

Research into the relation between thought and language has not provided incontrovertible support for the linguistic-relativity hypothesis; discrepant theoretical positions abound in this area. As Ervin-Tripp (1966) has indicated, the language-thought issue is continuously debated. Distinctions between language and thought are found in the work of such authorities as Church (1961), Furth (1964), Lenneberg (1964), Piaget (1961), and Vygotsky (1962), all of whom may be used as references to argue variously against the Bereiter-Engelmann position. Church (1961), for example, rejects an S-R associationistic-reinforcement view of language development and argues that children must gradually formulate their personal "constructions of reality" from various sense data they encounter. For Church, language categories do not determine thought processes among children. Rather, thought processes and language categories interact and accommodate to one another.

On the other hand, support for the strategy of improving abstract thought through systematic language training is found in the related work of Blank and Solomon (1968, 1969). These researchers, however, question the efficacy of group-oriented training and prefer the conditions made possible through individual training. Like B-E, Blank and Solomon have based their techniques on the observed language deficiencies of disadvantaged children, the most serious of which is the lack of an internal symbolic system functional for purposes of organizing and classifying stimuli.

Due to the complexity of the problems encountered in language-thought research with children, it is unlikely that theoretical issues engendered by this aspect of cognitive behavior will be quickly settled. Meanwhile, legitimate questions may be raised about this portion of the B-E language program rationale. While B-E imply that the learning of verbal labels helps the child to refine his perceptions of the environmental stimulus array, research fails to indicate that discriminatory power necessarily increases as a function of label acquisition (Lenneberg, 1961). Conversely, research data suggest that the acquisition of verbal responses facilitates verbal mediation, that is, a verbal stimulus (or series of verbal stimuli) mediates the selection of further verbal (or nonverbal) responses (Ervin and Miller, 1963). As Ervin-Tripp (1966) remarks, "the more distinctive the labels learned for the stimuli, the more readily are the labels learned, and the more quickly are later motor responses to the stimuli acquired" (p. 83). In effect, this phenomenon is relevant to both economy in learning and the long-term retention of learning—goals toward which the B-E program is oriented. Miller (1962) has also emphasized the importance of the grammatical properties of language in relation to the learning of verbal material. These properties apparently influence a learner's perception of verbal stimuli and how they are manipulated symbolically. Presumably, then, teaching strategies which highlight correct grammatical properties (as in the B-E program) would facilitate "correct" symbolic manipulations. On the other hand, there are data to show that the retention of verbal material is affected by both its semantic and syntactical properties (Mehler and Miller, 1964; Marks and Miller, 1964). Similarly, data suggest that sentence learning proceeds in stages, with the syntactical form being acquired *after* the semantic property is learned. If so, are B-E going about this process backwards?

Finally, language training geared toward the codification of stimulus dimensions (such as form, color, weight), a conspicuous feature of the B-E program, is apparently assumed to prompt the child to attend selectively to important features of the environment and problems posed by these features. This is not unlike a process designed to cultivate *learning sets,*[14] and support for this general procedure may be inferred from the literature on learning set acquisition (for example, Gagné and Paradise, 1961).

Moskovitz (1968) has severely criticized B-E in relation to a corollary assumption underlying the language program rationale: that lower-class black dialect interferes with processing and logical reasoning. That certain Afro-American dialect patterns differ from but are no less complex than standard English is indicated by many studies (Baratz and Shuy, 1969; Raph, 1967). These data and those associating linguistic variations with social class differences are striking. At issue, however, is whether these differences necessarily imply thought deficiencies. An objection may be voiced in some quarters to one implication springing from the B-E position: that standard English, a largely middle-class value, is *the* model for precision thinking and therefore marks a child's subcultural dialect as inferior.[15] A strategy for handling this delicate dialect problem is suggested by Cazden (1968). Teachers are advised to concentrate upon enlargement of the young child's language repertoire and to avoid the alteration of nonstandard linguistic forms except for the provision of a standard English *model.* Cazden believes that the emphasis should be upon standard English for learning purposes, but that intervention concerning the social functions of language may be self-defeating and irrelevant.

Related to the dialect problem are questions pertinent to the somewhat artificial nature of the language responses programmed by B-E. Children are, without exception, required to state loudly and completely all identity and second-order statements. This has the effect of inducing children to reflect in their vocalizations the same syntactical and grammatical properties as found in written language and, by definition, at a rather unnatural volume and pitch. This writer knows of no evidence to to suggest (1) that thinking, to be logical and refined, must take place in full, complete sentences; (2) that it is advisable to learn identical speaking and writing language patterns, or (3) that high intensity verbal

[14] A learning set may be defined as an orienting response which facilitates the learning of new, more complex material.

[15] B-E simply argue that certain language skills are necessary for all children if they are to operate effectively in school and society. At the very least, they are concerned that every child is able to exercise such basic skills when necessary. This line of thinking also permeates the Soviet Union's approach to preschool education. By the end of the fifth year of life children are expected to be able to pronounce correctly all the sounds in the Russian language. The correct use of standard Russian continues to be stressed from then onward (Chauncy, 1969). By definition, the Soviet Union is a worker society (classless at least in theory), and the emphasis there on correct language is extremely interesting in view of the value-laden language issues which currently exist in this country.

expressions per se are necessarily more easily discriminated or build stronger stimulus-response associations. With respect to the latter, there is the strong possibility that children may overgeneralize language responses so that loud, formal expressions occur in inappropriate contexts. In fact, some B-E program graduates have been observed to talk too loudly in the conventional primary grade classroom (Rowan, 1969).

Several other issues may be mentioned here briefly; one concerns whether children acquire a basic identity "operation" (see Chapter 6 by the simple verbatim repetition of statements. From a cognitive-developmental point of view, such an outcome is improbable, as is the achievement of other basic operations by way of rote learning experience. Another issue concerns the relationship of the language and reading phases of the B-E program. Ruddell (1963) has reported significantly greater prose comprehension when high-frequency patterns of spoken language structure are employed (versus low-frequency oral patterns). If so, the B-E strategy of stressing high-frequency patterns would favor subsequent comprehension *where* the reading material reflects the statement forms selected for teaching. Whether the B-E statement forms facilitate transfer to other forms found in children's prose has apparently not been directly researched.

In sum, the B-E language program rationale is based upon theoretical postulates concerning language, thought, and dialect that require close scrutiny. Conceivably, their theoretical rationale could be incorrect yet their techniques of language training valid, at least in terms of their stated purposes. While the delineation of issues above has not been exhaustive, it hopefully has illustrated some implicit features which may escape the attention of teachers and parents, particularly those who may be impressed by the authority denoted by highly specific curricula for young children.

Program Content and Presentation Strategies

The B-E program represents a selection of basic concepts and rule prototypes assumed to be imperative for the repertoire of a child who is to succeed with formal academics. One must assume that the analysis performed by B-E of successful primary grade academic achievement is accurate. Unquestionably this analysis, reported essentially in terms of subskills which build upon one another to culminate in reading, is one of the most specific and detailed to be placed in the public domain. In most respects the analysis is based upon logical deduction and opinion. It remains to be seen whether a logical programming of skill-building activities matches the psychological processes utilized by children in developing abstract reasoning skills. For example, it seems as though B-E have observed the capabilities of students who read well and successfully discriminate color and geometric form. Children who read poorly frequently do not demonstrate the latter skills. It is easy to conclude, therefore, that the route to reading success should include the teaching of color and form concepts. Whether or not such teaching is necessary to learning to read remains a question.

While the selection of certain class concepts for teaching may strike observers as arbitrary (for example, weapon) one must recognize the significance of the relational concepts and polar attributes in a young child's repertoire of meaning. Many, such as "or," "between," and "before-after," are frequently taken for granted by parents and teachers although rarely taught directly. According to the criteria for teaching relative concepts such as "few" and "some," established by Carroll (1964), the B-E strategies are valid. Further, children's concepts of phenomena such as "same" or "different" influence significantly their responses to discrimination tasks fundamental to reading readiness programs (Caldwell and Hall, 1969).

With respect to both language and concept teaching, certain process variables may provoke criticism. Moskovitz (1968), for example, charges that B-E have disregarded the natural, inductive process of language acquisition and require, quite inappropriately and unnaturally, children to produce complete sentences. Ordinarily, children establish successive approximations of complete sentences very gradually through interaction with a reinforcing model (parent). Imitation and expansion are fundamental processes in natural language learning (Brown and Bellugi, 1964), whereas the B-E process is more clearly a rote process in an artificial context. B-E argue, however, that to overcome the elliptical, restricted spoken English style of the disadvantaged child, standard English must virtually be taught as a foreign language. At issue is whether the developmental nature of native language learning is necessarily the model for teaching a second language. B-E have selected strategies consistent with those employed in contemporary foreign language instruction. These include: (1) presenting items to be learned in spoken form prior to their presentation in written form (the "natural sequence"), (2) using data obtained from an analysis of contrasts between telegraphic language style ("native language" for the disadvantaged child and the target language (standard English), (3) pattern drill to achieve overlearning (practice beyond the point of initial proficiency) where linguisitic patterns and phrases receive full attention and (4) a simulation of "real life" situations (classroom) where new language responses substitute for the use of native language (Carroll, 1963). It may be noted in passing that where second language listening comprehension is desired (an implicit priority in the B-E program) greater advantages accrue from training procedures whereby speaking precedes listening (Mace, 1966).

The effectiveness of didactic presentation of syntactical and grammatical rules in the B-E program, especially with respect to the transfer value of the rules, remains uncertain. Again, as compared to normal language learning, a didactic approach is artificial, even though conceivably much more economical *if* children achieve a functional understanding of the rules. Expressive language is seemingly based upon a system of rules learned inductively by children. This system is intuitively functional, that is, children apparently utilize these rules to understand and express phrases that they have never before heard or spoken. Thus, unique, but rule-based combinations of words are made, although a child is rarely able to verbalize the rules he uses (nor are many adults!).[16] Again, the issue is whether formal rule learning by young children in a didactic situation is sufficiently meaningful to facilitate expressive language development where new combinations of words are desired (versus proficiency with only a few statement forms). The rule learning approach generally has been questioned by Kamii and Derman (1969). These authorities believe that the imposition of rules is a less efficient teaching technique over the long term than are strategies which assist a child gradually to construct his own rules. The latter approach is directed toward the development of basic cognitive processes rather than the memorization of verbal abstractions.

Related to the above issue are the instructional strategies utilized for concept teaching. Concepts are taught to all children in the same stepwise fashion, thus allowing little, if any, provision for individual differences in learning style. Teachers are actually discouraged from giving other than cursory explanations, a style that presumably has contributed to the disadvantaged child's initial problem. (Recall the earlier discussion of this matter in Chapter 3.)

Perhaps more disputable is the pervasive concept teaching strategy which begins at the symbolic level rather than graduating to symbolism from concrete referents. That is, active sensory experiences are rarely programmed as referents for the derivation of abstract meanings and relations. As mentioned earlier, this sequence is basic to cognitive-developmental theory. Further, while concept teaching based upon deductive strategies or didactic presentations is generally more efficient, greater motivational and transfer effects often are associated with inductive,

---

[16] All languages, including dialects, have an implicit rule structure (Bailey, 1965). Original language production based upon this rule structure is discussed as generative or transformational grammar by the influential psycholinguist Noam Chomsky (1957).

discovery-oriented approaches (Jones, 1967).[17] Still, the issue concerns the experiential nature of the learning or its true effectiveness in terms of meaningfulness to the child (Rogers, 1967).[18]

Finally, the standardized arrangement of positive and negative examples of concepts for presentation is perhaps too inflexible for best results. For example, the concepts *break-fix* are taught by presenting a series of three positive examples (in sequence a doll, pitcher, and boy's arm are all broken, then fixed), interjected with a deviation (a tree branch is broken, but cannot be fixed), and end with a completely different meaning for the word *fix* (a misbehaving boy is told by his mother "I will fix you"). The general strategy of presenting positive examples followed by negative examples (nonexamples of the concept) to test for comprehension has support among educational psychologists (for example, McDonald, 1965, pp. 173–181). One must be concerned, however, about presenting a sufficent number of both positive and negative examples to a child. Reliable discrimination between exemplars and nonexemplars of a concept is perhaps the best indication of concept understanding. The Engelmann materials rarely meet this criterion and frequently introduce unnecessary confusion. If, as in the above example, a teacher wishes to introduce a disjunctive meaning ("I will fix a broken doll" versus "I will fix you, you naughty boy"), then more sophisticated materials must be devised.

In sum, the content of the B-E program is both highly selective and convergent. Inherent are issues related to language acquisition processes and concept learning processes the resolution of which is far beyond the scope of this book.[19] Absent are activities and materials formulated expressly for purposes of affective development and learning. Neither have any research data been provided as yet concerning the possible indirect effects the B-E program might have on children's attitudes and value orientations. (For example, higher self-esteem as a function of increased cognitive competence.) Lavatelli (1969), among others, has criticized the restrictive nature of this program and the limited number of verb tenses and statement forms found therein. Creativity development is, by implication, considered an unaffordable luxury. Most of the pivotal concepts in the program are, however, consistent with the objectives around which B-E learning activities have been constructed.

---

[17] Carroll (1964) points out that most concept learning tasks involve both processes, hence it is a matter of emphasis rather than either/or.

[18] Rogers defines "experiential learning" as that derived from significant, meaningful experiences. Its components include self-initiated movement, personal involvement, and self-evaluation.

[19] See Samuels, 1967, for a brief overview of psycholinguistic controversies.

The Learning Climate

The socio-emotional climate within which learning takes place is essentially a function of individual teacher characteristics. Teacher behavior varies on several dimensions of importance including *warmcold, systematic-disorganized,* and *dynamic-routine,* all of which are associated with pupil productivity in expected directions (Ryans, 1960). The B-E program virtually demands systematic and dynamic teacher behavior. It also has the effect of ascribing a highly authoritative role for the teacher: it is the teacher who plans and conducts all activities, answers most of the questions, and evaluates the adequacy of children's responses. This need not occur in an atmosphere lacking warmth and emotional support for children, although teacher-centered, highly structured classrooms are more likely to be perceived as nonsupportive by the naïve observer. Of more legitimate concern is the dependency that children may early develop toward the teacher. This concern is heightened if one believes that children should assume responsibility for their own learning as early as possible. Thus the question concerns whether children can learn skills deemed necessary by B-E without becoming overdependent upon teacher direction.

Bereiter (1967) has himself recognized this potential problem. He argues that in the public schools children generally must depend heavily upon their own initiative and learning style if they are to be successful. Unfortunately, they may also encounter less than ideal teachers along the way. Bereiter thus reasons that efforts directed toward the development of independent learning skills, persistence, and problem-solving strategies are well advised. Such efforts clearly require more attention in the B-E program (Bereiter, 1967).

One relevant strategy for the above purpose involves the programming of a series of gradually extended seatwork activities, each of which culminates in a reward. In effect one would thus be rewarding the child for this engagement in progressively longer independent study activities. Key response patterns would be increased persistence and decreased distractibility. It is this sort of augmentation strategy that has been suggested by Dr. Wesley Becker, the behaviorist now directing the Illinois program.[20]

Even in the original program format, however, reward strategies are stressed for purposes of maintaining rapport and pupil motivation. Teachers are advised to reward effort, task-involvement (versus play

---

[20] Such a strategy reflects the principle of *reinforcing successive approximations of desired behavior* so instrumental to behavioral analysis procedures. See Chapter 5. It should also be noted that during 1970 Becker and Engelmann will be relocating their operation at the University of Oregon in Eugene.

motives), group cohesiveness and cooperation. Shaming, coaxing, and derogation are to be avoided. The rewards suggested include both material (cookies, raisins, game privileges) and social (praise and recognition) ones, although B-E feel the real rewards for children will emanate from their newly learned skills. Disciplinary techniques advised, assuming their discreet use, include moderate physical punishment and social isolation, the effects of which are often unpredictable and fraught with negative side effects (Jones, 1967).

In summary, the B-E learning climate, like any other program climate, will vary according to teacher personality. By virtue of its authoritative format it conceivably could attract authoritarian teachers. The structure and "neatness" of the curriculum may also appeal strongly to insecure teachers. Unfortunately, no clear empirical data are yet available concerning the socio-emotional characteristics of either B-E teachers or children. Anecdotal reports indicate, however, that the children and teachers are generally enthusiastic, responsive, and secure; all participants seem to thoroughly enjoy what they are up to. Relevant research for the future hopefully will include the study of these children's self-concepts, anxiety responses, and intellectual achievement responsibility as well as the academic validity of the entire program.

SUMMARY

Structural pedagogy, as developed by Bereiter and Engelmann and applied to early education, marks a radical departure from conventional approaches. Its expressed purpose is to increase dramatically the probability of subsequent academic success for children from disadvantaged circumstances. The curriculum is geared toward the alleviation of critical deficits frequently observed to characterize such children. Language training provides the basic substance of the program. This training is intended to sharpen the child's use of language, particularly with respect to logical reasoning. Language training is extended into reading and arithmetic and is augmented by music activities. Hence the entire orientation is cognitive. Originally designed for four- and five-year-old children, efforts are now underway to extend B-E curriculum principles into the primary grades.

Superficially, the B-E program strikes many observers as atheoretical, that is, not based upon an organized system of related postulates and concepts that explain developmental learning. The program is implicitly founded on a rather strict application of associationistic (stimulus-response) learning theory, however, and the language program per se is rooted in a network of theoretical assumptions concerning language and cognition. Sequenced activities based upon pattern drill constitute the heart of the program. A rapid programming of symbolic auditory and visual input is preferred to enactive modes of learning.

On the basis of limited research, one may tentatively conclude that the B-E program is an impetus to cognitive development as measured by conventional instruments. Gains tend to be spectacular initially. Dissipation of these gains has been observed as later primary grades are reached. This gain reduction does not reach the point of indicating a complete long-term "wash-out," yet the phenomenon provokes several questions. One involves the permanency of the cumulative gains typically observed while children progress through the pre-primary two-year program. Another concerns the possible depressing effect of poor continuity from this program to conventional primary grade programs. Data regarding the effects, if any, of the B-E program on children's affective characteristics have not been provided by the early research.

A Pandora's box of complex theoretical language-cognition issues is opened by the B-E program, some of which are only touched upon in this chapter. Further research in psycholinguistics and verbal learning through auditory channels hopefully will provide a broader perspective within which to assess Bereiter and Engelmann's structural pedagogy more definitively.

References

Ahlfield, Kathy. "Pressure Cooker Teaching: How It's Working Out." *Nation's Schools,* 1969, 83, 58–62.

Ausubel, D. P. *The Psychology of Meaningful Verbal Learning.* New York: Grune and Stratton, 1963.

Ausubel, D. P. "How Reversible Are the Cognitive and Motivational Effects of Cultural Deprivation?" *Urban Education,* 1964, Summer, 16–35.

Bailey, Beryl. "Toward a New Perspective in Negro English Dialectology." *American Speech,* 1965, 11, 171–177.

Baratz, J. C., and R. W. Shuy (Eds.). *Teaching Black Children to Read.* Washington, D.C.: Center for Applied Linguistics, 1969.

Becker, Wesley, and Seigfried Engelmann. *University of Illinois Follow Through Approach: The Systematic Use of Reinforcement Principles.* Urbana: University of Illinois Press, 1968.

Bereiter, Carl. "Instructional Planning in Early Compensatory Education." *Phi Delta Kappan,* 1967, 48, 355–359.

Bereiter, Carl, and Seigfried Engelmann. *Teaching the Disadvantaged Child in the Preschool.* Englewood Cliffs: Prentice-Hall, 1966a.

Bereiter, Carl, and Seigfried Engelmann. "Observations on the Use of Direct Instruction with Young Disadvantaged Children." *Journal of School Psychology,* 1966b, 4, 55–62.

Bereiter, Carl, and Seigfried Engelmann. "The Educator and the Child Developmentalist: Reply to a Review." *Educational Leadership,* 1967, 25, 12–14.

Bernstein, Basil. "Social Structure, Language and Learning." *Educational Research,* 1961, 3, 163–176.

Blank, Marion, and Frances Solomon. "A Tutorial Language Program to Develop Abstract Thinking in Socially Disadvantaged Preschool Children." *Child Development,* 1968, 39, 379–390.

Blank, Marion, and Frances Solomon. "How Shall the Disadvantaged Child Be Taught?" *Child Development,* 1969, 40, 47–61.

Brown, Roger. "Language: The System and Its Acquisition." In R. Brown (Ed.), *Social Psychology.* New York: Free Press, 1966, 246–305.

Brown, Roger, and Ursula Bellugi. "Three Processes in the Child's Acquisition of Syntax." *Harvard Educational Review,* 1964, 34, 133–152.

Brown, Roger, and Jean Berko. "Word Association and the Acquisition of Grammar." *Child Development,* 1960, 31, 1–14.

Caldwell, Edward C., and Vernon C. Hall. "The Influence of Concept Training on Letter Discrimination." *Child Development,* 1969, 40, 63–72.

Carpenter, Thomas R., and Thomas U. Bussi. "Development of Self-Concept in Negro and White Welfare Children." *Child Development,* 1969, 40, 935–939.

Carroll, J. B. "Research on Teaching Foreign Languages." In N. L. Gage (Ed.), *Handbook of Research on Teaching.* Chicago: Rand-McNally, 1963, 1060–1110.

Carroll, J. B. "The Analysis of Reading Instruction: Perspectives from Psychology and Language." In E. R. Hilgard (Ed.), *Theories of Learning and Instruction.* National Society for Study of Education, 63rd Yearbook. Chicago: University of Chicago Press, 1964a, 336–353.

Carroll, J. B. "Words, Meanings, and Concepts: Part II. Concept Teaching and Learning." *Harvard Educational Review,* 1964b, 34, 191–202.

Carroll, J. B. *Language and Thought.* Englewood Cliffs: Prentice-Hall, 1965.

Cazden, Courtney B. "Some Implications of Research on Language Development for Pre-School Education." In R. D. Hess and Roberta Bear (Eds.), *Early Education.* Chicago: Aldine, 1968, 131–142.

Chauncey, Henry. *Soviet Preschool Education.* New York: Holt, Rinehart and Winston, 1969.

Chomsky, Noam. *Syntactic Structures.* s'Gavenhage, Holland: Mouton, 1957.

Chomsky, Noam. *Aspects of the Theory of Syntax.* Cambridge: M.I.T. Press, 1965.

Church, Joseph. *Language and the Discovery of Reality.* New York: Random House, 1961.

Day, D. E. "The Effects of Different Language Instruction on the Use of Attributes by Pre-kindergarten Disadvantaged Children." Paper read at American Educational Research Association Convention, Chicago, 1968 (February).

Deno, S. L., and J. R. Jenkins. "On the 'Behaviorality' of Behavioral Objectives." *Psychology in the Schools,* 1969, 6, 18–23.

Deutsch, Martin. *Social Intervention and the Malleability of the Child.* Fourth Annual School of Education Lecture, Cornell University, Ithaca, 1965.

Dickie, Joyce P. "Effectiveness of Structured and Unstructured (Traditional) Methods of Language Training." *Monographs of the Society for Research in Child Development,* 1968, 33, Serial No. 124, 62–79.

Diebold, A. R., Jr. "Review of Psycholinguistics." *Language,* 1964, 40, 197–260.

DiLorenzo, L. T., and R. Salter. "An Evaluative Study of Prekindergarten Programs for Educationally Disadvantaged Children: Follow Up and Replication." Paper read at American Educational Research Association Convention, Chicago, 1968 (February).

Engelmann, Seigfried. *The Basic Concept Inventory.* Chicago: Follett, 1967a.

Engelmann, Seigfried. "Relationship between Psychological Theories and the Act of Teaching." *Journal of School Psychology,* 1967b, 5, 93–100.

Engelmann, Seigfried. "Relating Operant Techniques to Programming and Teaching." *Journal of School Psychology,* 1968, 6, 89–96.

Engelmann, Seigfried. *Preventing Failure in the Primary Grade.* Chicago: Science Research Associates, 1969.

Engelmann, Seigfried, and Doug Carnine. *Distar Arithmetic I: An Instructional System.* Chicago: Science Research Associates, 1969a.

Engelmann, Seigfried, Jean Osborn, and Bonnie Lundeen. *Part-Whole Relationships: Learning Language.* Urbana: University of Illinois Press, 1968a.

Engelmann, Seigfried, Jean Osborn, and Bonnie Lundeen. *Action and Concept Stories: Learning Language.* Urbana: University of Illinois Press, 1968b.

Ervin, Susan, and W. R. Miller. "Language Development." In H. Stevenson (Ed.), *Child Psychology.* Chicago: University of Chicago Press, 1963, 108–143.

Ervin-Tripp, Susan. "Language Development." In Lois W. Hoffman and M. L. Hoffman (Eds.), *Review of Child Development Research,* Vol. II. New York: Russell Sage, 1966, 55–105.

Evans, Ellis D. "A Field Test of the Bereiter-Engelmann Preschool Language Curriculum." Research in progress, Seattle, 1970.

Feldman, Shirley, and D. Schmidt. "Effect of Auditory Training on Reading Skills of Retarded Readers." *Perceptual and Motor Skills,* 1968, 26, 467–480.

Fraser, C., Ursula Bellugi, and R. Brown. "Control of Grammar in Imitation, Comprehension, and Production." *Journal of Verbal Learning and Verbal Behavior,* 1963, 2, 121–135.

Friedlander, Bernard Z. "The Bereiter-Engelmann Approach." *Educational Forum,* 1968, 32, 359–362.

Fries, C. C. *Linguistics and Reading.* New York: Holt, Rinehart and Winston, 1963.

Furth, Hans. "Research with the Deaf: Implications for Language and Cognition." *Psychological Bulletin,* 1964, 62, 145–164.

Gagné, Robert. *The Conditions of Learning.* New York: Holt, Rinehart and Winston, 1970.

Gagné, Robert M., and N. E. Paradise. "Abilities and Learning Sets in Knowledge Acquisition." *Psychological Monographs,* 1961, 75, Whole No. 518.

Glaser, Robert. "Instructional Technology and the Measurement of Learning Outcomes." *American Psychologist,* 1963, 18, 519–521.

Gotkin, L. G. *Language Lotto.* New York: Appleton, 1966.

Gotkin, L. G. *Matrix Games.* New York: Appleton, 1967.

Hess, Robert D., and Virginia C. Shipman. "Early Experience and the Socialization of Cognitive Modes in Children." *Child Development,* 1965, 36, 869–886.

Hodges, Walter L. "Teaching Disadvantaged Children: A Review." *American Educational Research Journal,* 1966, 3, 313–314.

Hudgins, Bryce B., and Joseph Gore. "Classroom Recitation: The Effects of Interaction Patterns upon Learning." *Journal of General Psychology,* 1966, 75, 243–247.

Hutchinson, Barbara, and D. Clark. "Auditory and Visual Discrimination Skills of Normal and Articulation-defective Children." *Perceptual and Motor Skills,* 1968, 26, 259–265.

Hymes, James L. "Teaching Disadvantaged Children in the Preschool: A Review." *Educational Leadership,* 1967, 24, 463–467.

IPI. *Individually Prescribed Instruction.* Philadelphia: Research for Better Schools, 1967.

IPI. *Individually Prescribed Instruction: Education U.S.A. Special Report.* Washington, D.C.: Education, U.S.A., 1968.

Jones, Daisy, "The Implications of Linguistics for the Teaching of Reading." *Elementary English,* 1969, 46, 176–183.

Jones, J. Charles. *Learning.* New York: Macmillan, 1967.

Kamii, Constance, and Louise Derman. "The Engelmann Approach to Teaching Logical Thinking: Findings from the Administration of Some Piagetian Tasks." Ypsilanti, Michigan: Ypsilanti Public Schools, 1969 (February), 33 pp.

Karnes, Merle B., James A. Teska, and Audrey S. Hodgins. "A Longitudinal Study of Disadvantaged Children Who Participated in Three Different Preschool Programs." Urbana: Institute for Research on Exceptional Children, 1969.

Katz, J. J., and J. A. Fodor. "The Structure of a Semantic Theory." *Language,* 1963, 39, 170–210.

Kendler, T. S. "Development of Mediating Responses in Children." In J. C. Wright and J. Kagan (Eds.), *Basic Cognitive Processes in Children. Monographs of the Society for Research in Child Development,* Chicago: University of Chicago Press, 1963.

Kersh, B. Y., and Wittrock, M. C. "Learning by Discovery: An Interpretation of Recent Research." *Journal of Teacher Education,* 1962, 13, 461–468.

Kohlberg, Lawrence. "Early Education: A Cognitive-Developmental View." *Child Development,* 1968, 39, 1013–1062.

Lavatelli, Celia S. "An Approach to Language Learning." *Young Children,* 1969, 24, 368–379.

Lenneberg, E. H. "Color Naming, Color Recognition, Color Discrimination: a Reappraisal." *Perceptual Motor Skills,* 1961, 12, 375–382.

Lenneberg, E. H. (Ed.). *New Directions in the Study of Language.* Cambridge: M.I.T., Press, 1964, 65–88.

Lenneberg, Eric H. *Biological Foundations of Language.* New York: John Wiley, 1967.

Luria, A. R. *The Role of Speech in the Regulation of Normal and Abnormal Behavior.* New York: Pergamon, 1961.

McCormick, Molly, and Jean Osborn. *Language Through Songs.* Urbana: University of Illinois Press, 1969.

McDonald, Frederick T. *Educational Psychology* (2d ed.) Belmont, Calif.: Wadsworth, 1965.

Mace, L. "Sequence of Vocal Response-differentiation Training and Auditory Stimulus-discrimination Training in Beginning French." *Journal of Educational Psychology,* 1966, 57, 102–108.

Marks, L. E., and George E. Miller. "The Role of Semantic and Syntactic Constraints in the Memorization of English Sentences." *Journal of Verbal Learning and Verbal Behavior,* 1964, 3, 1–5.

Mehler, J., and G. A. Miller. "Retroactive Interference in the Recall of Simple Sentences." *British Journal of Psychology.* 1964, 55, 295–301.

Miller, G. A. "Some Psychological Studies of Grammar." *American Psychologist,* 1962, 17, 748–762.

Miller, Louise B. "Experimental Variation of Head Start Curricula: A Comparison of Current Approaches." Psychology Department, University of Louisville, Louisville, 1970.

Monsees, Edna K., and Carol Berman. "Speech and Language Screening in a Summer Head Start Program." *Journal of Speech and Hearing Disorders,* 1968, 33, 121–126.

Moskovitz, Sarah T. "Some Assumptions Underlying the Bereiter Approach." *Young Children,* 1968, 24, 24–31.

Osborn, Jean. "Teaching a Teaching Language to Disadvantaged Children." *Monographs of the Society for Research in Child Development,* 1968, 33, Serial No. 124, 36–48.

Osgood, C. E. and T. E. Sebeok. *Psycholinguistics: A Survey of Theory and Research Problems.* Bloomington: Indiana University Press, 1965.

Piaget, Jean. "The Genetic Approach to the Psychology of Thought," *Journal of Educational Psychology,* 1961, 52, 275–281.

Pick, Anne D. "Improvement of Visual and Tactical Form Discrimination." *Journal of Experimental Psychology,* 1965, 69, 331–339.

Raph, Jane B. "Language and Speech Deficits in Culturally Disadvantaged Children: Implications for the Speech Clinician." *Journal of Speech and Hearing Disorders,* 1967, 32, 203–214.

Reidford, P., and M. Berzonsky. "Field Test of an Academically Oriented

Preschool Curriculum." Paper read at American Educational Research Association Convention, New York, 1967 (February).

Rogers, Carl. "The Facilitation of Significant Learning." In Laurence Siegel (Ed.), *Instruction: Some Contemporary Viewpoints.* San Francisco: Chandler, 1967, 34–54.

Rounn, Helen (Ed.). "Heresy in Nursery School: The Bomb Throwers and Direct Teaching." *Carnegie Quarterly,* 1969, 17, No. 1, 2–3.

Rowan, Helen. "Heresy in Nursery School: The Bomb Throwers and Direct Teaching." *Carnegie Quarterly,* 1969, 17, 2–3.

Ruddell, R. B. *An Investigation of the Effect of the Similarity of Oral and Written Patterns of Language Structure on Reading Comprehension.* Doctoral Dissertation. Bloomington: Indiana University Press, 1963, 207 pp.

Rusk, Bruce. "Field-test of the Bereiter-Engelmann Preschool Curriculum in a Six Week-Headstart program." Paper read at American Education Research Association Convention, Los Angeles, 1969 (February).

Ryans, David. *Characteristics of Teachers.* Washington, D.C.: American Council on Education, 1960.

Samuels, S. J. "The Psychology of Language" *Review of Educational Research,* 1967a, 37, 109–119.

Samuels, S. Jay. "Attentional Process in Reading: The Effect of Pictures on the Acquisition of Reading Responses. *Journal of Educational Psychology,* 1967b, 58, 337–342.

Seifart, Kelvin. "Comparison of Verbal Interaction in Two Preschool Programs." *Young Children,* 1969, 24, 350–355.

Soares, Anthony T., and Louise M. Soares. "Self-perception of Culturally Disadvantaged Children." *American Educational Research Journal,* 1969, 6, 31–45.

Vygotsky, L. S. *Language and Thought: The Problem and the Approach.* Cambridge: M.I.T. Press, 1962.

Wakefield, Mary W., and N. J. Silvaroli. "A Study of Oral Language Patterns of Low Socioeconomic Groups." *Reading Teacher,* 1969, 22, 622–624.

Weiner, Paul S. "The Cognitive Functioning of Language Deficient Children." *Journal of Speech and Hearing Research,* 1969, 12, 53–64.

White, Robert W. "Motivation Reconsidered: The Concept of Competence." *Psychological Review,* 1959, 66, 297–333.

5

Behavior Analysis Procedures

In one way or another, all educational strategies are designed to modify behavior in desired ways. This is true whether one seeks a gross objective such as "positive growth and adjustment" or a specific one such as "the ability to discriminate visually the letters of the alphabet." In short, where objectives are sought, behavioral change is implied.

Since behavior never occurs in a vacuum, that is, always occurs in an environmental context, an educator obviously must attend to the characteristics of an environment which influence behavior. This chapter is concerned with those environmental influences which affect the rate at which a learner progresses en route to a given objective. It is the systematic study and manipulation of such influences that consumes the major attention of educators who take a behavioral analysis approach to teaching and learning.

Most generally, behavior analysis involves the application of principles and procedures for behavior modification where environmental conditions and events are systematically arranged in specific temporal relationships with specific behavior. These principles and procedures, independent of any subject-matter content, have been developed through a system for the measurement of behavior change. This measurement system is designed to enable a teacher to identify environmental events which influence the acquisition, maintenance, increase in strength, or disappearance of various types of responses or response patterns. It is this chapter's purpose to explain behavior analysis principles, how these principles can be applied to the behavior of young children, and representative research data that have been obtained through such application. In order to assist the reader toward an understanding of these principles, the conceptual system from which behavioral analysis procedures have been derived will first be described.

THE SYSTEM: BASIC CONCEPTS

Respondent and Operant Behavior

The technical system which encompasses principles of behavior analysis was born of laboratory experimentation in operant conditioning by B. F. Skinner (1938). Within the broad framework of associationistic S-R (stimulus-response) approaches to learning, Skinner early distinguished two classes of behavior: *respondent* and *operant*.[1] Respondent behavior is that which is elicited unconditionally by some known and observable stimulus. For example, a strategically placed hammer blow immediately below one's kneecap results in the familiar kneejerk response—one's knee *responds* to the hammer blow stimulus. Respondent behavior is basically reflex behavior. It thus involves responses over which voluntary control is ordinarily highly improbable.

---

[1] A third class, involving an overlap or interaction between operant and respondent behavior, has also been identified. This class will not be treated in this brief chapter. Further, since most classroom behavior with which teachers deal is primarily operant in nature, neither will the intricacies of respondent conditioning be examined here.

In contrast, *operant* behavior is volitional. Instead of being elicited predictably by some known stimulus, an operant response is emitted voluntarily, presumably to produce some effect on the environment. In other words, one operates intentionally on the environment to effect some change or result. Consider a child who asks his mother for a nickel. His asking behavior (verbalization of request) represents an operant response. So would any further act he performed using the nickel, such as buying a candy bar. If the child is successful, that is, receives the nickel after asking, he has produced a change in his environment.

Unlike respondent behavior, operant behavior is not necessarily associated with any known antecedent stimulus. Rather, it is influenced by the consequences which follow the behavior. Operant behaviors do, however, usually become associated with an antecedent stimulus condition. When this occurs, the antecedent establishes the occasion for an operant response to occur. As such, the antecedent becomes the *cue* for an operant response to be emitted; it does not elicit a response in the same sense as a hammer blow elicits a knee jerk.

Consider that, in the above example, the child asks for a nickel only when in the presence of a candy machine. This suggests that the candy machine has taken on antecedent cueing properties; that is, the machine's presence is necessary to establish the occasion for nickel-asking behavior. The observed relationships between the cue (candy machine) and the response (nickel-asking) would signal the development of a *discriminated operant* response. In other words, the child now makes a predictable response in the presence of a specific stimulus. This is due to his history of reinforcement—receiving a nickel—for making that specific response in the presence of that stimulus. It should be noted, however, that operant conditioning is concerned basically with providing a reinforcer after a response has occurred. A cue-response connection is not at issue; rather, it is the response per se which is strengthened by reinforcement. A legitimate description of operant conditioning may be made quite apart from specifying stimuli which precede a response. Despite this methodological point, the essence of a teacher's job, as we shall see, is the development of strong discriminant operants.

Reinforcement

For a discriminated operant to be developed and maintained over time, a further condition is necessary: a *reinforcing consequence*. That is, a response emitted in the presence of a set of antecedent stimuli must be followed by a *reinforcing stimulus*. Consider once again our example above. If giving the child a nickel *after* he has asked for it increases the probability that he will in the future emit the request under similar circumstances, the nickel may be defined as a reinforcing stimulus.

The truly important feature of operant conditioning is the relationship of an operant response (or series of operant responses) to its reinforcing stimulus (consequence). This relationship is said to be *contingent* if a reinforcing stimulus is presented when and only when the operant response is emitted. Reinforcement would thus depend upon the emission of a response. This concept is fundamental to the development and modification of behavior soon to be discussed under the rubric of *contingency management*. Finally, it must be noted that a stimulus which occurs subsequent to an operant response is a reinforcer *only* if the frequency of that operant response is maintained or increased over time. In other words, a reinforcer is determined by its effect upon response emission. Thus is defined an empirical concept of reinforcement (Bijou, 1964).

Positive and Negative Reinforcement   As behavior is conceived in terms of classes, respondent and operant, so may reinforcement be classified. Although any consequent stimulus is a reinforcer if response probability is increased, two primary classes of reinforcers may be distinguished: *positive* and *negative* reinforcement. Each involves a quite different method for the conditioning of operant behavior.

If a consequent stimulus, when added to a set of circumstances, increases or strengthens the probability of operant response occurrence, the stimulus is defined as a positive reinforcer. To illustrate, consider a small child who picks up from the kitchen floor a piece of cloth and hands it to his mother. The mother responds immediately by patting the child's head. The child is then observed to repeat his "picking-up" response, although this time it is performed upon a small piece of paper. Again, a loving head pat from his mother follows. A third item, a crust of bread, is then picked up and delivered by the child to his mother and still another head pat follows immediately. This observation plus the subsequent observation of similar kitchen behavior may permit the inference that head-patting (consequent stimulus) takes on the properties of a positive reinforcer. This would be true, however, *only* if head-patting had an observed effect on the maintenance or increased frequency of the child's "picking-up" response. (Our original example involving a child and a candy bar machine is also illustrative of positive reinforcement). While on the surface this concept may appear very simple, the point is that parents and teachers frequently assume that certain events have "reward value" when, in fact, they have none or may even carry aversive properties. Thus, it becomes necessary to observe carefully the effects, if any, a presumed reinforcer has upon operant response strength. Positive reinforcement, then, refers to events which, upon presentation, strengthen the probability that an operant response will recur in the future. Recent data indicate a pattern effect of continued positive reinforcement in which initially small changes in response frequency are generally followed by more rapid accelerations (Lindsley, 1969). This means that the effects of positive reinforcement may not always be self-evident early in a response acquisition process. Its cumulative effect over time is the significant criterion.

To be distinguished from positive reinforcement is the concept of negative reinforcement. If an antecedent stimulus, when *removed from* a situation following the occurrence of an operant response, increases the probability of response occurrence, it meets the criterion for a negative reinforcer. For example, consider a mother who tweaks her child's ear *until* he picks up a piece of paper from the floor. If removal of the ear tweak increases the strength of "picking-up" behavior, ear-tweak removal (consequent event) becomes a negative reinforcer. Note also in this example that ear-tweak removal would be *contingent* upon the operant response of picking up the paper. Such circumstances could ultimately result in active avoidance learning in that "picking-up behavior" may be executed in order to avoid an ear tweak. Perhaps a more cogent classroom illustration of negative reinforcement is the child who daily confronts a nagging, punitive teacher. If the teacher's nagging behavior, when directed toward this child, is (1) aversive to the child and (2) ceases only when he performs a given response (such as sitting quietly), the removal of the teacher's nagging may negatively reinforce that response. That is, the teacher's nagging increases the child's rate of responding (sitting still) because by so responding the child removes the teacher's reason for nagging.

Two additional concepts in the operant conditioning system warrant brief mention: *nonreinforcement* and *punishment.* Nonreinforcement refers to the absence of a reinforcing stimulus following an operant response. A withholding of reinforcement indefinitely, according to research-derived principles of behavior, leads gradually to the extinction of an operant response. That is, the response, no longer functional for the individual, is either dropped from his response repertoire or is superseded by a more effective response (a response which *is* reinforced). For example, consider a kindergarten child who receives his teacher's full attention every time he tugs at her skirt. If teacher attention has the effect of maintaining or increasing the strength of the child's skirt-tugging (operant response) such attention would be a positive reinforcer. Therefore, according to Skinner's position, failure to provide teacher attention (nonreinforcement) should have the effect of decreasing gradually the child's rate of skirt-tugging. If the child ceases this behavior entirely, extinction would be assumed. To facilitate extinction one might find it necessary, however, to make teacher attention contingent upon behavior incompatible with skirt-tugging. This would necessitate the reinforcement of constructive, non–skirt-tugging behavior using teacher attention.

Finally, punishment, as used in the operant conditioning vocabulary, refers most generally to the application of an aversive stimulus after an operant has been emitted. Thus, a child may be spanked following the performance of a voluntary act judged as inappropriate by his parents. Skinner has indicated that the effects of punishment are less predictable than the effects of reinforcement and require further investigation. Related study, however, shows the consequence of punishment to vary from no effect to a slight decrement of response strength to virtual suppression of the punished response (as well as other types of responses in the punished organism's repertoire).[2] The application of punishment has yet to be shown effective in eliminating (or "stamping out") a response, and the side effects of punishment are typically quite undesirable. The preferred and most effective behavioral modification strategies are those based upon positive reinforcement, nonreinforcement, and negative reinforcement. Although punishment is generally not advocated by those identified with behavioral analysis procedures, its contingent application has been studied in an attempt to decelerate hazardous, otherwise unmanageable children's behavior (Birnbrauer, 1968; Bucker and Lovaas, 1967; Tate and Baroff, 1966).

According to Lindsley (1969), punishment, if "effective," produces large initial changes in response frequency followed by successively smaller ones. One implication of this generalized pattern could be that if behavior change does not occur quickly as a consequence of a systematically applied punishing condition, the condition should be abandoned; it is unlikely to have any significant effect if continued and may only serve to complicate an already unfortunate situation.

Types of Reinforcement   As we have noted, a reinforcer is broadly defined as any stimulus event following a response (consequent stimulus event) that increases the frequency with which that response occurs.

---

[2] The literature on punishment is complex, and psychologists do not agree completely upon the definition of punishment. Among the most representative students of punishment, from whom the generalizations above have been taken, are Azrin and Holz (1966), Maier (1956), Skinner (1938), and Solomon (1964).

Many types of consequent events are possible, although basic categories for them have been identified (Bijou and Sturges, 1959). These categories are consumables (such as food or drink), manipulatibles (such as toys), visual and auditory stimuli (such as pictures or music), social stimuli (such as attention from others), and tokens. Consumable reinforcers, although very powerful, have been used largely in animal research, and their contingent use is neither ethical nor very practical in the classroom. The remaining four types, however, are clearly feasible for use in most classroom situations. In fact, with the possible exception of tokens, they have been used by teachers for centuries. In behavioral analysis, stress is placed upon the *systematic* (versus random and unscheduled) use of such types. Social stimuli have been shown to be a particularly strong type of reinforcement, especially in relation to young children. This is significant, for such stimuli (for example, teacher attention, teacher approval and disapproval) occur as a matter of course in any classroom. As we shall see, studies of the effect of systematic arrangement of social stimuli on children's classroom behavior represent a major class of behavior analysis research.

To the above five types of reinforcers may be added a sixth: high strength behavior (Meacham and Wiesen, 1969). Briefly, high strength behavior refers to behavior that "naturally" occurs with a high frequency and, as such, can be used to reinforce behavior with lower natural frequencies. This notion soon will be further clarified in reference to the *Premack principle* (Premack, 1959, 1965).

Reinforcement Schedules

Reinforcement can be either continuous or intermittent. In the first case, reinforcement would proceed each and every emission of an operant response. Data indicate that the acquisition of operant responses is expedited by continuous reinforcement (Ferster and Skinner, 1957). This suggests that in the early stages of learning, continuous reinforcement is highly desirable. Therefore, teachers are advised to reinforce continuously children's new learning to the extent that this tactic is practical.

Apart from carefully planned situations, continuous reinforcement is a rare phenomenon. More typical of real life situations is intermittent reinforcement where a reinforcing stimulus occurs only periodically. Skinner and his followers have explored in detail two dimensions of intermittent reinforcement. One dimension which may vary involves the *interval of time* between one reinforcement and the next. An interval schedule of reinforcement based on time may be fixed or variable.

A *fixed interval* schedule is one in which reinforcement is delivered or obtained (following a specific response) at standard time intervals, whether it be every five minutes or every five days. A report card full of "A's" received at the end of a six-week grading period might represent such a schedule, assuming that grades are a reinforcer. In contrast, a *variable interval* schedule involves nonstandard blocks of time, as in the case of reinforcement after 2 minutes, then not again until 20 minutes, and so on. A strategy whereby a teacher periodically strolls about the classroom administering praise to industrious students engaged in seatwork could exemplify the variable-interval schedule.

The second dimension of intermittent schedules is that which involves *ratio* reinforcement. Instead of time, the number of discrete responses performed constitutes the criterion for reinforcement. A *fixed ratio* reinforcement schedule is one whereby reinforcement follows the commission of a set number of responses. Reinforcements administered to a child after every tenth word he spells correctly, irrespective of time lapsed, would comprise a fixed ratio schedule. In contrast, a *variable ratio* schedule involves reinforcement after series of varying numbers of responses have been accomplished. For example, a child reinforced after spelling two words correctly, then not again until he has emitted three correct responses, then four, and so on would be operating on a variable ratio schedule.

One of the most significant contributions of this approach to the study of behavior is the identification of reliable relationships between reinforcement schedules and operant response rates. Each of the four general types of schedules discussed above has predictable effects on the frequency with which operant responses are emitted over time. Various combinations of ratio and interval schedules can also be made to produce specific effects.[3] All of this carries profound implications for those who desire systematically to develop and maintain specific behaviors of children. Generally, fixed ratio reinforcement is associated with fairly uniform response rates; response rate is primarily a function of ratio size, and a pause in responding is often observed after a reinforcement. Uniform response rates are also associated with variable ratio schedules. Further, behavior established under the latter is usually strongly resistant to extinction. This is significant for teachers, since a major goal in most classrooms is the development of academic responses that will continue to be emitted at an efficient rate even when

---

[3] Sixteen distinct schedules have been developed and validated by Ferster and Skinner (1957).

no reinforcement is available. Response rates may also be higher with variable ratio schedules because (1) reinforcements increase with a higher response output and (2) by the very nature of the schedule, a higher rate is reinforced. Consequently, a high rate of response will most probably occur again.

Fixed and variable interval schedules also result in typical response rate patterns. The former pattern generally involves an increase in response rate just prior to reinforcement and a decrease in rate immediately after, although rate is generally proportional to the interval length. Many a classroom teacher has observed an analogous phenomenon. Consider, for example, a class whose study rate skyrockets immediately before each weekly test, only to drop dramatically upon completion of this task. Or, consider the rapidity at which many children complete their classroom assignments as recess time nears, even when they are given ample time to complete assignments leisurely. This phenomenon can generally be avoided, if one wishes, by utilizing a variable interval schedule; a fairly stable or uniform response rate prevails under this type of schedule, and behavior subject to a variable interval schedule is also highly resistant to extinction (Ferster and Skinner, 1957).

To summarize, the cardinal feature of ratio schedules is that reinforcement increases proportionate to the frequency with which responses are made. Hence, the higher the response rate the more frequent the reinforcement. Conversely, as fewer responses are made, the probability of subsequent responding is lowered because of the decrease in reinforcement received—a phenomenon which may lead to a "vicious cycle" (Michael and Meyerson, 1962).

Moderate response rates are typical of interval schedules, but a principal characteristic of behavior reinforced on such schedules is its high degree of resistance to extinction. The "vicious cycle" problem is generally avoided as interval schedules tend to be self-corrective. In other words, a reduced response rate is increased by reinforcement which will eventually come, and a higher response probability is again restored.

Finally, behavior maintained by intermittent reinforcement schedules, especially the variable ratio type, tends also to be strongly resistant to extinction. In other words, response frequency will persist for lengthy periods despite lack of reinforcement. This generalization is implicit in the following comment made by a psychologist to a group of mothers concerned about the management of their preschoolers' persistent nagging behavior: "Remember, a single yes can undo a thousand no's!"

It is important to note that if reinforcers are intended to establish and maintain desired behavior they must be scheduled on a *contingent* basis. Supplying a hungry child with a cookie every fifteen minutes regardless of how he behaves *does not* make a contingency. This procedure would tend only to reinforce the behavior emitted immediately prior to reinforcement. If, for example, a child happened to be picking his nose at that point in time, nose-picking would likely be reinforced. Contingent reinforcement avoids chance conditions such as this.

Behavior analysis researchers have been much more concerned with manipulating reinforcement schedules and contingencies to observe their effects than with explaining why such effects are obtained. In fact, the entire approach is descriptive. Causal inferences and explanations are typically avoided, as they are speculative and involve phenomena not directly observable. Perhaps the major underlying principle is that any child will respond according to the reinforcements available to him. The task is to find valid reinforcers and schedule them appropriately in order to construct desirable response patterns in the child.

In principle, this approach may be likened to a tenet of long standing in psychology: the *empirical law of effect.* This "law," whose history extends formally to Thorndike (1913), indicates that "acts leading to consequences which satisfy a motivating condition are selected and strengthened, while those leading to consequences which do not satisfy a motivating condition are eliminated" (McGeoch, 1942, p. 574). In behavioral analysis, however, no assumption is made about internal motivating conditions or subjective feelings of satisfaction. Motivation is considered strictly from the standpoint of externally manipulative conditions.[4] Further, this approach emphasizes the contingent arrangement of consequences according to systematic schedules. This is one feature which differentiates the operant approach from other S-R psychologies. Another subtle modification of the law of effect has been made by Skinner, namely, that behavior is a function of consequences which have in the past followed behavior rather than a function of consequences which are going to follow behavior. The latter would introduce the notion of *expectancy,* a hypothetical phenomenon. Behavior analysis researchers, it must be stressed, restrict themselves to directly observable responses. It is reasoned that to do otherwise would involve a less than scientific approach to the study of behavior.

---

[4] When a pattern of behaviors has been acquired to the point where it occurs predictably, at a consistent rate under intermittent reinforcement, an individual gives the appearance of being "intrinsically motivated" to respond, or "self-motivated."

BEHAVIOR ANALYSIS IN EARLY CHILDHOOD EDUCATION

From an operant perspective, a classroom is considered as an environment of stimuli capable of developing, maintaining, and changing the responses of a learner. This control is achieved by a systematic arrangement of cues (materials, equipment, and the teacher's behavior) and reinforcers. Thus, a learner operates within a context of stimulus events and becomes a product of those events under specific temporal arrangements.

Stimulus events may be considered in terms of independent variables or factors which are manipulated in order to (1) assess their effect on behavior and (2) capitalize upon their potential to change behavior. Responses are those behaviors emitted by the learner that become influenced by specifiable stimulus events. By way of cueing and reinforcement procedures a teacher serves as a virtual architect of classroom behavior. In other words, strategies are devised to condition in desired ways a child's operant behavior to the environmental setting which the classroom represents. Of concern in this portion of the chapter are the general procedures appropriate for such conditioning. While technical variations on the theme of behavioral analysis or operant conditioning exist (Lindsley, 1968; Lovitt, 1968), the strategy suggested by Reese (1966) will illustrate for the reader the necessary basic components.

Specification of Final Performance

If one is to arrange combinations that facilitate behavioral development, he must have clearly in mind what behavior is to be established. Two requirements are thus imposed: a statement clearly defining the desired terminal behavior and a procedure for measuring the behavior. The reader will recall the similarity between this criterion and the behavioral objectives of Bereiter and Engelmann (1966). Behavioral objectives are a necessary, but insufficient condition to define a behavioral analysis approach. It is the second requirement, specifying a procedure for measuring the behavior, that is critical to this technology. Several alternative measurement strategies may be employed, and, aside from an acceptance of response frequency as a basic datum, complete agreement concerning their merits and validity is not apparent in the literature concerned with operant conditioning. Nevertheless, if conditioning procedures are to be arranged, terminal objectives must be clarified empirically.

Desired terminal behavior may be comparatively simple and may reflect immediate concerns, or it may be extremely complex and involve an extensive instructional task. Consider, for example, the difference between teaching a child to clean up after finger painting versus teaching him to read silently a grade level primer at a demonstrated rate of speed and comprehension. (Additional examples of terminal behavior, conceived in operant terms, follow in the next section.) Finally, while many objectives may be determined prior to initial behavioral assessment, goals and subgoals are frequently created only after such assessment.

Assessment of Entering Behavior

If procedures are to be instituted in order to help a child acquire stated terminal behaviors, one must have a starting point. In behavior analysis the best starting point is thought to be in relation to a child's response capabilities at the outset of training. This is extremely important in order to ensure early success in a program, that is, initially to provide a child with tasks the performance of which falls within his response repertoire at the point of entry. Entering behavior *must* be assessed if a teacher is to "start where the learner is." Once it has been determined where the learner is in relation to the broader objectives of a program, a sequence of activities may be tailored to the individual child.

A variety of procedures, formal and informal, may be used for the assessment of entering behavior. Ordinarily, procedures are selected to reveal response deficits which must be considered in program planning. Psychometric tests are rarely, if ever, used as indicators of response capabilities. Preferred is the direct and continuous observation of a child in a controlled situation (Werry and Quay, 1969). Also relevant may be checklist procedures designed to inventory precisely what a child can or cannot do. The point to remember is that assessment procedures are selected in relation to objectives peculiar to the existing circumstances.

To illustrate, suppose a teacher is confronted with a child who exhibits a high rate of antisocial behavior (such as pushing, hitting, and commandeering the property of other children). If, in this situation, one's immediate objective was to decelerate such behavior, a first task would be to observe the frequency with which the antisocial responses occur *and* the conditions under which these responses seem to occur. This task would be accomplished prior to the application of modification procedures and result in a *baseline* from which to gauge subsequent progress.[5] Only with a baseline to operate from could one empirically determine the effectiveness of his modification procedures. If, on the other hand, one is concerned with academic responses, such as counting from 1 to 100 or demonstrated skill in dealing accurately with rational concepts like "in-between" and "middle-sized," a checklist might be used. In these cases, one would note the child's initial span of counting responses and whether or not he responds correctly to tasks which require an understanding of object relations. This procedure would be preferred to the use of such global indicators of "readiness" as age or IQ, particularly for the purpose of planning educational activities.

Specific baseline statements may be conceived in several ways, depending upon the criteria represented by terminal objectives. For example, a teacher may be concerned with a child's rate of arithmetic responses (such as correct performance of two-digit addition problems). This teacher could count such responses as they occur under a specified set of circumstances, in terms of (1) number correct and (2) number of errors committed. The specified circumstances could involve presenting the child with a list of 20 addition problems to solve within a period of 10 minutes. Baseline would then be determined through this accounting procedure. Assume in this hypothetical situation that the child attempted only one problem and was in error. In terms of frequency, the child's *correct rate* could be described as zero; the teacher's task would then be to arrange conditions to increase this child's correct response rate. If the terminal objective is two correct addition responses per minute, conditions must be manipulated until such a rate is achieved. Once this has occurred, the task is that of maintaining the child's rate.

Technically speaking, a rate statement is the only type of statement acceptable to a committed operant methodologist. In this writer's view, however, one is not required to meet this criterion in order to apply the basic conditioning strategy. For example, one may be interested in helping a child develop the ability to recite the pledge of allegiance to the flag. The main concern here is that the child perform this response when appropriate. That he performs this verbal chain at "x" frequency per unit of time is not at issue. True, if instruction is successful, a child's rate has increased from none to one per school day, but whether the terminal objective needs to be stated in responses per unit of time is questionable. The critical aspect is that the objective is stated in terms

---

[5] In laboratory conditioning procedures, the term baseline generally refers to *operant level*, that is, the strength of a response prior to the introduction of conditioning procedures.

of what the child is able to do and the conditions which come to control the recitation response.

To summarize, the assessment of entering behavior serves two important functions. One is to provide behavioral data which may be used to determine a point of embarkation for instruction. The second function is to provide a baseline upon which observation concerning the rate of progress and procedural effectiveness may be based. This point of strategy marks the beginning of a continuous cycle of data gathering characteristic of operant or behavioral analysis procedures. Ordinarily, every effort is made to graph the results of assessment. Graphic tabulations enable a teacher to examine the flow of behavior through a specified period of time. While variations in assessment methods occur, continuous data gathering is imperative for purposes of educational diagnosis, programming, and teacher decision making (Lovitt and others, 1968).

Structuring a Favorable Situation[6]

This elegant principle refers specifically to the way in which the learning environment is arranged. Aspects of the environment (physical equipment, teacher behavior, learning materials) are arranged so as to maximize the probability that desired behavior will occur and to minimize the likelihood that incompatible behavior will occur. In other words, it is a matter of structuring in relevant ways the cues in whose presence the child will respond appropriately so that positive reinforcement may be administered. Applied successfully, this principle suggests a very broad implication for the motivation of behavior. If emission of correct responses early in a learning sequence can be facilitated, the frustration of failure and error may be reduced while success and self-confidence are bolstered.

Several levels of application of this principle may be noted. At a gross, nonetheless important level might be the arrangement of physical equipment in a nursery school or kindergarten classroom where play materials are not easily available to children while they are engaged in pre-academic or academic activities. Otherwise, "play responses,"

---

[6] "Structuring a favorable situation" may include or be preceded by a policy known as *adaptation,* that is, arranging events which have the effect of training an individual to behave so that conditioning may take place. For example, a child who will not stay in the classroom once he is placed there will not be available for conditioning; he must first be adapted to the classroom. Adaptation procedures are described elsewhere (Reese, 1966).

or responses incompatible with desired academic responses, might accelerate primarily due to teacher mismanagement.

A second level of application may involve the ways in which teacher-child and child-child interactions are carried out. Suppose a teacher is working in the beginning stages of developing among children "cooperative social responses." This broad aim might be reflected in a number of activities, including the self-selection of rhythm instruments for a music activity. If a teacher places a box of such instruments on the floor in the middle of a group of children, the probability that children will "grab and fight over" the instruments (responses incompatible with social cooperation) may be increased. If, on the other hand, the teacher passes from child to child asking that each take an instrument in turn, this probability is substantially lowered. More probable would be the emission of a desired social response which could be reinforced. It is important to note here a basic strategy characteristic in behavior analysis, a strategy nicely summarized by the old song, "Accentuate the Positive and Eliminate the Negative." Avoided also are situations which may lead to the reinforcement of an undesirable response. In the above case, a child may be "reinforced" for grabbing behavior if his grabbing succeeds in gaining for him a desired instrument.

A third level of application for the "favorable situation" principle concerns the arrangement of learning materials and feedback procedures. This necessitates a careful ordering of the sequence of stimulus events, in which sufficient cues are present to prompt a response. Practices based upon this level are relevant for a wide variety of activities ranging from reading (Staats, 1968) to training for originality (Maltzman, 1960). Also important is the nature of the feedback given to a child concerning the adequacy of his response and what might be done to improve it if needed.

It is attention to this third level of application that has resulted in the extensive use of programmed materials among those identified with operant conditioning methods.[7] The general features of programmed materials are threefold, although their collective objective concerns making learning as efficient as possible. First, materials are arranged in a graduated sequence so as to elicit the continuous active response of a learner. In some cases, elaborate machinery is utilized. For ex-

[7] It should be noted that the use of programmed materials is by no means exclusive to behavior analysis procedures. The concept of programming has been applied in a wide variety of classroom settings by educators with diverse pedagogical orientations. It is true, however, that Skinner (1954) is generally credited with having provided a principal impetus to recent programmed material development and use.

ample, a child may be required to press buttons which represent his answer to prerecorded oral questions, as in computer-assisted instruction. In contrast, a child may emit a marking or writing response to visually presented stimuli where no hardware is involved, as in a programmed workbook. The essential point is that a learner interacts constantly with carefully sequenced material.

A second major feature of programmed materials is that they provide for immediate confirmation or correction of a learner's response. In other words, the materials are designed so that a learner is informed or may inform himself immediately whether or not his response is correct by checking the appropriate source. A third feature of such materials is the opportunity they provide for individualization in terms of rate of progress. A learner may proceed through a programmed sequence as quickly or as slowly as he feels is necessary or most comfortable. Thus rapid learners and slow learners may proceed according to their own rate, the former being free to move ahead, the latter avoiding the frustrations of being pushed.

Programmed materials have been envisioned as one major solution to several problems inherent in most classroom settings (Skinner, 1968). Among Skinner's most serious criticisms include the relative infrequency with which learners are reinforced in school and the excessive delay between the time a behavior occurs and its reinforcement. Equally serious for Skinner are two additional problems: the aversive nature of many educational practices and the predominance of poorly sequenced curricula. In connection with the former, Skinner (1954, 1968) has remarked that, whether educators like it or not, most students today study to avoid the consequences of not studying. Even more striking he believes is the frequent apathy, withdrawal, and aggression of many school children, response patterns which Skinner attributes to the extensive use of aversive control techniques in most schools. With respect to curriculum sequencing, Skinner has maintained that many teachers feed material to students in such large, unmanageable chunks that it contributes to inefficient and ineffective learning. For Skinner this practice serves to establish a "natural condition" for failure.

Still another school problem identified by Skinner is the apparent tendency for teachers (and parents) to attend primarily to the undesirable behavior of children and to ignore the desirable. In effect, this personifies a behavior change system based upon aversive control; there is little systematic reinforcement for "good" behavior, but ample punishment for the "bad." Even casual observation tends to verify the insight conveyed by Skinner's critical contentions. Structuring a "more favorable situation" is a most acute requirement if many of the above problems are to be avoided.

Selection of Reinforcers

Once a situation has been structured so as to maximize the probability that desired responses will occur, the task is clear: reinforce positively the responses when they occur. One must ensure, however, that the reinforcing stimulus actually serves to strengthen behavior. That is, one cannot assume the reinforcing value of a stimulus—its value must be observed. Thus, the basic problem is to determine what controllable and demonstrably effective reinforcing events are available to a teacher.

Perhaps the most desirable, effective reinforcer for humans is success, that is, performing correctly and knowing that one has performed correctly. For success to be a reinforcer, however, conditions must be very precisely arranged, hence the rationale for programmed instruction. Daily experience with children suggests that success per se is not always an effective reinforcer; children frequently need to develop subsidiary behaviors before meaningful success may be achieved. For example, the success marked by the correct making of change in a monetary transaction may be sufficiently reinforcing to strengthen a child's change-making behavior. But the many subsidiary skills involved in this complex act must first be developed before this sort of real life success can be achieved.

Where success is not a reinforcing event, other reinforcers (even contrived ones) may be necessary. Social reinforcers such as praise, attention, and recognition may be arranged positively to influence behavior. Such social events are often considered as "natural reinforcers" because they pervade the course of much human interaction and unquestionably influence behavior; these social events generally acquire reinforcing properties early in the lives of most children. Occasionally, material reinforcers such as candy, toys, or even money may be required in order initially to establish behavior. Once behavior has been established by material reinforcers, however, it may be maintained by a transfer to more "natural" reinforcers.

An extremely utilitarian device for the selection of reinforcers is the *Premack principle* (Premack, 1959). This principle is based upon the notion that a child's high probability behavior may be used contingently to reinforce and thus increase his low probability behavior. In effect, this means that a child selects his own reinforcers. An example will illustrate. Suppose that within a classroom setting a child has the freedom to choose one activity from among ten available ones. Assume that his first choice was painting with water colors and his last choice was alphabet drill. Suppose further that over time the child was observed to paint with water colors whenever he had a free choice. By definition, water color painting would constitute a high probability behavior. Alphabet drill, by comparison, would be classified as a lower probability behavior. A teacher operating on the Premack principle might utilize water color painting as a reinforcing event *contingent* upon the execution of a prescribed amount of alphabet drill activity. In effect, the high probability behavior of the child would be used to increase the frequency and adequacy of the child's alphabet drill behavior. (This assumes the latter to be a functional objective.) In sum, an individual child must be observed carefully to determine his high probability behavior(s). Once high probability behaviors are identified, they may be used contingently to reinforce a child's low probability behaviors. The latter may be academic (spelling) or social (sharing playground equipment with others). For the record, productive use of this principle has been documented (Homme and others, 1963). Appropriate control over the behavior of nursery school children previously unresponsive to verbal directives or teacher requests was achieved by the systematic application of this practical reinforcement principle.

A generalized token or point-credit system based upon the Premack principle is frequently used in behavioral analysis classrooms. Such a system involves the arrangement of "credit," in terms of tokens or points earned, for the performance of certain behaviors at specified levels of quality. Thus points or tokens are awarded contingent upon the emission of responses consistent with instructional objectives. Points may be accumulated by a child to be traded in for items such as free time or other privileges. Free time enables a child to do with it whatever he wishes (engage in high probability behavior) within the specified limits of the classroom. A system such as this is therefore conclusive to the arrangement of highly effective reinforcing events. Research data illustrative of this system will be discussed shortly.

A reminder is in order. Since behavioral analysis subsumes an empirical concept of reinforcement, it is essential that the effects of arranged consequences be meticulously observed. This requires the continuous measurement of response rate over time so that consequent events may be verified as reinforcers. For example, if free-time tokens had no effect upon the frequency of a child's correct response performance over time (as compared to his frequency prior to the introduction of tokens), then another type of reinforcement would be sought. In any case, the selection of reinforcers is usually facilitated by the careful observation of individual children.

Behavior Shaping

From an operant conditioning point of view, the technique of producing new behavior—establishing new types of responses—is called *behavior shaping*. To shape behavior, response variations which resemble a desired behavior are reinforced selectively, while less relevant (or inappropriate) variations are not reinforced (extinguished). Thus new, more complex forms of behavior may be developed by reinforcing gradual changes in the type of response being made as it comes closer to the desired type of operant response. The underlying principle is that of *reinforcing successive approximations,* that is, reinforcing resemblances of the final desired response where such resemblances are in the direction of that ultimate goal. Once a new approximation has been acquired the lesser approximations are no longer reinforced.

A classic example of the shaping process is provided by a child learning to write cursive style. No child is likely to write spontaneously a perfect letter on the first attempt, even with a model letter to copy.[8] What will result is an approximation of the ideal. But, if the child's response produces a letter in the direction of the ideal, it should be reinforced. In short, to maintain cursive writing responses so that improvement may be made, the reinforcement of progressive approximations of the model letter(s) is essential. Both the informational and motivational functions of reinforcement would be lost if reinforcement were withheld until the child forms a perfect letter. In fact, such a performance in the absence of reinforcement would be unlikely.

Behavior shaping procedures may also be exemplified by a reference to children's language development. The spontaneous and correct pronunciation of most new words by a young child learning to talk is unlikely. A child's first attempts are more typically approximations of the desired response. The writer's own child, for example, first pronounced the word "rhododendron" as "rowdenon." This was a good approximation. Gradually, however, with the assistance of selective reinforcement (and a correct language model), the correct pronunciation was achieved. There are ample data to illustrate the application of shaping procedures to language development (for example, Staats,

---

[8] This would mean that a child's operant level for writing a model letter "y," for example, would be zero.

1968), but the principle purportedly applies to all classes of operant behavior.

Behavior shaping has been classified as an "art," since reinforcement must be used quite selectively in order to avoid certain basic problems (Sidman, 1962). For one thing, approximations must be reinforced immediately. Neither too many nor too few reinforcements should be given for an approximation of a desired terminal response. For another, a reinforcing agent (teacher) must observe a child carefully so that successive approximations may be clearly specified. Shaping procedures could easily fail if a teacher continues massively to reinforce approximations at a level lower than would indicate progress. Obviously, behavior shaping requires a clear statement of objectives and a clear understanding of what responses constitute approximations of it.

Further examples of the shaping principle applied to educational practice include (1) teacher praise of students when they have shown improvement (as in creative writing) even when this improvement falls short of a desired standard of competence; (2) allowing partial credit for the correct use of an arithmetic principle even though a mechanical error has led to an incorrect answer; and (3) reinforcement for a child who has selected the correct primary colors (red, blue, and green) for mixing to make the color brown, yet may have failed to mix the primary colors in correct proportion. In the latter example, if correct proportionate use of colors were the terminal behavior it would be self-defeating to continue the prolonged reinforcement of incorrect proportionate use. For shaping purposes, reinforcement would be withheld for the next higher level of paint-mixing response.

Once behaviors have been shaped appropriately, the task becomes that of maintaining the relevant responses in the learner's repertoire so that they are available when necessary. In many cases, maintenance at a low rate will be sufficient; in others, rate increases are desired. For example, once a child has learned to respond correctly to the question, "Where do you live?" It would probably be enough only to maintain it at sufficient strength so that the child will emit the response when necessary. With respect to behavior such as that desired during a "show and tell" time, however, a teacher may be interested in more than an indication of whether or not a child is capable of show and tell behavior—she may wish to increase the child's rate so that he participates voluntarily and frequently during each period set aside for that purpose. (It is after behavior has been established, incidentally, that the arrangement of intermittent reinforcement schedules to maintain or increase response frequency is critical.)

Shaping, as described above, is not always the crucial problem in a classroom based upon behavior analysis principles. In some instances, a child may already have a desired response but may fail to emit it under the desired stimulus conditions. This point can be illustrated by referring to certain aspects of the task of learning to read. For example, a child may bring a wealthy vocabulary of words to the school situation, most of which he pronounces correctly. Thus the problem is not shaping his verbal responses. Rather, the problem involves conditioning the child to emit verbal responses which correspond to verbal symbols (letters, words, and sentences) presented visually. This problem actually serves to define a core instructional endeavor for any educational approach based upon learning principles: *systematic discrimination training.* Most basically, discrimination training involves reinforcing a response in the presence of a stimulus (for example, reinforcing a child for saying "boat" in the presence of the word "boat") and not reinforcing a response emitted when the appropriate stimulus is absent (withholding reinforcement if a child says "boat" in the presence of the word "bat"). In this way correct stimuli will come to control a correct response with a high degree of probability. When this criterion is reached a stimulus qualifies as *discriminative.* Within the broad areas of language, academic, and social behavior, *discrimination repertoires* are gradually established. These consist of high probability responses which will be emitted when discriminative stimuli are presented (teachers' instructions, workbook exercises, creative art materials, reading primers, and so on).

It is in connection with discrimination training that *stimulus fading* techniques are frequently employed. To illustrate, consider a child who consistently errs in discriminating between the letters "b" and "d." Assume that a teacher wishes to program an extraneous cue to facilitate the acquisition of correct discrimination responses. In this example, the child's correct discrimination responses may be defined as a correct verbal response ("b" and "d") when letter symbols are presented visually. An extraneous cue in this case may take the form of assigning different colors to dramatize the half-circle at the base of each letter (the direction of this half-circle, left or right, represents the critical invariant feature for "b-ness" or "d-ness"). Suppose the b's half-circle was traced in red, with blue being assigned to d. A letter discrimination strategy could then be devised by the teacher whereby color serves as an additional prompt. Assume for the moment that, with color cues in evidence, the child makes a correct and reliable verbal response to each letter. The problem is now to "wean" the child from this extraneous cue; thus a fading technique is required. In this case color may gradually (and literally) be faded through prepared successive stimulus presentations, while reinforcement for correct responses is continued. The success of the fading technique would then be measured in terms of the child's correct rate subsequent to complete fading.

In summary, the nucleus of a behavioral analysis approach to teaching is a set of five principles. These principles are final performance specification, entering behavior assessment, design of a favorable situation in which behavior may occur, selection of reinforcements, and behavior shaping. These principles require considerable teaching skill for successful implementation. They are also independent of any specific academic content. Consider next, then, the role of the teacher and some examples of learning materials suitable to these principles.

Role of the Teacher and Instructional Materials   Several equally important functions must be served by a professional who uses behavior analysis procedures to increase the precision of her teaching: planning, data-taking, and contingency management. For successful educational practice a teacher is required to perform these functions subtly, yet actively. Planning involves both (1) a clear perspective on which pupil behaviors will need to be constructed and strengthened and (2) a careful programming of activities and learning materials. In early childhood settings conventional materials may be used extensively but always systematically. For basic academic training, selected programmed materials may be used more frequently than other types, as may teaching machine resources. In reading, for example, the *Sullivan Associates Program* (Webster Division, McGraw-Hill) has received close attention. Skinner's *Handwriting with Write and See* program (Lyons and Carnahan) is clearly designed for the progressive shaping of handwriting responses. For spelling, the *Programmed Spelling Series* (Behavioral Research Laboratories) may be viewed as a core set of materials. The *Sets and Numbers* program (Singer-Random House) is among the most applicable set of mathematics activities available. These are only a few examples of a growing number of programmed materials suitable for early academic training.

Of the educational alternatives currently applied to young children, it is behavioral analysis that necessitates the highest degree of teacher skill in data-taking. This is perhaps at once the greatest strength and greatest criticism of this alternative.

The task of continuous response measurement requires that a teacher translate all target behavior into frequency or rate statements and implement a recording system whereby behavioral changes are charted or graphed in relation to programmed events and reinforcing events. Elaborate forms have been devised for this purpose, some of which are quite complex and thus require special training for their proper use. There are some recent developments which indicate that pupils themselves may learn to record their own behavioral data sufficiently. This would reduce substantially a teacher's total burden in this regard.[9] Nevertheless, refined and efficient observational and recording skills are essential for a complete execution of the behavioral analysis approach. Only through the inspection of data obtained by continuous response measurement can functional relationships between manipulated events (materials and reinforcements) and pupil behavior be determined. Such measurement is also imperative in terms of identifying contingencies to be managed for more efficient learning. These skills may be impractical for teachers who have not received advanced training or those whose work does not involve relatively small groups of children. It is difficult for a single teacher to take continuous data on the responses of thirty to thirty-five children. Recently, however, progress toward these goals has been noted among conventionally trained teachers and beginning teachers in public school settings (Hall and others, 1968; Ward and Baker, 1968). Further, Lovitt (1968) has explicated several general guidelines for data-gathering well within the managerial capabilities of any concerned professional. Continuous response measurement problems aside, the principles of behavior analysis are applicable in any teaching situation.

BEHAVIORAL ANALYSIS RESEARCH

Most approaches to early childhood education deal with groups of children immersed in a combination of content and methodological variables. Periodic measures are then taken of the total program effects, and results are reported in terms of group averages. In contrast, a behavior analysis approach to research typically involves the singular manipulation of clearly specified variables in order that the effect(s) of such manipulation on an *individual child* can be assessed. *Continuous measurement* (response counting) through time is preferred to a policy of periodic measurement (such as end-of-program tests). It is argued that only through the singular manipulation of stimulus events and the continuous logging of performance can the optimum learning conditions for any given child be identified. Once these optimum conditions are identified they can be implemented to assist the child toward a maximum rate of educational progress. In this segment of the chapter,

[9] Mr. Harold Kunzelmann, Experimental Education Unit, University of Washington, 1969, personal correspondence with the author.

behavior analysis research techniques will be briefly discussed. Subsequently, some examples of this approach involving young children will be presented.

General Procedures

Research procedures pertinent to the behavioral analysis point of view are variously described as the experimental analysis of behavior (Skinner, 1966), the functional analysis of behavior (Haring and Lovitt, 1967), or analytic behavioral application (Baer, Wolf, and Risley, 1968). The first represents the parent strategy as developed by Skinner under intensely controlled laboratory conditions. As suggested earlier, the focal point of this approach is the rate of repeated occurrences of an operant response over time. This technique stands in contrast to that whereby finite samples of behavior are obtained at one point in time (as in psychological tests) and where such samples are used to infer some general human characteristic (such as intelligence, anxiety, achievement, or creativity). Response rate is preferred as the basic datum, because it is thought to be the best single indication of the probability that a given behavior will occur at a given time (Skinner, 1966).[10] All pertinent variables (for example, stimuli antecedent and subsequent to a response and the timing of the presentation of either) that affect the probability of a response or chain of responses in functional (observable and describable) ways must be considered. Subjects for analysis (whether human or infrahuman) are studied individually to determine what manipulations (made through real time) affect relative changes in response rate over time. Changes in response rate (probability) can then be related precisely to specific manipulations.[11] Thus may sequences of behavioral development be charted or progressive behavioral change be observed. Only measurement through time enables one to derive this sort of probability statement and a description of variables which influence response probability.

Since response frequency has the quality of an empirical event, that is, it is directly observable, it has the advantage of replacing many ambiguous terms such as "interest," "hyperactivity" and "shyness." For example, a child "interested" in art may talk about art and partake

[10] It is suggested that the best indication of the probability that a response will occur in the future under given conditions is the frequency with which it has occurred in the past under those conditions.

[11] To be admissable as evidence, a relationship between stimulus events and response rate must hold for all subjects in a given experiment, not for just a few or for the "average."

of art activities *frequently;* a "hyperactive" child may perform random motor responses such as head-jerking, arm-waving, jumping, and foot-tapping *frequently;* and a "shy" child may initiate social contacts with other children *infrequently* (Ferster and Perrott, 1968).

Standard research applications of the experimental analysis of behavior generally include the *reversal* technique. An example will illustrate. Consider a psychologist whose task it is to increase a child's rate of cooperative social behavior (defined in terms of sharing playground equipment) in a laboratory nursery school. This child is then observed over a period of several weeks for evidence of such behavior (baseline measurement). In this case, our psychologist observes that no cooperative social responses occur despite the existence of conditions generally favorable to such behavior. Hence, the child's baseline rate would be zero. The psychologist then decides to introduce an experimental variable, teacher attention (as defined by a smile and words of praise for the child), to be administered only when a cooperative social response (or an approximation thereof) is emitted by the child. During this period of selective reinforcement the teacher is directed also to withhold her attention from the child whenever he makes responses incompatible with cooperative social behavior. During this period the teacher is also requested to provide ample attention to children who do exhibit cooperative behavior, making sure that the uncooperative child witnesses her attentions. Gradually, the uncooperative child may be observed to increase his cooperative behavior to the point where, under appropriate conditions, cooperative responses occur at a stable rate. Behavior has changed. The question is whether or not change is truly a function of the teacher's procedure. To answer this, the experimental variable (teacher attention) must be discontinued to determine if the effected change is dependent upon it. If it is dependent, a decrease in rate of cooperative social behavior should be observed. If such a decrease is observed (a reversal), the experimental variable can again be introduced to see if a recovery in rate occurs. The observance of a recovery substantiates a functional relationship between teacher attention and cooperative behavior *for this child.*[12]

In summary, the reversal technique is a basic procedural design consisting of at least four elements: (A) baseline measurement; (B) introduction of experimental variable (for example, contingent rein-

---

[12] Since many behavioral modifications are valuable, it is not desirable to reverse a behavior in order to satisfy a methodological requirement. In the example above, a teacher may wish rather to maintain the child's cooperative behavior, in which case it may come under extra-experimental conditions (for example, positive social reinforcement from peers) and no longer be dependent solely upon teacher attention.

forcement); (A) reversal (withdrawal or modification of experimental variable); and (B) reinstatement (reintroduction of experimental variable). Behavior is measured continuously and directly throughout the procedure.[13]

While the reversal technique is common to the experimental analysis of behavior, it is neither always suitable nor necessary in applied settings. Yet both strategies (or variations thereof) involve the issue of *reliable* change, and all experimental variables must be specified for their correct execution. Generally, the attempt is made to relate procedures to operant conditioning principles, and most analyses are concerned with a demonstration of the durability or generality of behavior over time. Perhaps the principal difference between the experimental analysis of behavior (as conducted in the psychologist's laboratory) and applied behavior analysis rests with the degree to which control can be exercised over the many variables that influence behavior. Further, applied behavior analysis has, in practice, been more concerned with specifying variables that are "effective" for the modification of important behaviors (such as social and verbal responses) in their *naturally-occurring contexts* (including the classroom).

A Sampling of Behavior Analysis Research on Young Children

A large research literature has accumulated for the purpose of documenting the application of behavior analysis research to young children. It is true, however, that this approach to the study of behavior is not limited by age-level considerations nor is it species-specific. Some of the more dramatic and impressive applications of this approach have involved exceptional children, including those in conventional diagnostic categories such as mental retardation, brain injury, autism, and assorted behavior disorders and learning disabilities (Ullman and Krasner, 1965). Further, principles of operant conditioning have been applied successfully to the process of toilet training (Madsen, 1966), the extinction of temper tantrums (Williams, 1959), the improvement of children's regressive patterns of motor behavior and motor skills (Harris and others, 1964; Johnston and others, 1966), the reduction of operant crying behavior in young children (Hart and others, 1964), and the

---

[13] Nothing has been said here about the use of a *multiple baseline* design, that is, a procedure by which response changes in more than one operant class may be analyzed at one time. Multiple baseline technique is perhaps the most functional for behavioral analysis research workers. See Sidman (1960) and Baer and others (1968) for further comment on this technique.

management of hyperactive children (Patterson, 1966). In fact, from a context of operant conditioning and social learning principles, some of the most productive and practical techniques for classroom management and behavioral development, maintenance, and change have been created (Clarizio and Yelon, 1967).

Present space limitations make it possible to mention only a few illustrative analyses of children's behavior that are relevant to early childhood educators. Almost without exception, these analyses have included individual children or very small numbers of children for whom modification procedures have been tailored.

One classification of representative studies helpful for teachers is on the basis of whether given behavior is desirable or disruptive. As used here, desirable behavior is defined as behavior broadly compatible with children's educational progress and personal-social welfare; disruptive behavior may be thought of as behavior incompatible with these goals.

DESIRABLE BEHAVIOR

Studies which illustrate behavioral modifications broadly compatible with classroom learning are myriad, although longitudinal data specific to academic development in classrooms for young children are just beginning to appear. For general illustrative purposes, examples of research concerned with the attending responses of children, study behaviors, and self-management skills will be mentioned. Subsequently, the reader will be provided with data in relation to children's academic response repertoire, including language and reading. Finally, an example of social response modification will be considered.

Evidence that reveals the effects of a systematic program of social reinforcements upon attending behavior ("attention-span") is provided by Allen and others (1967). It was observed that a 4½-year-old nursery school boy never remained with any set of materials long enough to make constructive or creative use of them. Initially, social reinforcements were given immediately whenever the child engaged in a single activity for one continuous minute. Adult approval and attention were continued for as long as the child persisted with the activity. In contrast, attention was withheld for behaviors other than those relevant to persistence. A substantial decrement in the number of activity changes initiated by the child was observed within seven days after contingency implementation. Reversal and reinstatement procedures were executed with predictable results. The study is representative not only in terms of the "pre-academic" behavior established, but also in terms of the type of reinforcement typically used with young children.

A sequence of contingent and noncontingent reinforcements was arranged for a group of twelve preschoolers by Bushell and others (1968). Contingencies, represented by tokens for a variety of study behaviors (independent task involvement and completion, cooperative study, and attending to instruction) were arranged to establish a desired rate of study behavior. Once this rate was achieved, special privileges were then administered noncontingently—a procedure which quickly reduced the level of study behavior. A rapid recovery was charted, however, upon reinstatement of the original contingencies. The contributions of this study are at least threefold: (1) practical contingencies are feasible with larger groups of children; (2) practical observational techniques can be used to assess empirically the influence of reinforcement in the classroom; and (3) while study rates may increase for all children, individual differences in rate acceleration occur.

A second analysis of study behavior acquisition concerns the effects of contingent teacher attention upon the study responses of normal first- and third-grade pupils (Hall and others, 1968). At the outset of this study, all children demonstrated very low rates of appropriate study behavior. Initially, nonstudy behaviors were ignored while teacher attention was distributed contingently upon study responses (orientation toward appropriate objects or persons, such as classroom materials and reciting classmates, and participation in classroom discussions at the teacher's request). A full implementation of technical procedures (baseline measurement, contingent reinforcement, withdrawal and reinstatement of reinforcement) indicated a functional relationship between teacher attention and study responses. Further, as study response rate increased for these children their overall academic achievement tended to improve. Noteworthy in the Hall and others (1968) study was the reinforcement of successive approximations; teacher attention was established as a consequence of such responses as picking up a pencil and paper, opening a book to the correct page, and other approximations of the general operant class of "study behavior." Follow-up observation revealed that the "higher study rates" were in evidence even after the termination of formal research procedures.

Birnbrauer and others (1966a) have described a programmed learning classroom for children with various response deficits whereby a token system is used to facilitate self-management skills.[14] This study involved participant teachers who were faced in all cases with children ap-

[14] In behavioral analysis research, decisions to use concrete token systems are frequently made on the grounds that desired behavior may be established more quickly than under a system based upon intangibles.

parently "unmotivated to learn basic management and academic skills." Neither were the children in this study initially capable of the attentional responses and study skills considered as prerequisites for effective self-instruction. Resultant data indicated that persistence, resistance to distraction, cooperation, and study skills can be strengthened through a combination of competently organized sequences of learning activities and reinforcements. These researchers have also provided data concerning programmed instruction approaches to reading, writing, and arithmetic with retarded children (Birnbrauer and others, 1966b).

Language Behavior   Several experiments with preschool and primary grade children have illustrated a functional relationship between contingent reinforcement and rate of verbalization. For example, Salzinger and others (1962), using words per second as a criterion, found that greater numbers of reinforcements under a variable ratio schedule produced the most rapid rate accelerations and the greatest resistance to extinction (vis-a-vis slower deceleration when reinforcement is withheld). Of particular interest in this study is the finding that a "lower limit" or minimum number of reinforcements was necessary to produce a rate increase. An incidental finding was that baseline rates for the private nursery school children in the study were substantially higher than among their public school counterparts, most of whom were children from lower socioeconomic backgrounds.

Disadvantaged children were also involved in a related pair of studies (Hart and Risley, 1968; Reynolds and Risley, 1968). In the first of these, a systematic combination of teaching materials and environmental contingencies was effective for increasing the correct usage rate in spontaneous adjective-noun description. Thus a distinct class of verbal responses was influenced by conditioned learning principles. General spontaneous speech rate was influenced significantly by reinforcement contingencies in the second study (Reynolds and Risley, 1968), with the critical contingencies identified as material reinforcements administered in a context of social interaction.

Reinforcement applied contingently to the accurate *verbal imitation* responses of young children has also been explored (Brigham and Sherman, 1968). Systematic reinforcement of preschool children's accurate imitations of English words presented by an adult model was followed by an increased rate of accurate responses. A concomitant effect was also observed, namely, an increase in the accurate imitation of Russian words similarly presented even though these imitative responses were not at all reinforced. Contingency removal was followed by a reduction in imitation accuracy for both word classes. The apparent generalization effect obtained in this study suggests that reinforcement applied to a broad operant class (such as sound imitation) may have a "transfer effect." There is some question, however, about the permanency of the verbal behavior established in this study.

Along lines similar to the above study are data which indicate that successful vocalization shaping and echoic response development can be obtained with an initially mute child (Kerr, Meyerson, and Michael, 1966). Echoic responses (spontaneous imitation of model-produced sounds prior to the point at which sounds may be comprehended) are considered to be a significant stepping stone in language development (Vetter, 1969). Further study has shown that mixtures of verbal modeling cues, reinforcement, and attentional prompts are variously effective for producing increases in children's use of prepositions and syntactic discriminability (Bandura and Harris, 1966).

In summary, there is little question that language behavior is affected by conditioning principles. Wide varieties of response classes have been studied with generally impressive results. Data summarized elsewhere, however, suggest that operant training effects are greatest with respect to language phenomena such as the nature of topics one selects to discuss, vocabulary selection, general fluency, and verbal mediation (Ervin-Tripp, 1966). Further research is needed to examine the direct effects that operant conditioning procedures may have upon grammar (syntax and morphology), prosody, or phonology. Other sources may be consulted for an operant accounting of speech development (Skinner, 1957), language training (Schiefelbusch, 1967), contingency-based verbal behavior modification (Sapon, 1969), and remedial speech (Cook and Adams, 1966).

Reading Behavior　Extensions of operant conditioning principles to the acquisition of reading responses constitute another category of research activity. In this category of research activity, discrimination training has received major attention, because it is generally considered as the principal element of reading response acquisition. While the same general principles apply to both language learning and reading response acquisition (bringing verbal responses under the control of auditory and visual stimuli), the latter is judged as the more difficult of the two tasks (Staats and Staats, 1962). Not only does learning to read involve a rather sudden bombardment of requirements on children by adults, but the entire process is usually formalized, more compressed and rapidly paced, and often braced with less potent reinforcers than is language learning.

Variables influencing the acquisition rate of unit reading responses include stimulus-pairing strategies and reinforcement scheduling, and Staats and others (1964b) have demonstrated that the latter variable can make a substantial difference in rate of reading progress. A carefully designed reinforcement system and a unique presentation apparatus were utilized to teach male kindergarten-age children correct verbal responses to conventional reading characters. Of the multiple reinforcement schedule variations employed in their study, the rate advantage went to those which involved variable ratio reinforcement. Resumé accounts of this and subsequent research which illustrate the utility of operant principles for complex verbal and symbolic learning have since appeared in a major publication (Staats, 1968).

The correct reading response rate of a six-year-old "slow reader" has also been accelerated impressively by means of a contingency-managed tutorial mechanism (Whitlock and Bushell, 1967). Correct responses were reinforced by a procedure of continuous electronic recording as responses occurred. Correct response accumulations were revealed to the child by a counter located in the mouth of a paper clown placed adjacent to her. Various point denominations were exchangeable for a smorgasbord of "back-up" reinforcers such as coloring book activity and a picnic with the teacher. In this study it is difficult to separate reinforcement effects from other variables (such as close personal contact of teacher and child), but the rapid correct response acceleration demonstrated by the child indicates the importance of motivation in the acquisition and performance of complex skills.

Larger numbers of otherwise normal children with various reading disabilities have also been studied (Haring and Hauck, 1969b). Entering behavior assessments taken on male elementary children indicated reading performances ranging from one to five years below grade level. In order to increase correct reading response rate, individually programmed learning materials and reinforcement systems were established for each child. Within five months, reading grade level increases from one and one-half to four years were achieved. Prior to treatment these children's difficulties had been diagnosed in terms of hypothetical constitutional or genetic factors. Experimental results obtained by Haring and Hauck suggest rather that these difficulties may have reflected previously ineffective instructional procedures. These same researchers have reported a doubling and trebling of academic response rates among large numbers of disadvantaged children during a summer remedial program (Haring and Hauck, 1969a). Accelerations were produced through sequential reinforcement contingencies and a blending of programmed materials for reading and mathematics. More seriously disabled children have also been assisted by the behavioral reading programs of Hewett and others (1967) and the conditioning procedures of McKerracher (1967).

Cooperative Social Behavior   As academic behavior is valued, so is cooperative social behavior. Numerous examples of behavior analysis research reflect this value. Hart and others (1968) compared two conditions of adult social reinforcement in terms of their effects on the cooperative play of a preschool child. One condition involved random reinforcement administered during each school day for an extended period of time. The second involved reinforcement contingent upon cooperative play or approximations thereof. Noteworthy change in the frequency of cooperative play responses was associated only with the latter condition. Similarly, a female nursery school child whose behavior was best described as "isolated," that is, behavior incompatible with the constructive social play activities fundamental to nursery school programs, has been studied (Allen and others, 1964). Prior to the arrangement of contingent social reinforcement for social play, it was observed that most of the teacher attention directed toward the child was actually a consequence of behaviors such as erratic speech, play-like sleeping, and solitary play, all of which impeded social interaction with peers. Thus the possibility was strong that teachers had been reinforcing unwittingly the very behaviors they wished to modify. Subsequent to baseline charting, teacher attention (smiling at, talking to, giving help to, and affectionately touching the child) was administered contingent upon approximations of social interaction (such as parallel play, approaching another child, speaking to another child). None was provided during times when the child was alone. A continuous reinforcement schedule gradually succeeded by an intermittent one was effective in establishing and maintaining a higher rate of social interaction; contingencies were validated by way of the ABAB design discussed earlier.

Finally, Azrin and Lindsley (1956) have found that children working as pairs in a game situation can develop and maintain cooperative responses under contingent reinforcement conditions. This objective was achieved even in the absence of specific instructions for the children to cooperate.

UNDESIRABLE BEHAVIOR

As increases in desirable behavior have been associated with operant conditioning principles so have decreases in behavior incompatible with desirable classroom learning. For example, techniques such as removing social reinforcement for aggressive acts and providing social reinforcement for cooperative acts have been used successfully to reduce aggressive behavior among nursery school boys (Brown and Elliot, 1965). It was necessary, however, for the researchers to school the teachers involved in the contingent use of reinforcement. Early in the study, teachers also expressed general skepticism about the utility of reinforcement principles, until the results of their schooled actions led them to acknowledge the validity of these principles. Interestingly, greater decrements in verbal aggression (disparaging and threatening others) occurred in this study than occurred in physical aggression (pushing, hitting, holding). A plausible explanation is that teachers find it harder to ignore acts of physical aggression and thus may maintain such aggressive responses by attending to them.

Similar success in modifying the disruptive and assaulting behavior of a kindergarten boy has been reported (Sibley and others, 1969). Systematic contingencies, including teacher attention, nonreinforcement, and social isolation, were applied in relation to Spaulding's (1967) schedule for the analysis of coping behavior. Of special concern was this child's behavior during structured learning activities. Startling decrements in the frequency of undesirable behavior (with an accompanying increment in desirable behavior) were observed. This result is taken by the researchers to indicate a functional relationship between both classes of behavior and teacher interactions.

Relationships between teacher behavior (approving-disapproving) and primary grade pupil behavior (appropriate-disruptive) have also been clarified (Thomas and others, 1968). In general, increases in disruptive pupil behavior are associated with (1) the withdrawal of approval for appropriate behavior and (2) increases in teacher disapproval. Conversely, contingent teacher approval was associated with the production and maintenance of desirable classroom behavior.

One of the most extensive analyses of strategies suitable for the modification of children's problem behavior has been conducted "on the firing line." (Becker and others, 1967)[15] In this investigation, significant reductions in deviant behavior were associated with the application of general conduct rules in combination with social reinforcement. These investigators, however, have emphatically stated that differential social reinforcement, while very potent, is not a panacea for the solution

[15] These problem behaviors include such gross motor behaviors as leaving one's seat and running about the classroom to taking the property of other children to blurting out, screaming, and whistling in class.

of behavior management problems. In fact, several useful generalizations have been developed from their exploration. One is that the mere dispensation of rules for behavior does little, if anything, to maintain classroom control. Neither does simply ignoring deviant behavior. It is argued that these strategies must be supplemented by the reinforcement of behavior which is *incompatible with deviant behavior* (as cooperative social interaction is incompatible with physical aggression). Of further importance is the discovery that social reinforcement administered to an appropriately behaving child (a child working constructively, either independently or in cooperation with others) in proximity to a child behaving deviantly (distracting others) is very effective. A teacher who implements this strategy would not attend directly to a misbehaving child, and the possibility of reinforcing deviancy is therefore reduced. In addition, a deviant child who observes an appropriately behaving child being positively reinforced is likely to change his behavior to more closely approximate the model child.

As a final example of behavior analysis research, consider a situation in which a teacher was faced with the task of regaining control of an entire class composed of children with high rates of disruptive behavior (O'Leary and Becker, 1967). To reduce this disproportionate ratio of deviant to acceptable behavior, a contingency token system was conceived. Initially, points earned by children for specified acceptable behavior were immediately negotiable for a variety of back-up reinforcers. Savings periods were then gradually increased to the point where children were required to accumulate points for four days before "purchasing privileges" were granted. Carefully woven into this fabric of reinforcements was a pattern of traditional social rewards and group contingencies. Deviant behavior decreased from an average of 76 percent to 10 percent of all observed behavior during the experimental period. Accordingly, the frustration and time-consuming features of discipline problems were reduced, thus freeing the teacher to attend to academic skill development. This effect was, in turn, associated with reduced failure rates among the children. A subsequent attempt at replicating the effects of these procedures in a different classroom has also been successful (O'Leary and others, 1969).

To summarize, many behavior modification studies involving young children have dealt with the influence of reinforcement and cueing procedures on pre-academic, academic, and social behavior. Social reinforcement by adults has been demonstrated to be a very powerful influence on the behavior of young children. Thorough discussions of its contingent use in preschool and remedial settings have been written and may be consulted for further detail (for example, Baer and Wolf, 1968). Other types of reinforcers, such as token or point systems interlaced with material back-up reinforcers, also seem to have reliable effects. Although operant conditioning procedures have been particularly effective in modifying the behavior of deviant children and in the treatment of learning disabilities, they have been applied broadly to "normal" children. Most of the research to date indicates functional relationships between principles of operant conditioning and the acquisition of language, reading, and social responses. Gilbert (1962) may be consulted for an accounting of mathematics learning and operant principles.

Further data about behavior analysis programs for young children will undoubtedly emerge from institutions participating in the National Laboratory of Early Childhood Education, such as the University of Kansas. In fact, a Follow Through Model for compensatory education has been developed and is being implemented at Kansas and other locations throughout the country (Bushell, 1969). This model has been augmented by a procedure for systematic parent participation. Other programs include a preschool program at the University of Washington's (Seattle) Experimental Education Unit, the Juniper Gardens Project (Risley, 1969) and an operant-based program for the development of school readiness (requisite antecedent behaviors for school performance) among preschoolers (Sapon, 1968). Presumably, data from these programs will soon appear in the published literature on early childhood education.

CRITIQUE

Concepts of precision teaching developed from the work of Skinner and his followers represent an ambitious attempt to improve education by developing new models of instruction. This attempt is clearly based on the idea that practices prevalent in schools today are rarely attuned to the genuine problems of individualizing instruction. Nor have efficient curricular sequencing and contingent reinforcement systems been achieved on a wide scale. From a behavioral analysis perspective, constant experimentation is required to achieve these objectives. As we have seen, the ultimate goal in behavioral analysis is the precise specification of variables that may be manipulated to "optimize learning." Admirable as this goal may be, the educational practices derived from this perspective are not free from criticism. Nor can these practices be disassociated from certain crucial issues. The following discussion, although not exhaustive, constitutes a review of some major criticisms and issues associated with behavioral analysis.

Issues Related to a Scientific Concept of Behavior

A basic assumption upon which behavior analysis procedures rest is that fundamental laws govern the behavior of organisms. Scientific analyses are performed largely to identify these laws, including those which govern the behavior of children in educational settings. Behavior analysis is therefore patterned from a scientific conception of the child. A scientific conception of the child has not been readily accepted by many early childhood educators, nor by society generally for that matter. Skinner (1956) suggests that this resistance is perhaps due to the vanity of man. He believes that this vanity is exemplified by man's tendency to view himself in self-deterministic, free-will terms and as being blessed with inherent qualities which will help him conquer adverse circumstances in the pursuit of excellence. To acknowledge a scientific concept of behavior, that we are controlled by certain fundamental laws, is to surrender this and other facets of a democratic philosophy of human nature. Appealing as a democratic view of human nature may be, Skinner believes that human behavior is, in fact, controlled in many ways by environmental events. Experimental analyses of behavior are simply attempts to ferret out the ways in which behavior is controlled. There should be no reason, as Skinner argues, why knowledge of the laws of human behavior cannot be used to achieve better control of both our environment and ourselves. Control, then, becomes inevitable unless one depends entirely upon chance conditions to produce social improvement.

One immediate implication of the above scientific conception of human behavior concerns control in the form of education. If laws can be applied to control behavior in the classroom cannot such control be misused? To those who are fearful that the power to control may be misused Skinner offers at least three defenses: (1) expose fully the techniques of control so that *sub rosa* manipulations are neutralized; (2) restrict the use of physical force, coercion, or fear-inducing tactics; and (3) develop more refined skills among adults *and* children for purposes of better environment control, including education. Proponents of "open education" conceivably could argue that these defenses miss the real point, for at issue is any child's right to decide when, where, how, and under what conditions he will learn something. No such choice seems available when exacting objectives are determined in advance by an authority who further decides how the child shall be shaped. On the other hand, can an advanced technological society which depends, among other things, upon mass education for its advancement, afford to provide children the luxury of determining exclusively what, when, and where they will learn? Ausubel (1959), for example, has argued against the psychological soundness of curricula designed primarily according to children's professed desires. Ausubel believes that the rationale for curricula built upon the spontaneous desires of children is often based, at least in part, upon a faulty analogy derived from the study of nutrition: that nutrition is adequately maintained when infants are allowed to select their own diets. He also maintains that children's spontaneously expressed interests do not necessarily reflect all of their important needs. Ausubel further argues that breadth in a curriculum, an essential feature if we expect young children to expand existing interests and develop new ones, is unlikely if educational activities are delimited to meeting the transitory and frequently impulsive desires of the young.

A second issue involves the notion that a scientific conception of behavior fails to account for the individuality or uniqueness of children. In point of fact, those who take a scientific view of behavior do not deny that genetic or constitutional factors are reflected in the wide range of individual differences among children. These determinants are, however, recognized as not being subject to manipulation by behavior techniques. These techniques can be used to alter the environment in which behavior occurs; it is precisely this sort of change which characterizes behavioral analysis. A point to be made here is that the child's behavior—whether "normal" or deviant—is viewed as a product of environmental conditions. If a child has a learning problem, this problem is considered as an outgrowth of faulty environmental conditions, not as something inherent in the child for which teacher or parental responsibility can be denied. If put into practice, this notion represents a very constructive attitude and a positive departure from the frequent tendency to view children's problems as personal weakness or deficiency.

A third, related objection is sometimes raised in connection with operant conditioning: the inappropriateness of applying to human beings the behavioral modification techniques developed under laboratory conditions with animals. It is the author's experience that this objection has frequently and erroneously been taken to mean that human behavior is basically equivalent to the behavior of infrahuman species. While it is true that operant conditioning principles were originally developed through the laboratory study of animals, no serious student of behavior analysis known to this writer subscribes to the view that principles so developed can simplistically be applied to complex human behavior. However, it is also true that applied behavior analysis is frequently complicated by limitations in the control of variables or conditions so necessary to establish definitive functional relationships (Gewirtz, 1969). It is incumbent upon behavioral scientists to communicate these limitations clearly.

Broader issues in behavior analysis are associated more generally with S-R (stimulus-response) psychology as a whole. For example, positions about childhood learning and development built upon S-R concepts have long been viewed as mechanistic. This criticism is important to the extent that "mechanistic" implies (1) that children are simply passive reactors to the environment and (2) an apparent lack of concern within behavioral analysis for processes (cognitive and affective) that may mediate between environmental stimuli and overt responses. With respect to the first point, there is widespread disagreement among psychologists generally. For example, in contrast to the behavioral analysis view that the child learns by reacting to or being shaped by the environment is the cognitive-developmental view that the child actively constructs his own experience (see Chapter 7). Hence the issue concerns the basic nature of the child—an issue that has captured the attention of scholars for centuries.[16] Within psychological theory this issue has been translated into the question of whether operant conditioning actually contributes to our conceptualization of human growth. According to Langer (1969), for example, the answer is dependent upon the degree to which animal behavior and human behavior are comparable. It seems clear from the research that general principles of reinforcement applied across species yield similar results, but this finding need not be taken to indicate a simplistic nature of man.

The second point above—concerning psychological processes—is equally illustrative of disagreement among psychologists in matters related to child development theory and research. For those who take a strict behavioral analysis point of view, only overt (observable) behavior can be studied in a truly scientific way. Such behavior is presumed to be the content of psychological functioning. This position again stands in contrast to cognitive-developmental psychology in which overt behavior is taken to infer covert (unobservable) mental processes. Covert processes are then utilized to explain development. Thus, while supporters of behavior analysis will discuss behavior in terms of re-

---

[16] See Hitt (1969) for a recent articulation of the principal differences between behaviorism and existential psychology and the implications of these differences.

sponse rate, an empirical criterion, a cognitive-developmentalist may resort to hypothetical statements about qualitative thought processes that are not directly observable.

It is probable that the theoretical issues just described are of less immediate concern to educational practitioners than reservations they may have about the "coldly scientific" context in which behavioral analysis procedures may be executed. Possibly the observation of teachers who apply such procedures in the classroom has led to these reservations. Casual observation could conceivably result in a confusion between systematic contingency management and a teacher's feelings about children. Consider, for example, a child whose excessive dependency behavior (seeking help for every task he attempts) is being maintained by social reinforcement (teacher attention). If a decision is made to decrease dependency striving and increase independence striving, a goodly part of the strategy would necessitate removing the social reinforcement for dependency behavior. Nonreinforcement (planned ignoring) of this behavior might easily be misconstrued as "noncaring" teacher behavior by a naïve observer. This observer may believe that to reinforce a child positively regardless of the quality of the child's behavior (noncontingent reinforcement) or to help a child rationalize (find excuses for) inappropriate behavior is better for mental hygiene. Such techniques are often taken to indicate a "nurturant" teacher attitude. According to the behavioral analysis viewpoint, high rates of inappropriate or low quality behavior could result if these techniques were widely applied. The problem perhaps involves arriving at a teaching style which reflects a general accepting attitude toward children yet also reflects the clear and ethically appropriate management of contingencies for improving children's behavior. Concerning this issue the writer's primary concern is with the possibility that a precision teaching model constructed from behavior analysis principles might attract personnel already predisposed toward "cool and calculating" techniques of social interaction. On the other hand, there is no necessary reason for a cold, emotionally antiseptic atmosphere to pervade this or any other approach to early childhood education. Certainly it would be unfortunate for teachers and parents to equate systematic teaching with an emotional vacuum.

Finally, the operant approach is often criticized for its simplistic view of behavioral causation. For a teacher to consider behavior at any point in time in terms of a child's "reinforcement history," for example, is of limited value. No practical means for discovering a child's reinforcement history are available to teachers. One can only assume that high rates of free operant behavior are the result of past reinforcement.

Further, the deliberate avoidance of statements of causality in matters of educational diagnosis may disturb some observers. For example, consider the classic problem of underachievement, that is, a child who does not perform satisfactorily in terms of what is expected for him or what his past experience should predict for him. On the assumption that underachievement is a valid phenomenon, many educators and psychologists seek first to discover the cause(s) of this "problem." Interviews, tests, and case study procedures have traditionally been employed in the attempt to isolate the cause. Only by eliminating the cause of the problem will the problem be solved, according to this strategy. In contrast, it is maintained within behavior analysis that, apart from controlled experimentation, causation cannot be determined. Post hoc assumptions are avoided because they are untestable. In the case of the underachievement example, the problem for an operant methodologist is not to find the assumed cause (for example, "faulty" parent relations) in a post hoc fashion, but rather to modify the behavior of the child himself so as, for example, to increase the child's rate of persistent and constructive academic task responses. The focus is upon behavioral change instead of the etiology of behavior. As Clarizio and Yelon (1967) indicate, teachers are probably better advised to deal with behavior directly rather than with its causes. Several reasons may be advanced for the suggested strategy. Perhaps the most important of these reasons is that teachers are rarely trained to query the causes of behavior often considered obscure and perplexing even by experienced mental hygienists. Further, even if a cause is discovered, its treatment may be beyond the limits of a teacher's skill and ethical powers.

Additional Issues Concerning Reinforcement

Additional issues, most of which pertain more directly to the psychological outcomes and limitations of reinforcement, should be examined. For example, concern may be expressed about the narrowness of behavior change effected by operant techniques, that is, that while response frequency increases may be obtained in a singular response class (for example, attending to teacher instructions or initiating social contacts with other children), there is no guarantee that change will occur in other related response classes. Essentially this poses the issue of *allied* or *collateral change*. Few data relevant to this issue are as yet available, although there is some evidence to indicate that allied changes can occur (Buell and others, 1968; Kennedy and Thompson, 1967). Much more research is needed in this area. At this point in time it appears that reinforcement principles affect most clearly the way in which an individual selects and delimits his responses in the presence of specific cues, rather than the way in which he extends his repertoire rapidly across varied situations.

Still another issue worthy of note concerns the danger that the effects of reinforcement on learning may be oversimplified. Social learning theorists such as Bandura (1962, 1967, 1969) maintain that the ordering of reinforcement cannot claim to be the end-all of complex behavior development. The work of Bandura and his colleagues indicates that the modeling influences, independent of or in conjunction with direct reinforcing consequences, result in a wide variety of behaviors, including aggressiveness, fear development and modification, and nurturance. Imitation learning must be considered as a significant impetus to response acquisition. In fact, the contiguous sensory stimulation involved in imitation learning has been reported as a "sufficient condition for acquisition of most forms of matching responses" (Bandura, 1962). Bandura does not, however, exclude the role of *practice,* which is particularly important for the development of motor skills and where mere exposure to a model is insufficient. Nor does he deny the power of reinforcement for shaping the attentional responses of a learner. The point is that children acquire many responses by modeling their teachers or peers where deliberately arranged reinforcement contingencies are not apparent. It is apparent, however, that the development of broad classes of imitation responses are influenced measurably by reinforcement variables.

A notion related to the above issue is that many desirable behaviors may not be acquired efficiently by children, if at all, if one were to rely exclusively upon the method of reinforcing successive approximations (Bandura, 1962). Consider, for example, how long it would probably take to teach a child to perform a complex act like tying his own shoe in the absence of verbal cues and a model to imitate. With this in mind, one might argue that the stimulus events to which a child responds are as important, if not more so, than a reinforcement which may follow a response. Several studies indicate that children's discrimination learning frequently occurs quite suddenly in contrast to the incremental and gradual process implied by the successive approximations method (Rieber, 1966; Hill, 1965; Suppes and Ginsberg, 1963).

Still further reservations about simplistic application reinforcement systems have been expressed (Kuypers and others, 1968; Kagan, 1969; Maehr, 1968; Horowitz, 1967). For example, a token system, applied mechanically without attention to supplementary procedures and principles, may be self-defeating or only marginally effective. Kuypers and others (1968) report such a finding with reference to a behavior modification program for third- and fourth-graders. A successful token system apparently requires skill in both the integration of differential social reinforcement and behavior shaping. The former is particularly important, since frequently the goal of a token system is to increase the effectiveness of social reinforcers for children initially unresponsive to such "natural" reinforcement. A systematic pairing of token reinforcements and ample social reinforcement must occur, especially when delays exist between responding and token reinforcement. Teachers must be trained in the principles of behavior shaping and reinforcement scheduling if they desire to utilize token systems successfully.

Although the importance of social reinforcement is strongly emphasized in the operant conditioning literature, this type of reinforcement is not the last word in behavior modification. In fact, its influence is mediated by many variables (Horowitz, 1967; Stevenson, 1965; Zigler and Kanzer, 1962). For example, younger children are apparently more strongly influenced by social reinforcement than are older children. Girls seem generally more responsive to social reinforcement than boys. The extent to which a child perceives a dispenser of social reinforcement as a person with high status is still another mediating variable. Further variables include social class status of the child, the nature of the affective relationship between the child and a reinforcing adult, and the degree to which a child may have been previously deprived or satiated with social reinforcement in a given situation. In some cases, the nature of the task (simple versus complex, motor versus intellectual) may make a difference as also may the extent to which a child is anxious about his relationships with others or is strongly dependent upon adults for approval. Further, certain classes of behavior may be influenced more strongly by social reinforcement than others. Parton and Ross (1965), for example, report that social reinforcement does not uniformly facilitate the development of motor behavior in random samples of children. Taken together, these findings help to dramatize the need for a careful observation of individual children if appropriate reinforcers are to be selected and used effectively. For some children social reinforcement may have no apparent value whatsoever. Variables other than reinforcement may be much more critical in the development of complex behaviors.

The issue involved in much of the foregoing discussion relates to the limitation of reinforcement generally. According to Kagan (1969), reinforcement enlists a child's attention, furnishes excitement (when reinforcement is pleasant), and operates as an incentive to reproduce previously reinforced behavior. Although these functions are generally considered positive, Kagan maintains that two basic problems are inherent in the use of reinforcement. One is that a child is often tempted to predict the pattern of rewards or the schedule of reinforcement in operation during a learning activity. Once a child can predict the pattern and understands the relationship between his behavior and the reinforcing consequences (thus satisfying his curiosity) he may stop "playing the game." This may be particularly true for older children. Kagan's second caution is more theoretical in substance, nevertheless, noteworthy:

> It is important to appreciate that the term reinforcement has no independent definition and this fact alone should make us suspect of its integrity. A reinforcement is anything that will alter the probability of an action. If an event—no matter how bizarre—alters the probability of an action, it is a reinforcement. If it does not, it is not a reinforcement. If breaking balloons makes a child stay a little longer at the piano, then balloon breaking is a reinforcer. This definition is a little like defining dawn as the time when people begin to arouse themselves from their sleep. In a 24 hour winter night in Stavanger, Norway, dawn exists in a pitch black sky. A functional definition therefore, has obvious flaws. [Kagan, 1969, pp. 136–137.][17]

Other critics, such as Maehr (1968), are skeptical even about the motivational function of reinforcement, particularly when reinforcement occurs in the absence of challenging learning materials. Programmed materials, for example, can certainly be as unstimulating as an inadequate teacher. Certain qualities of learning materials, such as degree of novelty and degree of personal meaning to a learner, could conceivably obviate the need for a meticulously planned schedule of external reinforcement. Thus, the issue of *intrinsic* versus *extrinsic* motivation is raised.

Traditionally, intrinsic motivation has been thought of as "learning for learning's sake" or "learning reinforced by the positive affect which results from accomplishment or doing something well." The latter interpretation is reflected in an enormous amount of research on *achievement motivation* (Crandall, 1963). Educators have typically placed the highest value on intrinsic motivation; the efficacy or soundness of extrinsic motivation, that is, motivation prompted by tangible rewards intrinsic to a learning task has been doubted. Within be-

---

[17] The reader is encouraged to examine Kagan's logic. What he seemingly objects to is the tautological nature of an empirical concept of reinforcement. See Burgess and Akers (1966), whose ordering of definitions and propositions regarding operant behavior is an attempt to counter the charge that reinforcement principles are tautological.

havioral analysis a good deal of emphasis has been placed upon extrinsic reinforcement. An arrangement whereby tokens, negotiable for candy or other goodies, are provided upon evidence of academic performance is a good example of extrinsic reinforcement.

At least two concerns are expressed by those who question an emphasis upon extrinsic reinforcement. First, it is feared that if children are conditioned to receive (and expect) extrinsic reinforcements such as money, candy, and special treats, they will not wish to learn anything unless these incentives are provided. Second, it is argued that to program extrinsic reinforcements is to resort eventually to bribery or baiting of the child. While this writer knows of no evidence to validate these concerns, the issue merits clarification. In the first place, tangible reinforcements are typically used in behavior analysis programs only when "natural reinforcers" such as praise and successful accomplishment are ineffective. In fact, a principal objective in such programs involves conditioning children to be more sensitive or responsive to natural reinforcement. This is illustrated clearly in the study of token reinforcement systems mentioned earlier (Kuypers and others, 1968). Furthermore, after initial learning, reinforcement schedules are typically "leaned out" in an operant conditioning strategy so that continuous extrinsic reinforcement is no longer necessary. A possible overemphasis upon such material reinforcers as tokens and candy is also avoided in situations where "free time" is used as a reinforcing consequence (Osborne, 1969). This means that a child can accumulate various amounts of time, contingent upon constructive academic or social behavior, to utilize as he wishes for free play, art work, puzzle games, or any high strength behavior appropriate to the classroom. Teachers obviously have used this strategy for years. In behavior analysis its use is systematized to accelerate educational progress.

Regarding the second issue mentioned above, "bribery," there may be a substantial difference between *leading* a child by saying, "If you do this; then you can have this," and structuring a situation that results in a response being made which can *then* be reinforced. Operant methodologists typically avoid the former condition, for it may condition a dependence upon verbal cues. In broader perspective, however, one might question whether or not everyone behaves in anticipation of some sort of consequence, a phenomenon not far removed, if at all, from "bribery." In this connection, the writer is reminded of Max Weber's (1930) discussion of capitalism and the Protestant Ethic. Weber points that, according to this Ethic, the accumulation of material goods through hard work, self-sacrifice, and thrift serves as an indirect indication of the probability of being "saved." Some may consider this the ultimate in reinforcement contingencies. The point is that consequences *do* follow behavior; applying operant principles to education is simply an attempt to make the consequences positive rather than negative, or effective rather than ineffective.

SUMMARY

As applied to early childhood education, behavioral analysis may appropriately be considered as (1) a method for studying school environments and (2) a set of principles for behavioral modification. The success of this conceptual approach is dependent upon a systematic arrangement of cues and reinforcement contingencies. By virtue of these arrangements children are conditioned to establish and maintain desired rates of academic and social behavior.

In a behavioral analysis approach, every attempt is made to maximize the effects of positive reinforcement on learning. The importance of reinforcement in the learning process has been widely recognized and is not confined to behavior analysis. However, the behavior analysis view is that only through the contingent use of reinforcement can desired behavior be shaped predictably. As such, a critical teaching skill is required, namely, the prudent timing of reinforcements. Equally important, however, is skill in educational programming, that is, the efficient sequencing of learning activities so as to maximize the probability of successful academic progress for a learner.

Aside from precise contingent reinforcement, perhaps the most distinguishing features of a behavioral analysis approach are the type of data collected by a teacher and the methods used for collecting such data. Response frequency (increase and decrease) is the primary object of study. In contrast, practically all other strategies in education rely upon testing procedures to measure end-of-instruction competence summative evaluation). Within a behavioral analysis strategy, response rate measures are taken by means of precise observation and/or recording measures controlled by a child, who thereby records his own progress. The use of programmed materials to which children actively respond facilitates continuous response measurement. Programmed materials are therefore frequently preferred to standard materials, although careful arrangements of any learning materials may be suitable. Most broadly, the practical objectives of programs built upon behavior analysis principles are twofold: (1) to increase the range and frequency of appropriate academic and social responses and (2) to decrease the range and frequency of task-inappropriate or undesirable responses.

Ultimately, however, a behavior analysis approach would have a child so proficient in self-management and basic academic skills that he can pursue his own learning productively and independently. If, in this regard, the criteria of sound programming, continuous response measurement, and contingent reinforcement are met, then the ideal of individualized instruction for each child can be realized.

While behavioral analysis principles are firmly based in academic psychology, new procedures and techniques are continually being developed. A continual reassessment of standard procedures and the development of new ones often produce a lag between laboratory and educational practice. As new procedures are applied to education, research into the complexities of contingency management and programming is required. However, the available data about children's early school learning and the modification of behavior problems strongly suggest that a behavioral analysis framework is a most fruitful alternative to traditional methods for those who value precision teaching.

References

Allen, K. Eileen, B. M. Hart, J. S. Buell, F. R. Harris, and M. M. Wolfe. Effects of Social Reinforcement on Isolate Behavior of a Nursery School Child. *Child Development,* 1964, 35, 511–518.

Allen, K. Eileen, Lydia B. Henke, Florence R. Harris, Donald M. Baer, and Nancy J. Reynolds. "Control of Hyperactivity by Social Reinforcement of Attending Behavior." *Journal of Educational Psychology,* 1967 (August), 58, 231–237.

Ausubel, David P. "Viewpoints from Related Disciplines: Human Growth and Development." *Teachers College Record,* 1956, 60, 245–254.

Ausubel, David P. "Viewpoints from Related Disciplines: Human Growth and Development." *Teachers College Record,* 1959, 60, 245–254.

Azrin, N. H., and W. C. Holz. "Punishment." In W. K. Honig (Ed.), *Operant Behavior.* New York: Appleton, 1966, 380–447.

Azrin, N. H., and O. R. Lindsley. "The Reinforcement of Cooperation between Children." *Journal of Abnormal and Social Psychology,* 1956, 52, 100–102.

Baer, Donald, and Montrose Wolf. "The Reinforcement Contingency in Preschool and Remedial Education." In R. Hess and R. Bear (Eds.), *Early Education.* Chicago: Aldine, 1968, 119–129.

Baer, Donald, Montrose Wolf, and Todd Risley. Some Current Dimensions of Applied Behavior Analysis. *Journal of Applied Behavior Analysis,* 1968, 1, 91–97.

Bandura, Albert. "Social Learning through Imitation." *Nebraska Symposium on Motivation.* Lincoln: University of Nebraska Press, 1962, 211–269.

Bandura, Albert. "The Role of Modeling Processes in Personality Development." In W. W. Hartup and Nancy L. Smothergill (Eds.), *The Young Child.* Washington, D.C.: National Association for the Education of Young Children, 1967, 42–57.

Bandura, Albert. "Social-learning Theory of Identificatory Processes." In D. A. Goslin (Ed.), *Handbook of Socialization Theory and Research.* Chicago: Rand McNally, 1969, 213–262.

Bandura, Albert, and Mary Bierman Harris. "Modification of Syntactic Style." *Journal of Experimental Child Psychology,* 1966, 4, 341–352.

Bandura, Albert, and Frederick J. McDonald. "Influence of Social Reinforcement in the Behavior of Models in Shaping Children's Moral Judgments." *Journal of Abnormal and Social Psychology,* 1963, 67, 274–281.

Barclay, J. R. "Effecting Behavioral Change in the Elementary Classroom: An Exploratory Study," *Journal of Counseling Psychology,* 1967, 14, No. 3, 240–247.

Barrish, Harriet H., Muriel Saunders, and Montrose M. Wolf. "Good Behavior Game: Effects of Individual Contingencies for Group Consequences on Disruptive Behavior in the Classroom." *Journal of Applied Behavior Analysis,* 1969, 2, 119–124.

Becker, Wesley S., Charles H. Madsen, Carole R. Arnold, and Don R. Thomas. "The Contingent Use of Teacher Attention and Praise in Reducing Classroom Behavior Problems." *Journal of Special Education,* 1967, 1, 287–307.

Bensberg, G. J., C. N. Colwell, and R. H. Cassel. "Teaching the Profoundly Retarded Self-help Activities by Behavior Shaping Techniques." *American Journal of Mental Deficiency,* 1965, 69, 674–679.

Bereiter, Carl, and Seigfried Engelmann. *Teaching the Disadvantaged Child in the Preschool.* Englewood Cliffs: Prentice-Hall, 1966.

Bijou, S. W. "An Empirical Concept of Reinforcement and a Functional Analysis of Child Behavior." *Journal of Genetic Psychology,* 1964, 104, 215–223.

Bijou, S. W. "Behavior Modification in the Mentally Retarded." *Pediatric Clinic North America,* 1968, 15, 969–987.

Bijou, S. W., and D. M. Baer. "The Laboratory-experimental Study of Child Behavior." In Paul M. Mussen (Ed.), *Handbook of Research Methods in Child Development.* New York: Wiley, 1960, 140–197.

Bijou, S. W., and D. M. Baer. "Some Methodological Contributions from a Functional Analysis of Child Development." In Lewis P. Lipsitt and Charles C. Spiker (Eds.), *Advances in Child Behavior and Development,* Vol. 1. New York: Academic Press, 1963, 197–231.

Bijou, S. W., and D. W. Baer. "Operant Methods in Child Behavior and Development." In W. K. Honig (Ed.), *Operant Behavior.* New York: Appleton, 1966, 718–789.

Bijou, S. W., R. F. Peterson, and M. H. Ault. "A Method to Integrate Descriptive and Experimental Field Studies at the Level of Data and Empirical Concepts." *Journal of Applied Behavioral Analysis,* 1968, 1, 175–191.

Bijou, Sidney W., and P. S. Sturges. "Positive Reinforcers for Experimental Studies with Children." *Child Development,* 1959, 30, 151–170.

Birnbrauer, J. S. "Generalization of Punishment Effects—a Case Study." *Journal of Applied Behavioral Analysis,* 1968, 1, 201–212.

Birnbrauer, J. S., S. W. Bijou, M. M. Wolf, and J. D. Kidder. "Programmed Instruction in the Classroom." In L. P. Ullman and L. Krasner (Eds.), *Case Studies in Behavior Modification.* New York: Holt, Rinehart, and Winston, 1966b, 358–363.

Birnbrauer, J. S., and others. "Classroom Behavior of Retarded Pupils with Token Reinforcement." *Journal of Experimental Child Psychology,* 1966a, 2, 219–236.

Bloom, Richard. "The Contribution of an Operant Perspective to Studying Pre-School Environments." *Merrill-Palmer Quarterly* (In press, 1970).

Brigham, Thomas A., and James A. Sherman. "An Experimental Analysis of Verbal Imitation in Preschool Children." *Journal of Applied Behavioral Analysis,* 1968, 1, 151–158.

Brison, David. W. "A Non-talking Child in Kindergarten: An Application of Behavior Therapy." *Journal of School Psychology,* 1966, 4, 65–69.

Brown, Paul, and Rogers Elliot. "Control of Aggression in a Nursery School Class." *Journal of Experimental Child Psychology,* 1965, 2, 103–107.

Bucker, B., and O. I. Lovaas. "Use of Aversive Stimulation in Behavior Modification." In M. R. Jones (Ed.), *Miami Symposium on the Prediction of Behavior: Aversive Stimulation.* Coral Gables: University of Miami Press, 1967.

Buell, Joan, Patricia Stoddard, Florence R. Harris, and Donald M. Baer. "Collateral Social Development Accompanying Reinforcement of Outdoor Play in a Preschool Child." *Journal of Applied Behavioral Analysis,* 1968, 1, 167–174.

Burgess, Robert L., and Ronald L. Akers. "Are Operant Principles Tautological?" *The Psychological Record,* 1966, 16, 305–312.

Bushell, Don, Jr. *Behavior Analysis: A Research Approach to Follow Through.* Washington, D.C.: Department of Health, Education, and Welfare, 1969.

Bushell, Don, Jr., Patricia Ann Wrobel, and Mary Louise Michaelis. "Applying 'Group' Contingencies to the Classroom Study Behavior of Preschool Children." *Journal of Applied Behavioral Analysis,* 1968, 1, 55–62.

Cantrell, R. P., Mary Lynn Cantrell, C. M. Huddleston, and R. L. Woolridge. "Contingency Contracting with School Problems." *Journal of Applied Behavior Analysis,* 1969, 2, 215–220.

Clarizio, Harvey F., and Steven L. Yelon. "Learning Theory Approaches to Classroom Management: Rationale and Intervention Techniques." *Journal of Special Education,* 1967, 1, 267–274.

Cook, Charlotte, and Henry E. Adams. "Modification of Verbal Behavior in Speech Deficient Children." *Behavior Research Therapy,* 1966, 4, 265.

Crandall, Vaughn J. "Achievement." In H. W. Stevenson (Ed.), *Child Psychology.* Chicago: University of Chicago Press, 1963, 416–459.

Day, Willard F. "Radical Behaviorism in Reconciliation with Phenomenology." *Journal of the Experimental Analysis of Behavior,* 1969, 12, 315–328.

Ervin-Tripp, Susan. "Language Development." In Lois W. Hoffman and M. L. Hoffman (Eds.), *Review of Child Development Research.* New York: Russel Sage, 1966.

Ferster, C. B. "Reinforcement and Punishment in the Control of Human Behavior by Social Agencies." *Psychiatric Research Reports,* 1958, 10, 101–118.

Ferster, C. B., and Mary C. Perrott. *Behavior Principles.* New York: Appleton, 1968.

Ferster, C. B., and B. F. Skinner. *Schedules of Reinforcement.* New York: Appleton, 1957.

Franks, Cyril M., and Dorothy Susskind. "Behavior Modification with Children: Rationale and Technique." *Journal of School Psychology,* 1968, 6, 75–88.

Gage, N. L., and W. R. Unruh. "Theoretical Formulations for Research on Teaching. *Review of Educational Research,* 1967, 37, 358–370.

Gewirtz, Jacob L. "Mechanisms of Social Learning: Some Roles of Stimulation and Behavior in Early Human Development." In David A. Goslin (Ed.), *Handbook of Socialization Theory and Research.* Chicago: Rand McNally, 1969, 57–212.

Gilbert, T. F. "Mathematics: The Technology of Education." *Journal of Mathematics,* 1962, 1, 7–73.

Grunbaum, Adolf. "Causality and the Science of Human Behavior." *American Scientist,* 1952, 40, 665–676.

Hall, R. Vance, Diane Lund, and Delores Jackson. "Effects of Teacher Attention on Study Behavior." *Journal of Applied Behavior Analysis,* 1968, 1, 1–12.

Hall, R. Vance, Marion Panyan, Delores Rabon, and Marcia Broden. "Instructing Beginning Teachers in Reinforcement Procedures Which Improve Classroom Control." *Journal of Applied Behavioral Analysis,* 1968, 1, 315–322.

Haring, N. G., and Mary Ann Hauck. "Contingency Management Applied to Classroom Remedial Reading and Math for Disadvantaged Youth." Olympia, Washington: *Department of Institutions Research Report,* 1969a, 41–45.

Haring, N. G., and Mary Ann Hauck. "Improved Learning Conditions in the Establishment of Reading Skills with Disabled Readers." *Exceptional Children,* 1969b, 35, 341–352.

Haring, N. G., and T. C. Lovitt. "Operant Methodology and Education Technology in Special Education." In N. G. Haring and R. L. Schiefelbusch (Eds.), *Methods of Special Education.* New York: McGraw-Hill, 1967.

Harris, Florence, Montrose Wolf, and Donald Baer. "Effects of Adult Social Reinforcement on Child Behavior." In W. W. Hartup and Nancy L. Smothergill (Eds.), *The Young Child.* Washington, D.C.: National Association for the Education of Young Children, 1967, 13–26.

Harris, F. R., M. K. Johnston, C. S. Kelley, and M. M. Wolf. "Effects of Positive Social Reinforcement on Regressed Crawling of a Nursery School Child." *Journal of Educational Psychology,* 1964, 55, 35–41.

Hart, B. M., K. E. Allen, J. S. Buell, F. R. Harris, and M. M. Wolf. "Effects of Social Reinforcement on Operant Crying." *Journal of Experimental Child Psychology,* 1964, 1, 145–153, and Academic Press, Inc.

Hart, Betty M., Nancy J. Reynolds, Donald M. Baer, Eleanor R. Brawley, and Florence R. Harris. "Effect of Contingent and Non-contingent Social Reinforcement on the Cooperative Play of a Preschool Child." *Journal of Applied Behavioral Analysis,* 1968, 1, 73–78.

Hart, Betty M., and Todd Risley. "Establishing Use of Descriptive Adjectives in the Spontaneous Speech of Disadvantaged Preschoolers." *Journal of Applied Behavioral Analysis,* 1968, 1, 109–120.

Hartup, Willard W. "Peers as Agents of Social Reinforcement." In W. W. Hartup and Nancy L. Smothergill (Eds.), *The Young Child.* Washington, D.C.: National Association for the Education of Young Children, 1967, 214–228.

Hewett, Frank, E. Raft, and D. Mayhew. "An Experimental Reading Program for Severely Emotionally Disturbed, Neurologically Impaired and Mentally Retarded Children." *American Journal of Orthopsychiatry,* 1967, 37, 35–49.

Hewett, Frank, and others. "The Santa Monica Project: Evaluation of an Engineered Classroom Design with Emotionally Disturbed Children." *Exceptional Children,* 1969 (March), 35, 523–529.

Hill, S. D. "The Performance of Young Children on Three Discrimination Learning Tasks." *Child Development,* 1965, 36, 425–436.

Hitt, William D. "Two Models of Man." *American Psychologist,* 1969, 24, 651–658.

Holland, J. G. "Teaching Machines: An Application of Principles from the Laboratory." *Journal of the Experimental Analysis of Behavior,* 1960, 3, 275–287.

Holland, J. G., and B. E. Skinner. *The Analysis of Behavior.* New York: McGraw-Hill, 1961.

Homme, L. E., P. C. deBaca, J. V. Devine, R. Steinhorst, and E. J. Rickert. Use of the Premack Principle in Controlling the Behavior of Nursery School Children. *Journal of the Experimental Analysis of Behavior,* 1963, 6, 544.

Horowitz, Frances D. "Social Reinforcement Effects of Child Behavior." In W. W. Hartup and Nancy L. Smothergill (Eds.), *The Young Child.* Washington, D.C.: National Association for the Education of Young Children, 1967, 27–41.

Hundziak, M., R. A. Maurer, and L. S. Watson, Jr. "Operant Conditioning in Toilet Training of Severely Mentally Retarded Boys." *American Journal of Mental Deficiencies,* 1965, 70, 120–124.

Johnston, Margaret, Carolyn Kelley, Florence Harris, and Montrose Wolf. "An Application of Reinforcement Principles to Development of Motor Skills of a Young Child." *Child Development,* 1966, 37, 379–387.

Kagan, Jerome. "An Essay for Teachers." *Young Children,* 1969, 24, 132–142.

Kennedy, Daniel A., and Ina Thompson. "Use of Reinforcement Techniques with a First Grade Boy." *Personnel and Guidance Journal,* 1967, 46, 366–370.

Kerr, N., L. Meyerson, and J. Michael. "A Procedure for Shaping Vocalizations in a Mute Child. In L. P. Ullman and L. Krasner (Eds.), *Case Studies in Behavior Modification.* New York: Holt, Rinehart, and Winston, 1966, 366–370.

Kunzelmann, Harold. "Viewing the Learning Process." Seattle: University of Washington Child Development and Mental Retardation Center, 1969.

Kuypers, David S., Wesley C. Becker, and K. Daniel O'Leary. "How to Make a Token System Fail." *Exceptional Children,* 1968, 35, 101–108.

Langer, Jonas. *Theories of Development.* New York: Holt, Rinehart and Winston, 1969.

Lindsley, Ogden. *Public Address on Precision Teaching.* Tacoma, Wash., 1968 (November).

Lindsley, Ogden. *Public Address on Behavior Therapy.* University of Washington, Seattle, 1969 (May 22).

Lovitt, Thomas C. "Operant Conditioning Techniques for Children with Learning Disabilities." *Journal of Special Education,* 1968, 2, 283–289.

Lovitt, Thomas C., and Karen A. Curtiss. "Academic Response Rate as a Function of Teacher- and Self-Imposed Contingencies." *Journal of Applied Behavior Analysis,* 1969, 2, 49–54.

Lovitt, Thomas C., and others. "A Demonstration Project to Train Programming and Contingency Management Advisors." Olympia, Wash.: Department of Institutions Research Report, 1969, 35–40.

McGeoch, J. A. *The Psychology of Human Learning.* New York: Longmans, 1942.

McKerracher, D. W. "Alleviation of Reading Difficulties by a Simple Operant Conditioning Technique." *Journal of Child Psychology and Psychiatry,* 1967, 18, 51–56.

Madsen, C. H., Jr. "Positive Reinforcement in the Toilet Training of a Normal Child: A Case Report." In L. P. Ullman and L. Krasner (Eds.), *Case Studies in Behavior Modification.* New York: Holt, Rinehart and Winston, 1966, 305–307.

Madsen, C. H., Jr., W. Becker, and D. Thomas. "Rules, Praise, and Ignoring: Elements of Elementary Classroom Control. *Journal of Applied Behavior Analysis,* 1968, 1, 139–150.

Maehr, M. L. "Some Limitations of the Application of Reinforcement Theory to Education." *School and Society,* 1968, 96, 108–110.

Maier, Norman R. F. "Frustration Theory: Restatement and Extension." *Psychological Review,* 1956, 63, 370–388.

Maltzman, Irving. "On the Training of Originality." *Psychological Review,* 67, 229–242, 1960.

Meacham, Merle L., and Allen E. Wiesen. *Changing Classroom Behavior.* Scranton: International Textbook, 1969.

Michael, Jack, and Lee Meyerson. "A Behavioral Approach to Counseling and Guidance." *Harvard Educational Review,* 1962, 32, 382–402.

O'Leary, K. D., and W. C. Becker. "Behavior Modification of an Adjustment Class: A Token Reinforcement Program." *Exceptional Children,* 1967, 33, 637–642.

O'Leary, K. Daniel, Wesley C. Becker, Michael B. Evans, and Richard A. Saudargas. "A Token Reinforcement Program in a Public School: A Replication and Systematic Analysis." *Journal of Applied Behavior Analysis,* 1969, 2, 3–14.

Osborne, J. Grayson. "Free-time as a Reinforcer in the Management of Classroom Behavior." *Journal of Applied Behavior Analysis,* 1969, 2, 113–118.

Parton, D. A., and A. O. Ross. "Social Reinforcement of Children's Motor Behavior: A Review." *Psychological Bulletin,* 1965, 64, 65–73.

Patterson, G. R. "An Application of Conditioning Techniques to the Control of a Hyperactive Child." In L. P. Ullman and L. Krasner (Eds.), *Case Studies in Behavior Modification.* New York: Holt, Rinehart, and Winston, 1966, 370–375.

Patterson, G. R., R. Jones, J. Whittier, and M. A. Wright. "A Behavior Modification Technique for the Hyperactive Child." *Behavior Research Therapy,* 1965, 2, 217–226.

Premack, David. "Toward Empirical Behavior Laws: I. Positive Reinforcement." *Psychological Review,* 1959, 66, 219–233.

Premack, David. "Reinforcement Theory." In D. Levine (Ed.), *Nebraska Symposium on Motivation.* Lincoln: University of Nebraska Press, 1965, 123–180.

Reese, Ellen P. *The Analysis of Human Operant Behavior.* Dubuque, Iowa: Wm. C. Brown Company, 1966.

Reynolds, Nancy J. and Todd Risley. "The Role of Social and Material Reinforcers in Increasing Talking of a Disadvantaged Preschool Child." *Journal of Applied Behavioral Analysis,* 1968, 1, 253–262.

Rieber, Morton. "The Role of Stimulus Comparison in Children's Discrimination Learning." *Journal of Experimental Psychology,* 1966, 72, 263–270.

Rieber, Morton. "Mediational Aids and Motor Skill Learning in Children." *Child Development,* 1968, 39, 559–567.

Risley, Todd. *Juniper Gardens Nursery School Project.* Project underway at the University of Kansas, Lawrence, 1969.

Salzinger, Suzanne, K. Salzinger, Stephanie Portnoy, Judith Eckman, Pauline Bacan, M. Deutsch, and J. Zubin. "Operant Conditioning of Continuous Speech in Young Children." *Child Development,* 1962, 33, 683–695.

Sapon, S. M. "Contingency Management and Programmed Instruction in the Preschool." *Audiovisual Instruction,* 1968, 13, 980–982.

Sapon, S. M. "Contingency Management in the Modification of Verbal Behavior in Disadvantaged Children." *International Review of Applied Linguistics,* 1969 (In press).

Schiefelbusch, R. L. (Ed.). *Language and Mental Retardation.* New York: Holt, Rinehart and Winston, 1967.

Sibley, Sally A., Martha S. Abbott, and Betty P. Cooper. "Modification of the Classroom Behavior of a Disadvantaged Kindergarten Boy by Social Reinforcement and Isolation." *Journal of Experimental Child Psychology,* 1969, 7, 203–219.

Sidman, Murray. *Tactics of Scientific Research.* New York: Basic Books, 1960.

Sidman, Murray. "Operant Techniques." In Arthur J. Backrack (Ed.), *Experimental Foundations of Clinical Psychology.* New York: Basic Books, 1962.

Skinner, B. F. *The Behavior of Organisms: An Experimental Analysis.* New York: Appleton, 1938.

Skinner, B. F. "The Science of Learning and the Art of Teaching." *Harvard Educational Review,* 1954, 24, 86–97.

Skinner, B. F. "Freedom and the Control of Men." *American Scholar,* 1956a, 25, 47–65.

Skinner, B. F. "Some Issues Concerning the Control of Human Behavior." *Science,* 1956b, 124, 1056–1066.

Skinner, B. F. *Verbal Behavior.* New York: Appleton, 1957.

Skinner, B. F. *Science and Human Behavior.* New York: Macmillan, 1961.

Skinner, B. F. "What is the Experimental Analysis of Behavior?" *Journal of the Experimental Analysis of Behavior,* 1966a, 9.

Skinner, B. F. "Contingencies of Reinforcement in the Design of a Culture." *Behavioral Science,* 1966b, 11, 159–166.

Skinner, B. F. *The Technology of Teaching.* New York: Appleton, 1968.

Solomon, R. L. "Punishment." *American Psychologist,* 1964, 19, 239–253.

Spaulding, R. "A Coping Analysis Schedule for Educational Settings (CASES)." Education Improvement Program. Durham, N.C.: Duke University Press, 1967.

Staats, Arthur W. *Learning, Language, and Cognition.* New York: Holt, Rinehart and Winston, 1968.

Staats, Arthur W., Judson R. Finley, Karl A. Minke, and Montrose Wolf. "Reinforcement Variables in the Control of Unit Reading Responses." *Journal of the Experimental Analysis of Behavior,* 1964b, 7, 139–149.

Statts, A. W., K. A. Minke, J. R. Finley, M. Wolf, and L. O. Brooks. "A Reinforcer System and Experimental Procedure for the Laboratory Study of Reading Acquisition." *Child Development,* 1964a, 35, 209–231.

Staats, Arthur W., and Carolyn K. Staats. "A Comparison of the Development of Speech and Reading Behavior with Implications for Research." *Child Development,* 1962, 33, 831–846.

Stevenson, H. W. "Social Reinforcement of Children's Behavior." In Lewis P. Lipsitt and Charles C. Spiker (Eds.), *Advances in Child Development and Behavior,* Vol. 2. New York: Academic Press, 1965, 97–126.

Stevenson, H. W. and S. A. Allen. "Variables Associated with Adults' Effectiveness as Reinforcing Agents." *Journal of Personality,* 1967, 35, 246–264.

Suppes, Patrick, and R. A. Ginsberg. "A Fundamental Property of All-or-none Models: Binomial Distribution of Responses Prior to Conditioning with Application to Concept Formation in Children." *Psychological Review,* 1963, 70, 139–161.

Tate, B. G., and G. S. Baroff. "Aversive Control of Self-injurious Behavior in a Psychotic Boy." *Behavior Research and Therapy,* 1966, 4, 281–287.

Thomas, Don R., Wesley C. Becker, and Marianne Armstrong. "Production and Elimination of Disruptive Classroom Behavior by Systematically Varying Teacher's Behavior." *Journal of Applied Behavior Analysis,* 1968, 1, 35–45.

Thorndike, Edward L. *The Psychology of Learning.* New York: Teachers College, 1913.

Tiktin, Susan, and Willard W. Hartup. "Sociometric Status and the Reinforcing Effectiveness and Children's Peers." *Journal of Experimental Child Psychology,* 1965, 2, 306–315.

Ullman, L. P., and Leonard Krasner (Eds.). *Case Studies in Behavior Modification.* New York: Holt, Rinehart and Winston, 1965.

Valett, R. F. "A Social Reinforcement Technique for the Classroom Management of Behavior Disorders." *Exceptional Children,* 1966, 33, No. 3, 185–189.

Vetter, Harold J. *Language Behavior and Communication.* Itasca, Ill.: F. E. Peacock, 1969.

Wann, T. W. (Ed.). *Behaviorism and Phenomenology.* Chicago: University of Chicago Press, 1964.

Ward, Michael H., and Bruce L. Baker. "Reinforcement Therapy in the Classroom." *Journal of Applied Behavioral Analysis,* 1968, 1, 323–328.

Wasik, Barbara H., Kathryn Senn, Roberta H. Welch, and Barbara R. Cooper. "Behavior Modification with Culturally Deprived School Children: Two Case Studies." *Journal of Applied Behavior Analysis,* 1969, 2, 181–194.

Weber, Max. *The Protestant Ethic and the Spirit of Capitalism.* London: G. Allen, 1930.

Werry, John S. and Herbert Quay. "Observing the Classroom Behavior of Elementary School Children." *Exceptional Children,* 1969, 35, 461–467.

Whelan, Richard, and Norris Haring. "Modification and Maintenance of Behavior through Systematic Application of Consequences." *Exceptional Children,* 1966, 32, 281–285.

Whitlock, Carolyn, and Don Bushell, Jr. "Some Effects of 'Back-up' Reinforcers on Reading Behavior." *Journal of Experimental Child Psychology,* 1967, 5, 50–57.

Williams, Carl D. "The Elimination of Tantrum Behavior by Extinction Procedures." *Journal of Abnormal and Social Psychology,* 1959, 59, 269.

Willoughby, Robert H. "The Effects of Time-out from Positive Reinforcement on the Operant Behavior of Preschool Children." *Journal of Experimental Child Psychology,* 1969, 7, 299–313.

Zigler, Edward, and Paul Kanzer. "The Effectiveness of Two Classes of Verbal Reinforcers on the Performance of Lower- and Middle-class Children." *Journal of Personality,* 1962, 30, 157–163.

6
Piagetian Influences

Much of the contemporary attention to children's cognitive development is closely associated with the stimulating ideas of Jean Piaget, a Swiss epistemologist. Piaget began his ingenious study of child development with the careful observation of his own three children. From this beginning his investigations were gradually extended to other children and have resulted in the publication of vast numbers of papers, monographs, and books.

Piaget's conceptual system for the description and classification of children's cognitive development has been formulated independently of American psychology. As adequate translations of this system from the French language have slowly been made available, Piagetian concepts have become visible on a broad scale to American psychologists and educators. There is no doubt that these concepts have made an indelible impression on the psychological and educational literature in this country.

While impressive, the collective works of Jean Piaget represent an extremely dense conceptual network. An examination of this network is at best arduous and subject to error. In part this is due to certain semantic difficulties with Piagetian terms and various ambiguities which pervade the theory. Further, because the theory is not yet complete, subtle revisions occur frequently thus creating difficulties for the consumer. Regardless, in this chapter the writer will attempt to encapsulate the major features of Piagetian theory, provide a sampling of Piaget-based research, and illustrate some ways in which this theory and research have influenced curriculum development and instructional strategies for early childhood education.

THE SYSTEM

Of fundamental concern to Piaget and his colleagues at Geneva has been the identification of processes which underlie and govern qualitative changes in thinking throughout the course of development. This concern begins with a definition of mature intelligent behavior as the ability to reason and think critically in objective, abstract, and hypothetical terms.[1] Reasoning ability is conceived by Piaget to be superordinate; that is, it rests at the top of a hierarchy of subordinate elements which are its developmental predecessors. These progressively complex predecessors are said to emerge in a distinct sequence. Certain groupings of them define qualitatively distinct states of intellectual growth, beginning in infancy with sensory-motor coordinations and ending with the aforementioned formal reasoning ability.

Among the factors which influence this progression are neurological maturation in concert with physical and social experience. A fourth

---

[1] Implied here is an intimate relationship, at maturity, between thought processes and the properties of formal logic (Hunt, 1961).

factor of influence is, in effect, motivational and is termed *equilibration* by Piaget. Equilibration refers to a process by which a developing child seeks greater cognitive balance or stability at successively higher levels as new learnings are reconciled with the old. This adaptive reconciliation is further defined by an interaction of two processes or mechanisms of behavior change: *assimiliation* and *accommodation.*

When, at any given point in time, new data are integrated in a coordinated way within one's existing conceptual repertoire, one has *assimilated.* For example, consider a young child whose structure of meaning with respect to the class concept *bird* is limited to what birds do, namely, fly. If he then perceives a flying bat as a bird, he has assimilated the new experience with reference to his present comprehension level. The complementary process of accommodation may be engaged, however, when the child immediately finds that the object is not a bird, rather a mammal (disequilibrium). His conceptual understanding of bird must be refined to handle this apparent incongruity; he accommodates his reference system to fit external reality more accurately. A myriad of such interactions is necessary for a child gradually to come to terms with physical reality. This example serves to illustrate the developmental intimacy between perception and orderly cognitive functioning based upon logical operations. Perceptual development, according to Piaget, is governed by the principle of successive liberation; that is, with age a child becomes less and less a pawn of the dominant properties of the stimulus field as he explores this field perceptually. In turn, the content and processes of *thinking* are less perceptually bound with age.

The raw data from which the above concepts of behavior change have been inferred are supplied by the observation of children in their natural environments and the creative application of Piaget's *methode clinique.* The latter technique involves primarily (1) systematic observation of an individual child's interactions with his environment and (2) a patterned inquiry, interview style, into the reasons a child is able or prefers to give for an event he has observed, either in daily life or in an experimental setting. [Obviously (2) is possible only after a child's language development enables him to respond to questions.] For example, a balloon may be blown up in the presence of a child and released to zoom about the room. Subsequently the child would be probed by an investigator for any explanation(s) he might advance for this phenomenon. Or, two plasticine balls of equal size and weight may be shown to a child and, in full view, then rolled into a pancake. The line of questioning to follow might involve asking the child whether (and why) the transformed ball is "less than," "equal to," or "greater" in weight than the nontransformed one. Customarily, children of various ages are confronted with identical problems and questions. Children's responses are then classified on the basis of the logic (or its lack) inherent in them. The Genevan school has not, however, limited its inquiry to concepts of physical causality, space, and number. Age-based trends in moral judgment and play have also been identified (Piaget, 1932, 1951). Throughout these avenues of study Piaget has assigned a major proportion of his interest to the active role children themselves take in making sense out of their world. The resultant theory is essentially a commentary on the inductive learning processes of children.

The Sequence of Development

The sequence through which a child's cognitive structures evolve begins with a state of egocentrism and ideally culminates in a state of perspectivism (Langer, 1969). Egocentrism, in Piaget's terms, refers most generally to the inability of a child to distinguish his viewpoint from that of others and to differentiate himself from his actions. In other words, it is a lack of discrimination between the subjective and the objective. Piaget's concept of childhood egocentricity thus differs from that held by most of us. An egocentric adult is so disposed, not because he is unable to consider the other fellow's view, but because he does not wish to. Piaget's child is egocentric because he cannot behave otherwise. This immaturity in cognition is gradually superseded by greater objectivity and the ability to think reflectively. It is the order in which this evolution proceeds that is the hallmark of Piagetian theory. As characterized by Piaget, this order has at least two features: *invariance* and *cumulative development*. By *invariance* is meant that the sequence of development has a fixed, defined order; to reach point Z in development a child must have started with A and proceeded through B, C, D, E, and so on. Further, this order is said to be the same for all children (hence a genetic conception of thought development), although individual differences in rate are possible and likely.

The notion of *cumulative development* is closely related to invariance. By this is meant that the quality of a child's cognitive behavior at any point in time is dependent upon the quality of the sensory-motor and symbolic experience relevant to a particular cognition which has preceded it. It is therefore assumed that cognitive structures develop and become more finely attuned (complex) by way of underlying processes which reflect the interaction of genetic and experiential forces. Cognitive structures (organized components of intelligent behavior) which define behavior at one point in development (stage) are incor-

porated into those of a later period (stage); thus they are hierarchically arranged and, by definition, qualitatively distinct. The qualitatively
distinct periods involved by Piaget are the *sensory-motor stage* (birth
to two years), the stage of *preoperational thought* (two to seven years),
concrete operational stage (seven to eleven years), and the period of
formal operations (eleven years and beyond).[2]

SENSORY-MOTOR PERIOD

It is during the first two years of life that sensory-motor coordinations
(looking at things heard, grasping at things seen and heard, manipulating things seen) form the action basis for subsequent symbolic thought.
Gradually, reflexive behavior gives way to goal-seeking sensory-motor
enactments and budding concepts of time, space, and causality. Piaget
has found it necessary to subdivide this period into six substages, the
last of which marks the transition to symbolic thought as we normally
envision it. That is, the acquisition of basic language skills marks a shift
in orientation from sensory-motor to symbolic thought. (We may note
here that the symbolic content of logical thought requires the differentiation of a signifier—a verbal symbol, for example—and the object or
event which the signifier represents.) Illustrative would be a child
learning the difference between the word "apple" and its actual concrete referent. It is further necessary to note, however, that for Piaget
thinking operations do not emerge as a direct function of language.
Neither is language considered totally relevant to the explanation of
thinking operations and their development.

The developmental importance of the sensory-motor period can
hardly be overstressed. Among the most significant learnings reported
by Piaget to occur during this stage is the concept of the object, or
object permanence. That is, through environmental interactions the
infant discovers that objects do not "disappear" when out of sight;
objects maintain their existence even though they are not in the infant's
presence.[3] All subsequent logical thought development is thought to
hinge in part upon this discovery. Closely related during the sensory-
motor stage is the development of the ability to perceive certain aspects
of the environment as substantively invariant; that is, while objects
or people may appear in different contexts their identity does not
change. For example, father is father whether dressed in work clothes,
pajamas, or bathing suit; milk is the same whether in a bottle, cup, or

---

[2] These age brackets are general approximations and should not be interpreted re-
strictively.

[3] Flavell and Hill (1969) maintain that the charting of the evolution of object permanence may be Piaget's single most important contribution.

dish. A third significant development during the sensory-motor stage is learning that certain actions have certain effects on the environment —rudiments of the concept of causality. Overall, there is a gradual differentiation of self from nonself (determining what is "me" and what is "not me"), a trend which leads the infant from a totally self-centered existence to one successively more object-centered (Tuddenham, 1966). New means to achieve apparently desired outcomes (intentionality of purpose) may be observed, such means being the product of mental combinations not possible during the first year and a half of life. Imitation of observed behavior also becomes more and more complex and occurs even in the absence of contiguous models (deferred imitation). This further reflects the increased memory skills of the child.

PREOPERATIONAL STAGE

Accelerated language development and concomitant advances in conceptual meaning occur early in the preoperational period, thus freeing the child from the limitations of interaction based solely upon motor activity. While symbolic mental activity persists from this point onward, the preoperational child is still faced with limitations in thinking which can be overcome only through maturation and experience. For example, the child's conceptual behavior is dominated by his perceptions—his understanding (and misunderstanding) is based largely upon what can be seen contemporaneously. As Flavell (1963) has put it, the child's judgments are based upon his perception of "before the eye reality." To illustrate, suppose a child is shown two rows of kitchen matches, containing five matches each, with the matches of one row spaced at larger intervals than the other. In this situation, a common tendency for a preoperational child is to behave as though the more widely dispersed row actually contains more matches ("This row has more because it is longer!") Such a phenomenon is usually observed even when the two rows are equally distributed and then one is altered spatially while the child looks on. For the child it is as if he is unaware, or cannot comprehend, that the quantity of objects remains unchanged despite changes in contextual appearance. In other words, the child fails to *conserve* number in the fact of irrelevant transformations. Similar failures are noted in regard to object properties such as weight, length, and volume. In these cases it is not object identity that the child fails to conserve, rather basic properties of objects.

A second feature illustrative of early preoperational development is the child's attendance to only one object property or experience at a time, that is, a categorization of objects and experiences on the basis of single characteristics. For example, a cooking pan is either tall or wide—it does not possess height and width simultaneously. Or a banana may be big or it may be yellow, it may be green or it may be small, but a group of bananas will not be conceived along the multiple dimensions of big, yellow bananas and small, green bananas. Multiple classification is thus seen to be beyond the child's power of combinatory thought. Similarly, the child experiences great difficulty in establishing super-ordinate conceptual categorizations, as in problems which require the achievement of higher order abstractions. For example, while a pre-operational child may acknowledge that a squash is a vegetable, he may indicate that if all the squash in the world were eaten there would be no more vegetables. In this case the subordinate class squash is seem-ingly equivalent to its superordinate class, vegetable. In short, the child does not apprehend the multiple classes subsumed under the concept. Problems such as these exemplify the difficulty preoperational children have in assigning more than one attribute to one object. Further illus-trative is an anecdote from this writer's own recent experience. A four-year-old was asked if he had a "mommy" and a "daddy" to which he replied affirmatively. Negative replies were obtained, however, to other questions such as, "Is your mommy a wife?" and "Is your daddy a son?"

Still another characteristic of preoperational thought is what Piaget terms *transductive reasoning*—reasoning from the specific to the spe-cific or from the particular to the particular. This often takes the form of determining (apparently) cause-effect relations simply on the basis that one event may follow another in time, or through some remote functional properties which may associate objects and events, or that since one event (Y) is caused by another (Z) the relationship is recip-rocal (Y causes Z). An example of such reasoning was apparent in an interchange one Sunday afternoon between the writer and his three-year-old daughter. Jennifer: "Daddy, what day is it today?" Daddy: "It's Sunday." Jennifer: "No—it can't be Sunday. We didn't go to Sun-day School today!"

Still further aspects of the period, all of which reflect precausal think-ing, are *animism* (the tendency to attribute life or consciousness to in-animate objects, particularly where movement may be observed such as a cloud moving or a mountain stream rushing over a bed of pebbles); *artificialism* (the tendency to conceive of all objects in the world as the product of human creation and made for our own purposes), and *realism* (the tendency to view such psychological phenomena as dreams and pretenses as concrete, real occurrences). These latter three tendencies are said to be functions of general egocentrism. There exists no other view or experience for the child but his own. Events psychological and real are not well discriminated; wishful thinking and pretense are frequently confused with objective reality.

While the preoperational period encompasses roughly five years, the latter two or three years in this stage (ages 4 or 5 to 7) are marked by an acceleration in symbolic functioning (Flavell, 1963). Although absolute perceptions and subjectivity in judgment still prevail, certain important abilities gradually make their appearance. First, cognitive structures are elaborated by a grouping of objects in terms of elementary relationships. For example, concepts such as milk, milkman, cow, dairy, and farm may be integrated on the basis of functional relationships. Similarly, toward the end of the preoperational period, objects may be grouped according to common properties in terms of classes. For example, potatoes and meat may be subsumed under the class concept *food;* men and women are members of the class concept *people.*[4] Classification rules used by a child during this period are rarely verbalized, however, an item taken by Piaget to indicate nonawareness of the formal criteria for classification. Thus a child's perceptually-bound thinking, while often correct, is called *intuitive.* Children continue to utilize single-dimension classification strategies, that is, when confronted with a group of paper animals and plants (each group further characterized by two different sizes, large and small), the child is likely to classify by class membership or size, not both. Finally, the onset of quantitative thinking means that the child can handle relationships founded upon numerical order. This involves a transition from counting actual objects to the use of numbers as symbolic referents. For example, a child may count two apples on his left, two on his right, and add them to produce four apples. Eventually, the abstraction 2 + 2 is generalized, that is, not limited to or dependent upon four specific objects.

CONCRETE OPERATIONS

Around the age of 6 or 7 the intuitive thought transitional period is superseded by the next higher step in the developmental ladder: *concrete operations* (so called because logical operations—mental acts of reasoning—are performed on real, or concrete objects and events). The distinguishing characteristic of this stage is that objec-

---

[4] An interesting corollary to this is the appearance of classification items on conventional intelligence tests. For example, it is not until around age 7 that a majority of children are observed to respond with higher-order abstractions to questions such as, "In what way are a peach and a pear alike."

tivity and logic are increasingly applied in thinking. Deductive reasoning is now possible although the starting point for thinking is always the real.

One major operation emerging during this third stage of development is based upon the logical rule of *transitivity,* that is, the passage from one state or point to another along a conceptual continuum. This operation is critical to the continued development of number concepts and involves, for example, the arrangement of objects (or referents) in a series of "less than" or "greater than." Thus *serial ordering* or *seriation* may be performed and represented symbolically as in transitivity of length or weight. For example, if $X > Y$ and $Y > Z$, then $X > Z$. Or, a representational instance of this might be, "If Tom is heavier than Dick and Dick is heavier than Harry, then who is heavier, Tom or Harry? *Concrete* transitivity involves making inferences about the relations among actual objects whereas both of these examples indicate *formal* transitivity. That is, in each preceding example a relational inference must be drawn from the verbally-stated hypothetical premise. The concrete-operational forerunner to a functional comprehension of formal transitivity is the seriation of observable object properties (Murray and Youniss, 1968).

A second important concrete-operational ability is based upon *class inclusion,* by which (1) in regard to part-whole relationships the part and the whole can be thought about independently, and (2) multiple classification is possible. Technically, the operation involved is termed *combinativity,* that is, an operation in which two classes can be combined into one comprehensive class which subsumes both. Suppose a child is presented with a box of twenty-five wooden pencils (twenty-one yellow and four black). He is then asked to indicate whether there are more yellow pencils or more wooden pencils. The concrete operational child will ordinarily answer correctly in contrast to his preoperational counterpart, who will likely center upon the dominant stimulus and answer "yellow pencils." In short, the younger child experiences difficulty in dealing with the parts and the whole simultaneously. Symbolically, this translates to a relation now seemingly understood in the concrete operational stage: If $X = Y + Z$, then $X - Y = Z$. Multiple classification is also illustrated in the pencil example; namely, a pencil can be both yellow and wooden. Further it can be grouped, together with a metal ball-point pen and other equivalent items into the abstract class *writing instrument.*

A third operation critical to logical thinking is termed *reversibility,* to which a dual meaning is assigned. First, that for every action there exists one which cancels it (for example, the arithmetical operations of addition and multiplication can be reversed by subtraction and division, respectively). And second, that one can return to the original starting point of a thought sequence devoted to problem solving, that is, reversal of a thought process. For example, subclasses of plants can be combined into a superordinate class (and re-separated if necessary, into subordinate classes). Thus, correct answers may be given to questions such as, "If all the plants in the world were to die would there be any flowers left?"[5]

Reversibility is thought by Piaget to be a prerequisite for the important conservation concept. Essentially, a conserving child is one who recognizes that certain properties of objects remain unchanged despite certain changes made in the objects themselves (for example, two 12-inch pizza pies remain equivalent in, say, weight and mass, despite one having been cut into four pieces, the other into eight). According to Piaget, conservation ability develops toward successively more complex levels in a fixed sequence—mass, weight, then volume—and is therefore not an all or none concept.

A final example of concrete-operational thinking to be offered here is that based upon the principle of *associativity*. This principle is equivalent to the possibility that one may reach the same point or objective by different routes. Symbolically, this may be represented as $(W \cdot X) \cdot (Y \cdot Z) = (W \cdot X \cdot Y) \cdot Z = W \cdot (X \cdot Y) \cdot Z$, and so forth, or $(5 + 1) + (3 + 6) = (5 + 1 + 3) + 6 = 5 + (1 + 3) + 6$, and so on. In other words, the child is able to recognize different ways for combining parts and that an identical solution to a problem may be reached through two (or more) different means. A concrete example of associativity might be a child mixing paints where (red + black + yellow) = brown. As long as additive quantities are held constant the order in which the ingredients are mixed makes no difference in the final outcome.

In summary, the concrete operational child is capable of (1) logical seriation, (2) class inclusion, (3) the recognition of equivalence (for example, objects of varying size and color can be of equal weight—height does not necessarily denote increased weight), (4) the exercise of reversibility in thought (for example, tracing a transformational sequence back to its point of origin to account for change in appearance), (5) conservation, and (6) associativity. Piaget stresses that such competence does not imply conscious awareness of these underlying formal principles of thought. Rather, thought during this period is gov-

---

[5] Two forms of reversibility are distinguished: reversibility of relations (reciprocity) and reversibility of classes (inversion). These two forms are purported to merge into one operation during the final stage of development (formal operations).

erned by them. It is the next, and final stage of development during which "explainer thinking" emerges.

FORMAL OPERATIONS

Whereas operations prior to age 10 or 11 have been oriented toward concrete phenomena in the immediate present, they now move toward the potential or hypothetical and the non-present. Operational thought systems become integrated to form structures from which hypotheses can be generated and logical conclusions deduced on a verbal symbolic level (sans concrete props). The ability to perform combinatorial analysis (combine in thought several rules, operations, or variables to solve problems) becomes apparent, as does the ability to formulate and execute symbolic plans of action. Logical form can be examined apart from the content of a situation or statement, and potential relations among objects may be imagined. To illustrate, consider the child's ability to deal effectively with syllogisms involving a major premise, a minor premise, and a conclusion:

> Every virtue is laudable; kindness is a virtue; therefore kindness is laudable.

In the formal operational stage, the child is capable of reasoning (and explaining) that where a conclusion necessarily follows the premises and the premises are true, the conclusion must also be true. The child also becomes capable of detecting logical incongruities in hypothetical contexts. For example, consider what is wrong with the following: "The five-year-old shell of a three-tailed turtle who lived for over a hundred years was found on a mountain top." A child prior to the stage of formal operations would likely respond by saying, "Turtles don't live on mountain tops," "Turtles have only one tail." In contrast, the formal operational child would be capable of ferreting out the logical contradiction and answering accordingly.

Piaget suggests that the adolescent's proclivity for criticizing and theorizing arises from new cognitive power; that is, he can now envision alternatives to the way things are done (child-rearing, education, government) and advance hypotheses for their improvement. This newly-acquired power in turn feeds the idealism of youth. When idealism is combined with neatly-packaged solutions to complex problems without due consideration of practical limitations of such solutions, it represents the last "high water mark in egocentrism" (Flavell, 1963; Elkind, 1967). Finally, during this period the child becomes capable of evaluating the quality (logic) of his own thought (termed second-order or reflective thinking).

Piaget's system of thought development is infinitely more complex and detailed than the above summary may indicate. Hopefully, however, the reader is by now sufficiently equipped to appreciate the general dimensions of Piaget's system. Aside from Piaget's own writing, many secondary sources are available for a more advanced study of the theory (Baldwin, 1967; Flavell, 1963; Furth, 1969; Hunt, 1961; Maier, 1965).

Two further notions regarding Piagetian theory require some elaboration prior to a sampling of research on the system which follows shortly. One concerns a problem with normative-descriptive approaches generally. A second concerns Piaget's stance on the relationship of language to thought. Consider first Piaget's normative (age-related) description of development. Development so described can rarely be associated with anything more specific than a child's "natural environment." Thus statements concerning children's abilities are technically a description of what children actually do at various ages, not what they may be able to do. In many cases, the "natural environment" may not do a very efficient nor effective job in programming experiences which would maximize developmental potential. One might expect some variation in developmental rate to be associated with qualitative variations in environmental experience. Further, one might argue that some, if not a great many, normative-descriptive data represent behavior that could be quite different if children were taught otherwise. This point is basic to much of the "training research" to be discussed shortly.

Another problem with normative-descriptive approaches, particularly when they are stage-based, is the implication that development is subject to a predetermined unfolding process. A position based upon predeterminism can easily lead to the view that educational intervention is of minor value in the developmental process (Sullivan, 1968). Further, the generalized emphasis upon age-based behavior may lead one to operate according to central tendencies in development and to overlook the wide range of individual differences in development, including the sources of such variation. Again, these thoughts are pertinent to the ensuing discussion of educational implications.

The language-thought issue previously encountered in Chapter 4 is also imbedded in Piaget's theory, and some attention to this issue may contribute further to the reader's perspective. According to one source, Piaget is "perhaps the only exponent of logical intelligence who does not see language as an intrinsically necessary element of operational thinking" (Furth, 1969, p. 109). Piaget also rejects the proposition that language is a sufficient condition for the development of thinking operations, although he acknowledges that language may be necessary for the operations of formal logic. It is true, of course, that Piaget has studied children's verbal behavior extensively. This study does not attend specifically to language acquisition, however, except to demonstrate that the developmental characteristics of logical thought are not joined in definite ways with successive advances in linguistic ability (Furth, 1969). In other words, the specific relationship of operational structure to linguistic structure is vague. But, if anything, language for Piaget is structured by logic instead of the reverse. Thus, in the Piagetian framework, the formation of operational structures is neither dependent upon nor necessarily assisted by the social transmission of spoken language.[6]

An example of verbal thinking may help to clarify the above point of view. Suppose a five-year-old from Wichita were asked: "Are there more Wichitans or more Kansans?" According to Piagetian theory, the child would probably answer "More Wichitans!" In a couple of years, however, the correct answer likely would be routine. As Furth (1969) explains,

> In connection with this Piaget-type problem of class inclusion we may ask what language contributes as an integral part of the problem situation. Since the question was framed in linguistic symbols, linguistic competence is of course a prerequisite in this situation. Moreover, the child's general knowledge or lack of knowledge of embedded class systems is expressed by the verbal reply. But is the verbal reply or any linguistic skill in general an intrinsic part of this knowledge of classes? To this question Piaget replies with an unequivocal no. He finds no theoretical reason for bringing in language nor is he able to interpret any known evidence to the effect that language in itself is a decisive contributory factor in developing the first operations. [Hans G. Furth, *Piaget and Knowledge: Theoretical Foundations,* © 1969, p. 119, Prentice-Hall, Inc.]

For this writer, a portion of the problem created by Piaget's stand on the above phenomenon is that Piaget has not proposed an explicit theory of language acquisition. In the absence of this it is extremely difficult

---

[6] For evidence, Piaget cites his own work; support comes from independent research such as Furth's (1969) study of deaf children. Furth has shown that "mature intelligence" develops in the absence of early linguistic experience and a verbal symbol system. Also pertinent is a conclusion from conservation training studies that while verbal training for nonconservers can promote attention to task-relevant features, it does not in itself result in the acquisition of operations involved in conservation ability (Sinclair-De-Zwart, 1969). In contrast, Bruner (1964) argues in favor of a functional relationship between a child's achievement of symbolic representation (representation of past events on a symbolic level) and the development of conservation skills. The entire issue is far from settled at this point.

to evaluate the language-thought relationships as outlined by Piaget, much less develop specific implications for teaching language. On the whole, one interested in facilitating cognitive development through language training finds little encouragement from Piagetian theory, at least in terms of the initial development of thinking operations. This is yet another point basic to the training research to be discussed shortly. As we shall see, certain modifications of Piaget's position are necessitated if language training is to play an important role in the development of logical intelligence.

RESEARCH

Introductory Comment

Piagetian theory has been exceptionally heuristic. It has been applied to the study of both "normal" mental development and mental deficiency (Woodward, 1965; McManis, 1969). Consequently, a vast number of studies inspired by Piagetian theory has been poured into professional journals during the past decade, and most studies have been concerned specifically with Piaget's concepts of cognitive and moral development (for example, Breznitz and Kugelmass, 1967). All research workers, to one degree or another, have attended to the validity of Piaget's system, although some believe that the predominant concern has been with a verification of the observations from which Piaget has built his theory rather than with systematic tests of the theory itself (Skager and Broadbent, 1968). The issue of validity is, of course, central to any extrapolation from the system for purposes of instruction and curriculum development.

Many of the early studies consisted mainly of replicating Piaget's original experiments with different and larger numbers of children (for example, Elkind, 1961, 1964). For the most part experimenters have attempted to avoid the pitfalls inherent in Piaget's *methode clinique* in order to quell the criticisms of "hard-core empiricists." Perhaps because of the intriguing and ingenious tasks suited to the study of concrete operational thought and the central role of conservation in cognition, children ages 5 to 10 have been studied most frequently.[7] This age bracket also includes the normative period during which

[7] Studies concerned with conservation far outweigh those which have dealt with classification and seriation. Very little evidence pertinent to formal operations has accumulated. It has been reasoned that this gap in the research may be due to (1) the notion that a complete elaboration of the theory at the formal-operational level is comparatively recent and (2) that many aspiring researchers may have been frightened away by the complex propositions of symbolic logic that are involved at this level (Skager and Broadbent, 1968).

children make the transition from preoperational (intuitive) to logical thought. Transition mechanisms seem to have aroused the curiosity of many psychologists, perhaps because they are among the least clearly articulated aspects of the theory.

As we shall see, Piaget-based studies taken together highlight at least two important research variables. First, the responses of children to Piaget-type tasks vary substantially according to the amount and relevance of information provided them and the kinds of questions posed to them. Since these tasks are, in effect, devices for the measurement of behavior, it should be kept in mind that the inferences made from behavior so measured are only as valid as the measurement techniques themselves. Thus the entire theory, like others, is a function of the methods used to obtain data. In Piaget's case, the data are assumed to be cognitively-based responses. Second, many of the studies related to theoretical validation highlight issues such as the relationship between perception and logical thinking and the relationship of language to thought. These issues are rooted in theoretical conflicts between the Geneva school and those who approach cognitive development from a modified perspective (for example, Bruner and others, 1966).

The following research review, however brief, is intended to provide the reader with a perspective useful for the interpretation of educational implications drawn from Piagetian theory. In no way is this review exhaustive; more inclusive and detailed accounts are available elsewhere (Hunt, 1961; Wallach, 1963; Flavell, 1963; Sigel, 1964; Baldwin, 1967; Sullivan, 1967). No attempt will be made to examine Piaget's original research, as his work appears in widely available publications (see References for studies by Piaget and Inhelder and Piaget).

Replication and General Validation Studies

Basic issues in the replication research have included the sequences of logical operation appearance, the age at which children perform tasks on the basis of logical thought (concrete or formal), and the degree to which operations are generalized or interdependent (Ammon, 1969). While studies are not easily categorized, it is true that the broad trends in cognitive development championed by Piaget are generally supported by data from a wide variety of sources. Examples include the trend from precausal to causal thinking (Safier, 1964), age trends in the mastery of concrete operational thinking (Dudek, Lester and Goldberg, 1969; Smedslund, 1964), and qualitative shifts in children's thinking during the general age periods specified by Piaget (Davol and others, 1967). More specifically, Murray (1968) has confirmed the relationship of age to conservation acquisition, and the order in which Piaget believes conservations are acquired (the orderly sequence of mass, weight, then volume conservation) has been successfully replicated (Uzgiris, 1964).

Further support for Piaget's idea of sequential progression in thought has come from the study of distance conservation and the understanding of spatial coordinates (Shantz and Smock, 1966) and transitivity and serial ordering (Murray and Youniss, 1968). Such evidence has been taken to confirm the more general concept of invariant sequence which for most cognitive-developmentalists is a basic power center of Piaget's theoretical system.

Many "validation" studies have dealt with the specific ages at which children's concepts are functional. From his original work, for example, Piaget has concluded that children normally acquire the concept of probability around age 7 or 8. American researchers, however, have reported reliable and appropriate probabilistic behavior for children as young as age 3 and 4 (Davies, 1965; Goldberg, 1966). As Stevenson points out, this discrepancy may be explained by the fact that Piaget places the ability to *verbalize* the concept at the later age, an ability preceded by a correct intuitive use of the concept. Neither the Davies nor the Goldberg studies required correct verbalizations. Rather, nonverbal assessments were used. Age descriptions discrepant with Piagetian theory also appear in the earlier work of Braine (1959). Concepts of transitivity and position order were located at a point roughly two years earlier than Piaget would have us believe. Braine's methods were also essentially nonverbal—an item taken by Smedslund (1963) as a distortion of Piaget's criterion for genuine transitivity. With "improved" tests Smedslund replicated Piaget's original contention regarding the emergence of concrete transitivity.

A novel approach to the assessment of Piaget's system is that represented by computer-assisted study (Gyr and Fleisher, 1967; Gyr, Brown and Cafagna, 1967). Models simulating the properties of Piaget's three successive cognitive stages have been written as a computer program which, in turn, can be utilized in conjunction with experimental problem-solving activities across age levels. This rigorous procedure has produced data generally consonant with the qualitative stage distinctions advanced by Piaget and may signal a new direction in validation research.

Age-related qualitative changes in spatial concept development have also been documented; however, children's performance at different "levels" or "stages" is frequently dependent upon task specificities (Dodwell, 1963). Such variations have also been noted among adolescents who apparently do not manifest formal operational thought uniformly (Case and Collinson, 1962). Regressive responses more typical of earlier stages (preoperational or concrete-operational) may occur, particularly on tasks which require for their performance information and verbal skills not yet assimilated. The question becomes one of the uniformity and interdependence of thinking operations at a given level. In support of Piaget are findings that positive interrelationships exist among various Piaget task performances (children ages 4 to 11) and that mastery of approximately three-fourths of concrete-operational tasks is observed by age 8 (Smedslund, 1964).[8] That qualitatively equivalent logical operations are not always apparent at various "stages," however, may have some bearing on a critique of Piaget by Kagan and Henker (1966). These critics have questioned the general application of some Piagetian principles, because the success of such application depends heavily upon the extent to which the ideas being explored are grounded in direct experience.

To the efforts of research workers most interested in general replication have been added those of investigators concerned explicitly with the methodological variables in Piaget-based child study (Achenbach, 1969; Griffiths and others, 1967; Gruen, 1966; Nunmedal and Murray, 1969; Pratoomraj and Johnson, 1966; Rothenberg, 1969; and Smith, 1968). Representative of these investigations is that of Griffiths and others (1967), who examined the relational concept repertoires ("more," "same," "less") of children ages 4 and 5 (normally transitional). Widespread confusion among children with regard to the concept "same" was discovered. Consequently, the investigators recommended that if one intends to utilize classical (verbal) conservation testing techniques with children he should first determine his subject's ability to discern similarities and make appropriate use of "same." Otherwise, one's results could be an artifact of questioning. In short, it would become difficult to determine whether (1) a child cannot conserve, (2) a child can conserve but is unable to decipher a question, or (3) he can neither conserve nor decipher a question.[9]

---

[8] This finding should not be interpreted to mean that all children will demonstrate equal performances at a given age. It is more applicable to Piaget's thesis concerning a general cognitive-developmental factor. Further, task performance differences are associated with socioeconomic status (Dodwell, 1961; Rothenberg and Courtney, 1969).

[9] Braine and Shanks (1965) agree that the cognitive competence level of a child may be underestimated by unsuitable question-asking procedures, yet some researchers maintain that very little effect can be attributable to the kind of question asked (Pratoomraj and Johnson, 1966). This counterargument is made more extreme by Youniss and Furth (1965, 1966) who contend that verbal sophistication has little bearing upon the utilization of a logical transitivity operation. The latter studies, however, involved direct instruction and are therefore not technically comparable to conventional descriptive Piagetian studies. A further item of note has come from the observation that, for a sample of disadvantaged children, an understanding of the concepts more, less and same may be a necessary but insufficient condition for number conservation (Halasa, 1969).

Still other Piaget-based studies can be taken to illustrate some difficulties with theory. Recall that Piaget pictures the child below age 7 or 8 as markedly deficient in number concepts and the ability to deal with circumstances involving uncertainty and change. Data gathered by Ginsburg and Rapoport (1967) suggest that younger children (age 4) are much more quantitatively adept than Piaget would have us believe, even though they may not have attained number conservation (Rothenberg and Courtney, 1969). A higher rate of correct probability judgments among four- and five-year-olds than Piaget would predict has also been observed by Goldberg (1966). Both the Ginsburg and Rapoport (1967) and Goldberg (1966) studies included tasks different from classical Piagetian techniques and therefore raise the possibility that task variables are critical to an interpretation of the theory.[10] Further, the cueing procedures utilized by investigators are seemingly another source of response variation among children. Possible contaminating effects of task-irrelevant cues (verbal and physical representation) have been associated with children's transitivity inferences (Coon and Odom, 1968), performance on double seriation tasks (serial ordering of a group of geometric designs along the dual dimension of size and color brightness) (Shantz, 1967), and conservation responses (multiple classification) (Sigel, Saltz, and Roskind, 1967). Neither did the latter study support the notion that conservation ability emerges at a specific stage in the cognitive-developmental process. And finally, the method of presenting concept class instances (visual versus verbal) apparently influences the Piagetian-task performance of children in transition from intuitive to concrete operational thought (Bruner, 1964).

In sum, research has provided credible data to support much of the sequential development of cognition as outlined by Piaget. However, to the extent that variations in tasks (including amount and kind of information provided to children, the nature of questions posed to them, and the positioning of objects for observation or manipulation by the child) produce variation in children's observed behavior, cautionary progress in theory development is advised. Until methodological problems are solved, there remains the possibility that certain theoretical features are artifacts of testing.

---

[10] The Ginsburg and Rapoport study (1967) involved was a cross-sectional comparison of children aged 4, 7, and 12 concerning their ability to estimate proportions (for example, estimation of the proportion of X's in a visually presented poster board matrix of X's and O's). Younger children demonstrated an occasional tendency toward under- and overestimation, but on the whole accuracy was not found to differ according to age. Goldberg's (1966) task involved a decision-making procedure whereby children were rewarded for correct responses and were not required to understand terms such as "most likely."

Extension Research

While methodological skirmishes continue, some investigators have utilized Piagetian concepts to study issues and behavioral phenomena heretofore unexplored by the Geneva school. A prime example is the work of David Elkind, a professor of psychology at the University of Rochester. Elkind's line of attack has involved mapping the developmental terrain of perceptual behavior as it relates to reading. Elkind began with a developmental study of decentration, the results of which were most adequately explained by Piaget's perceptual operations (Elkind and Scott, 1962). Data from subsequent studies revealed increased ability (with age) for children to perceive part-whole relationships and explore unstructured perceptual materials systematically (Elkind, Koegler, and Go, 1964; Elkind and Weiss, 1967). Similar age effects were noted for types of concept acquisition (Elkind, Van Doorninck, and Schwarz, 1967) and successively more difficult conceptual orientation shifts (Elkind, 1966).[11] All results have been interpreted neatly in terms of Piaget's theoretical anatomy, specifically that member of the anatomy known as decentering.

This accumulation of data has provided Elkind with a springboard for studying the complex relationship of perceptual activity to reading. Elkind argues that two of our most predominantly used methods of reading instruction may be inconsistent with perceptual development, at least in terms of teaching the "average six-year-old" without having first provided perceptual pre-training. The "look-say" method, according to Elkind, requires of a child responses which are inconsistent with development in *schematization*. It is not until about age 7 and beyond that children are normally able to coordinate part-whole relationships (such as letter-word) so that each maintains both its identity and interdependence. Neither does the phonics approach escape Elkind's analysis unscathed. Successful phonics learning depends, believes Elkind, upon the spontaneous ability to reverse figure and ground (*perceptual reorganization* in the Piaget system). In other words, a child must come to terms with two related phenomena: (1) more than one sound is represented by one letter (letter *a* for example) and different letters can represent the same sound (letter *s* and *c* as in "snake" and "circus," for example); and (2) learning the equivalences of upper- and lower-case letters and manuscript and cursive letters. As Elkind states,

---

[11] Conceptual orientation shift behavior refers to the changes a child can make in his classification strategy during inductive concept formation activities, for example, the ability to shift from a classification of objects on the basis of function (uses) to their concrete properties and vice versa.

In all of these instances, the real problem lies in the recognition that the same element can represent different things and that different elements can represent the same thing. . . . [this] is then directly analogous to that faced by the child in reversing figure and ground when viewing an ambigous figure (such as the famous Rubin-Vase Profile). That such an assumption is not fortuitous is shown by the fact that slow readers are deficient in the ability to reverse figure and ground in comparison with average readers of comparable mental ability. [Elkind, 1967c, p. 360]

The implication of Elkind's work is that training in perceptual reorganization and/or schematization may facilitate the reading process. At the least, assessment of perceptual behavior may be dictated for children who early experience reading difficulties.

The apparent advantages of perceptual training are shown by a recent study of inner-city second-grade Negro children (Elkind and Deblinger, 1969). The children in one group were engaged in a program of non-verbal perceptual exercises over a period of fifteen weeks. A second group of children, matched with the perceptual trainees on the basis of reading achievement and initial perceptual ability, underwent training for the same period of time with a conventional reading series. At the end of the training period the perceptual training group demonstrated a significantly higher level of word and word form recognition skills than did the control group. These data are taken to supply validity for the training techniques developed by Elkind from Piagetian thought.

A second example of extension research favorable to Piaget is provided by DeVries (1969), whose interest was the responses of children (aged 3 to 6) to a generic identity problem. Three groups of children each viewed a specific "transformation" of one live animal (cat or dog) into another "animal" (rabbit, dog, or cat) by way of masking techniques; in other words, one animal was made to look like another by placing a mask on its face. The children first viewed the original animal, watched the animal's tail while the experimenter screened the masking operation from the child's view, and then were offered the entire animal again for inspection. Children were then queried with regard to their interpretation of this apparent transformation. At issue here is the concept of identity constancy, that is, that invariance characterizes the extant identity of a living substance. DeVries's analysis led to two important conclusions. First, that the concept of qualitative invariance is acquired sequentually with age (a definitive sequence throughout the age range 3 to 6 was documented). Second, the achievement of this concept precedes the development of quantitative invariance (children are capable of handling generic identity problems earlier than problems involving quantitative invariance). These findings are relevant as support for Piaget's distinction between identity and conservation. Qualitative invariance is thought to be linked hierarchically with the earlier development of object permanence and may be one key mechanism in the trend away from egocentricism. This study does share problems in common with others based upon Piagetian interviewing technique, namely, the semantics of questions and the suggestibility of children where children may unintentionally be led by a questioner to make a "desired response." On the face of it, however, this study is significant theoretically and further illustrates the clever nature of Piaget-type tasks.

Behavioral Correlates

One traditional and pervasive approach to the description of behavior by psychologists has been the *correlational* approach. Various measurements are taken from the same individuals within a selected population and then correlated, usually to (1) investigate individual differences comprehensively, (2) discover broad patterns in behavior or common characteristics which may define basic, species-specific dimensions of behavior, and (3) identify characteristics or combinations of characteristics which may lead to the more efficient prediction of behavior. Thus a teacher may be assisted toward a better understanding of, say, anxiety, by recognition of (1) what other characteristics of children are associated with variations in this emotional response, (2) what responses may combine with this attribute to define more basic personality patterns or (3) whether this constant (anxiety) is relevant to making predictions about, say, academic achievement. Occasionally, correlational studies are also used as clues to empirical interrelationships among theories that are linked abstractly to one another.

All of these concerns have been implicit in a series of studies by Goldschmid (1967, 1968) which exemplifies the behavioral-correlates approach within a Piagetian framework. Both studies utilized conservation among first- and second-grade children as the criterion of cognitive functioning. Their combined results show higher levels of conservation ability to be associated with (1) higher IQ, chronological age, and vocabulary, (2) more favorable peer and teacher ratings, (3) less maternal domination, and (4) greater objectivity in self-evaluation. Results of the 1967 study also led to the suggestion that emotional maladjustment may impede the acquisition of the conservation concept. This suggestion is reminiscent of Neale's data (1966) which indicate a significantly greater degree of egocentrism among institutionalized emotionally disturbed children as compared to "normal" peers.

Correlational data like those above pose interpretation difficulties. They cannot legitimately be stretched to infer cause-effect relationships, only a "going-togetherness." Thus the data above indicate only a positive "going-together" of characteristics generally thought desirable in our society (a phenomenon sometimes described by the phrase, "Those what has, gets!"). Perhaps more importantly, these data provide indirect evidence for the principle, *all aspects of development interact.* As Piaget and others have maintained, the developmental process represents a complex interdependence of system components. However, this seemingly obvious principle may too often be overlooked by teachers and parents.

Longitudinal examinations of the relationship between Piagetian concept attainment and the academic behavior of children are rare. What little has been done to date does, however, indicate that this is a promising area for study. With regard to the prediction of spelling and arithmetic achievement, comparable power has been found for a Piagetian concept test and a conventional intelligence test (Freyberg, 1966). A combination of these two measures achieved even greater prediction efficiency in this study of children aged 6 to 9. This suggests that school achievement is related to areas of conceptual development not tapped by standard mental tests.

A similar conclusion has been reached by Dudek, Lester, and Goldberg (1969), who also analyzed relationships between Piagetian and conventional psychometric methods for the measurement of intelligence.[12] High (.52 to .62) correlations between the Piagetian developmental scales and standard IQ measures were obtained, and both scales were equally effective for the prediction of primary-grade achievement. This was interpreted to mean that, while both assessment methods measure a "great deal in common," each test accounts for elements of intelligent behavior not measured by the other. Multiple correlations of .70 to .80 were found between the two assessment methods combined and school achievement.

It is quite possible that Piagetian-derived scales (with their principal emphasis upon reasoning processes) measure more of what has been

---

[12] Utilized in their study were Piaget tests of space and time concepts, artificialism, animism, realism, objectivism, class inclusion, seriation, and conservation of quantity and surface. Conventional IQ measures included the WISC and Lorge-Thorndike Intelligence Scale. Academic achievement was measured by teachers' grades and the California Achievement Test.

termed "fluid intelligence" (Cattell, 1963; Horn, 1968). The former concept of intelligence refers to a pattern of abilities involving central neural organizations and mental processes less bound to specific learning and acculturation experience. In contrast, crystallized intelligence is thought to reflect more particularized experience, including education and other fairly orderly cultural influences. These two kinds of intelligence are not mutually exclusive. Rather it is a matter of the proportion of influence reflected by each (physiological versus cultural). This is, however, a viable distinction which may help to explain correlational data obtained from the use of Piagetian and conventional IQ scales. It may also be useful in regard to research concerning the effects of direct teaching on logical structure development. We will return to this point later.

Another recent Piaget-based correlational study involved the relationship of reversibility in thought to intelligence (as measured conventionally) (O'Bryan and MacArthur, 1969). Creativity has been envisioned in the research literature as an intricate combination of abilities and attitudes which culminate in the production of original or unusual solutions to problems. O'Bryan and MacArthur (1969) reasoned that reversibility, claimed to generate from flexibility of hindsight and foresight, should demonstrate some relationship to the flexibility in thought purportedly measured by tests of creativity or divergent production (Torrance, 1963). Extensive statistical analyses of test scores from nine-year-old boys yielded two reversibility factors—reversibility of classes (inversion) and reversibility of relations (reciprocity)—which correlated most strongly with creative performance and intelligence test performance, respectively. This supports tentatively the dual nature of reversibility contended by Piaget to develop during the concrete-operational period. Possibly the differentiated reversibility factors also underlie different forms of intelligent behavior, such as convergent and divergent problem solving, and may serve as a cue for the design of further studies.

Finally, that abilities involving seriation, correspondence, and conservation (not typically measured by conventional scales) are positively correlated with academic behavior of early school children (arithmetic achievement) is substantiated in studies by Dodwell (1961) and Hood (1962).

Test Development

As the above examples attest, Piaget-inspired studies generally have involved transitional and concrete-operational children. One of the few attempts to validate Piaget's views about infant development has involved the construction of test items to assess sensory-motor response patterns (Uzgiris and Hunt, 1966). This work indicates that hierarchical development does occur during the sensory-motor period as Piaget contends, that is, that successful performance on advanced items is preceded by a sequential success on earlier items where item placement is dictated by the theory. Further support for the hierarchical hypothesis has resulted from the construction and use of scales for the measurement of object permanence and classificatory development (Decarie, 1965; Kofsky, 1966). In the later study, however, it was found that the exact order of mastery varies widely; some children failed early items only to pass later, more difficult ones. This phenomenon could reflect difficulties in the theory, in test item construction, or both.

Among the most massive efforts to measure precausal thinking in children ages 4 to 12 (N = 500) is that of Laurendeau and Pinard (1962). Impressive resemblances to Piaget's earlier findings on precausality were observed, including evidence of a stage-sequence nature for children's phenomenal explanations. Responses to the Laurendeau and Pinard scales uniformly reflected three primary stages (apart from children's refusal to answer or their complete incomprehension of a question): (1) children who provide exclusively precausal explanations; (2) children who utilize precausal and objective causal factors simultaneously; and (3) children who show no evidence of precausality.[13] Trend analyses culminated in at least two important conclusions regarding the evolution of each form of precausal thinking. First, of those children around age 4 who were capable of responding to the question, all depended upon precausal explanations. Second, vestigial precausal thinking was variously apparent until the age of ten, after which no further primitive responses appeared. In a self-critique, Laurendeau and Pinard admit the possibility of artifactual results, the difficulties of inferring reasoning processes from limited verbalizations, and the relatively remote nature of some problems from children's daily experience. In final analysis, however, they interpret the main body of their data as support for developmental stages in causal thinking based upon the *substitution* process. In other words, precausal beliefs are substituted (replaced) gradually and in segments by more physical or objective interpretations. This reflects the more general transition from egocentrism to an objective dissociation of self and environment.

---

[13] Animism and artificialism were discovered as the most frequent forms of precausal thinking and observing, although there was also evidence of realism.

The reader may wish to field test for himself the Laurendeau and Pinard scales and examine the validity of their stage-relevant data classification system. Several issues regarding such validity might be raised. For example, of what influence are the subtle reinforcements of children by adults on children's precausal thinking? Adults often resort to anthropomorphic measures to control children's behavior ("Don't kick the chair. You will hurt it!"). Adults also tend to encourage animistic thinking in various ways ("Love the nice dolly! You want the dolly to like you, don't you?") Or, adults may convey animistic concepts by implication ("She's a beautiful ship, isn't she?"). Further, the influence of religious instruction could easily give rise to concepts of divine artificialism that are by no means unique to young children.

Finally, two parallel forms of a *conservation scale,* composed of six tasks each, have been developed for use by psychologists and educators (Goldschmid and Bentler, 1968). Performance on this scale is positively related to school grades (most notably arithmetic, social studies, science, and physical education) and therefore may be valuable in terms of refining the procedures of psychological diagnosis and prediction. According to Piagetian theory, conservation tasks are relevant during the period of the elementary grades because they best exemplify intellectual behavior at that time. Further, unlike conventional measures of intellect, incorrect responses on a conservation scale may provide information as valuable as correct answers; failure would indicate that the property of reversibility has not yet been incorporated in thought. For these and other reasons related to measurement and test-construction theory, Piaget's system applied to the assessment of cognitive functioning is promising indeed (Sullivan, 1967).

Training Studies

Of perhaps greatest interest to education (and ultimately of greatest significance to Piagetian theory) are explorations into the influence of specific instruction and general schooling experience upon cognitive growth (logical thinking). There are several practical questions which may clarify an educator's interest in this domain. For example, if a teacher is to embark upon a learning experience the success of which requires of the learner mastery of the number conservation concept which the learner fails to demonstrate, can the learner be "taught" to conserve? If so, what techniques are most efficacious for this purpose? Another practical concern is with the transfer value or generalizability of specific training. For example, if a learner demonstrates weight conservation in one situation can it be assumed that this ability will be demonstrated in a second, more novel situation requiring the same basic operation? Or, does weight conservation ability necessarily relate in any way to the ability to conserve volume? Will these two abilities require experiences peculiar to each, or is formal experience even a significant factor? More broadly, is it possible through training to accelerate the entire process of conceptual development in the interests of more comprehensive, in-depth education (assuming a decision that such an objective is "good")? Most of these questions and others like them have not yet been followed by unqualified answers. Nonetheless, the pursuit of data relevant to them has been a popular activity.

It will be recalled that Piaget is not strongly disposed toward the view that didactic experience is a significant determinant of cognitive change; his emphasis is upon the active role a child takes to assimilate from and accommodate to the environment only those cognitions which are manageable. Thus, Piaget warns against force feeding by external sources. One might argue, however, that if the cognitive capacity of the child were precisely known, appropriately-sized chunks of experience could be arranged so as to build in economical ways a healthy cognitive system. Training research seems increasingly to be conducted with this in mind. A typical procedure is to determine, through pretesting, the extent of a child's conserving ability, after which conservation training tasks are introduced.[14] If, through comparatively short-term learning experiences, a reliable conservation ability develops or a change in the developmental sequence as outlined by Piaget is noted, considerable difficulties are posed for the basic theory.

The initial wave of training studies was generally consistent with the prevailing Piagetian viewpoint that systematic pedagogy is of modest, if not questionable value for accelerating children's cognitive development (Flavell, 1963; Wallach, 1963; Smedslund, 1963a). Illustrative is an early study by Smedslund (1963b), in which it was concluded that unless children already have some notion of invariance, training procedures result in little or no cognitive improvement up through the age of seven. One implication of studies like this is that educational experiences relevant to conservation, for example, should be delayed until a child shows evidence of invariance. Or, one might take a more direct route in order to assess the effects of direct instruction, namely, systematic training and practice in reversibility, an operation said by Piaget to be a prerequisite for conservation. The latter strategy has been

[14] Training for conservation is by far the most frequently attempted modification strategy. Thus children identified as "nonconservers" or "partial conservers" are treated variously so that the influence of experiential phenomena may be evaluated. Obviously, little purpose would be served by using children who already conserve.

successful for the achievement of number conservation among children ages 6 to 8, in contrast to strategies based upon rote arithmetical operations (Wallach and Sprott, 1964; Wallach, Wall, and Anderson, 1967). From the second Wallach study it was also concluded that to conserve successfully children must not only recognize reversibility but avoid being misled by irrelevant cues. Significantly, the Wallach children did not transfer their achieved number conservation skill to a substance (liquid) conservation task.

The transfer failure noted above leads to the implication that while a specific conservation skill may be "taught," it may remain splintered, that is, nongeneralizable to other contexts. This suggestion has been supported by Beilen and Franklin (1962), who trained first- and third-grade children to solve area measurement problems. Problem-solving skills developed during training by the older children were transferred successfully to a new set of area measurement tasks, an effect not observed for the younger children. Presumably the older children had the advantage of being well-grounded in concrete-operational thought while the first-graders were not. The results of the Beilen and Franklin study are thus consistent with the Genevan belief that until fundamental operations are mastered they will not be widely generalized. In other words, while younger children may correctly solve problems for which they are specifically trained, they are not likely to solve new problems successfully until they have learned to conserve "naturally."[15] Further empirical support for this generalization comes from Murray (1968), who trained nonconserving children in the five-to-eight age range to conserve length. Murray's check on the transfer effects of this training led him to question the value of premature instruction. Such instruction may, claims Murray, simply result in a masking by verbal responses of a conceptual deficit that has the "magnitude of nonconservation itself" (Murray, 1968, p. 86).

A further exploration into the mystery of conservation acquisition involved a comparison of different procedures for teaching the principles of correspondence and conservation to nonconserving kinder-

[15] This facet of Piagetian theory involves a puzzling set of contentions. One contention is that a given concrete operation may not be generalized into all contexts, that is, will reflect situational specificity, particularly in the early stages of concrete-operational thought. The other, broader notion is that basic cognitive operations, such as conservation, underlie *all* forms of logical thinking once a stage of operational thought is reached. The weight of the evidence seems to indicate, however, that conservation skills are acquired in "bits." Gottfried (1969), for example, reports that for children ages 6 to 9 number conservation performance was superior across-the-board to length conservation performance. This suggests a hierarchy of difficulty not unlike that applicable to substance conservation (mass, weight, volume).

garten children (Feigenbaum and Sulkin, 1964). The principal cue for training was Piaget's notion that the understanding of number concepts is contingent upon number conservation ability, which, in turn, is based upon the principle of one-to-one correspondence. Results indicated that teaching correspondence can facilitate impressively the number conservation concept when (1) an actual opportunity is given to manipulate the objects involved (beads in the vase task) and (2) irrelevant visual stimuli are removed by blindfolding the learner (recall the similarity of this teaching technique to Montessori's principle of sensory isolation). A teaching strategy based exclusively upon providing reinforcement (knowledge of results) to children for their addition and subtraction responses was ineffective. This finding is consistent also with the data of Wallach and others (1967).

The Feigenbaum and Sulkin (1964) study seemingly validates Piaget's sequential idea and at the same time provides a commentary on the success of direct instruction. It also attends to the cogence of perceptual cues and their elimination, a factor which crops up in a variety of research contexts. If one considers this in relation to most of the validation studies discussed earlier, firm support (at least on the face of it) for a basic Piagetism is in evidence: that younger children operate primarily on a "before-the-eye-reality" basis. The problem is, however, that some researchers are unwilling to accept this as evidence that children who so operate are incapable of logical thought. Hence, once again issues involving interrelationships among perception, verbalization, and logical thinking are raised.

Perhaps more research like that of Halpern's (1965) will help to clarify the above interrelationships. Halpern found in a study of five- to seven-year-olds that errors in solving problems of inference were most frequent in situations where perceptual data directly contradicted logic. It was concluded that residual perception-bound thought may still occur in certain situations even after the emergence of concrete-operational thought. Assumedly this residue would be most apparent during the early phases of concrete-operational thought. At the very least, this implies that teachers will do well to arrange carefully the cues with which children of this age period are confronted in learning situations.

That cue arrangement is an important variable is apparent in the work of Gelman (1969), who gave discrimination learning set training on length and number tasks to a group of nonconserving five-year-olds. Gelman observed virtual error-free performance among her subjects on specific length and number conservation subsequent to training; roughly 60 percent correct nonspecific transfer conservation response (mass and liquid amount) was also obtained. Durability of training was also apparent two to three weeks after training. Gelman concluded that conservation "failure" among young children can be a function of their inattentiveness to pertinent quantitative relationships and overattentiveness to irrelevant aspects of conservation tasks.

Several of the training studies heretofore discussed are representative of a pervasive search for valid teaching strategies. This search has resulted in a definition of several variant approaches; yet the results of these approaches do not fall into neat, consistent patterns. The most widely researched strategies are based upon verbal instruction (which often includes verbal rules provided to children), cognitive conflict, and task analysis. Most frequently, researchers compare two or more of these approaches in terms of immediate outcomes and transfer value. Let us briefly consider, in order, these approaches.

Significant conservation training effects using a verbal rule approach with nonconserving or transitional children have been achieved by several researchers; however, no evidence for the transfer of conservational skill is provided in these studies (Beilen, 1965; Smith, 1968). Verbal training has also been successful for the achievement of specific symbolic representations (Beilen, Kagan, and Rabinowitz, 1966). In contrast, number conservation was not induced through the use of verbal rule instruction with children ages 3 to 6 (Mermelstein and Meyer, 1969). The results of the above studies are perhaps not as discrepant as they may appear, for the issue seems to involve whether a generalized conservation ability can be developed through predominantly verbal instruction.

Presently, the efficacy of verbal didactic instructional measures is questionable in reference to the development of logical structures. It is entirely possible, however, that differences in children's background experience and the extent to which verbal instruction is integrated with other forms of guided experience will affect training outcomes considerably. Certainly there is sufficient evidence to conclude that children's mastery of Piaget-type concepts is not necessarily contingent upon lengthy passages of time. For example, kindergarten and first-grade children have developed through guided experience a functional concept of specific gravity at a rate contrary to predictions from Piaget's theory (Ojemann and Pritchett, 1963). In addition, five-year-olds have been taught class inclusion operations successfully (Kohnstamm, 1963), and a multivariate conservation training technique for preschoolers has been conducted effectively (Young, 1969). That children may learn concepts more readily than Piaget supposes is also suggested by Looft and Charles (1969), whose direct instructional approach resulted in the rapid development of a generalized nonprecausal concept of life among children aged 7 to 9.

A variation in training procedures more consistent with Piagetian theory than direct instruction is based upon the cognitive-conflict hypothesis. Cognitive conflict (discrepancy between what is in one's current conceptual repertoire and what is observed in the environment) is thought to trigger the acquisition of new or more refined concepts. In theory, cognitive conflict disturbs equilibrium (produces dis-equilibrium), which the child then strives to re-establish by somehow resolving discrepant events or acknowledging a point of view different from his own. The conflict resolution idea has been advanced explicitly by Smedslund (1961), among others, although controversy surrounds its utility for the explanation of conservation acquisition (Winer, 1968). Some support for the value of cognitive-conflict experience has accumulated (Gruen, 1965; Brison, 1966). In the Gruen (1965) study it was found that such experience combined with verbal pre-training was superior to direct, reinforced practice in teaching number conservation skill to children ages 4 to 6. An important question, however, is whether cognitive conflicts per se will necessarily motivate behavior pursuant to conceptual change among all children. Or, can incentive conditions other than or in addition to conflict resolution increase the effects of training?[16]

One of the few acceleration studies relevant to this question involved the training of kindergarten children on substance-conservation tasks (Brison, 1966). These children were pretested for their entering verbal concepts (more, less, some), conservation ability, and preferred mode of explanation (the tendency, if any, for a child to examine causes when formulating an explanation for an observed event). Matched nonconservers were assigned to one of two groups—control and experimental. The latter received conservation training during which conflict was induced and an external incentive for correct performance (juice to drink) was provided. Brison reports significant training effects in terms of reversibility manifest in accurate substance conservation. Further, in contrast to many studies, correct transfer to substances (sand, clay) other than that used in training (liquid) was observed. Brison has suggested that his incentive condition may have enhanced the motivation of his children, at least to the point of more concentrated attention.

Brison's data are teasing indeed. It must be noted, however, that uniform training effects were not achieved. Roughly 30 percent of his experimental subjects failed to conserve despite training. One might argue that those who did develop conservation were either (1) "ready" to

---

[16] Questions such as these are particularly important in view of an underlying assumption of most training studies, namely, that children are equally motivated to respond to training. Precise commentary on individual differences in motivation is not apparent in the Piagetian literature.

profit from instruction and/or (2) influenced positively by the incentive, while those who failed were not. This reasoning is grossly circular, however, and begs the real question. Increased attention to individual differences in training research seems warranted.

A third variation on the training research theme is based upon task analysis (Gagné, 1965) or substructure analysis (Sigel, Roeper, and Hooper, 1966). This involves a careful analysis of complex task performance, as in conservation of substance, in terms of successive subskills which are prerequisite for success. This is extremely important from a theoretical standpoint, for if pre-training for subskill development makes no difference in subsequent conservation training strong evidence for a maturation-dependent view would be available.

With these thoughts in mind, a training procedure based upon a task analysis of weight and length conservation was devised by Kingsley and Hall (1967). Five-and six-year-olds, well below Piaget's normative standard for such conservation, were trained to criterion (successful weight and length conservation) with this approach. No more than nine 20-minute sessions were programmed for this purpose. Positive transfer to substance conservation was also observed. Since this is one of the more dramatic instances of positive training effects, it is surprising that additional studies of its type have not appeared in the literature. It should be noted, however, that conservation training studies which resemble the task analysis approach have been performed with similar success (Bearison, 1969; Sigel, Roeper, and Hooper, 1966). Bearison (1969) has highlighted the importance of a child's "quantitative set" to respond to conservation problems while Sigel and others (1966) point to the oft-overlooked necessity of pre-training procedures in operations such as multiple classification and reversibility.[17]

Most modification studies may be criticized from the standpoint of assessing only the immediate or short-term effects of training. Thus a critic might question whether the apparent changes are maintained over longer periods of time. Of the few studies which have been addressed to this issue, those conducted by Bearison (1969) and Jacobs and Vandeventer (1969) are most impressive. In the latter study, for example, first-graders were subjected to individualized and highly structured training techniques to solve double classification problems (taking into consideration two different stimulus dimensions simultaneously, such as color and form, when inferring logical relations). Trained children

[17] The basic assumption of this sort of approach—that the concept of conservation is necessarily achieved once a child has met the prerequisities for conservation—has recently been challenged (Mermelstein and Meyer, 1969). This challenge is apparently based on the notion that the whole is greater than the sum of its parts.

scored significantly higher than controls for both a criterion test and a transfer test immediately after training. This significant advantage was still in evidence four months later when a retention and second transfer test were administered to the two groups.

While several of the above-mentioned studies indicate that specifically arranged experience can facilitate cognitive development along Piagetian lines, there are others whose results are counter to this trend. For example, verbal rule instruction techniques have been ineffective for purposes of number conservation development among preoperational children (Mermelstein and Meyer, 1969). Neither were three alternative teaching techniques effective for this purpose (cognitive-conflict strategy, a language activation method, and a multiple-classification technique). It was concluded that, due to basic cognitive limitations, children aged 3 to 6 are unlikely to profit from specific planned experience. Presumably maturational intersensory processes are implicated as well as individual children's learning styles. Contradictory data such as these are not atypical and thus serve to remind a student of Piaget that many features of the theory require further study.

To conclude briefly, at least three variables apparently mediate the effectiveness of training: the type or class of problem (for example, weight, conservation, multiple classification, transitivity of length), the instructional technique used (for example, inductive-discovery, deductive-rule demonstration, direct reinforcement), and the developmental level of the child (subskills which are brought by the child to the training session) (Sigel and Hooper, 1968). To this should probably be added the child's current state of intersensory development (to the extent that this represents something in addition to "subskills"). Training effects at the level of intuitive and early concrete-operational thought are somewhat equivocal, particularly in regard to the transfer of training. Novel strategies have been devised, however, and their further application should help to clarify existing questions.

The ambiguity which presently pervades this facet of the Piaget-based research may be interpreted as a problem for those who would build curricula for young children on Piaget's theory. We will examine this problem further in a later section.

The Effects of General Schooling

More general are those studies which have attempted to cull out the influence of schooling upon the development of operational thought. Generally these studies constitute attempts to assess Piaget's thesis that interaction with the total environment, rather than specific teaching, is the instrumental factor for conservation acquisition.

For example, Goodnow and Bethon (1966) compared the conservation skills (weight, volume, and surface) and combinatorial reasoning skill of unschooled Hong Kong children to schooled American children in the same age range. It was found that variation in schooling was not associated with differences in conservation skill; however, lack of schooling was associated with lowered combinatorial reasoning ability. These results were interpreted to mean that children very likely acquire conservation skills in the "normal course" of development through their experiences with the physical environment. The greater degree of abstract thought, or mediational thought, required by combinatorial reasoning tasks is thought to be more strongly affected by academic events in the classroom, including perhaps a model (teacher) after whom one can pattern one's thinking.[18] This finding may also be taken to imply that conservation skills are not affected greatly by instruction. The broadest conclusion from this study is that schooling (or its lack) affects various thinking operations differentially.

A second comparison of schooled and nonschooled children (ages 6 and 9) was also based upon the criterion of conservation skill (Mermelstein and Shulman, 1967). These data indicate that, with age, schooling is increasingly associated with verbal proficiency on conservation tasks. That is, schooled children were significantly more successful on tasks requiring a verbal explanation with respect to conservation. Virtually all of the Piagetian probing techniques are verbally grounded, and these researchers found question-phrasing variations to influence certain performance items markedly. Such results suggest again that carefully designed language training (or even general language stimulation) may facilitate Piagetian task performance. If so, some difficulty would be created for Piaget's position on language and thought. In general, however, further studies of the effects of schooling are needed to help sort out this and other issues. To date, comparisons have been gross, have failed to control for variables such as intelligence, and rest heavily upon inference.

Summary Comment

Illustrated in the above discourse is an exchange of theoretical and methodological parries and thrusts characteristic of the Piagetian litera-

---

[18] Another way to view this is in terms of a distinction between *arranged* and *unarranged* experience. Basic cognitive structures of concern to Piaget could be those which develop as a function of unarranged experience. Or, still another interpretation is that Piaget explores the "spontaneous" features of development (learning) which are essentially universal for all children as opposed to "nonspontaneous" learnings as represented by formal school experience and other idiosyncratic phenomena.

ture. In many cases, studies defy comparison due to a wide variation in tasks utilized and controls exercised. This in turn poses an obstacle to any synthesis activity. Considerable support exists for Piagetian contentions regarding the sequence of logical thought development, especially among studies which have employed methods and materials similar to Piaget's originals. This is notably the case for the development of conservation skills. At the same time, there exist wide variations in the age of skill emergence and the age at which training is successful. Many independent studies indicate that children are dealing successfully with operations earlier than reflected by Genevan data.

Whether the total developmental sequence outlined by Piaget is genuinely invariant is not as yet proven. Possibly "invariance" is more a function of the increasing difficulty level of tasks or problems faced by children than it is a mechanism inherent in the human organism. Certainly as difficulty level increases subskills of greater specificity and technicality become commensurately more important. That differential subskills bear close examination is prompted by the frequent finding that a given child may operate simultaneously at several levels of logical thought (for example, preoperationally in some areas and concrete-operational in others). This poses difficulties for the simple classification of a child within a constricted stage of development.

Among other issues awaiting further investigation are those related to Piaget's concepts of motivation, the mechanisms of transition from one "stage" to another, the perception-logical thinking relationship, individual differences, the precise role of experience in cognitive development, and the permanence of training effects. As these issues are more thoroughly explored, it is likely that even greater complexity in developmental patterns will be observed.[19]

CURRICULUM IMPLICATIONS

It is fair to say that Piagetian theory is a theory in the making. Add to this the fact that important theoretical problems clog various aspects of the Piaget system and one could argue that curricular derivations from the theory are premature. Ammon (1969), for example, quite clearly states that the empirical basis of Piagetian theory has not been sufficiently established to make practical application advisable. Even Piaget

---

[19] That conceptual development is more complex than suggested by original Piagetian thought is exemplified by the study of classification logic and number concept acquisition (Dodwell, 1962), conservation and number differentiation (Zimiles, 1966), and weight conservation (Nunmedal and Murray, 1969).

himself has not addressed systematically the possible pedagogical applications of his theory. Neither do Piaget's writings reflect any real concern with the problems of educators. In fact, Piaget has expressed some irritation over what is termed the "American question," namely, education to accelerate cognitive development. Yet the appeal of Piagetian theory has led to developmental and educational implications for early education which run the gamut from general (for example, Ginsberg and Opper, 1969; Hunt, 1961; Sigel, 1969) to specific (for example, Sonquist and Kamii, 1967; Lavatelli, 1968; Picard, 1969). Further, Piagetian theory has been utilized as a framework around which to organize a Follow Through program for educationally disadvantaged children (Weikart and Erickson, 1969). This program includes the development of curriculum content around such areas as temporal and spatial relations, seriation, causality, classification, and conservation.

Generally, in statements of the educational implications of Piagetian theory, a cluster of basic principles are stressed. Included are emphases upon: (1) active, self-discovery, inductively oriented learning experiences whereby a child is able to perform transformations on materials from the environment (where direct teaching is necessary, it follows rather than precedes periods of manipulation and exploration); (2) arrangement of moderately novel experiences which capitalize upon and facilitate stage-relevant thinking operations but simultaneously accommodate to the child's present intellectual style; (3) a variety of patterned and enriched concrete sensory experiences; (4) the symbolization of manipulative, play, and aesthetic experiences; (5) provision of a variety of models for imitative learning; (6) a high rate of interpersonal interaction among children with ample opportunity for role playing, a sharing of different viewpoints, and corrective discussions led by adults under appropriate circumstances; and (7) the use of the clinical method to study children's progress (specifically for the purpose of noting the process through which a child may go en route to a problem solution).

The common focus for statements of implications is upon the quest for ways to govern children's environmental encounters so that intellectual potential is maximized—particularly with respect to analytical or causal thinking. This involves an issue, hinted at earlier, which is based largely upon the way one interprets Piaget: a systematic provision of intellectual content to increase the scope and quality of intelligence (early cognitive enrichment) versus allowing "natural" cognitive development to ensue while assisting with socio-emotional growth (Kohlberg, 1968). Piaget's own views on this issue are not crystal clear, although several authorities have recently stressed Piaget's interactionism in order to reduce this ambiguity (Kohlberg, 1968; Langer, 1969). Perhaps the following excerpt from Piaget will help the reader in this regard:

> The goal in education is not to increase the amount of knowledge, but to create the possibilities for a child to invent and discover. When we teach too fast, we keep the child from inventing and discovering himself— Teaching means creating situations where structures can be discovered; it does not mean transmitting structures which may be assimilated at nothing other than a verbal level. [Piaget, in Ripple and Rockcastle, 1964, p. 3]

Thus, at the nursery and kindergarten level, for example, the aim would not be to teach concrete operations, but rather to provide experience with their prerequisites so that operativity will subsequently flower (Kamii and Radin, 1967).

One feature of Piaget's system has been the explicit analysis of concepts (such as conservation) and principles or operations (such as reversibility and transitivity) that parents and teachers either take for granted or deal with only indirectly during the course of education. It is perhaps this same feature which has directed the attention of those educators identified with Piagetian theory toward applications in the areas of mathematics and the physical sciences. Of most concern to this chapter, however, are curricular frameworks based upon Piaget's growth sequence. Of these, the efforts of Dr. Constance Kamii and her colleagues in Ypsilanti, Michigan, are among the most exemplary (Kamii, 1968; Kamii and Radin, 1967; Sonquist and Kamii, 1967).

The Ypsilanti Piaget-Based Curriculum for Early Education

Kamii (1968) feels that Piagetian theory is a useful curriculum base for at least two main reasons: (1) it delineates for teaching purposes the cognitive abilities critical for the scope of elementary school academic activities; and (2) it creates an in-depth developmental perspective on the subject-matter activities at this level. For Kamii, a principal conceptual guideline is to assist children through a process of prerequisite skill construction. Three comprehensive classes of objectives have been established—socio-emotional, perceptual-motor, and cognitive. Into this triad is fused a fourth objective, language development. Cognitive objectives have been drawn specifically from Piaget. Socio-emotional objectives spring indirectly from Piaget's concept of social collaboration. Cues for perceptual-motor goals have been provided by Kephart (1960), who shares with Piaget the view that orderly cognitive functioning depends upon normal sensory-motor underpinnings. Kamii believes that educational development will be superior to that occurring in non-Piagetian curricula because it can proceed on the basis of broad abilities (for example, classification and conservation) that transcend specific subject matter. For illustrative purposes, consider the following objectives (cognitive domain only):

A. The Development of Physical Knowledge: Learning about the nature of matter:
    1. Knowledge of the properties of objects which are encountered in the environment (such as weight, form, texture).
    2. Development of a repertoire of actions which can be performed appropriately on objects when unfamiliar materials are explored (such as squeezing, folding, shaking, tearing).
B. The Development of Social Knowledge: Structuralizing the effects of social action and accommodating to social convention.
    1. Knowledge of social information (for example, social or occupational roles).
    2. Knowledge of norms for social conduct (for example, table etiquette, cooperative play).
C. The Development of Logical Knowledge: Logico-mathematical and spatio-temporal operations.
    1. Classification: The ability to group objects together through a coordination of their quantitative and qualitative aspects (colors, forms, animals, plants, and so on). Pre-classification relationships are stressed for preoperational children, including grouping according to "sameness" (perceptual criteria), "similiarity" (perceptual and conceptual criteria), and "going-togetherness" (conceptual criteria).
    2. Seriation: The ability to compare and arrange objects along a peculiar dimension (for example, the coordination of transitive relationships with reference to length, color, temperature). Preoperational ordering activities (pre-seriation) would include quantity (such as "a lot" and "a little"), size (such as "large" and "small"), and quality (such as "cold" and "hot").
    3. Number: The ability to arrange objects on the basis of one-to-one correspondence (groups of cups and saucers, pencils and erasers, toy cars and trucks, and so on).
    4. Space: The ability to structure topological space out of which develops the concepts of Euclidean space (for example, "here-there," "front-back," "over-under;" reproduction of object placement in proximity relationships such as

copying a bead-string design; spatial transformations such as disarranging a coordinated multi-block design and correctly rearranging it; and the structuring of representational space, such as copying shapes using paper and crayon).

5. Time: The ability to develop representationally temporal sequences based upon causal and means-ends relationships (for example, *before* the rain it is dry, after the rain it is wet; to buy a gum ball from a machine the penny is inserted *first,* the handle is pulled *next,* and the gum ball is taken out *last; if* you drop the glass on the cement, *then* it will break).

D. Representation: Learning symbolization to make language meaningful.

1. Symbolization through *imitation* (using the body to represent objects, as in pretend activities), *make-believe* (using objects to represent still other objects, as in using a box of sand to represent a cake), *onomatopeia* (producing sounds to represent objects, as in "buzz-buzz" to represent a bee), *three-dimensional models* (for example, constructing a block house or building a clay animal), and *two-dimensional representations* (drawing pictures and identifying objects and action events portrayed graphically). It is in the representational area that Kamii and her colleagues attribute great significance to sociodramatic play, particularly imitation, as such play establishes "*the* bridge between sensorimotor intelligence, and representational intelligence" (Kamii, 1968, p. 16). In this connection Kamii has drawn heavily upon the work of Smilansky (1968).

2. Language Representation: The ability to represent through language the objects in one's environment and physical, social, and logical knowledge. This includes assisting the child to induce the syntactical and morphological rule structure of his language and to gain skill in the use of synonyms, antonyms, and homonyms. (Recall Piaget's thesis that non-verbal representations, as in imitation, facilitate language level representation).

The above objectives have been presented because they, rather than specific content, are the more important distinguishing features of a Piaget-based curriculum. As Kamii (1968) points out, "literally anything" in a child's natural environment can be utilized to teach Piagetian knowledges and representations. This approach also lends itself to the establishment of a flexible and creative learning environment. The "knowledge-representation" integration of a common household object is explicitly conveyed in the following:

> . . . knowing an object involves knowing it in a social sense, in a physical sense, in a logical sense, and in a representational sense . . . a glass (for example) should be known socially (e.g., it is used to drink milk, but not to drink soup) and physically (it breaks, it rolls, it is transparent, etc.). Glasses should also be known logically (they can be classified with certain objects, seriated according to size, and quantified so that there will be enough glasses for all the children in the class. They should also be known spatially in terms of "top-bottom," "in-out," "round-straight," linear ordering, etc. An example of knowing a glass in a temporal sense is the sequence of washing it, drying it, and putting it away. [Kamii, 1968, p. 17a]

While a detailed specification of process-oriented objectives may be the cardinal feature of a Piaget-based curriculum, it is also true that such objectives are correlated with developmental (sequential) and methodically executed teaching strategies. For example, seriation (pre-seriation) activities first include manipulations of uncoordinated and small series of three or four objects. This step is followed by perceptual seriation exercises, and finally by operational seriation (logical-symbolic with no trial-and-error involved). For a more specific look at the sequential nature of teaching strategies, consider the areas of number concept acquisition and the development of classification structures.

Preparing Children for Number Concept Acquisition

Kamii (1969) maintains that, for elementary number concept acquisition (a precursor to conservation) a teacher must assist the child to establish through sensory-motor action patterns a logical structure of number such that this structure is "more powerful" than the child's spatial intuition. Activities for this purpose are sequential, beginning with the grouping of common objects (such as beans, bottle caps, and buttons) and making gross comparisons between unequal groups of objects. The latter involves first the use of terms such as "a lot" and "a little"—the terms "more" and "less" are introduced after the former set has been mastered. To make this sort of quantity-comparison more interesting and meaningful, story contexts may be provided by the teacher in which children are asked to give a boy doll "a lot of beans because he is very hungry" and a girl doll "a little because she is not hungry" (Kamii, 1969, p. 7).

Grouping and comparing activities are followed by the "arranging, disarranging, and rearranging" of a set of objects where spatial arrangement, not quantification, is of concern. An example of this might involve a child's working with ten drinking straws. After having made a row ("fence") with the straws at the teacher's request, the child may be asked to figure out a different way to arrange the straws. Once something different has been devised (possibly a geometric design) the child would be asked whether he can remake the original "fence" (row). The purpose of all of this is to promote mobility in thought and the ability to begin anticipating the outcome of certain actions. Repetition of this basic sequence of manipulations presumably leads to an internalization of the action so that it can be performed symbolically. In short, objects can be returned to their original configuration.

A third step in the number acquisition sequence involves linear ordering, that is, a lining up of objects in order to copy a model in an exact fashion. Working with duplicate sets of toys, for example, a teacher may position one set on a table and then ask the child to arrange his toys on his table so that they look exactly like the model. The important thing here is that the child attend to the relative positions of objects in the series, not simply make pairs of objects. According to Piaget's theory, this sort of activity is difficult for young children and involves its own sequence from nonequivalence to equivalence. Yet, because it prompts a child to achieve ordinal correspondence between two sets of objects, the linear ordering activity is extremely important in the learning sequence.

A shift to more precise set comparisons is marked by the introduction of a fourth activity, namely, provoked correspondence. This involves *qualitative* one-to-one relationships between objects. Examples would include equal numbers of bottles and bottle-caps or cups and saucers. Again, according to the theory, children find it easier to develop quantitative one-to-one correspondence with such materials than with two sets of bottle-caps or cups alone. Equivalence may be established by having the child take "just enough" caps for bottles; it may be re-established by adding (or subtracting) an extra bottle or two to the array and having the child do what is needed to have enough caps for all the bottles. Finally, a teacher may ask the child to place all bottle caps in an empty drawer (thus destroying the one-to-one correspondence), after which the child is asked further, "If we were to place our bottle caps back on our bottles, will we have enough caps for all these bottles (or will there be a bottle without a cap, or a cap without a bottle)?" Such a question is thought to require of the child his attention upon both the act of regaining correspondence and the outcome of such an act. If successful, the act is an integral part of the child's preparation for *reversibility in thought* which is a prerequisite to conservation.

The fifth activity to assist the child to develop a logical structure for number is temporal correspondence. This involves one-to-one correspondence built upon "simultaneity and temporal sequence" (Kamii, 1969, p. 14). That is, the simultaneous manipulation of corresponding objects by teacher and child so that a temporal accounting of these objects may be performed in the child's presence. As in the case of provoked correspondence, three kinds of activities are pursued. First, equivalence is established. Working with two sacks of hard candy and two drinking glasses, for example, a teacher would ask the child to drop a candy in his glass each time the teacher drops a candy in hers. Candy-dropping must be synchronized by way of vocal cues (for example, "ping," "ping," "ping."). This is necessary to counter a tendency for children to believe that the two sets are not numerically identical. When a desired number is reached the teacher stops to ask the child whether they both have the same number of candies in their glasses. Subsequently, the teacher would add one or two candies to her glass and ask the same question. The child may then perform the necessary actions to re-establish equivalence. Countless variations are possible for a teacher to establish nonequivalence. The third phase in this activity would require the teacher to pour her candies into a different container (larger or smaller) and ask the child if he were to take the "new" container would he have the same amount as in the other glass. The child would also be asked to explain why. If unable to deal with the conservation question the child would be asked that if he were to put the displaced candies back into their original glass would he and the teacher have exactly the same number of candies. If unsure, the child may be encouraged to verify this by extracting a candy from each glass simultaneously. In this way he could determine whether the glasses became empty at the same time (Kamii, 1969, p. 16).

The whole purpose of the above strategy is to base teaching upon the child's internal thought processes instead of his overt behavior. For Piaget, numbers comprise a logical structure which must be constructed by the child himself. The sequence above is illustrative of the processes which the child must initiate—ordering and grouping objects and deciding whether to cease or repeat actions—in order to develop this structure. According to Kamii (1969), this stands in contrast to the more common belief of educators that numbers are a property of a group of objects which must be abstracted to be learned.

Educating Children for the Development of Classification Structures

Another example of curricular activities is Lavatelli's (1970) program for the development of classification structures. Such structures in-

volve several characteristics which must be translated into separate
operations and arranged according to level of complexity in ways consistent with the child's developmental sequence. This sequence of operations begins with children's identification of object properties (for
example, form, color, or size of blocks) and object-matching on the
basis of two or more properties (for example, form, color, *and* size).
The underlying purpose is the development of skill in extracting the
common property of a class of objects and extending the class to incorporate all objects which may possess that property.[20]

A second step in the process of classification structure development
requires that the child apply the above skill. Now, however, the child
must be mindful of two or more object properties as he seeks an object
to complete a set of objects. The medium for such activity is a matrix
puzzle comprised of pictures. Matrix activity is initiated by having the
child respond to a "puzzle" involving pictures of "two large red flowers
and a small yellow flower in the top horizontal row, and two large red
apples and a blank space for which the child must select a card picturing
one small yellow apple from a number of choices of flowers and apples"
(Lavatelli, 1970, pp. 89–90). The difficulty level of these analogy-type
problems is gradually increased to the point where a child must attend
to three variables or attributes simultaneously. According to Piaget,
the young child solves such puzzles on a perceptual rather than upon a
conceptual or logical basis, but a basic purpose of such activity is to
provide opportunities for a teacher to learn something about the conceptual level a child may be operating on.

From multi-property classification exercises, in the Lavatelli (1970)
curriculum the child proceeds to activities arranged to promote the
recognition of complementary classes. Suppose a child is confronted
with ten pictures of vegetables, two of which are carrots. Will he be
able to separate this set into no more than *two* classes of vegetables,
carrots and vegetables–not carrots? Complementary classes are defined by such a separation. The relationship involved is helpful for
children's understanding of what is and what is not included in a given
class. In other words, when carrots (or sparrows or shoes) are discussed,
a complementary class is understood (vegetables–not carrots, birds–
not sparrows, clothing–not shoes) and that the specified class and its
complement together comprise the total class. An important feature of
this is the more general concept of negation, which is also treated, al-

[20] Lavatelli also recommends that appropriate verbal activities should accompany these
actions so that grammatical structures are modelled in sequence. In this case the sequence
would begin with simple declarative sentences, followed by transformations which would
include coordinate sentences containing directives for more than one action.

though much differently, in the Bereiter-Engelmann curriculum (Chapter 4).

A fourth step in Piaget-based classification activity requires that the child take whole classes "apart" to determine subclasses and make comparisons of "all" and "some." Suppose a child is working with ten wax crayons, two green and eight orange. The "whole class" in this case is wax crayons. Subclasses would be green wax crayons and orange wax crayons. All-some relations may be pinpointed by precision questioning by the teacher in combination with crayon-manipulation by the child. Understandings to be developed would include that there are more wax crayons than orange crayons, some of the wax crayons are orange and some (fewer) are green, and that all crayons, regardless of color, are wax. But the broader understanding, of course, would be a generalized concept of class-subclass relations. Such understanding requires time and experience with a wide variety of objects suited to this type of activity. As in the preceding classification skills, the child's transactions begin at the sensory-motor level, progress to the level of imagery (mental and pictorial), and eventuate in verbal behavior in which phenomena are dealt with in words. The latter requires memory of the critical facts in a transaction.

The fifth set of activities in the classification sequence calls for two skills on the child's part (Lavatelli, 1970). First, he must be able to abstract the common property of an object class ("intension"). The second skill involves extending a class to incorporate all objects that possess the given property ("extension"). Both memory and the prediction of events are involved. Suppose a child is provided with a mixed collection of "mini-toys"—cars, soldiers, dogs, and marbles—and four boxes into which he may deposit toys that are "alike in some way" (using *all* the toys). Here the common property for each class must be abstracted, remembered, and applied to each toy that he places into a specific class. As in other classification skills, the intension-extension combination develops sequentially. Younger children begin by grouping on the basis of spatial configuration instead of abstracted properties. Gradually, criterial attributes are used as the basis for grouping, although children generally do a lot of "criterion-matching" during a classification activity before they achieve a consistent set to follow through an entire grouping exercise using the same criterion.

While step number five above depends heavily on the use of prestructured materials, there are generally many occasions for object-grouping activities and defining relations between objects during the course of a school day. For example, in the art corner a teacher may identify common properties of objects such as paint brushes, paints, crayons, towels, and the like. Children may be asked first to put all the "things-we-make-pictures-with" on the table. Later would come something like, "Let's put all the art materials in separate boxes. Here are four boxes. Let's put the materials that are alike in some way, that go together in some way in each of these boxes." More than one classification scheme is usually possible (for example, color, function or use, composition), although a child must classify all objects.

Skill in abstracting common properties is a precursor to the sixth point of orientation in classification structure development: locating objects concordant with the intersection of two classes. Stimulus materials for this task could include pictures of a blue truck, a yellow truck, a red truck, a green truck, and an orange truck all aligned horizontally. For accompaniment, in a vertical row would be pictured a red scarf, a red ball, a red lollipop, a red pencil, and a red book. The child's task here is to select from among a separate group of pictures (which include all of the aforementioned objects) the one to place in a blank space where horizontal and vertical rows intersect in matrix fashion. Thus he must simultaneously note the object property common to objects in both rows and identify a picture that contains both properties. In this example, "truck-ness" is the property common to the horizontal row, "red-ness" the common property of the vertical row. Hence, the choice of a red truck from among the separate group of pictures would meet this criterion. Abstracting ability, memory, and a concept of simultaneous membership are all requisite for success (Lavatelli, 1970).

The classification activities series culminates in experience with permutation problems, that is, making all possible combinations of a given number of elements. Such arrangements in the abstract are basic to a formal study of algebra, but at the early childhood level, of course, the experience is based upon concrete manipulations. An example would include the discovery by a child that a doll whose wardrobe consists of two blouses in green and white and two miniskirts in green and white actually has four combinations of outfits. The point is not that a child derive a law or formula for the combination of elements in a set. It is rather that he perform actions upon real objects which constitute the groundwork for the later development of mental structures.

The sequence described above has not, to this writer's knowledge, been tested longitudinally to verify the long-range vertical transfer effects its devisor believes possible. It is basically consistent with Piagetian thought on the evolution of skills and logical structure, although Lavatelli has also drawn upon the work of Bruner (1964) to formulate her position. Suggested training activities in these skill areas combined with a variety of similarly oriented informal play experiences assumedly would assist children to become more capable logical thinkers than they otherwise would be. Kamii's (1969) and Lavatelli's (1970) work on number acquisition and classification structure, respectively, together illustrate developmentally-based teaching strategies and a curriculum sequence considered by authorities as basic Piagetian contributions (for example, Ginsburg and Opper, 1969; Sigel, 1969). Perhaps the most paradoxical feature of strategies such as those outlined above is inherent in the theory from which they have been derived. As Mermelstein and Meyer (1969) have noted, a deliberate ordering of experiences may be subject to the law of diminishing returns. Piaget's child constructs his own reality; he will not necessarily assimilate material in an order presented to him, even if it is logical. Nor will he necessarily assimilate all of what is presented. The procedures outlined above, however, clearly would provide children with a concrete, sensory-motor base for thinking operations.

To conclude, a Piaget-derived curriculum differs from most other cognitively-oriented curricula on at least four counts (Kamii, 1968). First, Piagetian theory provides a comprehensive structural organization for major knowledge areas: physical (feedback from objects), social (feedback from people), and logical (the internal consistency of an individual child's logical system). This analysis further leads to a separation of content variables (such as, food, glassware, musical toys) from process variables (such as, classification and seriation). Second, a curriculum so based assumes intelligence as a process (versus a stacking of facts) and therefore employs varied content to refine the cognitive structures of children at successive developmental stages. Third, it permits a matching of curricular activities to preoperational and transitional children who are in cognition qualitatively different from the adult. And fourth, it separates representation from the three basic dimensions of knowledge. It is argued that while representation may be a necessary condition for knowledge, it is not sufficient. For example, one may teach a child words such as *green, round, more, small,* and *eight* but cannot be assured that the child's ability to use these words logically will be positively affected; sensory-motor action concepts must come first.

With emphasis upon (1) procedures for the discovery of reality, (2) the integration of familiar social concepts, (3) a building of tasks according to individual learning style (for example, a child's initial preference for grouping objects) rather than imposing one "unnatural" to him, (4) the logical structure of number, (5) the sequential structuring of spatial concepts, (6) temporal reasoning, and (7) sociodramatic play to develop symbolic representation, a Piaget-based curriculum is seen by many cognitive psychologists to be the most developmentally-relevant procedural system for maximizing cognitive potential. The continued concentration of program activities upon building logical structures by strengthening the processes which underlie them seems quite consistent with data culled from training research. This further buttresses the sequential approach.

A final noteworthy feature of a Piaget-derived curriculum is a two-dimensional evaluative strategy: formative and summative. (Variations on this theme are seen elsewhere, as in Stern, 1969, and behavior analysis procedures). Formative evaluation is a process of continual, ongoing assessment and, in the Piagetian sense, would rest heavily upon procedures subsumed under the *methode clinique*. In contrast, summative evaluation is terminal assessment at the end of a given unit of time or instruction. Formative evaluation serves a particularly useful purpose in approaches which attempt to individualize instruction and to continually check procedural validity and pupil progress; it is a natural outgrowth of the belief that educational methods are most effective if consistent with the thought patterns indigenous to a given stage of cognitive development. Without formative evaluation, this attunement would be unlikely, especially where individual differences in developmental rate are manifest.

CRITIQUE

No one can deny that Piaget has contributed significantly to the study of child development. Accolades are plentiful. A 1963 Merrill-Palmer Institute Symposium and recent collection of essays (Elkind and Flavell, 1969) are representative of tributes, including the uniqueness of Piaget's research strategy, the vast number of empirical questions which have been given birth by the theory, his articulated views on the propellant value of "intrinsic" motivation,[21] and his system as a source of intellectual ferment. Such ferment is positive in terms of producing new cognitive wine in new conceptual bottles. Nor have Piaget's contributions been limited to straight cognition. Studies of children's moral judgmental capabilities have been stimulated in novel ways by the Geneva school (Berkowitz, 1964).

Criticism also abounds, however, a preview of which has been at-

---

[21] It should be noted here that Piaget has by no means cornered the market on intrinsic motivation. American psychologists have developed independent views of motivation not far afield from equilibration theory.

tempted in the earlier research review. On a specific theoretical level, reasoned critical treatises, most of which address contradictions within Piaget's system, have appeared on play (Sutton-Smith, 1966), motor development (Ausubel, 1966), and psycho-logic (McLaughlin, 1963). The hypothetical structures nurtured by Piaget represent a complex maze of inferences that may never be mastered sufficiently through empirical study. Compound problems in research methodology and divergent interpretations which are made of the same data cloud and occasionally chill the enthusiasm of students.

The interplay which has transpired among Piaget, his followers, and his critics frequently takes on the character of a semantic game whereby those who challenge Piagetianism may be accused of not knowing what Piaget really means by a given term. Yet one wonders occasionally if Piaget himself knows what he means. In defense of Piaget, Flavell (1963) attributes the discrepant experimental results reported periodically in the literature to be, in part, a function of the attitude and depth of understanding a researcher may have with regard to Piaget's theory. But Piaget has altered his views from time to time. This, plus the difficulties inherent in translating a special psychological vocabulary from French to English, perhaps accounts for a portion of the problem.[22]

Several other points of criticism can be identified. For example, not much attention has been paid to individual differences apart from associating Piaget task-performance variation with variations in measured intelligence and emotional stability. Piagetians have not been noticeably receptive to the possibility that the phenomena studied by them may be subject to explanations more parsimonious than those couched in the latticework of the theory (for example, Ausubel, 1965; Farnham-Diggory and Bermon, 1968). Very little systematic study has yet been devoted to the effect of "natural" reinforcement on children's cognitive behavior. Dissatisfaction exists with Piaget's views on thinking, language, and symbol formation (Ausubel, 1968) and double classification behavior (Jahoda, 1964), to mention two additional specific sore points. And Sigel and Hooper (1968) believe that Piaget's conviction about the hierarchical and integrative nature of thought development must be held in abeyance as it lacks definitive empirical support. Finally, the reader interested in serious conceptual digging may wish to apply his thinking tools to the issues provoked by the Geneva-Harvard controversy (Inhelder and others, 1966).

Neither is full agreement apparent as to the educational implications

---

[22] Elkind (1969) suggests that one primary difficulty has been maintained by Piaget's own turgid writing style.

of Piaget. Lavatelli (1968), for example, very stoutly points out that perceptual training would not be stressed in a Piagetian preschool curriculum. This notion may be supported, in part, by the failure of perceptual training (Montessori cylinder block training) to enhance the conservation skills of kindergarten children (Ball and Campbell, 1970). Phillips (1969), however, sees perceptual-motor training techniques as quite basic to weld the relationship between sensory-motor constructions and intellectual performance. In addition, Elkind (1967) sees Piaget-derived perceptual training as basic to the process of learning to read. And, while Engelmann (1967) believes that Piaget has provided little of use to educators (save a specification of certain skills that children are not normally taught), Sigel (1969) believes that any educational innovator would be negligent not to examine in depth the relationships of Piaget's "model" to education.

Among the most thorough of recent Piagetian critiques are those of Sullivan (1967,1968). Sullivan has rated Piaget a solid hit on at least two counts: the potential of Piaget's stage observations for developing tools to assess intellectual capacity and the value of Piaget's probing techniques to assess learning outcomes in a developmental curriculum. For Piaget, correct answers are subsidiary to the means by which a child arrives at an answer; a child's level of understanding is the important variable. Teachers, above all, must appreciate that pat solutions given by children may be "correct," but provide no guarantee that the true basis of a problem is understood.

Sullivan's favorable impressions with regard to Piaget-derived evaluation techniques are supported elsewhere (Skager and Broadbent, 1968). Consider the following:

> [There are] at least two significant advantages in using measures derived from developmental theory. First, as criteria the measures would have great generality. The skills measured ought to be consistent with the long-term goals of many different approaches to instruction. Second, theoretically based measures would be less likely to be perceived as biased toward a particular ideology about curriculum content. [Skager and Broadbent, 1968, p. 6]

These authorities, however, are careful to point out that Piagetian theory (and thus Piagetian measures) may not be applicable to every variety of educational program. Skager and Broadbent believe that an instructional program must be oriented toward the development of cognitive skills if Piagetian theory (and measures) are to be relevant.

Returning once again to the Sullivan (1967, 1968) critiques, we find skepticism concerning the assistance that Piaget's stage theory can provide for the structuring and sequencing of curriculum content and activities. By this Sullivan means that Piaget's epistemology and developmental model have too frequently been accepted uncritically, particularly with reference to Piagetian stages as a definition of educational readiness. In Sullivan's view, a Piagetian concept of readiness is very narrow and has little value for educators. Several facets of Piagetian theory may be combined to demonstrate this narrowness. The first is Piaget's conviction that a gradual accumulation of general age-related daily life experience is necessary for development. There can be no substitute for this; thought structures therefore cannot be taught. Second, while cognitive development accrues through a child's daily activity, language is of relatively little importance in terms of logical thought operations. A teacher therefore will be wasting her time, Piagetians maintain, by attempting to "explain" Piagetian problems to a child. In short, if a child at a given age is unable to demonstrate mastery of an operation, it cannot be taught. Thus a teacher must wait until a child is able to demonstrate mastery, but then, of course, the operation no longer needs to be taught. This impasse is characteristic of stage-dependent theory in general, namely, that somehow time and general experience will "take care of development."

Protagonists for the Piagetian viewpoint would likely counter the above criticism by arguing that although operations per se cannot be taught, prerequisite skills can (for example, Churchill, 1961). Further, they would maintain that, given appropriate chunks of general experience, children will develop insight in due time. If so, the major reason for school, at least in terms of cultivating cognitive structures, would be to provide better general age-related experience than a child could get in his natural environment. This is not a particularly optimistic view and leaves educators with the further problem of defining general age-related experience in terms compatible with Piaget. The reader has earlier been presented with examples of how this problem might be solved and how prerequisite skill development is programmed.

The above counterargument may itself be subject to the challenge that a curriculum planned deliberately to present sensory and conceptual data to a child is virtually antithetical to Piaget's entire framework. Recall that, for Piaget, cognitive development is a matter of continuous interaction with an environment that allows a child to pick and choose, thereby regulating his own adaptational process. Taken to the extreme, this would imply that the child must construct his own reality and will define automatically his own sequence for learning. If one accepts this developmental tenet, then direct teaching, apart from training for social convention, has no legitimate place at all in the world of Piaget's child.

A further criticism of those who have taken Piagetian theory as a basis for educational planning concerns the capacity of the theory to prescribe an atmosphere for learning (discovery-exploratory activity in a permissive, tension-free environment). Sullivan (1967), for example, feels any such prescription is based on "pure extrapolation" from the least authenticated part of the theory: equilibration. Sullivan extends his criticism to suggest that much of Piaget's current popularity is due to a congruity between the theory and the current discovery learning "mystique" which pervades American education.[23] That is, instead of seeking a rationale from Piagetian theory for the guidance of educational activities, the theory is being used as a justification for practices presently in vogue among social and educational theorists.[24]

In contrast, Duckworth (1964) believes that the necessity for a child to do his own learning, to manipulate, question, compare, and reconcile discrepant events—all based upon the equilibration concept—is perhaps *the* commanding message from Piaget to educators. This message is by no means new, however, for it was central to the writings of John Dewey over thirty years ago. Regardless, the notion that concrete-manipulatory activity is a necessary prerequisite to concept learning (for example, conservation of weight) has not been proven. In fact, it has been challenged decisively (Murray, 1969).

The ambivalence of many American psychologists toward Piagetian theory as a source of educational implications is aptly summarized by Cohen (1966). Piaget's "preoccupation" with cognition and the current inadequacy of his theory to account for the socio-emotional life of the child, much less the influence of anxiety on adaptation, troubles Cohen.[25] She also believes that, apart from the emphasis upon novelty and variety in a learning environment, Piaget actually has little to say to educators about motivation. This view is echoed by Bruner (1959) who feels that Piagetian theory fails to account specifically for the diverse goals toward which children and adolescents strive. It must be noted, however, that no psychological theory has proved capable of explaining completely and unambiguously human development and learning. Nor

[23] The reader is encouraged to consult Bruner (1961) and Ausubel (1961) for alternative views on this purported mystique.

[24] A more general concept involved here is basic to a recent discussion of educational change (Skager and Broadbent, 1968). It is contended that decisions regarding changes in curriculum and instruction are more likely to be influenced by philosophical arguments and "professional salesmanship" than by what research workers would consider "hard empirical evidence."

[25] Piaget's alleged "preoccupation" with cognition is deceiving. He clearly maintains that affect and intelligence cannot be disassociated. Rather, he believes that these two phenomena are complementary for all of human behavior (Piaget, 1967b). It is true, however, that Piaget emphasizes the influence of cognitive development on affectivity instead of the reverse (Shantz, 1969).

has such theorizing led to the solution of our major educational problems, many of which revolve around children's attentional and motivational processes.

Finally, in rebuttal to Cohen (1966), it should be noted that fully developed educational strategies based upon Piagetian theory actually do *not* neglect socio-emotional objectives. For example, systematic attention has been paid to such affective dimensions as intrinsic motivation, curiosity, self-confidence, creativity, self-control, and interpersonal relationships (Kamii, 1970). All of these affective components of behavior are consistent with the Piagetian viewpoint, even though the pivotal concepts of the Geneva group are cognitive in nature. In reality, cognitive and socio-emotional behaviors are inseparable, and this is nowhere more clearly indicated than in Piagetian theory.

SUMMARY

Jean Piaget's genetic approach to thought development represents one of the most thoroughly articulated and influential theories in contemporary psychology. According to this theory, the human organism strives toward higher and higher levels of cognitive integration as physical reality is confronted and adapted to. Adaptation is sequential and invariant, and four successive levels or developmental stages comprise this sequence. The first—the sensory-motor stage—encompasses roughly the first two years of life, during which the infant learns to coordinate sensory inputs, develops the concept of object permanence, and achieves a gross level of intentional goal-directed activity. The preoperational stage then supersedes and represents an extended period of transition of higher-level cognitive functioning. During this second period the child's thought is strongly dominated by absolute perceptions; his principal cognitive task is mastery of the symbol.

Around the age of seven the third, or concrete-operational stage of development is attained. Thinking during this stage is still stimulus-bound but takes on logical properties such as reversibility, transitivity, multiple classification, associativity, and the conservation concept. Thus, the mastery of classes, relations, and quantities defines the basic cognitive tasks of the school-age child (Elkind, 1967b).

Another transition in thought occurs between the ages of ten and twelve, a transition which terminates in formal operational thought. This fourth stage is marked by the ability to think reflectively and perform hypothetico-deductive operations.

Taken together, these successively complex stages, which involve hierarchies of cognitive structures, are utilized by Piaget to describe how particular contents of behavior are produced at particular ages. Piaget's primary interest has been in the quality (kind) of cognitive operation that culminates in action, not whether an action is necessarily "successful" for a child in terms of adult criteria. Thus, Piaget's views are among those most explicit with regard to the distinction between product and psychological process. An astonishing amount of space in the child development research literature is now being consumed by Piaget-inspired studies. General support has accumulated for the concept of sequential growth; however, many details of the theory remain to be examined thoroughly. While many types of Piagetian studies have been executed, those concerned with the effects of training and schooling are usually of greatest interest to educators. Through such research have been identified a number of specific variables for educators to account for in the design of learning environments to facilitate cognitive growth. Unfortunately, research on the possible long-term advantages of a Piaget-based education for young children is not available at this time.

Several unresolved issues exist with respect to precise curriculum building from the Piagetian blueprint, although valuable cues can be taken from this blueprint for such purposes as the specification of educational objectives and the assessment of children's cognitive development. The blueprint further demands the careful attention of educators to active, discovery-oriented learning experiences which prepare the child for logical, causal thinking. In general, however, a Piaget-based approach to early education does not provide much support to those who would seek to accelerate children's intellectual development or provide curative experiences for children whose development is retarded (Kohlberg, 1968).

Despite many unknowns, enthusiastic support is growing for the Piaget-based curriculum as a generally superior orientation for early education. Enthusiasts stress at least three dimensions of curriculum planning. These include the use of the sequence of developmental acquisition to guide the content and timing of educational material, a preference for self-directed exploratory learning over didactic techniques, and an emphasis upon social interaction within the peer group for the enhancement of qualitative cognitive growth (Hooper, 1970).

References

Achenbach, Thomas M. "Conservation of Illusion—Distorted Identity: Its Relation to MA and CA in Normals and Retardates." *Child Development,* 1969a, 40, 663–680.

Achenbach, Thomas M. "Conservation Below Age Three: Fact or Artifact?" Proceedings of the 77th Annual Convention, American Psychological Association, 1969b, 275–276.

Altemeyer, Robert A., Daniel Fulton, and Kent M. Berney. "Long-Term Memory Improvement: Confirmation of a Finding by Piaget." *Child Development,* 1969, 40, 845–858.

Ammon, Paul R. "Logical Thinking in Children: Research Based on Piaget's Theory." (A Review), *American Educational Research Journal,* 1969, 6, 293–295.

Ausubel, David P. "Learning by Discovery: Rationale and Mystique." *Bulletin of the National Association of Secondary School Principals,* 1961, 45, 18–58.

Ausubel, David P. "Neobehaviorism and Piaget's Views on Thought and Symbolic Functioning." *Child Development,* 1965, 36, 1029–1033.

Ausubel, David P. "A Critique of Piaget's Theory of the Ontogenesis of Motor Behavior." *Journal of Genetic Psychology,* 1966, 109, 119–122.

Ausubel, David P. "Symbolization and Symbolic Thought: Response to Furth." *Child Development,* 1968, 39, 997–1001.

Baldwin, Alfred. *Theories of Child Development.* New York: Wiley, 1967.

Ball, Thomas S., and Mary L. Campbell. "Effect of Montessori's Cylinder Block Training on the Acquisition of Conservation." *Developmental Psychology,* 1970, 2, 156.

Bearison, David J. "Role of Measurement Operations in the Acquisition of Conservation." *Developmental Psychology,* 1969, 1, 653–660.

Beilen, Harry. "Learning and Operational Convergence in Logical Thought Development." *Journal of Experimental Child Psychology,* 1965, 2, 317–329.

Beilen, Harry, and J. C. Franklin. "Logical Operations in Area and Length Measurement: Age and Training Effects." *Child Development,* 1962, 33, 607–618.

Beilen, Harry, and Jacob Kagan. "Pluralization Rules and the Conceptualization of Number." *Developmental Psychology,* 1969, 1, 697–706.

Beilen, Harry, Jerome Kagan, and Rhea Rabinowitz. "Effects of Verbal and Perceptual Training on Water Level Representation." *Child Development,* 1966, 37, 317–329.

Berger, Ellen T., and others. "The Development of Causal Thinking in Children with Severe Psychogenic Learning Inhibitions." *Child Development,* 1969, 40, 503–516.

Berkowitz, Leonard. *The Development of Motives and Values in the Child.* New York: Basic Books, 1964.

Braine, M. D. S. "The Ontogeny of Certain Logical Operations: Piaget's Formulation Examined by Nonverbal Methods." *Psychological Monographs* 1959, 73, No. 5.

Braine, M. D. S., and B. L. Shanks. "The Development of Conservation of Size." *Journal of Verbal Learning and Verbal Behavior,* 1965, 4, 227–242.

Breznitz, Shlomo, and Sol Kugelmass. "Intentionality in Moral Judgment: Developmental Stages." *Child Development,* 1967, 38, 469–479.

Brison, D. W. "Acceleration of Conservation of Substance." *Journal of Genetic Psychology,* 1966, 109, 311–312.

Brison, D. W., and E. V. Sullivan (Eds.). *Recent Research on the Acquisition of Conservation of Substance.* Educational Research Series (No. 26). Toronto: The Ontario Institute for Studies in Education, 1967.

Bruner, Jerome S. "Inhelder's and Piaget's *The Growth of Logical Thinking:* A Psychologist's Viewpoint." *British Journal of Educational Psychology,* 1959, 50, 363–370.

Bruner, Jerome S. "The Act of Discovery." *Harvard Educational Review,* 1961, 31, 124–135.

Bruner, Jerome S. "The Course of Cognitive Growth." *American Psychologist,* 1964, 19, 1–15.

Bruner, Jerome S., and others. *Studies in Cognitive Growth.* New York: Wiley, 1966.

Case, D., and J. M. Collinson. "The Development of Formal Thinking in Verbal Comprehension." *British Journal of Educational Psychology,* 1962, 32, 103–111.

Cattell, Raymond B. "Theory of Fluid and Crystallized Intelligence: A Critical Experiment." *Journal of Educational Psychology,* 1963, 54, 1–22.

Churchill, E. M. *Piaget's Findings and the Teacher.* London: National Froebel Foundation, 1961.

Cohen, Shirley. "The Problem with Piaget's Child." *Teachers College Record,* 1966, 68, 211–218.

Coon, Robert C., and Richard D. Odom. "Transitivity and Length Judgments as a Function of Age and Social Influence." *Child Development,* 1968, 39, 1133–1144.

Davies, Carolyn M. "Development of the Probability Concept in Children." *Child Development,* 1965, 36, 779–788.

Davol, Stephen H., Edward Chittendon, Marjorie L. Plante, and Jane A. Tuzik. "Conservation of Continuous Quantity Investigated as a Scaleable Development Concept." *Merrill-Palmer Quarterly,* 1967, 13, 191–199.

Decarie, T. T. *Intelligence and Affectivity in Early Childhood.* New York: International Universities, 1965.

DeVries, Rheta. "Constancy of Generic Identity in the Years Three to Six." *Monographs of the Society for Research in Child Development,* 1969, 34, Serial No. 127.

D'Mello, Sydney, and Eleanor Willemson. "The Development of the Number Concept: A Scalogram Analysis." *Child Development,* 1969, 40, 681–688.

Dodwell, P. C. "Children's Understanding of Number Concepts: Characteristics of an Individual and of a Group Test." *Canadian Journal of Psychology,* 1961, 15, 29–36.

Dodwell, P. C. "Relation between the Understanding of the Logic of Classes and of Cardinal Number in Children." *Canadian Journal of Psychology,* 1962, 16, 152–160.

Dodwell, P. C. "Children's Understanding of Spatial Concepts." *Canadian Journal of Psychology,* 1963, 17, 141–161.

Duckworth, Eleanor. "Piaget Rediscovered." *Journal of Research in Science Teaching,* 1964, 2, 172–175.

Dudek, S. Z., and others. "Relationship of Piaget Measures to Standard Intelligence and Motor Scales." *Perceptual and Motor Skills,* 1969, 28, 351–362.

Elkind, David. "Children's Discovery of the Conservation of Mass, Weight, and Volume: Piaget Replication Study II." *Journal of Genetic Psychology,* 1961, 98, 219–227.

Elkind, David. "Discrimination, Seriation, and Numeration of Size and Dimensional Differences in Young Children: Piaget Replication Study VI." *Journal of Genetic Psychology,* 1964, 104, 275–296.

Elkind, David. "Conceptual Orientation Shifts in Children and Adolescents." *Child Development,* 1966, 37, 493–498.

Elkind, David. "Piaget's Conversation Problem." *Child Development,* 1967a, 38, 15–28.

Elkind, David. "Egocentrism in Adolescence." *Child Development,* 1967b, 38, 1025–1034.

Elkind, David. "Piaget's Theory of Perceptual Development: Its Application to Reading and Special Education." *Journal of Special Education,* 1967c, 1, 357–361.

Elkind, David. "Piagetian and Psychometric Conceptions of Intelligence." *Harvard Educational Review,* 1969, 39, 319–337.

Elkind, David, and Jo Ann Deblinger. "Perceptual Training and Reading Achievement in Disadvantaged Children." *Child Development,* 1969, 40, 11–20.

Elkind, David, and John H. Flavell (Eds.). *Studies in Cognitive Development.* New York: Oxford, 1969.

Elkind, David, R. Koegler, and E. Go. "Studies in Perceptual Development: II. Part-Whole Perception." *Child Development,* 1964, 35, 81–90.

Elkind, David, M. Larson, and W. Van Doorninck. "Perceptual Decentration Learning and Performance in Slow and Average Readers." *Journal of Educational Psychology,* 1965, 56, 50–56.

Elkind, David, and L. Scott. "Studies in Perceptual Development I: The Decentering of Perception." *Child Development,* 1962, 33, 619–630.

Elkind, David, William Van Doorninck, and Cynthia Schwarz. "Perceptual Activity and Concept Attainment." *Child Development,* 1967, 38, 1153–1161.

Elkind, David, and Jutta Weiss. "Studies in Perceptual Development III: Perceptual Exploration." *Child Development,* 1967, 38, 553–561.

Engelmann, Siegfried. "Teaching Formal Operations to Preschool Children." Unpublished manuscript, University of Illinois, 1966.

Engelmann, Siegfried. "Cognitive Structure Related to the Principle of Conservation." In D. W. Brison and E. V. Sullivan (Eds.), *Recent Research on the Acquisition of Conservation of Substance.* Toronto: Ontario Institute for Studies in Education, 1967, 53–72.

Farnham-Diggory, Sylvia, and Maurice Bermon. "Verbal Compensation, Cognitive Synthesis, and Conservation." *Merrill-Palmer Quarterly,* 1968, 14, 215–227.

Feigenbaum, K. D., and H. Sulkin. "Piaget's Problem of Conservation of Discontinuous Quantities: A Teaching Experience." *Journal of Genetic Psychology,* 1964, 105, 91–97.

Festinger, Leon. *A Theory of Cognitive Dissonance.* Evanston, Ill.: Row, Peterson & Company, 1957.

Flavell, John H. "Piaget's Contributions to the Study of Cognitive Development." *Merrill-Palmer Quarterly,* 1963a, 9, 245–252.

Flavell, John H. *The Developmental Psychology of Jean Piaget.* Princeton: Van Nostrand, 1963b.

Flavell, John H., and John P. Hill. "Developmental Psychology." *Annual Review of Psychology.* Palo Alto, Calif.: Annual Reviews, Inc., 1969, 1–56.

Freyberg, P. S. "Concept Development in Piagetian Terms in Relation to School Attainment." *Journal of Educational Psychology,* 1966, 57, 164–168.

Furth, Hans G. "Concerning Piaget's View on Thinking and Symbol Formation." *Child Development,* 1967, 38, 819–826.

Furth, Hans G. *Piaget and Knowledge.* Englewood Cliffs: Prentice-Hall, 1969.

Gagné, Robert. *The Conditions of Learning.* New York: Holt, Rinehart and Winston, 1965.

Gelman, Rochel. "Conservation Acquisition: A Problem of Learning to Attend to Relevant Attributes." *Journal of Experimental Child Psychology,* 1969, 7, 167–187.

Ginsburg, Herbert G. "Children's Estimates of Proportions." *Child Development,* 1967, 38, 205–212.

Ginsburg, Herbert, and Sylvia Opper. *Piaget's Theory of Intellectual Development.* Englewood Cliffs: Prentice-Hall, 1969.

Ginsburg, Herbert, and A. Rapoport. "Children's Estimates of Proportions." *Child Development,* 1967, 38, 205–212.

Goldberg, Susan. "Probability Judgments by Preschool Children: Task Conditions and Performance." *Child Development,* 1966, 37, 157–167.

Goldschmid, Marcel L. "Different Types of Conservation and Nonconservation and Their Relation to Age, Sex, I.Q., MA, and Vocabulary." *Child Development,* 1967, 38, 1229–1246.

Goldschmid, Marcel L., and P. M. Bentler. "The Dimensions and Measurement of Conservation." *Child Development,* 1968, 39, 787–802.

Goodnow, J., and G. Bethon. "Piaget's Tasks: The Effects of Schooling and Intelligence." *Child Development,* 1966, 37, 573–582.

Gottfried, Nathan W. "The Relationship between Concepts of Conservation of Length and Number." *Journal of Genetic Psychology,* 1969, 114, 85–91.

Griffiths, Judith A., Carolyn Shantz, and Irving Sigel. "A Methodological Problem in Conservation Studies: The Use of Relational Terms." *Child Development,* 1967, 38, 841–848.

Gruen, Gerald E. "Experiences Affecting the Development of Number Conservation in Children." *Child Development,* 1965, 36, 963–979.

Gruen, Gerald E. "Note on Conservation: Methodological and Definitional Considerations." *Child Development,* 1966, 37, 977–983.

Gyr, J. W., J. S. Brown, and A. C. Cafagna. "Quasi-formal Models of Inductive

Behavior and Their Relation to Piaget's Theory of Cognitive Stages." *Psychological Review,* 1967, 74, 272–289.

Gyr, J. W., and C. Fleisher. "Computer-assisted Studies of Piaget's Three Stage Model of Cognitive Development." *Psychological Reports,* 1967, 20, 165–166.

Halasa, Ofelia. "A Developmental Study of Number Conservation Attainment among Disadvantaged Children." Paper read at American Educational Research Association Meeting, Los Angeles, 1969.

Hall, Vernon C., and Gwendolyn J. Simpson. "Factors Influencing Extinction of Weight Conservation." *Merrill-Palmer Quarterly,* 1968, 14, 197–210.

Halpern, Esther. "The Effects of Incompatibility between Perception and Logic in Piaget's Stage of Concrete Operations." *Child Development,* 1965, 36, 491–497.

Hood, H. B. "An Experimental Study of Piaget's Theory of the Development of Number in Children." *British Journal of Psychology,* 1962, 53, 272–289.

Hooper, Frank. "An Evaluation of Logical Operations Instruction in the Preschool." Paper presented at a conference entitled "Conceptualizations of Preschool Curricula," City University of New York, 1970 (May 22–24).

Horn, John L. "Organization of Abilities and the Development of Intelligence." *Psychological Review,* 1968, 75, 242–259.

Huey, J. Frances. "Learning Potential of the Young Child." *Educational Leadership,* 1965, 23.

Hunt, J. McV. *Intelligence and Experience.* New York: Ronald, 1961.

Hunt, J. McVicker. "Piaget's System as a Source of Hypotheses Concerning Motivation." *Merrill-Palmer Quarterly,* 1963, 9, 263–275.

Inhelder, Barbel, Magali Bovet, Hermine Sinclair, and C. D. Smock. "On Cognitive Development." *American Psychologist,* 1966, 21, 160–164.

Inhelder, Barbel, and Jean Piaget. *The Early Growth of Logic in the Child: Classification and Seriation.* New York: Harper and Row, 1964.

Jacobs, Paul I., and Mary Vandeventer. "The Learning, Transfer, and Retention of Double Classification Skills by First-graders." Paper read at American Educational Research Association Meeting, Los Angeles, 1969.

Jahoda, G. "Children's Concepts of Nationality: A Critical Study of Piaget's Stages." *Child Development,* 1964, 35, 1081–1092.

Kagan, Jerome, and Henker, Barbara A. "Developmental Psychology." *Annual Review of Psychology,* 1966, 1–50.

Kamii, Constance K. "Evaluating Pupil Learning in Preschool Education: Socio-Emotional, Perceptual-Motor, and Cognitive Objectives." Ypsilanti, Mich.: Ypsilanti Early Education Program, 1968.

Kamii, Constance. K. "Preparing Preschool Children for the Acquisition of Elementary Number Concepts." In *Proceedings of the New England Kindergarten Conference,* Lesley College, 1969.

Kamii, Constance K. "An Application of Piaget's Theory to the Conceptualization of a Preschool Curriculum." Paper presented at a conference entitled "Conceptualizations of Preschool Curricula," City University of New York, 1970 (May 22–24).

Kamii, Constance K., and Norma L. Radin. "A Framework for a Preschool

Curriculum Based upon Piaget's Theory." *Journal of Creative Behavior,* 1967, 1, 314–324.

Kephart, Newell C. *The Slow Learner in the Classroom.* Columbus: Merrill, 1960.

Kessen, William, and C. Kuhlman (Eds.). "Thought in the Young Child." *Monographs of the Society for Research in Child Development,* 1962, 27, 176 pp.

Kingsley, Richard C., and Vernon C. Hall. "Training Conservation through the Use of Learning Sets." *Child Development,* 1967, 38, 1111–1126.

Kofsky, Ellin. "A Scalogram Study of Classificatory Development." *Child Development,* 1966, 37, 191–204.

Kofsky, Ellin, and Sonia F. Osler. "Free Classification in Children." *Child Development,* 1967, 38, 927–937.

Kohlberg, Lawrence, Judy Yaeger, and Else Hjertholm. "Private Speech: Four Studies and a Review of Theories." *Child Development,* 1968, 39, 691–736.

Kohnstamm, G. A. "An Evaluation of Part of Piaget's Theory." *Acta Psychologica,* 1963, 21, 313–315.

Kohnstamm, G. A. *Teaching Children to Solve a Piagetian Problem of Class Inclusion.* Uitegevess, Netherlands: Mouton, 1967.

Langer, Jonas. *Theories of Development.* New York: Holt, Rinehart and Winston, 1969.

Laurendeau, M., and A. Pinard. *Causal Thinking in the Child.* New York: International Universities, 1962.

Lavatelli, Celia Stendler. *Early Childhood Curriculum: A Piaget Program.* Boston: American Science and Engineering, 1970.

Lavatelli, Celia Stendler. "A Piaget-derived Model for Compensatory Preschool Education." In Joe L. Frost (Ed.), *Early Childhood Education Rediscovered.* New York: Holt, Rinehart, and Winston, 1968, 530–544.

Lavatelli, Celia Stendler. "An Approach to Language Learning." *Young Children,* 1969, 24, 368–376.

Looft, William, and Don C. Charles. "Modification of the Life Concept in Children." *Developmental Psychology,* 1969, 1, 445–446.

McLaughlin, G. H. "Psycho-logic: A Possible Alternative to Piaget's Formulation." *British Journal of Educational Psychology,* 1963, 33, 61–67.

McManis, Donald L. "Comparisons of Gross, Intensive, and Extensive Quantities by Normals and Retardates." *Child Development,* 1969, 40, 237–254.

Maier, Henry W. *Three Theories of Child Development.* New York: Harper and Row, 1965.

Mermelstein, Egon, and Edwina Meyer. "Conservation Training Techniques and Their Effects on Different Populations." *Child Development,* 1969, 40, 471–490.

Mermelstein, Egon, and Lee Shulman. "Lack of Formal Schooling and the Acquisition of Conservation." *Child Development,* 1967, 38, 39–52.

Merrill-Palmer Institute Symposium. "Contributions of Piaget to Developmental Psychology." *Merrill-Palmer Quarterly,* 1963, 9, 243–285.

Murray, Frank B. "Cognitive Conflict and Reversibility Training in the Acquisition of Length Conservation." *Journal of Educational Psychology,* 1968, 59, 82–87.

Murray, Frank B. "Stimulus Abstractness and the Conservation of Weight." Proceedings of the 77th Annual Convention, American Psychological Association, 1969, 627–628.

Murray, John P., and James Youniss. "Achievement of Inferential Transitivity and Its Relation to Serial Ordering." *Child Development,* 1968, 39, 1259–1268.

Neale, John M. "Egocentrism in Institutionalized and Noninstitutionalized Children." *Child Development,* 1966, 37, 97–101.

Nunmedal, Susan G., and Frank B. Murray. "Semantic Factors in Conservation of Weight." Paper read at American Educational Research Association Meeting, Los Angeles, 1969.

O'Brien, Thomas C., and Bernard J. Shapiro. "The Development of Logical Thinking in Children." *American Educational Research Journal,* 1968, 5, 531–542.

O'Bryan, K. G., and R. S. MacArthur. "Reversibility, Intelligence, and Creativity in Nine-year-old Boys." *Child Development,* 1969, 40, 33–45.

Ojemann, R. H., and K. Pritchett. "Piaget and the Role of Guided Experiences in Human Development." *Perceptual-Motor Skills,* 1963, 17, 927–940.

Peel, E. A. "Learning and Thinking in the School Situation." In R. E. Ripple and V. N. Rockcastle (Eds.), *Piaget Rediscovered: A Report of the Conference on Cognitive Studies and Curriculum Development.* Ithaca: Cornell University School of Education, 1964.

Phillips, John L., Jr. *The Origins of Intellect: Piaget's Theory.* San Francisco: Freeman, 1969.

Piaget, Jean. *The Moral Judgment of the Child.* New York: Harcourt, 1932.

Piaget, Jean. *Play, Dreams, and Imitation in Childhood.* New York: Norton, 1951.

Piaget, Jean. *The Child's Conception of Numbers.* New York: Humanities Press, 1952a.

Piaget, Jean. *The Origins of Intelligence in Children.* New York: International Universities, 1952b.

Piaget, Jean, and Barbel Inhelder. *The Child's Conception of Space.* London: Routledge, 1956.

Piaget, Jean, Barbel Inhelder, and Alina Szeminska. *The Child's Conception of Geometry.* New York: Basic Books, 1960.

Piaget, Jean. *On the Development of Memory and Identity.* Worcester, Massachusetts: Clark University Press, 1967a, 42 pp.

Piaget, Jean. *Six Psychological Studies.* New York: Random House, 1967b.

Picard, A. J. "Piaget's Theory of Development with Implications for Teaching Elementary School Mathematics." *School Science and Mathematics,* 1969, 69, 287–296.

Pratoomraj, Sarvat, and Ronald C. Johnson. "Kinds of Questions and Types of Conservation Tasks as Related to Children's Conservation Responses." *Child Development,* 1966, 37, 343–354.

Ragan, William B., and Celia B. Stendler. *Modern Elementary Curriculum.* New York: Holt, Rinehart, and Winston, 1966.

Ripple, R. E., and V. N. Rockcastle (Eds.). *Piaget Rediscovered: A Report of the*

Conference on Cognitive Studies and Curriculum Development. Ithaca: Cornell University School of Education, 1964.

Roemischer, Miriam D. "A Structural Analysis of Selected Aspects of Jean Piaget's Theory of Cognitive Development." *Educational Horizons,* 1969, 47, 127–136.

Rothenberg, Barbara B. "Conservation of Number among Four- and Five-year-old Children: Some Methodological Considerations." *Child Development,* 1969, 40, 383–406.

Rothenberg, Barbara B., and Rosalea G. Courtney. "Conservation of Number in Very Young Children." *Developmental Psychology,* 1969, 5, 543–547.

Rothenberg, Barbara B., and Jean H. Orost. "The Training of Conservation of Number in Young Children." *Child Development,* 1969, 40, 707–726.

Safier, G. A. "A Study in Relationships between the Life and Death Concepts in Children." *Journal of Genetic Psychology,* 1964, 105, 283–294.

Shantz, Carolyn U. "Effects of Redundant and Irrelevant Information on Children's Seriation Ability." *Journal of Experimental Child Psychology,* 1967, 5, 208–222.

Shantz, Carolyn U. "Essays on Equilibrium." *Merrill-Palmer Quarterly,* 1969, 15, 295–304.

Shantz, Carolyn, and Charles Smock. "Development of Distance Conservation and the Spatial Coordinate System." *Child Development,* 1966, 37, 943–948.

Siegelman, Ellen, and Jack Block. "Two Parallel Scalable Sets of Piagetian Tasks." *Child Development,* 1969, 40, 951–956.

Sigel, Irving. "The Attainment of Concepts." In M. L. Hoffman and L. W. Hoffman (Eds.), *Review of Child Development Research,* Vol. I. New York: Russell Sage, 1964, 209–248.

Sigel, Irving E. "The Piagetian System and Education." In David Elkind and John Flavell (Eds.), *Studies in Cognitive Development.* New York: Oxford University Press, 1969, 465–489.

Sigel, Irving, and Frank Hooper. *Logical Thinking in Children.* New York: Holt, Rinehart and Winston, 1968.

Sigel, I. E., A. Roeper, and F. H. Hooper. "A Training Procedure for Acquisition of Piaget's Conservation of Quantity: A Pilot Study and Its Replication." *British Journal of Educational Psychology,* 1966, 36, 301–311.

Sigel, Irving E., Eli Saltz, and William Roskind. "Variables Determining Concept Conservation in Children." *Journal of Experimental Psychology,* 1967, 74, 471–475.

Sinclair-De-Zwart, Hermina. "Developmental Psycholinguistics." In D. Elkind and J. Flavell (Eds.), *Studies in Cognitive Development.* New York: Oxford, 1969, 315–336.

Skager, R. W., and L. A. Broadbent. *Cognitive Structures and Educational Evaluation.* Center for the Study of Evaluation of Instructional Programs. Berkeley: University of California Press, 1968.

Smedslund, Jan. "The Acquisition of Conservation of Substance and Weight in Children, V: Practice in Conflict Situation without Reinforcement." *Scandinavian Journal of Psychology,* 1961, 2, 156–160.

Smedslund, Jan. "Development of Concrete Transitivity of Length in Children." *Child Development,* 1963a, 34, 389–405.

Smedslund, Jan. "The Effect of Observation on Children's Representation of the Spatial Orientation of a Water Surface." *Journal of Genetic Psychology,* 1963b, 102, 195–201.

Smedslund, Jan. "Concrete Reasoning: A Study of Intellectual Development." *Monographs of the Society for Research in Child Development,* 1964, 29, Serial No. 93, 1–39.

Smedslund, Jan. "The Development of Transitivity of Length: A Comment on Braine's Reply." *Child Development,* 1965, 36, 577–580.

Smedslund, Jan. "Performance on Measurement and Pseudomeasurement Tasks by Five- to Seven-year-old Children." *Scandinavian Journal of Psychology,* 1966, 7, 81–92.

Smedslund, Jan. "Conservation and Resistance to Extinction: A Comment on Hall and Simpson's Article." *Merrill-Palmer Quarterly,* 1968, 14, 211–214.

Smilansky, Sarah. *The Effects of Sociodramatic Play on Disadvantaged Preschool Children.* New York: Wiley, 1968.

Smith, Jan D. "The Effects of Training Procedure upon the Acquisition of Conservation of Weight." *Child Development,* 1968, 39, 515–526.

Sonquist, Hanne D., and Constance K. Kamii. "Applying Some Piagetian Concepts in the Classroom for the Disadvantaged." *Young Children,* 1967, 22, 231–246.

Stendler, Celia B. "Aspects of Piaget's Theory That Have Implications for Teacher Education." *Journal of Teacher Education,* 1965, 16, 330–335.

Stern, Carolyn. "Evaluating Language Curricula for Preschool Children." In M. A. Brottman (Ed.), *Language Remediation for the Disadvantaged Preschool Child.* Monographs of the Society for Research in Child Development, 1968, 33, Serial No. 124, 49–61.

Sullivan, Edmund V. *Piaget and the School Curriculum: A Critical Appraisal.* Ontario Institute for Studies in Education, University of Toronto, Bulletin No. 2, 1967.

Sullivan, Edmund V. "Piagetian Theory in the Educational Milieu: A Critical Appraisal." Unpublished manuscript, Ontario Institute for Studies in Education, University of Toronto, 1968.

Sutton-Smith, Brian. "Piaget on Play: A Critique." *Psychological Review,* 1966, 73, 104–110.

Torrance, E. Paul. *Education and the Creative Potential.* Minneapolis: University of Minnesota Press, 1963.

Tuddenham, R. D. "Jean Piaget and the World of the Child." *American Psychologist,* 1966, 21, 207–217.

Uzgiris, I. C. "Situational Generality of Conservation." *Child Development,* 1964, 35, 831–841.

Uzgiris, I. C., and J. McV. Hunt. *Ordinal Scale of Infant Development.* Presented at 18th International Congress of Psychology, Moscow, 1966.

Wallach, Lisi, and R. L. Sprott. "Inducing Number Conservation in Children." *Child Development,* 1964, 35, 1057–1071.

Wallach, Lisi, A. Jack Wall, and Lorna Anderson. "Number Conservation: The

Roles of Reversibility, Addition-subtraction, and Misleading Perceptual Cues." *Child Development,* 1967, 38, 427–442.

Wallach, Michael A. "Research on Children's Thinking." In H. W. Stevenson (Ed.), *Child Psychology.* Chicago: University of Chicago Press, 1963, 230–276.

Weikart, David, and Marian J. Erickson. *Cognitively Oriented Follow Through Project.* Ypsilanti, Mich.: Eastern Michigan University and Ypsilanti Public Schools, 1969 (March).

Winer, Gerald A. "Induced Set and Acquisition of Number Conservation." *Child Development,* 1968, 39, 195–205.

Wohlwill, J. F. "From Perception to Influence: A Dimension of Cognitive Development." *Monographs of the Society for Research in Child Development,* 1962, 27, Whole No. 83, 87–106.

Wohlwill, Joachim F. "Piaget's System as a Source of Empirical Research." *Merrill-Palmer Quarterly,* 1963, 9, 253–262.

Wohlwill, J. F., and M. Katz. "Factors in Children's Responses on Class-inclusion Problems." Paper presented at Society for Research in Child Development, New York, 1967.

Woodward, Mary. "The Application of Piaget's Theory to Research in Mental Deficiency." In Norman R. Ellis (Ed.), *Handbook of Mental Deficiency.* New York: McGraw-Hill, 1965, 297–324.

Wright, John C. "Toward the Assimilation of Piaget." *Merrill-Palmer Quarterly,* 1963, 9, 277–285.

Wright, J. C. "Cognitive Development." In F. Falkner (Ed.), *Human Development.* Philadelphia: Saunders, 1966, 367–376.

Young, Beverly. "Inducing Conservation of Number Weight, Volume, Area, and Mass in Pre-school Children." Paper read at American Educational Research Association Meeting, Los Angeles, 1969.

Youniss, James, and Hans G. Furth. "The Influence of Transitivity on Learning in Hearing and Deaf Children." *Child Development,* 1965, 36, 533–538.

Youniss, James, and Hans G. Furth. "Prediction of Causal Events as a Function of Transitivity and Perceptual Congruency in Hearing and Deaf Children." *Child Development,* 1966, 37, 73–82.

Zimiles, Herbert. "The Development of Differentiation and Conservation of Number." *Monographs of the Society for Research in Child Development,* 1966, 31, Whole No. 108.

7

The British
Infant School Movement
and Miscellaneous Programs

THE BRITISH INFANT SCHOOL MOVEMENT

An increasing interest among educators in "informal education" for
young children has been noted during the past several years (Barth and

Rathbone, 1969). This interest has been stimulated by knowledge of innovative educational practices that have been implemented in selected British infant schools. Infant schools in England and Wales are generally equivalent to the kindergarten–primary grades in American school systems; they enroll children from the ages of five to seven or eight. From the infant schools children go on to junior schools, designed to accommodate children until the age of eleven.

A document which has apparently done much to direct the attention of American education to the British infant school movement is a government-sponsored study of early education in England known as the Plowden Report (1967). This report actually represents two salient concerns: (1) a survey of the status of early education in England, and (2) proposals for needed educational reform. Among other things, this elaborate document includes favorable references to the informal classroom procedures that are followed in about one-third of the infant schools in England. These procedures are generally viewed as the outgrowth of a "tradition of revolution" which has gradually occurred in England over the past few decades.

This tradition of revolution has several key elements (Featherstone, 1967a). One is a wide latitude of freedom among school personnel to determine what will go into a curriculum—a freedom which if exploited can contribute substantially to educational reform. A second element of this tradition has involved a gradual role shift among the governmental educational officials responsible for overseeing public instruction. This change is from an "inspector-evaluator" role to an "advisory" role, and has been especially noticeable in the schools of Leicestershire County, England. It is in Leicestershire County that experimentation with informal educational procedures began in earnest several years ago. A third influence in the infant school tradition of revolution is based upon insights from contemporary developmental psychology that have shaped English educators' concepts of children's learning and motivation. And it is Piagetian psychology that is most widely recognized as the source of these insights.

The following comments concerning British infant school practice are based primarily upon those schools which have patterned themselves on the Leicestershire County Plan; it should therefore be remembered that these comments do not apply to all British infant schools. For purposes of discussion, the term *new infant school* will be used.

General Features

One appropriate source for a descriptive assessment of evolutionary "new" infant school practices is provided by L. G. W. Sealey (1966).

For nine years (1956–1965), Sealey served as an advisor to the Leicester-shire County Schools. Sealey's advisory strategy was organized around "growth points," that is, program components which exude evidence of change. Using growth points as stepping stones, Sealey's personal involvement with Leicestershire County schools led him to function as an intermediary among teachers who shared the desire to enlarge and sharpen mandates for change. As forces for change were thus mobilized, mutually supported new patterns for learning were created. It should be noted, however, that change has characteristically occurred in infant schools as a product of teacher initiative and creativity, not of the proposals developed by "experts" outside the classroom.

The Integrated Day Among the most significant new patterns reported by Sealey to have developed from a growth point is the integrated day.[1] In an integrated day, no class lessons based upon prescribed time allotments are found. Rather, classrooms are typically organized into various learning centers—one for general purpose activity, a second for science and mathematics, a third for visual arts, and a fourth for reading and language arts (Sealey, 1966). Some classrooms may also be equipped with programmed learning materials and other supplements. The personnel of new infant schools believe that, aided by subtle teacher guidance, children will accept the responsibility to synthesize their own learning experiences—some of which may be fleeting, others of which may encompass several weeks of related activity. Neat, tidy, and fettered teacher-centered learning activities are therefore rare. Children's productivity is believed to be directly associated with teacher skill in planning and organizing the learning centers, although children are typically enlisted to assist in this planning. Sealey maintains that it is perhaps not so much the physical and curricular rearrangements that are important in infant schools as it is the freedom to experiment and change that such rearrangements allow. The following example of an integrated learning experience will perhaps provide the reader with a general idea of this important feature of infant school practice.

> When a class of seven-year-olds notice[s] the birds that come to the bird table outside the classroom window, they may decide, after discussion with their teacher, to make their own aviary. They will set to with a will, and paint the birds in flight, make models of them in clay or paper mache, write stories and poems about them and look up reference books to find out more about their habits. Children are not assimilating inert ideas but are wholly involved in thinking, feeling and doing. The slow and the bright

[1] Teacher-initiated change notwithstanding, much of the credit for this concept is given to an American advisor in Leicestershire County, Dr. Anthony Kallet.

share a common experience and each takes from it what he can at his own level. There is no attempt to put reading and writing into separate compartments; both serve a wider purpose, and artificial barriers do not fragment the learning experience. [Plowden Report, 1967, p. 199. Reproduced by permission of Her Majesty's Stationery Office.]

The sort of project described above lends itself to a full deployment of interest centers, individual interests and levels of conceptual involvement, independent as well as cooperative planning and thinking, and task-oriented social interaction. Work flow need not be interrupted by artificial time barriers and subject-matter divisions. Furthermore, with such a pupil-centered orientation the teacher can be free to spend more time with individual children as needed. On the face of it such a policy should rate high in its potential for dealing with the wide range of individual differences typical of any classroom group.

Other accounts of infant school practices, notably those practices in Leicestershire County, are consistent with the pattern suggested above. Hawkins and Hawkins (1964), for example, have noted that children spend a majority of their time pursuing activities of their own choice. The Hawkins' also agree that in new infant schools integrated learning episodes take precedence over specified periods for separate subject orientations. This point can be used to clarify an instructional principle inherent in the example of bird study described earlier. Instead of being confronted successively with reading, art, arithmetic, and writing periods, children are free to engage themselves in painting or ceramics, nature study or experimentation, writing stories about these experiences, and exchanging stories in order to read about the activities their peers have pursued. In a classroom of thirty children, thirty different classroom activities may be occurring simultaneously, although small clusters of children are often seen working together on "mutually absorbing" tasks. The following account, based upon the personal observation of Yeomans (1969), exemplifies further the panorama of new infant school activities based upon the integrated day concept:

Forty to forty-five children, ages 5 through 7, attached to the room, but not necessarily in it, with one teacher.

Focal-points, consisting of tables, chairs, bookshelves, bins, lockers, pegboards, sinks, a carpentry bench, a clay table, a stove, easels, and a sand table, all placed around the walls or in the middle of the room, or out on the terrace if the weather was good.

Two girls in the "Wendy House" (a child-sized playhouse), dressed in Victorian costumes, serving "tea" to each other and to passers-by.

A "green-grocers" store (small booth and bright-colored awning) in which a 7-year-old and his 5-year-old helper are selling stage fruits, for stage money, to a line of customers being particular about the change.

A small individual reading alone in a nook partitioned off from the outer bustle by screens that double as bookshelves.

Two boys and a girl sawing and sandpapering wood on the carpenter's bench on the terrace.

Three others painting at easels on the terrace.

An animal-lover feeding the hamster; another observing the tadpoles in an aquarium.

A group of six at tables in the center of the room with the teacher, working with attribute blocks and plastic and wooden shapes which, when combined correctly, make geometric patterns in either two or three dimensions.

An older and a younger child at another table reading aloud to each other.

A group of four making clay animals at the clay table.

This does not account for all 45, for the others were out of the room engaged in various projects. Teaching was taking place, but in unorthodox ways. The teacher had an eye for everything and everyone, but the children typically sought her aid on problems that were occupying them. She would visit a group of children writing stories and help them with their spelling; or hear an individual read aloud; or suggest another way of pressing clay into a mould; or invite someone she thought had been doing puzzles long enough to try reading this book. Older children were helping younger ones and then turning back to their own work. [Reprinted from pages 13 and 14 of *Education for Initiative and Responsibility*, by Edward Yeomans. Copyright 1967 by the National Association of Independent Schools.]

The sort of action described above would not be possible without a wide variety of multipurpose "raw materials" for learning. Such materials need not be expensive nor necessarily prepared in advance for specific purposes. It is the criterion of variety in materials suitable for the children's "natural learning environment" that is important. A teacher has the responsibility to see that such materials are used constructively; constructive use of classroom materials can occur at different times and different levels depending upon children's intentions and their perceptions of the properties of such materials. There is no established formula for an integrated day; diversity in the degree of structure, in groupings, and in content in infant school classrooms is the rule, rather than the exception (Yeomans, 1969).

Vertical Groupings A second "growth point" has evolved from a modification of grouping practices. In lieu of instructional groups formed "homogeneously" according to age, measured intelligence, or other arbitrary criteria, the policy of *vertical* or "family" grouping is preferred in many new infant schools. This means that classes are composed of children varying in age from five to seven or eight, all of whom intermingle for learning and recreational activities.[2] It also means that a child is likely to spend his entire infant school life with one teacher, or two teachers who work together sharing the responsibility for two classes. This "unclassification" makes it possible for a cross-section of an entire school population to be represented in each classroom. Infant school teachers have reported that such an organization emphasizes individuality rather than disguises individuality under the cloak of artificial age and/or ability-grouping practices. Vertical grouping also eliminates the great block of time required each year for a teacher to become acquainted with successive classes. Thus a teacher may grow increasingly aware of pupil needs and learning styles over a two- to three-year period of acquaintance with children and their parents.

Not all "new" infant schools practice vertical groupings, nor is there a consensus about the advantages of this organizational concept (Blackie, 1967). In final analysis the method of organization is surely less significant than the quality of infant school teaching faculties. Nevertheless, members of the Central Advisory Council for Education (England), whose studies culminated in the "Plowden Report" mentioned earlier, were impressed by the "liveliness and good quality" of the activity in infant schools so organized. For members of this Council the advantages of vertical groupings outweigh the disadvantages, at least for purposes of infant school education.[3] Supportive evidence for this practice is largely anecdotal, and no particular advantage for double or triple age grouping has been reported in infant school practice.

Additional Components of Infant School Practice The *integrated day* and *vertical groupings* mark two of the most significant new infant school growth points. Other policies have evolved, however, as several reports have indicated (Blackie, 1967; Sealey, 1966; Yeomans, 1969). Of these policies, that broadest in scope concerns a refocus of educational objectives. Specific, convergent, and factual outcomes have been assigned a substantially lower priority in favor of a "thought-process" orientation. In other words, a greater relative value has been placed upon inductive thinking and the development of problem-solving strate-

[2] The reader may recall the rationale for this strategy proposed formally by Montessori (see Chapter 2).

[3] Possible disadvantages include the possibility of children being exposed in an extended way to the same weaknesses of a given teacher, an overpowering of younger children by older class members, and limited adult contact. All of these could easily be avoided or remedied by alert professionals, however.

gies. This value has implications for the provision, selection, and use of materials, and evidence of these implications is provided by Yeomans' (1969) earlier example of diverse classroom activity. Further, as Yeomans (1969) has put it, a child's work manner—the quality of his self-control and responsibility—is considered more relevant for educational development than the absolute level of academic achievement a child has reached.

A conceptual accent in the mosaic of new infant school policy concerns an avoidance of the work-play dichotomy purported to be so firmly entrenched in traditional schools. The potential of children's play for the achievement of worthwhile learning objectives and the general value assigned to play activity is clearly communicated by the following passage:

> Play is the central activity in all nursery schools and in many infant schools. This sometimes leads to accusations that children are wasting their time in school: they should be working. But this distinction between work and play is false, possibly throughout life, certainly in the primary school. Its essence lies in past notions of what is done in school hours (work) and what is done out of school (play). We know now that play—in the sense of 'messing about' either with material objects or with other children, and of creating fantasies—is vital to children's learning and therefore vital in school. Adults who criticise teachers for allowing children to play are unaware that play is the principal means of learning in early childhood. It is the way through which children reconcile their inner lives with external reality. In play, children gradually develop concepts of causal relationships, the power to discriminate, to make judgments, to analyze and synthesize, to imagine and to formulate. Children become absorbed in their play and the satisfaction of bringing it to a satisfactory conclusion fixes habits of concentration which can be transferred to other learning. [Plowden Report, 1967, p. 193. Reproduced by permission of Her Majesty's Stationery office.]

It may be mentioned in passing that the above view is a fundamental component of traditional American nursery school practice. Further, educational practice based upon the work-play dichotomy has been identified as one of several variables associated with differences in children's creative output (Torrance, 1963). That is, a low frequency of divergent thinking responses has been noted in classrooms characterized by an "austere, no-fun" atmosphere and where school activities, apart from recess, are clearly labeled by teachers as work to be "endured."

Also consistent with the "pupil-centeredness" of infant school practice is a third policy accent: an attitude among teachers that children can be trusted to do their own learning.[4] Coercive measures designed to force children's learning are avoided. So are artificial incentives. Preferred are motivational strategies which capitalize on children's exploratory responses and natural curiosity. This trust in the child's capacity for initiative and responsibility has undoubtedly been fostered by improved professional relationships between classroom teachers and their superiors. According to Blackie (1967), a major force behind the infant school revolution is the conviction that teachers will do their best work if allowed to exercise their initiative and judgment at every feasible opportunity. In short, greater teacher productivity is likely when liberty and responsibility are delegated to them by administrators than when teachers are tightly directed, circumscribed, and obligated to follow a set program.

Another feature of new infant school practice that has impressed many American observers is the apparent lack of obsession among teachers with children's futures. Instead, the prevalent teaching value is placed upon making the most of a child's current learning situation. In other words, the enrichment of children's lives in infant school takes precedence over a concern about what they will be able to do at the end of one, two, or three years. This is several degrees away from most American approaches, which generally gauge program effectiveness in terms of long-range results. It would be a mistake to assume, however, that infant school teachers have shed the responsibility for children's school futures. It seems to be more a matter of a commitment to the idea that the best assurance a child has for the future is a meaningful, absorbing, and productive present.

Finally, a serious effort has been sustained over the years to establish compatible school-parent relationships. From all reports, communications between parents and teachers, parental support of and satisfaction with school practices, and parent visitation in the schools are frequent and generally positive.

Commentary on Innovative Practices

According to Susan Williams (the director of Gordonbrock Infant School in London, 1967), the greatest difference between the "new" and "old" infant school approach is a matter of taking cues from children to guide learning versus coming to them with a lesson prepared in

---

[4] Observers of American educational practice, by contrast, conclude that if teachers' attitudes can be inferred from their classroom behavior, American teachers generally do not believe that children can be trusted to do their own learning. See Rogers (1967) for a treatment of this issue.

advance. This requires that the teacher be alert at all times for signs of "readiness" which may issue from the children. Thus while overall planning and master objectives are always but subtly present, specific advance planning is played down. New teachers are advised above all to *talk with the children* to find out about their interests and past experiences. Occasionally, lessons of a more "formal nature" are conducted with small groupings of children who are "ready" for such an experience. Rules exist, but largely to prevent chaos. While a play-like atmosphere seems to dominate new infant school classrooms, teachers generally insist that children must either write or talk about what they have done. This can be considered as something of a system of accountability. An order to the child's learning is assumed, that is, concrete experiences *precede* labeling or describing. Such an order, it may be recalled, is consistent with a Piagetian view of developmental learning; as mentioned earlier, new infant school practices are most generally based upon cognitive-developmental theory. Both the Plowden Report (1967) and Blackie's (1967) *Inside the Primary School* contain frequent references to Piagetian concepts for educational strategy. For many British educators, these concepts represent the best of what is known about the nature of children's development. Cognitive-developmental theory also points up the need for individual approaches to learning. It is the need for individualization around which the entire infant school movement has been organized.

A Sampling of Problems and Issues   Lest one conclude that what has developed in selected British infant schools is an educational "Shangri-La," several problems impede the potential of this "revolution" (Hawkins and Hawkins, 1964; Blackie, 1967; Yeomans, 1969). Some of these problems are beyond the immediate control of teachers; others are perhaps inherent in any attempt at "open education." In the first category is the problem of overcrowded classrooms. As class enrollments increase, so does the density of demands for teachers to (1) plan, coordinate, and integrate individual learning activities and (2) assist each child frequently and constructively.[5] With such a high demand density, teachers may not conduct a sufficient number of task-oriented discussions nor provide adequate and frequent summaries of activities (Hawkins and Hawkins, 1964). Both of these latter techniques are recognized as important for children's learning. Obviously, not just any teacher is capable of coordinating a classroom of thirty to forty children in which

[5] Crowded classroom conditions in many infant schools are apparently a function of (1) statutory restrictions (one new teacher for every 40 new children in 1964) and (2) teacher shortage.

genuine pupil-centered instruction is applied. Success in any case is highly dependent upon individual teaching skill; new infant school methods, like any other educational methods, are not foolproof. As Blackie (1967, p. 50) has remarked, "No method is better than the teacher who is using it." This remark does not mean that method is irrelevant and that all children really need is a "good" teacher. Rather, new infant school methods are thought to take good account of both subject matter and the nature of children. Therefore, these methods should be "better" in the hands of a strong teacher than would other methods in the same teacher's hands—methods which account for neither subject matter nor the course of children's development. Whether infant school teachers are better than, say, American primary teachers is a moot question. What is impressive to this writer about the infant school movement, however, is the dedication of school faculties to self-analysis and continued improvement.[6] It is remarkable that so many English teachers can apparently implement a style of education considered applicable only in small classes.

Considering that infant school teachers have been delegated such heavy responsibility for curriculum development and that individual teacher skill is so critical for infant school success, the problem of monitoring the infant school enterprise can be raised. In other words, what measures have been taken to prevent anarchy or a proliferation of incompetent teaching? Observers generally have not expressed fear that practices will deteriorate without close control. Possibly this is because several "checkpoints" exist for purposes of monitoring the system. These checkpoints are represented by (1) separate organizational authorities which, in combination, facilitate school and classroom inspection, (2) the widespread exchange of teaching ideas, and (3) formal procedures for school and curriculum improvement, extensive in-service training practices, and means for teachers to control their own work (Blackie, 1967).[7]

Another problem, particularly notable throughout the Leicestershire experiment, is a frustrating and elongated period of transition from a formal to a self-directed instructional approach. This "period of adjustment" for both teacher and children could hardly be used as a logical argument against the policy of open education, but it does point up a

[6] Hawkins and Hawkins (1964) report, for example, that new infant school teachers regularly visit each other's classrooms to evaluate practices and share new ideas. Such visitations are virtually unheard of in American schools.

[7] These organizations include Her Majesty's Inspectorate of Schools, Local Education Authorities, and the Schools Council for the Curriculum and Examinations. For details on the structure and functions of these bodies see Blackie (1967) and/or the Plowden Report (1967).

hazard to be overcome. Perhaps more critical is the transition for children from the informal atmosphere of an infant school to a traditionally-operated junior school. Few reports have as yet treated this transition on any systematic empirical basis, and most observers express concern over the lack of school continuity in many parts of England. There is some evidence that junior school practices are becoming more "relaxed."[8] Yet junior schools in general represent a vivid contrast to the Leicestershire County infant school concept. Perhaps the most concrete evidence for junior school change is the gradual abolishment of the traditional "eleven-plus" examination. The "eleven-plus" achievement test has for years been administered to children as they complete their junior school education. British educators have then used the results of this achievement battery to determine the direction of children's secondary school education. Children who fail this test are virtually excluded from a secondary education which would qualify them for eventual college or university opportunities. The intense pressures of the "eleven-plus" examination have apparently contributed in the past to inflexible curricula, to a lack of experimentation and innovation in the schools, and to various undesirable social and economic side effects among children who fail.

Evaluation in Infant School Practice   According to Sealey (1966), many infant school innovations have been introduced gradually and unsystematically. Perhaps because of this, formal research evaluations were rare during Sealey's tenure as advisor (1956–1965). Sealey reports that, in lieu of psychometric assessment, four evaluative criteria have operated to foster the growth of "creative" infant school practice:

1. Judgment as to whether or not teachers and children desire to continue a new procedure.
2. Judgment concerning the extent to which "sense of fun" is engendered by new learning experiences.
3. Judgment about the ability of new learning situations to involve children actively and induce persistence.
4. Judgment as to the degree a new experience or procedure helps a teacher to be more responsive to individual needs of children.

Underlying this approach is a generalized belief that appropriate means to evaluate the purported outcomes of new infant school practice are not currently available. As Barth (1969) puts it, the assumption con-

---

[8] Implicit in this "relaxation" is the assumption that what is desirable for the infant school population is equally desirable for the junior school population, an assumption which requires close examination.

cerning evaluation is at least twofold: (1) that the best measure of a child's work is his work itself; and (2) that one needs to observe the cumulative effects of experience over long periods of time before evaluation of a child's progress is relevant. For the latter purpose, anecdotal records—"jottings"—are taken continually to log the characteristics and progress of individual children. As these jottings accumulate it is believed that a teacher can develop a comprehensive academic and social portrait of individual children from which teaching cues can be gleaned. Thus pupil evaluation is less a matter of accounting a child's achievement than a matter of seeking data for planning purposes.

A de-emphasis of traditional means for pupil evaluation, especially standardized achievement testing, may be disturbing to educators who value technical evidence, such as empirical statements of validity and reliability. In England, however, this trend toward less formal evaluations may continue if the recommendations of the Plowden Report (1967) are accepted:

> We have considered whether we can lay down standards that should be achieved by the end of the primary school but concluded that it is not possible to describe a standard of attainment that should be reached by all or most children. Any set standard would seriously limit the bright child and be impossibly high for the dull. What could be achieved in one school might be impossible in another. We have suggested . . . that, with the ending of selection examinations, teachers—and parents—will need some yardstick of the progress of their children in relation to what is achieved elsewhere. Without it teachers may be tempted to go on teaching and testing in much the same way as they did before. We therefore envisage that some use will continue to be made of objective tests within schools. Such tests can be helpful—and then norms can serve on a basis of comparison—as long as they are used with insight and discrimination and teachers do not assume that only what is measurable is valuable. [Plowden Report, 1967, pp. 201–202. Reproduced by permission of Her Majesty's Stationery Office.]

Research Evidence   As the above discussion indicates, systematic research into new infant school practice has not been plentiful. The results of a few general surveys, some of which are cited in the Plowden Report (1967), have been published. There are also some data tangential to the question of infant school effectiveness. Examples include studies of the influence of infant–junior school transition on reading achievement (Shields, 1969) and the relationship between anxiety and ability grouping (streaming) in progressive and traditional schools (Levy, Gooch, and Kellmer-Pringle, 1969). At the present time, however, one must be content with anecdotal reports, including those of infant school personnel who assure outsiders that the infant schools "work."[9]

Although from many points of view this state of affairs may be unsatisfying, independent (albeit subjective) observational reports of infant school operations do seem to be reliable—at least observers indicate in their reports that they are seeing and being impressed by the same general features (Featherstone, 1967abc; Schlesinger, 1966; Hawkins and Hawkins, 1964).

According to most observers, the highest relative levels of achievement attained by infant school pupils are in the arts. High degrees of inventiveness with wood, cloth, and clay, a sharp increase in the number of children who elect to pursue instrumental music, and evidence of creative body movement are reported.[10] But it is the skill in reading and free writing shown by infant school children that seemingly produces the most awe among American observers. This is largely because no "classes" in reading and writing are held. Teaching in these skill areas generally is confined to an individual basis, with many methods and materials placed at the disposal of teachers and children. The guiding principle is firmly to enjoin and coordinate reading and writing with moment-to-moment learning activities. According to the reports of new infant school teachers, if a child does not learn readily he is rarely the object of worry or increased instructional effort. This provides a sharp contrast to the "uptightness" observed among many American teachers and parents, a tension that may serve to increase rather than solve a child's learning "problem." This relaxed attitude combined with informal approaches to reading instruction is viewed as instrumental to the extremely low incidence of nonreaders in the new infant schools.

Observers also report favorably upon the "good beginnings" in mathematics and science among infant school children.[11] Hall and Armington (1967) maintain that, by comparison, many of the Leicestershire infant schools are "far ahead" of their American counterparts in multibase arithmetic. These observers believe that English classrooms represent a more favorable learning climate and greater flexibility with respect to "readiness" for learning than do most American classrooms. According to Hall and Armington, infant school children are neither re-

---

[9] It is unlikely that research into the effects of the numerous variables which operate interactively in infant school classrooms will be anything but complex, although behavioral-analysis procedures (Chapter 5) would be fruitful.

[10] According to Blackie (1967) the infant school revolution actually began during the 1930s with new approaches for teaching of art and new methods of physical education.

[11] Programmed materials for these two subjects are sometimes utilized in the infant schools, but their use is more common in junior schools.

strained from pursuing advanced learnings nor are they coerced to participate in formal drill. In contrast, many kindergarten children in the U.S. are prevented from learning to read on the grounds that "reading is not taught until first grade." Although favorably impressed with the flexibility in new infant schools, Hall and Armington (1967) do remark that the technology of some language-based activities is weak; for example, a lack of focus upon the development of phonetic analysis skills has been mentioned. They further note that the noticeable variation in quality among the Leicestershire schools makes it very difficult to derive sound generalizations about general classroom operations and their effectiveness. Similar reservations are expressed by Yeomans (1969), whose report on Leicestershire County schools indicates that sustained work in certain areas (for example, history, literature) was not apparent.

Anecdotal reports, however thoughtful, unfortunately are not a substitute for systematic evaluation. For empiricists, there is presently little "clean" evidence to validate (or deny) the effectiveness of infant school practices. However, this writer knows of nothing which suggests that new infant school practices are disadvantageous to children's subsequent progress in the junior school and beyond. Further, conventional research techniques, especially group testing, with their focus upon product are not entirely consistent with the new infant school focus upon *process*. A rethinking of research questions and procedures appropriate to a process orientation is needed. Perhaps this will soon result in the identification of more specific antecedent-consequent relationships within new infant school classrooms.

It is possible that faith in the value of pedagogical change or belief in the success potential of new methods among teachers may have influenced the outcome of the infant school movement in positive ways. Yet, it is the fundamental value of classrooms patterned after the Leicestershire experiment that continues to impress visitors: a reasoned reorganization of the total early school framework to facilitate the intellectual and emotional emancipation of children. As Yeomans (1969) indicates, the real strength of Leicestershire may be an avoidance of formulae, convergent systems, and pedagogical conformity. There has been no obsession to "prove" that one theory or method is better than another. All theories are considered and utilized as deemed appropriate to the situation; the classroom teacher remains the best judge of applicability. Thus far, personnel of the British Infant Schools have demonstrated that open education apparently works, even in large classes, therefore providing an object lesson for American educators. Conditions must be right, however, and a most important condition is that teachers be allowed to exercise the same responsibility and initiative that are wanted for pupils (Yeomans, 1969).

Examples of Infant School Philosophy in the United States

Apart from scattered public and private schools or classroom and laboratory programs in colleges of education, there is not overwhelming evidence of "open education" in the United States. Two steps in this direction, however, are symbolized by the Vermont Design for Education and the Head Start Follow Through plan for "Continuing Growth" presented by the Education Development Center (Newton, Massachusetts). The latter has perhaps been most explicitly influenced by British Infant School practices.

Educational Development Center: Continuing Growth Plan   EDC's "Continuing Growth" Plan (Armington, 1968) is an attempt to realize an educational environment that (1) eliminates the "persistent contradiction" between educational practices and educational ideals and (2) paves the way for children to achieve "personal fulfillment." The achievement of these two objectives requires that any school faculty receive encouragement and reinforcement for the development of its own unique identity (individuality). Experimentation and personal freedom are seen (1) as necessary role enactments for school personnel and (2) as a substitute for enactments constrained by prescribed curricula. The purpose of this shift from "prescription" to "freedom" is to effect improved responsiveness by teachers to individual children's needs and to individual teaching styles.

Two "key elements" form the conceptual substance of this Continuing Growth Plan: the open classroom and the advisory service. An open classroom is defined by EDC in terms of openness in communication (dialogue), classroom organization, time, and space. Most fundamentally, openness applies to *self* (teachers as well as children). Teaching methods and conditions are primary concerns; intellectual content is secondary. Communication skills, intellectual curiosity, self-confidence, and responsibility are among the favored educational aims in this plan. The characteristics of a classroom necessary for the attainment of such aims include (1) a rich variety of learning materials, (2) freedom to plan one's own activities, (3) an interdisciplinary approach to "work," (4) flexibility in scheduling, (5) cooperative interchange among pupils, and (6) a supportive teacher role. The latter involves both careful observation of and active participation in classroom life.

Life in open classrooms is further sustained by the second "key element" mentioned above: the "Advisory." The Advisory consists of a team of advisors—not supervisors—which performs a variety of functions to implement the open classroom philosophy and develop specific practices consistent with this philosophy. Advising, as a concept, is built upon three principles. One is the principle that changes in educational practice are only effective when teachers feel the need for and desire to change. Thus, the Advisory purports to enhance and capitalize upon the readiness for change exhibited in a given situation. Members of the Advisory must therefore be accessible at all times and immediately responsive to invitations for advisory services. A second principle is based upon a "way of working" with teachers. This involves both a responsiveness to the demands of specific situations and an attempt to help teachers realize their full capabilities. The third principle is defined in terms of various integrated advisory functions: direct services (seminars, provision of curriculum materials, parent education, and so on), research and curriculum development services, the provision of a workshop and resource center within which consultations may ensue, and the communication of ideas, problems, and needs among classroom teachers.

The number of schools currently participating in EDC's Continuing Growth Plan is not large: in 1968–1969, only five New England communities were involved. Neither has the Continuing Growth Plan operated sufficiently long to permit meaningful evaluation. Protagonists at EDC, however, report that several conclusions can be made on the basis of their work to date. First, that a "large percentage" of educational personnel and parents with whom EDC has worked demonstrate an affinity for the open education philosophy and have worked actively for its application. Secondly, that as the application of this philosophy is extended to larger numbers of classrooms, the Advisory becomes progressively more important. This means that an expansion of advisory services is necessary if more frequent and direct contact with teachers is desired. Finally, the success of the Advisory depends upon the full and unified support of school administrations and parents. Thus, EDC recommends that each local school district develop and execute its own high quality "Advisory."

Vermont Design for Education   The State of Vermont has developed a student-centered philosophy of education very similar to that underlying the British Infant School movement. The Vermont philosophy includes an integrated set of principles related to the motivation of behavior, human relations, and individual psychology. It also leads one to emphasize the learning process rather than the teaching process. This distinction is a matter of degree rather than kind, although it is based implicitly on the postulate that one does not teach children. Instead, one arranges conditions which are conducive for children to learn. Immediately the issue of optimal conditions arises. For the Vermont Design, a humanistic teacher-student relationship is the most basic condition. The following principles have been cultivated from this premise:

1. A student must be accepted as a person.
2. The teacher's role must be that of a partner and guide in the learning process.
3. All people need success to prosper.

A second related component of the Vermont Design is based on the concept of individual differences. For example:

4. Education should be based upon the individual's strong, inherent desire to learn and make sense of his environment.
5. Educators should strive to maintain the individuality and originality of the learner.
6. Emphasis should be upon a child's own way of learning— through the discovery and exploration of real experiences.
7. A child's perception of the learning process should be related to his own conception of reality.
8. A child should be allowed to work according to his own abilities.
9. Expectation of children's progress should be individualized if individualization in instruction is sought.

A third philosophical constituent of the Vermont Design involves the need for effective personal and social growth through educational experience:

10. One of the most important human accomplishments is the formulation of a basic set of values by which to guide daily living.
11. Schools should establish a context within which children are able to learn from one another.
12. The development of a sense of responsibility should be encouraged for every child.

The Vermont Design is basically an abstract and general statement of principles, yet this statement is generally consistent with the open education point of view. Similar philosophical stirrings have been reported in New York, New Jersey, the teacher education program at Wheelock College (Boston), City College of New York, and the University of North Dakota, to mention a few (Barth and Rathbone, 1969).[12]

Summary Comment

The infant school movement most clearly represents a philosophy of education and child growth which translates to a child-centered, inductive approach to learning. This movement has occurred gradually and only in selected areas of England, nevertheless its impact is being felt worldwide. Infant school rhetoric, as several have observed (for example, Featherstone, 1967a; Hall and Armington, 1967), is virtually identical to that associated with progressive education in the United States, a movement that began several decades ago but never seemed to flourish here in pure form.

Perhaps cynical observers will say that there is actually little genuine innovation reflected in the infant school movement. Broadly speaking, from a standpoint of both philosophy and pedagogy, many of the major ideas of open education have been espoused and practiced in this country for years, although admittedly not on a large scale.

Tempting as it may be to suggest that infant school philosophy is a reaction against a purported "dehumanization" of the educational process, such a conclusion is probably an oversimplification of the issues. The infant school movement has developed over an extended period of time and under peculiar sociological, economic, and pedagogical circumstances. It is probably premature for American educators freely to implant such a philosophy and accompanying pedagogy here without (1) a full understanding of these circumstances and (2) specific delineations of the qualities which set superior infant school classes apart from mediocre ones (Featherstone, 1967c). With due respect to caution, there is little reason to think that American children are so different from their English peers that a Leicestershire Experiment here would be doomed to failure. Educational Development Corporation's Continuing Growth Plan represents just such an experiment and bears watching by all professional early childhood educators.

Perhaps one of the greatest hazards of the open education movement

[12] An impressive document generally aligned with the open education movement has also been published by the Provincial Committee on Education in Ontario, Canada, entitled *Learning and Living* (1968). A principal strength of this document is its impressive list of specific recommendations—258 in number—for change in the entire educational complex of Ontario.

is the mostly implicit tendency for its protagonists to render value judgments about formal pedagogy that are undeserved. This writer, for example, has sensed that many supporters of informal education judge their approach as warm, open, flexible, and therefore "good," while formal education is dismissed as cold, authoritarian, rigid, and therefore "bad." Though many open educators may disdain teacher control techniques, the fact remains that children's learning (both type and degree) is controlled by the selection (or exclusion) of learning materials and the selective reinforcement of behavior—both are inevitable in any classroom setting. As Barth (1969) puts it, the real problem facing informal education is to define clearly and specifically the division of responsibility for learning that is unequivocally encountered in any adult-child relationship.

In addition to the need for empirical research, several important questions about infant school practice need clear answers. For example, when each child determines by individual choice how he will use his time, is there a danger of excessive random activity (Yeomans, 1969)? In other words, who is accountable if a given child does not achieve the praiseworthy, if ambiguous, aims of informal education? If there are certain curriculum "universals" (content areas) that all children need to share, can these be left to personal choice? Is there, as Barth (1969) suggests, a danger that infant school practices will be "haphazard, disordered, and misunderstood" unless they are guided by a clear theoretical framework? To what extent does the emphasis upon intuitive teaching and evaluation conflict with educators' attempts to build a science of teaching? To what extent is informal education, with its potential strengths and weaknesses, consistent with a society's national goals? Why, as it is often claimed, does the educational "establishment" in England and the United States seemingly resist change in the direction of broad-scale open education? How does one best prepare teachers and children for a successful open education experience? Are infant school children developing greater independence and responsibility, as is generally claimed? Is the near-idyllic existence of new infant and junior school children too far divorced from the realities of life for it to be the best sort of learning experience?

Perhaps these questions will be answered to our satisfaction during the next few years. Meanwhile there is much to commend in the efforts of British educators to provide a school community in which children may live as children—to discover, to create, to experience the pleasure and excitement of cooperative learning—in short, to make child-centered education work.

MISCELLANEOUS APPROACHES RELATED TO EARLY CHILDHOOD EDUCATION

This book has been concerned primarily with broad strategies for early education generally. There have appeared, however, a number of programs or approaches to child study and education which are of interest to most students of early childhood education. The remainder of this chapter includes brief descriptions of approaches specific to three relatively distinct areas: education for emotional development, perceptual-motor training for children whose learning progress is slow, and infant education. The first area may be linked most broadly with self-development theory in psychology. The second area, perceptual-motor training, has involved most clearly the relationship of perceptual-motor development to academic achievement. Infant education, the third topic to be considered in this portion of the chapter, may be thought of as an extension of a societal concern for the effects of very early experience, particularly in relation to the prevention of problems linked with environmental deprivation.

Education for Self-Development

While the cognitive education trail is being systematically blazed throughout the country, one might ask if equally systematic attention has been given to education for emotional development. A belief widely held among early childhood educators is that a child's self-concept— his perception of himself as a competent person of worth—must be nurtured in the preschool and early school years if that child is successfully to meet academic and social demands. This thesis was tightly bound with the original early childhood education movement, but few programmatic attempts have appeared to implement it. In other words, the humaneness of nursery-kindergarten teachers and a benevolent no-pressure environment have been viewed as imperative to foster emotional growth, but systematic attempts to "teach for" such an outcome have been rare. An exception to this is the human relations approach developed by Ralph Ojemann at the University of Iowa, although its focus has for the most part been on older children (Ojemann, 1958). The emotional education banner has also been flourished variously and at different times by many others (for example, Dinkmeyer and Drei-kurs, 1963; Drews, 1966; and Prescott, 1938). Related concerns are reflected in the mushrooming literature on education and mental health (for example, Clarizio, 1969; Seidman, 1963; Torrance and Strom, 1965) and the study of children's anxiety, especially as it may affect learning (for example, Sarason and others, 1960; Ruebush, 1963).

The Human Development Program Among the approaches specific to children as young as age 4, the *Human Development Program* (Bessell and Palomares, 1967; Bessell, 1968) has appealed to educators who identify broadly with humanistic psychology. Bessell and Palomares (1967) have taken the position that remedial means are not the best way to approach the many emotional problems which face adolescents and adults; remediation in their view has simply not been sufficiently effective for the solution of these emotional difficulties. Rather, Bessell and Palomares prefer to apply preventative mental health techniques during childhood, before these problems are developed. The task as they see it involves helping children to develop a sound emotional outlook which increases cumulatively their resistance to society's many pestilent features, including aversive human interaction in the schools. A first step in this process is to help the child overcome his fears about such things as his safety, his acceptance by others, his helplessness, and his lack of power. Thus, freedom from fear is seen as a basic prerequsite for sound learning and development.

At least three specific problems contributing to children's fears are taken by Bessell and Palomares to suggest a framework for emotional education: inadequate understanding of the cause-effect relationships in social interaction, insufficient understanding of the motives underlying human behavior, and low self-confidence. These problem areas in combination have provided the stimulus for their human development curriculum, the objectives of which include the achievement of improved (1) *social interaction* skills (understanding and accepting others), (2) *self-awareness* (insight into and acceptance of one's own feelings), and (3) *mastery* (achievement of responsible competence). Also basic to this tripartite framework are the further objectives of self-control and personal authenticity.[13]

The medium for human development education as interpreted by Bessell and Palomares is the "Magic Circle." This circular arrangement puts eight to twelve children and the teacher in a smaller (inner) circle with the remaining children seated in a larger, concentric circle. The inner circle of children is the participating body. Members of the outer circle observe. Circle membership varies from day to day as the teacher

[13] A published curriculum for four- and five-year-old children is now available (Bessell and Palomares, 1967). Higher program levels for the primary grades have been developed and are in press at the time of this writing. Materials for grades 4–6 are being planned.

initiates topics for discussion (twenty-minute periods daily) relevant to the three main process themes. Up to six weeks are devoted in one block to a given theme. The clarification and analysis of children's feelings and perceptions take precedence over a focus on the content of children's verbalizations; consistent attempts are made, however, to help children build a more effective vocabulary for the expression of feeling. Bessell (1968) believes that younger children are not yet "at war" with themselves as are most adults and therefore they exude a spontaneity that sustains the activity of the Magic Circle. Bessell is also convinced that children (1) will respond favorably to opportunities for sharing in decision-making processes, (2) can assume leadership roles (for Bessell the golden age of leadership development is the period from six to eight years), and (3) will help others, including the teacher, in constructive ways if only they are allowed to. Therefore the program is designed to shift leadership responsibility gradually from the teacher to the children. Consequently, leadership tasks may then be shared by the children. However, this shift does not begin until the primary grades. Bessell (1968) maintains that the key to successful human relations training is *involvement.* He thus suggests an equation for this purpose: *as responsibility is divided, involvement is multiplied.* In short, Bessell is convinced that to promote self-responsibility definite opportunities for this must exist in the classroom. The Human Development Program therefore represents a semistructured effort to capitalize upon children's social nature and their resources for cooperative personal assistance in order for children to achieve self-responsibility.

Comment The enthusiasm with which the Bessell program has reportedly been received by teachers (at this time primarily in the western U.S.) is perhaps a testimonial to the need many teachers perceive for organized human development activities for young children. Anecdotal data from teachers who have utilized the program in their classrooms indicate a reduction in discipline problems, higher motivation, greater verbal expressiveness, and smoother social interaction among children. Bessell himself reports data from a school system in Los Cruces, New Mexico, that indicate "slightly higher" academic achievement and a reduced absentee rate among children who have experienced the program.[14] The fact is that, at the time of this writing, no carefully designed and executed research has been done about the program, although opportunities for evaluation are plentiful. To assist in

---

[14] Howard Bessell, personal correspondence, 1969.

this regard, Bessell and Palomares (1967) have designed a rating scale for teacher use in assessing behavioral changes associated with the program. Observational and self-report techniques can also be used for this purpose. A teacher should fully recognize the theoretical basis for the program which is essentially a mix of neo-analytic and self-actualization personality theories (Adler, 1927; Horney, 1950; Rogers, 1942). Further, the success of the program most certainly demands sensitivity, acceptance, empathy, and group leadership skills from the teacher. It may be that the principal issue facing Bessell (who is himself a trained and experienced clinical psychologist) is not his program as much as it is the training of those who may elect to use it. Particularly dangerous would be a situation in which a teacher uses such a program to attempt psychotherapy or group-encounter activities with children. These activities are insufficiently understood even by many professionally-trained therapists. And there is a more basic issue involved: whether schools should even attempt to promote affective development through organized educational experiences. Perhaps in Bessell's favor, however, is the fact that many of the highly visible contemporary critics of education—John Holt, Paul Goodman, Edgar Friedenberg, and Jules Henry, for example—share an intense concern over the lack of attention to the feelings of children in our schools.[15]

Neither can research into self-concept development be overlooked by educators. Techniques for the measurement of young children's self-concepts and self-evaluative tendencies are beginning to appear (for example, Dreyer and Haupt, 1966). Self-concept measures secured from kindergarten children, according to Wattenberg and Clifford (1964), are significantly predictive of reading progress two and one-half years later. Other data suggest that self-acceptance is a prerequisite for the acceptance of others (McCandless, 1967). Coopersmith (1967) believes that the antecedents of self-esteem rest with adult-child relations in the preschool years. Collectively, evidence like this may serve as reinforcement for efforts such as Bessell and Palomares' to help children formulate a clear, positive self-image. Many questions remain to be answered, including whether incidental human-relations training will help children to achieve a positive self-concept, the extent to which the self-concept is a *determinant* of behavior, and whether the concept of the self-concept is itself valid (Lowe, 1961).

---

[15] A remarkable increase of articles, research and otherwise, pertinent to the clarification of children's feelings, has occurred recently in the child development literature. See, for example, Ellisor (1969); Gilbert (1969); Long (1969); Ojemann (1967); Peck (1967); Perkins (1969); and Sonntag (1969).

Perceptual-Motor Training

Kephart's Program   Several programs centered on the perceptual-motor foundations of academic achievement have appeared in the past decade. Most of these programs have been recommended by their originators primarily for children whose academic progress is slow. One such program is that developed by Kephart (1960). Kephart's basic thesis is that a logical sequence of perceptual-motor development precedes the elaboration of cognitive achievements. In other words, Kephart believes that cognitive operations are an outgrowth of perceptual manipulation which, in turn, is preceded by systematic motor explorations. For Kephart, motor movement generalizations—balance and posture, locomotion, contact responses (reaching, grasping, and releasing), and receipt and propulsion skills—represent the bases for all subsequent perceptual and cognitive development. Learning disorders among children who are otherwise not intellectually impaired are, Kephart believes, founded in poorly developed motor generalizations or the motor explorations which become differentiated from these generalizations. The quality of a child's differentiated motor explorations is, in Kephart's view, a function of *laterality* (left-right differentiation), *directionality* (projection of laterality into objective space), and *body image*.[16] Kephart further believes that the quality of a child's body image is significant with respect to the perception of environmental stimuli and the selection of responses when environmental events impinge upon the child. Finally, Kephart stresses the critical importance of *perceptual-motor matching* responses (as in copying letters) which require for their performance sound ocular pursuit skills, discrimination skills, and the ability to make use of motor-muscular feedback.

To test the relationship of perceptual-motor skills to school achievement, a developmental survey was constructed to measure these skills (Roach and Kephart, 1966). The use of this survey has resulted in several types of evidence, including (1) a positive correlation (.65) between scores on the perceptual-motor survey and teachers' ratings of academic achievement, and (2) the fact that a large percentage (85 percent) of a sample of "nonachieving" children scored very poorly on the examination. These data have not been taken as a claim that all achievement problems are rooted in or associated with perceptual-motor disorders, but Kephart believes that a good many such problems are. For the remediation of achievement problems suspected to have a basis in per-

---

[16] Directionality involves a translation by the child of the right-left differentiation within (laterality) to right-left discrimination of objects external to the self. Body image refers to the picture a child has of his own body.

ceptual-motor deficits (for example, reading reversals), Kephart has prescribed a set of training techniques. These techniques were devised in relation to the aforementioned motor generalizations and include techniques for laterality and directionality training (Kephart, 1960; Chaney and Kephart, 1968).

Comment   Kephart's contention for a logical, orderly sequence to development is broadly supported by independent studies of perceptual-motor behavior (Buktenica, 1969; O'Donnell, 1969). Further, Kephart's developmental survey is unique in terms of the checkpoints it provides to educators concerned specifically with the assessment of children's perceptual-motor development. Certainly perceptual-motor development is important in its own right, quite apart from any connection it may have with academic behavior. Although Kephart's data about perceptual-motor development and school achievement are correlated, they are insufficient for the validation of a reliable relationship between these two variables. Neither have Kephart's carefully programmed training techniques been validated through research to the point where confidence in their remedial power has been established. It is in fact surprising to this writer that so little independent research has apparently been performed with the Kephart materials.[17] There may be much more direct routes to the development of academic subskills than that which Kephart has mapped for teachers. Meanwhile, followers of Kephart may have to rely upon tangential supportive data such as that of Kahn and Birch (1968). Kahn and Birch report a positive correlation between auditory-visual integrative competence and reading skill among elementary school children. In addition, the use of training procedures broadly similar to those advocated by Kephart and patterned on standard normative motor development data appears promising. McCormick and others (1969) have applied perceptual-motor training procedures to children who varied in measured intelligence and reading achievement. In this study, patterned perceptual-motor training was not followed by reading achievement gains by children of average intelli-

[17] One of the few independent researches into Kephartian assumptions and training procedures is that of Ball and Edgar (1967). These data indicate a positive effect of Kephartian sensory-motor training on motor generalizations relevant to *body image* among normal kindergartners. No attempt, however, was made to relate body image development to academic or intellectual variables. The interested reader may also wish to consult the case report of an "underachieving" boy who was subjected to Kephartian perceptual-motor training in combination with academic training (consisting largely of cursive letter tracing). It was concluded in this report that academic improvement (increased reading comprehension and decreased letter reversals) was associated with improved gross motor coordination and perceptual-motor matching (Early and Kephart, 1969).

gence already reading at grade level; however, such training did result in reading gains among children below average in IQ and who were initially reading below grade level.

One broader implication of Kephart's thinking is that a general program to enhance the development of basic movement skills of all preschool and primary-grade children might be incorporated into routine "physical education" activities (Smith, 1968). Such a proposal, implicitly reminiscent of Kephart's views, is the "Movement Exploration" program for elementary schools (Hackett and Jensen, 1966). At the time of this writing, however, no research data on the specific academic effects of broad movement training are known to the author.

Frostig's Approach A second approach to the assessment and developmental training of perceptual behavior has been established by Marianne Frostig and her colleagues (Frostig and Horne, 1964). Frostig defines perception as the "ability to recognize stimuli," an ability which subsumes, (1) the receipt of sensory impressions (both external and internal), (2) the interpretation of these impressions, and (3) the collation of impressions with past experience. She further maintains that the age span of three and one-half to seven and one-half years is the optimal period for maximum visual-perceptual development. Frostig's primary concern is for children whose perceptual development "lags" and who therefore do not have a secure basis for academic learning. For Frostig, perceptual development rate is almost entirely independent of intelligence, although she reports a positive correlation between perceptual disability and emotional disturbance. Whether emotional disturbance is a cause or a result of perceptual problems is not easily determined. Frostig generally avoids the issue of causation, although she admits that such factors as minimal brain dysfunction and sensory deprivation possibly lead to perceptual dysfunction. In short, Frostig's emphasis is upon diagnosis and remediation of specific perceptual deficits.

Visual-perception subfunctions isolated by Frostig include: (1) eye-hand coordination, (2) figure-ground perception, (3) form constancy, (4) position in space, and (5) spatial relationships. Her efforts to develop a diagnostic test and a program for perceptual subfunction training resulted from the observation that many children with general learning problems also demonstrate perceptual disabilities. Specific test content was therefore selected on the basis of those perceptual skills important to school performance, especially reading. In this connection, Frostig contends that roughly 20 to 25 percent of beginning first-grade children are insufficiently mature in perceptual development to make successful academic progress without "undue effort." Hence Frostig maintains that her program can be useful for the routine developmental training of normal kindergarten and first-grade children. This recommendation is made even though her techniques were originally devised for remedial purposes. Since Frostig believes that the "golden age" for perceptual training is during the late preschool and early school years, training is advised at this time in order best to prepare children for higher-order cognitive development. Frostig is careful to point out the limitation of this training, however, and does not guarantee that children who undergo this experience will operate successfully at higher cognitive levels.

Frostig's program is not confined to visual-perception training. It also includes procedures for the enhancement of gross and fine muscle coordination, body image, and eye movement. Neither does Frostig limit her educational therapy to diagnosed visual-perception deficits. Her broader clinical strategy is built upon cues from additional measures of individual differences including the Wepman Test of Auditory Discrimination, the Wechsler Intelligence Scale for Children, and the Illinois Test of Psycholinguistic Abilities (Frostig, 1967).

Comment   Most accounts in the literature specific to Frostig testing and training have been advanced by Frostig and her colleagues (for example, Frostig, Lefever, and Whittlesey, 1964; Frostig and Horne, 1965). There are some indications in the perceptual-motor literature that both the test and training program are being used with increased frequency, but reports of this increased use vary widely in their scope and quality. With respect to the visual-perception–achievement relationship, both Olson (1966) and Gill and Herdtner (1968) provide Frostig with moderate support. Olson (1966) found the Frostig materials to be "of some value" in predicting general achievement among second-graders. He also uncovered scattered relationships between Frostig scores and specific reading abilities. As for the prediction of academic achievement, however, Olson voices more confidence in conventional instruments such as intelligence scales. While Gill and Herdtner (1968) found perceptual performance generally to be positively correlated with academic success, this relationship was stronger for girls than boys.

At this writing, only a few studies involving the application of Frostig training techniques have been published. These studies have also generally been limited to samples of exceptional children. For example, in two investigations with retardates, significant visual-perception skill improvement as a function of Frostig training has been found (Allen, Dickman, and Haupt, 1966; Talkington, 1968). Unanswered in studies such as these, however, is the question of *transfer:* whether perceptual skill improvement is associated with academic gains.[18] Such studies

[18] This involves the issue of *allied change* discussed in Chapter 5.

are necessary further to clarify the relationship of visual perception and reading achievement, including the degree and specificity of perceptual skill required (see Olson and others, 1968). Unfortunately, the appropriateness of the Frostig test for this clarification has been seriously challenged (Olson, 1968). Olson's statistical analysis of Frostig test data leads one to question Frostig's claim that the test measures five separate and critical visual-perception skills. Instead, the test seems to measure one common perceptual factor (Olson, 1968).

The Delacato Technique   Easily the most controversial of training approaches within the area of sensory-motor functioning is that based upon the theory of neurological organization (Delacato, 1963, 1966). Out of this theory Delacato has attempted to develop a totally new concept of remediation technique, particularly with reference to reading and language problems. Delacato sees such problems as manifestations of deficiencies in neurological organization, that is, incomplete or inadequate neurological cell differentiations and arrangements. In contrast, intellectual and sensory-motor superiority are for Delacato valid indices of complete neurological organization. This basic tenet of Delacato's theory has led him to argue that a diversity of sensory-motor and cognitive "dysfunctions" can be treated by imposing on one's nervous system a program of "nonsurgical" exercises. These exercises, including cross-pattern creeping and walking, a prescribed position for sleep, and various lateralization activities, are claimed to result in a reorganization of critical nerve cells. Once this occurs, Delacato maintains, improved sensory-motor functioning will follow. These procedures have been advocated by their inventor for the treatment of brain-injured and severely retarded children as well as for average children with specific learning disabilities. By implication, the program would supposedly accelerate or otherwise facilitate normal developmental processes for all children.

Comment   The principal supportive evidence for the neurological reorganization approach has been Delacato's own clinical data. By and large these data have been anecdotal (versus statistical) and have failed to meet the legitimate requirements of scientific study. Despite the ambiguities and weaknesses in Delacato's reporting procedure, his techniques have been publicized favorably in many popular magazines (Robbins, 1967). The scientific community, in contrast, has received favorably neither Delacato's theory nor his claims concerning treatment effects. Hudspeth (1964) was among the early skeptics who addressed the implausibility of the Delacato position, especially with reference to children's reading behavior. More recently, a joint statement on

Delacato has been issued by the American Academy of Pediatrics and American Academy of Neurology (1968). The writers of this statement are particularly critical of Delacato's undocumented contentions regarding the "cure" of neurologically handicapped children and the "extreme demands" placed upon parents in fulfilling their roles as remedial agents. The responsibility has thus been placed upon Delacato and his colleagues to provide evidence which validates both his theory and the training techniques derived from it.

To this writer's knowledge, Delacato has not yet answered satisfactorily the challenges of his critics. Meanwhile, independent inquiries into Delacato's original claims have appeared. Two such inquiries based on neurological organization theory have been performed by Robbins (1966, 1967), who himself studied at Delacato's Institutes for the Achievement of Human Potential. Neither inquiry has provided support for Delacato's neurological organization theory generally nor the neurological organization–reading skill relationship, specifically. According to Robbins' data, reading skill is related neither to creeping ability, laterality, nor exposure to the Delacato training program. This conclusion held for both normal and retarded readers at the primary and intermediate grade levels. A similar conclusion, that Delacato treatment per se is of little benefit to the reading readiness of kindergarten children, has been made by Stone and Pielstick (1969). These researchers did, however, observe a slight increase in performance on the Frostig Developmental Test of Visual Perception among children who experienced Delacato training. Hence it is possible that such training may result in some advantage concerning "lower" sensory-motor development, but it is not clear whether this possible advantage is related in a functional way to reading readiness or progress in reading achievement. The principal issue once again involves transfer of training. As Wingert (1969) has shown, improved and relatively permanent visual-motor skills (as measured by the Frostig Tests) may be achieved through training but do not necessarily carry over to reading skills.[19]

Clearly what is needed at this time is more carefully controlled research into Delacato's neurological training program. Careful research evaluation of the Kephart and Frostig programs is also needed, although these two approaches are more plausible scientifically than is Delacato's. Kephart and Frostig have not made the same radical assumptions about development as Delacato. Neither have their reporting procedures attracted the wrath of allied professionals. At this point, an atti-

---

[19] A thorough critique of experimentation regarding the function of neurological organization and reading behavior has been provided by Glass and Robbins (1967).

tude of critical objectivity toward these approaches is mandatory. This attitude is conveyed effectively in the following excerpt:

> Some of the training procedures recommended by these programs (Kephart, Frostig, Delacato) are competitive but not contradictory. For example, for the typical school-age reading disability case, it is likely that Kephart would utilize "angels in the snow" as a training procedure, while Delacato would recommend crawling. Here the choice is based principally on the question of which offers greater efficiency (Le Winn, 1966). *But in some instances, the competitive recommendations would be flatly contradictory.* For example, if a retarded reader lacked a well-defined handedness, Delacato would probably promote the development of "single-handedness" by discouraging the use of the subdominant hand. This is precisely what Kephart would not recommend. In fact, Kephart feels that in some cases a strongly developed handedness serves to compensate for, and may even mask, a serious deficiency in internal awareness of left and right.[20] The existence of a methodological conflict is also suggested by Ayres, who commented, "One also wonders if we need . . . to have two sides of the body to work together adequately, before we establish hand dominance" (1964). In the Frostig program (1964, 1965), early attention is given to identifying right and left parts of the body on pictorial representations and on the self. Kephart, on the other hand, would not use the designations right and left in such early training, nor would he emphasize pictorial representations. Moreover, he feels that many children deficient in internal awareness of left and right can reliably name the sides of their bodies solely on the basis of external characteristics (Kephart, 1960, p. 45).
>
> Viewed from the perspective of developing specific skills or as purely recreational activities, the further proliferation of sensory-motor programs poses few problems. However, when the sensory-motor activity is designed to affect an underlying central process, presumably deficient or disturbed in certain types of clinical cases such as reading disability, such conflicts are of considerable clinical and ethical importance. Individual therapeutic successes, however dramatic, do not provide proof of the correctness of the theory upon which it is based. Further proliferation of techniques, schools and even "cults" can only compound the confusion that already exists in this field. [Ball and Edgar, 1967, pp. 393–394][21]

[20] Delacato equates laterality with the child's pattern of handedness, eyedness, and footedness. For Kephart, handedness and laterality are linked, but they are not one and the same thing (Kephart, 1960). For a comprehensive discussion of laterality concepts, see Palmer (1964).

[21] Only a small sample from the literature on perceptual-motor theory and training has been reviewed in this chapter. Perceptual influences on early school behavior constitute an extremely viable area for further study. The interested reader is encouraged to consult the following references for this purpose: Ames (1969); Bibace and Hancock (1969); Dudek (1969); Edgar (1969); Falik (1969); Gill and others (1968); Mann (1969); O'Donnell and Eisenson (1969); Rice (1969); and Sparrow (1969).

Infant Stimulation

For one inclined to accept a broadly liberal concept of early child-hood education the subject of infant stimulation is laced with many pro-vocative implications. Recent investigations of the effects of infant "education" represent not only an extension of the "renaissance" dis-cussed in Chapter 1, but an extension of long-standing interest among psychologists in such areas as learning in infancy, maternal and sensory deprivation, and variations in early socialization practices.[22] These interests and others provide a background for several research programs for infant stimulation. Most of these recent programs are intended to prevent retardation thought to have an environmental source. This re-search activity also involves questions related to how and to what extent the course of normal development might be accelerated. This writer pre-fers to leave to his readers the matter of philosophical or ethical judg-ments concerning infant education. Thus, this segment of the chapter will be limited to a brief description of illustrative programs and, where applicable, their results.

Two programs of study from which early returns are available are those of White (1968) and Painter (1968). White (1968) begins with the premise that the basic objective of an educational system is to maximize each individual's ability to cope with "life's various problems." The achievement of this goal, White reasons, is impossible until educators attend to the entire course of postnatal development instead of limiting their concern to the events which begin at age 5 or 6. White acknowl-edges that much more research into early development is needed in order to reap any dividends that may follow from this broadened atten-tion. Thus, White has elected to study infants from birth through about age 8 months in order to build a stock of data from which rich educa-tional hypotheses may be formulated and tested.

Most recently White has attempted to assess the extent to which very early development can be influenced by differential rearing conditions. Preliminary data taken from the study of an enriched infant environ-ment have led White to invest his confidence in developmental plastic-ity, that is, the notion that developmental processes, especially those perceptual-motor in origin, do not just "happen" but are influenced measurably by environmental conditions.[23] For example, the condition of "extra handling" (tactile stimulation) is reported to have resulted in

[22] See, for example, Caldwell (1964), Casler (1961), Yarrow (1961), and Orlansky (1949) for reviews of studies related to these topics.

[23] Four early perceptual-motor functions have been isolated in White's infant studies: visually directed reaching, visual attention, visual accommodation, and blinking in re-sponse to an approaching visible object.

increased visual attention responses among infants. Advances in reaching behaviors (prehension) and visual attention were also observed (ultimately, although not initially) to be affected positively by an enriched visual environment and increased infant opportunity for object manipulation and movement.

From these and other data extracted from his "modification-enrichment" studies, White (1968) has testified to the "enormous importance" of the first five months of life for perceptual-motor development. He has also concluded that enrichment procedures influence the course of early development in remarkable ways. Unknown as yet are the answers to such important questions as (1) What minimal amounts and kinds of stimulation are necessary for normal development? (2) At what point does stimulation cease to be salubrious and may even become hazardous? (3) Does early enrichment necessarily produce changes (advantages) that are more long-term in nature?

While White's work has involved "normal" subjects, Painter (1968, 1969) has dealt with infants who would be classified by most educators as "disadvantaged." Briefly, Painter administered a structured program of stimulation to a group of infants (8–24 months old) in their own homes. This year-long program consisted of early language, conceptual, and sensory-motor training. End-of-year comparisons were made between the experimental infants and a group of controls (infants initially equal in developmental and socioeconomic status but who did not experience any special training). Standard developmental criteria were used for this comparison, including the Stanford-Binet and assorted language-conceptual tasks. In general, the results indicated developmental superiority for the training group. On the basis of these findings Painter has concluded that (1) specific early intervention can make a positive difference in total development; and (2) the home environment provides a suitable medium (vehicle) for such intervention. At this point in time we cannot say, of course, whether the apparent gains of Painter's experimental infants will hold throughout the preschool years or whether early training in infancy will be an antecedent to successful school achievement. As one wag has put it, "Are subnurseries really necessary?"

Even larger scale social action projects are the infant stimulation programs of Caldwell and Richmond (1968) and Robinson (1968). These research workers have taken the position that sound and systematic "education" is feasible as early as the first year of life and may be indispensable if inadvertent learning deficiencies are to be prevented. High frequency adult contact, a variety of manipulable play materials, exploratory freedom, rich cultural experiences, health care, verbal stimulation, and family educational services are among the principal components of these programs; all components are coordinated with successive levels of development. Optimistic early returns have been provided by these researchers, particularly in terms of "eliminating" to a large extent the developmental disadvantages frequently associated with lower socioeconomic status. Although the Caldwell and Richmond (1968) program has been limited largely to children from the age of six months to three years, Robinson's (1968) program allows for infants as early as the neonatal stage (these are typically the infants of working mothers). Both of these vanguard programs should provide an abundant source of longitudinal data on early learning and development. These and other continuing studies—for example, the Yale Child Study Program (Provence, 1969), the Harlem Research Center Project (Palmer, 1969), the Florida Parent Education Program for infant stimulation (Gordon, 1969), the Ypsilanti Home Stimulation Program for Infants (Weikart, 1970), and the Infant Education Research Project (Schaefer and Aaronson, 1970)—have the potential to produce trenchant changes in the thinking of early childhood educators.

The Early Training Project   A step away from infant education is the *Early Training Project* (Gray and Klaus, 1968; Klaus and Gray, 1968). This Project is important, however, due to its concern with the problem of environmentally-based progressive retardation, a concern central to infant stimulation projects. This broad gauge intervention program was conceived from a summer pilot project (1961) that yielded fragmentary and disappointing results with deprived children bound for the first-grade. In the words of the researchers, this intervention was "too little, too late." Thus, a five-year program was initiated in 1962 with both preschool children (age 3) and their parents as participants. The intervention package, including home visitation procedures for parent education, has included materials and activities thought to be most closely associated with successful school performance.[24] Special attention was given to the systematized use of equipment (such as puzzles, painting and coloring materials, and rhythm instruments), adult-child interactions (reinforcement patterns or schedules), and the timing of language and concept-building activities. Summers were devoted to group activities; the winter program was executed primarily through the home visitations.

For research purposes, Klaus and Gray (1968) devised two combinations of summer and winter programs for experimental children. They

---

[24] A detailing of materials and procedures for their use has been provided by Gray and others (1966).

also arranged for two control groups. Some eighty children in all were thus studied. An attempt was made to modify specific aptitudes and attitudes among the experimental-group children. Many instruments were used to assess change, including the Stanford-Binet, the Peabody Picture Vocabulary Test, reading readiness tests, achievement test batteries, and various original attitudinal measures. Achievement test batteries were also used once the children had entered school.

A wealth of data has resulted from the Early Training Project, although only a few major findings will be reported here. First, modestly positive and statistically significant effects were observed for the experimental children throughout the period of the Project. This included the second year of public schooling. Secondly, the more widespread and apparently reliable differences between the experimental- and control-group children occurred in cognitive, rather than in affective behavior. This is perhaps due in part to the lesser degree of sophistication characteristic of personal-social behavior assessments. Nevertheless, this second finding is indicative of the potentially more difficult problems facing intervention programs designed to influence motivational response-pattern development. Third, the researchers concluded that the earlier intervention procedures are implemented the greater their influence is likely to be. Moreover, state Klaus and Gray (1968), the greater the initial deprivation the more probable it is that intervention (or its lack) will make a difference.

The Early Training Project is significant methodologically if for no other reason than that its formulators have anticipated many of the problems which are thought to impede success in Project Head Start (see Chapter 3). This Project has also indicated longer-term results than is typically the case for most programs. Further follow-up data on this Project and other research and demonstration activities are contemplated at the Demonstration and Research Center for Early Education (DARCEE) in Nashville, Tennessee.[25]

SUMMARY

This chapter summarizes a variety of contemporary influences in early childhood education, ranging from the British infant school movement to infant stimulation. A most noteworthy feature of the former

[25] Two additional significant demonstration projects concerned with assisting impoverished children are Martin Deutsch's program at the Institute of Developmental Studies in New York and Herbert Sprigle's Learning to Learn School. See Grotberg (1969) for brief descriptions of these projects.

movement is the genuine commitment to informal, child-centered education that it represents. Concepts of organization and instruction such as the integrated day, vertical groupings, and education for thought-process development characterize this movement; the movement's protagonists believe that such conceptual guidelines are much more consistent with the course of children's cognitive and affective development than are "traditional, lock-step" approaches. Although conventional research and evaluation procedures have not been applied widely in the changing British infant schools, most anecdotal reports from teachers and outside observers reflect a basic enthusiasm and confidence in the power of "open education" to produce desirable outcomes. Although there are many similarities, both philosophically and psychologically, between new infant school practice and the concept of American progressive education, more widespread acceptance and support of child-centered policies has seemingly occurred in the British schools. Two American versions of British infant school practice, the Educational Development Center's "Continuing Growth Plan," and the Vermont Design for Education warrant close watching by educators in this country.

Additional topics examined in this chapter include programs for children's emotional education and perceptual-motor development. Few systematic attempts to foster emotional growth are apparent at this writing, although an increasing amount of space in the early education literature is being devoted to the views of teachers and psychologists concerned with children's feelings and modes of emotional expression. Perhaps the most serious issue to be reckoned with in this regard is the distinction between education and psychotherapy, particularly in view of the possibility that teachers may easily tread on psychological grounds they have not been trained to cultivate.

Programs for perceptual-motor development tend most frequently to be remedial in nature, that is, applied to children whose academic progress is slow or who manifest various sorts of learning disabilities. Perceptual-motor training is generally based on the assumption that certain basic perceptual-motor skills underlie a child's academic response repertoire. As a whole, research conducted on these programs has been spotty and inconclusive, a fact perhaps too often overlooked by educators quick to implement new remedial procedures in the schools.

This chapter was concluded with a brief discussion of infant stimulation programs. Obviously, many ethical issues are associated with the concept of systematic intervention during the earliest years of life; however, the supporters of this concept have based their views upon generally sound psychological rationales. Longitudinal research on infant education has not yet reached a stage in which decisive comment on the extended effects of stimulation programs is advised, but preliminary findings indicate that systematic stimulation does influence general early development in measurable ways.

References

Adler, Alfred. *Practice and Theory of Individual Psychology.* New York: Harcourt, 1927.

Allen, R., I. Dickman, and T. Haupt. "A Pilot Study of the Immediate Effectiveness of the Frostig-Horne Training Program with Educable Retardates." *Exceptional Children,* 1966, 33, 41–42.

American Academy of Pediatrics and American Academy of Neurology. "Joint Executive Board Statement on the Doman-Delacato Treatment of Neurologically Handicapped Children." *Sight-Saving Review,* 1968, 38, 148–154.

Ames, Louise Bates. "Children with Perceptual Problems May Also Lag Developmentally." *Journal of Learning Disabilities,* 1969, 2, No. 4, 205–208.

Armington, David E. "A Plan for Continuing Growth." In *Descriptions of Follow Through Programs.* Washington, D.C.: U.S. Department of Health, Education, and Welfare, Office of Education, 1968, C-1-12.

Ausubel, David P. *Theory and Problems of Child Development.* New York: Grune and Stratton, 1958, 86–88.

Ball, T. S., and Clara Lee Edgar. "The Effectiveness of Sensory-motor Training in Promoting Generalized Body Image Development." *Journal of Special Education,* 1967, 1, 387–395.

Barth, Roland S. "Open Education." *Theory and Philosophy of Education,* Kensington, Australia, 1969.

Barth, Roland S., and Charles H. Rathbone. "Informal Education." *The Center Forum,* 1969, 3, 108.

Bessell, Harold. "The Content is the Medium: The Confidence is the Message." *Psychology Today,* 1968, 2, 32–35ff.

Bessell, Harold, and Uvaldo H. Palomares. *Methods in Human Development.* San Diego: Human Development Training Institute, 1967.

Bibace, Roger, and Karen Hancock. "Relationships between Perceptual and Conceptual Cognitive Process." *Journal of Learning Disabilities,* 1969, 2, No. 1, 19–30.

Blackie, John. *Inside the Primary School.* London: Her Majesty's Stationery Office, 1967.

Buktenica, N.A. *Visual Learning.* San Rafael, Calif.: Dimensions Publishing Co., 1969.

Caldwell, Bettye M. "The Effects of Infant Care." In M. L. Hoffman and Lois W. Hoffman (Eds.), *Review of Child Development Research.* New York: Russell Sage, 1964, 9–88.

Caldwell, Bettye M., and Julius B. Richmond. "The Children's Center in Syracuse, New York." In Caroline A. Chandler, Reginald S. Lourie, and Anne De Huff Peters (Eds.), *Early Child Care: The New Perspectives.* New York: Atherton Press, 1968, 326–358.

Casler, L. "Maternal Deprivation: A Critical Review of the Literature." *Monographs of the Society for Research in Child Development,* 1961, 26, No. 2., Whole No. 80.

Cazden, Courtney B. "Interview with Susan Williams." *ERIC Report,* PS001615, 1967, 19 pp.

Chaney, Clara M., and Newell C. Kephart. *Motoric Aids to Perceptual Training.* Columbus: Merrill, 1968.

Clarizio, Harvey F. (Ed.). *Mental Health and the Educative Process.* Skokie: Rand McNally, 1969.

Cohen, David K. "Children and Their Primary Schools: Volume II." *Harvard Educational Review,* 1968, 38, 329–340.

Coopersmith, Stanley. *The Antecedents of Self-esteem.* San Francisco: Freeman, 1967.

Delacato, Carl. *The Diagnosis and Treatment of Speech and Reading Problems.* Springfield, Ill.: Charles C Thomas, 1963.

Delacato, Carl. *Neurological Organization and Reading.* Springfield, Ill.: Charles C Thomas, 1966.

Denison, Joseph W. "Perceptual Influences in the Primary Grades: An Alternative Consideration." *Journal of School Psychology,* 1968–69, 7, 38–46.

Dinkmeyer, Don C., and Rudolf Dreikurs. *Encouraging Children to Learn: The Encouragement Process.* Englewood Cliffs: Prentice-Hall, 1963.

Drews, Elizabeth Monroe. "Self-Actualization: A New Focus for Education." In *1966 Yearbook, Association for Supervision and Curriculum Development.* Washington, D.C.: National Education Association, 1966, 99–126.

Dreyer, Albert S., and Dorothy Haupt. "Self-evaluation in Young Children." *Journal of Genetic Psychology,* 1966, 108, 185–197.

Dudek, S. Z. "The Validity of Cognitive, Perceptual-motor, and Personality Variables for Prediction of Achievement in Grade I and Grade II." *Journal of Clinical Psychology,* 1969, 25, 165–170.

Early, George H., and Newell C. Kephart. "Perceptual-motor Training and Academic Achievement." *Academic Therapy Quarterly,* 1969, 4, 201–206.

Edgar, Clara Lee. "Effects of Sensory-motor Training on Adaptive Behavior." *American Journal of Mental Deficiency,* 1969, 73, 713–20.

Ellisor, Mildred. "Classroom Opportunities to Express Feelings." *Childhood Education,* 1969, 45, 373–378.

Falik, Louis H. "The Effects of Special Perceptual-motor Training in Kindergarten on Reading Readiness and on Second Grade Reading Performance." *Journal of Learning Disabilities,* 1962, 2, No. 8, 10–17.

Featherstone, Joseph. "Schools for Children." *The New Republic,* 1967a (Aug. 19), 17–21.

Featherstone, Joseph. "How Children Learn." *The New Republic,* 1967b (Sept. 2), 17–21.

Featherstone, Joseph. "Teaching Children to Think." *The New Republic,* 1967c (Sept. 9), 15–19.

Featherstone, Joseph. "Report Analysis: Children and Their Primary Schools." *Harvard Educational Review,* 1968, 38, 317–328.

Frostig, Marianne. "Testing as a Basis for Educational Therapy." *Journal of Special Education,* 1967, 2, 15–34.

Frostig, Marianne, and David Horne. *The Frostig Program for the Development of Visual Perception.* Chicago: Follett, 1964.

Frostig, Marianne, and David Horne. "An Approach to the Treatment of Children with Learning Disorders." In Jerome Hellmuth (Ed.), *Learning Disorders,* Vol. I. Seattle: Special Child Publications, 1965, 293–305.

Frostig, Marianne, D. W. Lefever, and J. R. B. Whittlesey. "A Developmental Test of Visual Perception for Evaluating Normal and Neurologically Handicapped Children." *Perceptual and Motor Skills,* 1961, 12, 383–384.

Frostig, Marianne, D. W. Lefever, and J. R. B. Whittlesey. *The Marianne Frostig Development Test of Visual Perception.* Palo Alto, Calif.: Consulting Psychologists Press, 1964.

Gilbert, Doris C. "The Young Child's Awareness of Affect." *Child Development,* 1969, 40, 629–640.

Gill, Newell, and L. L. Herdtner. "Perceptual and Socioeconomic Variables, Instruction in Body-orientation, and Predicted Academic Success in Young Children." *Perceptual and Motor Skills,* 1968, 26, 1175–1184.

Gill, Newell T., Thomas J. Herdtner, and Linda Lough. "Selected Perceptual and Socio-economic Variables, Body-orientation Instruction, and Predicted Academic Success in Young Children." *Childhood Education,* 1968, 45, 52–54.

Glass, G. V., and M. P. Robbins. "A Critique of Experiments on the Role of Neurological Organization in Reading Performance." *Reading Research Quarterly,* 1967, 3, 5–51.

Gordon, Ira J. "Stimulation Via Parent Education." *Children,* 1969, 16, 57–59.

Gray, Susan W, and Rupert A. Klaus. "The Early Training Project and Its General Rationale." In Robert D. Hess and Roberta Meyer Baer (Eds.), *Early Education.* Chicago: Aldine, 1968, 63–70.

Gray, Susan W., and others. *Before First Grade.* New York: Teachers College, 1966.

Grossman, Len, and Donald H. Clark. "Sensitivity Training for Teachers: A Small Group Approach." *Psychology in the Schools,* 1967, 4, 267–271.

Grotberg, Edith. *Review of Research: 1965–1969.* Washington, D.C.: Office of Economic Opportunity, 1969.

Hackett, Layne C., and Robert G. Jensen. *A Guide to Movement Exploration.* Palo Alto, Calif.: Peek Publication, 1966.

Hall, William P., and David Armington. "Leicestershire Revisited." *ERIC Report,* PS00617, 1967, 16 pp.

Hawkins, David, and Frances Hawkins. "Leicestershire: A Personal Report." *Elementary Science Study Newsletter,* 1964 (June), 1–3.

Horney, Karen. *Neurosis and Human Growth.* New York: Norton, 1950.

Hudspeth, J. "The Neurobehavioral Implausibility of the Delacato Theory." In M. P. Douglass (Ed.), *Claremont Reading Conference Yearbook,* 1964, 126–131.

Ismail, A. H., and J. J. Gruber. *Motor Aptitude and Intellectual Performance.* Columbus: Merrill, 1967.

Kahn, D. and H. Birch. "Development of Auditory-visual Integration and Reading Achievement." *Perceptual and Motor Skills,* 1968, 27, 459–468.

Kephart, Newell C. *The Slow Learner in the Classroom.* Columbus: Merrill, 1960.

Kershner, John R. "Doman-Delacato's Theory of Neurological Organization Applied with Retarded Children." *Exceptional Children,* 1968, 34, 441–450.

Klaus, Rupert A., and Susan W. Gray. "The Early Training Project for Disadvantaged Children: A Report after Five Years." *Monographs of the Society for Research in Child Development,* 1968, 53, Serial No. 120.

Learning and Living. Report of the Provincial Committee on Aims and Objectives of Education in the Schools of Ontario. Toronto: Ontario Department of Education, 1968.

Levy, Philip, Stan Gooch, and M. L. Kellmer-Pringle. "A Longitudinal Study of the Relationship between Anxiety and Streaming in a Progressive and a Traditional Junior School." *British Journal of Educational Psychology,* 1969, 39, 166–173.

Long, Nicholas J. "Helping Children Cope with Feelings." *Childhood Education,* 1969, 45, 367–372.

Lowe, C. Marshall. "The Self-Concept: Fact or Artifact?" *Psychological Bulletin,* 1961, 58, 325–336.

McCandless, Boyd R. *Children: Behavior and Development* (2d ed.) New York: Holt, Rinehart and Winston, 1967, Chap. 6.

McCormick, Clarence C., Janice N. Schnobrich, and S. Willard Footlik. "The Effect of Perceptual-motor Training on Reading Achievement." *Academic Therapy Quarterly,* 1969, 4, 171–176.

Mann, Gloria T. "Reversal Reading Errors in Children Trained in Dual Directionality." *Reading Teacher,* 1969, 22, 646–648.

O'Donnell, P. A. *Motor and Haptic Learning.* San Rafael, Calif.: Dimensions Publishing Co., 1969.

O'Donnell, Patrick A., and Jon Eisenson. "Delacato Training for Reading Achievement and Visual Motor Integration." *Journal of Learning Disabilities,* 1969, 2, No. 9, 10–16.

Ojemann, Ralph. "Basic Approaches to Mental Health: The Human Relations Program at the State University of Iowa." *Personnel and Guidance Journal,* 1958, 36, 198–206.

Ojemann, Ralph H. "Incorporating Psychological Concepts in the School Curriculum." *Journal of School Psychology,* 1967, 3, 195–204.

Olson, A. V. "Relation of Achievement Test Scores and Specific Reading Abilities to the Frostig Developmental Test of Visual Perception." *Perceptual and Motor Skills,* 1966, 22, 179–184.

Olson, A. V. "Factor Analytic Studies of the Frostig Developmental Test of Visual Perception." *Journal of Special Education,* 1968, 2, 429–433.

Olson, A. V., and others. *A Multivariate Analysis of First Grade Reading Achievement Reading Readiness, and Intelligence.* Athens, Georgia: University of Georgia Research and Development Center, 1968.

Orlansky, H. "Infant Care and Personality." *Psychological Bulletin,* 1949, 46, 1–48.

Painter, Genevieve. *Infant Education.* San Rafael, Calif.: Dimensions Publishing Co., 1968.

Painter, Genevieve. "The Effect of a Structured Tutorial Program on the Cognitive and Language Development of Culturally Disadvantaged Infants." *Merrill-Palmer Quarterly,* 1969, 15, 279–293.

Palmer, Frances H. "Learning at Two." *Children,* 1969, 16, 55–57.

Palmer, R. D. "Development of a Differentiated Handedness." *Psychological Bulletin,* 1964, 62, 257–272.

Peck, Robert F. "What Should We Teach Elementary School Children about the Principles of Human Behavior?" *Journal of School Psychology,* 1967, 5, 235–240.

Perkins, Hugh. "Clarifying Feelings through Peer Interaction." *Childhood Education,* 1969, 45, 379–380.

Plowden, Lady Bridget, (Chairman). *Children and Their Primary Schools: A Report of the Central Advisory Council for Education* (England), Vol. 1. London: Her Majesty's Stationery Office, 1967.

Prescott, Daniel. *Emotion and the Educative Process.* Washington, D.C.: American Council on Education, 1938.

Provence, Sally. "A Three-pronged Project." *Children,* 1969, 16, 53–55.

Rice, James A. "Confusion in Laterality: A Validity Study with Bright and Dull Children." *Journal of Learning Disabilities,* 1969, 2, No. 7, 29–34.

Roach, E. G., and N. C. Kephart. *The Purdue Perceptual-motor Survey.* Columbus: Merrill, 1966.

Robbins, M. P. "A Study of the Validity of Delacato's Theory of Neurological Organization." *Exceptional Children,* 1966, 32, 517–523. [See CD Abst. V. 41 Feb.-April, 1967 (#1 & 2) p. 3]

Robbins, M. P. "Test of the Doman-Delacato Rationale with Retarded Readers." *Journal of the American Medical Association,* 1967, 202, 87–91.

Robinson, Halbert B. "The Frank Porter Graham Child Development Center." In Caroline A. Chandler, Reginald S. Lourie, and Anne De Huff Peters (Eds.), *Early Child Care: The New Perspectives.* New York: Atherton Press, 1968, 302–312.

Rogers, Carl. *Counseling and Psychotherapy.* Boston: Houghton Mifflin, 1942.

Rogers, Carl. "The Facilitation of Significant Learning." In Laurence Siegel (Ed.), *Instruction: Some Contemporary Viewpoints.* San Francisco: Chandler Publishing Company, 1967, 37–54.

Rogers, Vincent R. "English and American Primary Schools." *Phi Delta Kappan,* 1969, 51, 71–75.

Ruebush, Britton E. "Anxiety." In Harold W. Stevenson (Ed.), *Child Psychology.* Chicago: University of Chicago Press, 1963, 460–516.

Sarason, Seymour, and others. *Anxiety in Elementary School Children.* New York: Wiley, 1960.

Schaefer, Earl, and Mary Aaronson. "Infant Education Research Project: Method and Implications." Paper presented at a conference entitled,

"Conceptualizations of Preschool Curricula," City University of New York, 1970 (May 22–24).

Schlesinger, Joy. "Leicestershire Report: The Classroom Environment." *ERIC Report,* PS001616, 1966, 14 pp.

Sealey, L. G. W. "Looking Back on Leicestershire." *ESI Quarterly Report,* 1966, Spring-Summer, 37–41.

Seidman, Jerome M. (Ed.). *Educating for Mental Health.* New York: Crowell, 1963.

Shields, M. "Reading and Transition to Junior School." *Educational Research,* 1969, 11, 143–147.

Smith, H. M. "Motor Activity and Perceptual Development: Some Implications for Physical Educators." *Journal of Health, Physical Education, Recreation,* 1968, 39, 28–36.

Sonntag, Joyce. "Sensitivity Training with Gifted Children." *Gifted Child Quarterly,* 1969, 13, 51–57.

Sparrow, Sara S. "Reading Disability and Laterality." *Proceedings, 77th Annual Convention, American Psychological Association,* 1969, 673–674.

Stone, Mark, and N. L. Pielstick. "Effectiveness of Delacato Treatment with Kindergarten Children." *Psychology in the Schools,* 1969, 6, 63–68.

Talkington, L. W. "Frostig Visual Perception Training with Low-ability-level Retarded." *Perceptual and Motor Skills,* 1968, 27, 505–506.

Torrance, E. Paul. *Education and the Creative Potential.* Minneapolis: University of Minnesota Press, 1963.

Torrance, E. Paul, and Robert D. Strom (Eds.). *Mental Health and Achievement.* New York: Wiley, 1965.

Wattenberg, W., and C. Clifford. "Relation of Self-concepts to Beginning Achievement in Reading." *Child Development,* 1964, 35, 461–467.

Weikart, David. *Ypsilanti Home Stimulation Program for Infants.* Personal correspondence, 1970.

White, Burton L. "Informal Education during the First Months of Life." In Robert D. Hess and Roberta M. Bear (Eds.), *Early Education.* Chicago: Aldine, 1968, 143–169.

Wingert, Roger C. "Evaluation of a Readiness Training Program." *Reading Teacher,* 1969, 22, 325–328.

Yarrow, Leon J. "Maternal Deprivation: Toward an Empirical and Conceptual Evaluation." *Psychological Bulletin,* 1961, 58, 459–490.

Yeomans, Edward. *Education for Initiative and Responsibility.* Boston: National Association of Independent Schools, 1969.

8
Major Issues Revisited

The title song from a popular motion picture of the sixties *(Alfie)* contains a phrase very appropriate to the concern of this book, namely, "What's it all about?" A study of the preceding seven chapters should provide the reader with a variety of viewpoints in regard to this question. The basic value assumption underlying the viewpoints discussed in this book is that early childhood education is a good thing. However, this assumption must be qualified. Opinions differ on what kind of early childhood education is desirable, and some authorities have questioned the value of educational intervention beyond general enrichment for preprimary children (Elkind, 1969; Harris and Fisher, 1969). Without exception, adults make decisions about what is desirable for the education of young children. Adults then act to establish conditions which, at least in theory, will achieve desired goals. It is to research activity that one turns to determine as best as is possible what degree of success has been attained. Whenever research activity entails a comparison of one approach to another (as is frequently the case), there is an implicit competition factor involved which eventually boils down to the question, "Which program or what combination of experiences is best for children?" Such a question answered without qualification would surely be an oversimplification. The answer depends upon many variables, including one's preferred goals and the nature or needs of the children involved, and therefore is not easily achieved. Possibly the question will never be answered to the satisfaction of all people. The purpose of this chapter is to reconsider some major problems and issues in order to stimulate the reader's own thinking about programs for early childhood education.

Interrelated issues of major status from Chapter 1 involve goals, content, timing, methodology, instructional personnel, and general rationale for early childhood education. In the course of the book many other issues have been raised, including those related to research strategies, language and thought, the nature of learning and development, and the control of behavior. To do justice to all issues would require a chapter of immense proportions. Hence, only the problem of goals and the major issues of *what, how, when, who* and *where* will receive primary attention. This chapter will conclude with a discussion of problems related to research and ethics in early childhood education.

GOALS FOR EARLY CHILDHOOD EDUCATION

The creators of any approach to the education of young children must consider both immediate and long-range objectives. In practice, the latter are likely to be general and abstract while the former are more frequently specific. Unfortunately, the relationship of short- and long-term objectives is not always clear. Regardless, various mixes of philosophical and psychological thought are apparent in most goal statements. Broadly speaking, there seems not to be much conflict among those who prescribe alternative educational strategies with respect to long-term goals. For example, few would oppose the notion of "education for the development of maximum individual potential," although this, as well as any other objective, represents a value judgment (in this case based on the democratic idea). Other longer-term objectives that accompany this broad goal include such behavioral outcomes as autonomy and independence of judgment, ability to think critically, personal initiative and responsibility, self-respect, and respect for the rights and property of others. Such a listing could go on for pages, but the focus of the early childhood educator must, by necessity, be upon the foundations of these behaviors, which may be established during the early years. This notion, of course, is based upon the further assumption that the events of the early years are indeed critical for long-term personal development: that is, early experiences can make a measurable difference in what occurs later in the developmental sequence.

The importance of an educational and social philosophy for the purpose of establishing objectives cannot be overemphasized. If we place early childhood education in a total context of organized developmental education, a philosophy will be needed to answer many questions. Examples of such questions include what the characteristics of a "good life" should be, the extent to which different social, ethnic, or ability groups should receive different kinds of education, what constitutes a "proper" balance between individuality and social and intellectual conformity, and whether the school should encourage children and youth to change (improve) the social order (Furth, 1958). These "should" kinds of questions are inescapable.

Whether made explicit or not, the answers to "should" questions are manifest in the behavior of those who accept (assume) responsibility for the educational guidance of children. Many examples specific to the content of the present book can be cited, including whether "preschool" children should receive formal academic training and the extent to which all children should be required to "master" given areas of subject-matter content. Perhaps the most basic philosophical issue, however, relates to compensatory education: Should we intervene in the lives of these children and, if so, what should be the nature of this intervention? Many psychologists and educators have already answered both questions, but as yet universal agreement on these answers does not exist. In this connection, Cronbach (1969) suggests that confusion exists regarding the two basic ways an environmental modification can be helpful to children. One way involves the construction of an "optimal maintenance environment" so that children's growth can be promoted in the best possible fashion. The second way is to create a "special intervention environment" for the period of time necessary in order to develop children's readiness for the conventional environment. Once this readiness has been achieved, then special treatment can be terminated. Currently, the major source of disagreement among educators is in terms of the philosophical basis for deciding which kind of environment is most suitable for this or that group of children. Issues related to social-class value differences are also involved and will be clarified later in the chapter.

The "intervention or not" question raised above can serve to illustrate at least two related problems. First, an answer to this question depends in large part on prior philosophy-based decisions regarding the long-term characteristics of a desirable adult existence. Thus, a clear definition of an adult role that has value to both the individual and society is needed (Cronbach, 1969). Second, the "intervention or not" question helps to demonstrate the intimate relationship of philosophy to psychology. The role of psychology in selecting (and eliminating) goals for early childhood education is, like that of philosophy, crucial. Hopefully, from the psychological study of children's learning and development come data that contribute to the efficiency and effectiveness of education. Psychological questions range from a concern with the description of children's "natural" development (for example, Piaget) to the broad concern of determining the outcomes (for example, cognitive and affective) of deliberately arranged experiences. Once an answer to a psychological question is found, any decision to use it for educational planning requires a value judgment. Thus, philosophy and, in many cases, ethics again enter the picture.

Apart from some independent set of criteria, a discussion of the goals issue is limited to individual programs or approaches. For example, the major goals around which the Montessori curriculum for young children is organized are motor competence, sensory discrimination skills, basic academic skills, and personal autonomy. The structural pedagogy of Bereiter and Engelmann has been designed to produce an acceleration of language development, reading skills, and computational skills. Behavior analysis procedures, in practice, are oriented toward the development of self-management skills. A Piaget-based curriculum is geared primarily toward the cultivation of children's logical thinking. In short, emphases *are* different and can be arranged along several continua, including cognitive, affective, and psychomotor. The purpose of the present discussion, however, is not to review in detail the stated goals of these programs. Rather, the goals issue will be discussed more broadly in terms of how psychology may contribute to decisions regarding goals and to the evaluation of organized strategies for early education. Three basic ideas will be presented. The first two are the result of systematic analyses by psychologists. The third is essentially supplementary and represents perhaps more than anything else the writer's own value system. All three ideas, however, are intended to stimulate the reader's thinking about goals for early childhood education.[1]

[1] The larger issue of the relationship of goals for early childhood education to national goals will not be considered here, as this section is intended simply to provide different

Basic Behavior Repertoire

One framework within which to plan, analyze, and evaluate strategies for early childhood education is based upon the concept of a *basic behavior repertoire* (Staats, 1968). This concept refers to fundamentals of the spoken language, including syntax and grammar, attentional responses (including responsiveness to verbal cues), primary discrimination skills, and the various sensory-motor skills that are required for play and manipulative activities. It is argued (Staats, 1968) that such a repertoire is a necessary foundation for any child's subsequent learning success (cognitive, social, and emotional), especially in formal educational environments as they are presently constituted. In other words, the quality of basic repertoire acquisition affects children's ability to profit from later training, specifically the rate and quality of their subsequent school learning. Thus, a hierarchical approach to development and learning is implicit in Staat's thinking. Hierarchical development, it will be recalled, is inherent in both a Montessorian and a Piagetian approach to child development. Staats, however, has formulated this concept of hierarchical learning from a background of S-R theory and research. Staats believes that this concept is but one of several aspects of his new accounting of learning and behavior, especially of language acquisition.

The basic behavior repertoire described above has been broken down into several major components, as the following outline will indicate. Staats (1968, pp. 397–469) should be consulted for a more thorough discourse and rationale.

1. Basic Language Repertoire
   a. Phonemes and phonemic combinations (unit speech responses which comprise the sounds of language—this component of the repertoire must extend to an ability to link phonemes for purposes of word and sentence construction).
   b. Imitative speech responses (the ability to produce imitative sounds, a "fundamental" for reading response acquisition).
   c. Labeling speech repertoire (essentially a matter of vocabulary development whereby a child is sufficiently capable of responding with appropriate labels to environmental stimuli).
   d. Motor behavior under the control of verbal stimuli (ability to control one's own motor responses by verbal means and to follow the verbal instructions of others when appropriate).

---

viewpoints from which to consider goals. If the reader desires to consider developmental theory as the basic reference point for goal determination, a review of Chapter 6, "Piagetian Influences," is recommended.

  e. Basic set of word meanings (broad comprehension of the semantic properties of words used in daily child-adult interaction).
  f. Word association (a broad scope of grammatical word associations whereby standard sentence constructions and verbal sequences assist memory and reasoning).
  g. Number repertoire (basic counting responses where correct orders of verbal responses prevail).
2. Attention
  a. "Sense placing" responses (for example, looking, feeling) under stimulus control (for example, verbal instructions) to permit effective sensory stimulation.
  b. Discrimination skills (refined attention which results in differential responding, such as attending to critical attributes which differentiate stimuli by form and color through simultaneous and successive comparison).
3. Sensory-Motor Skills
  a. General balance and coordinated movement through space.
  b. Eye-hand coordination.
  c. Imitation responses (including ability to discriminate the actions of other persons, the stimuli that control such actions, and when imitation is appropriate).
4. Motivation (including responsiveness to "natural reinforcers," such as praise and social approach, and "self-reinforcers," such as successful task accomplishment, which are relied upon in the classroom for purposes of maintaining attention, persistence, and the like).

Staats (1968) argues that the acquisition of the basic behavior repertoire in itself is complex and depends heavily upon the systematic application of several principles, including instrumental discrimination learning and reinforcement (see Chapter 5). It is further argued that our present educational system has been designed with the assumption that children come to school with a basically sound repertoire. That is, the elementary school curriculum, including kindergarten, begins with tasks whose successful achievement depends upon skills like those outlined above. Most of these skills are acquired in the home (well or poorly) with parents as the agents responsible for child training. Educators have seemingly operated on the premise that parents can do such training. Staats, however, seriously questions this premise. He maintains that parents, whose abilities to teach children vary greatly, have themselves rarely encountered systematic training in techniques for conducting successful training. Staats further maintains that in society it has generally been expected that parents will deal with a great variety of training problems, some of which are very difficult (for example, mentally and physically handicapped children). The problem, as Staats sees it, is that parents have typically not been provided with sufficient knowledge, skills, and materials to help in the solution of these training problems. In view of this, Staats concludes that our current educational system reflects little regard for the foundation upon which it rests, namely, early childhood learning.

There are many implications of the Staats (1968) position, including the extension of compulsory public education downward so that a child's basic repertoire can be earlier assessed and refined. For the moment, however, the reader is encouraged once again to consider the alternatives to early education described in this book with the *basic behavior repertoire as a criterion for analysis.* If preschool or preprimary programs, including compensatory strategies, are purported by their designers to prepare children in better ways for formal academic experiences, such a criterion is useful. Of course, this notion is based on the assumption that Staats has correctly identified a foundation of skills essential for a child's subsequent progress in schools as they are presently constituted.

The Developmental Task Concept

A second potentially helpful approach to the development and evaluation of early childhood education programs concerns a system of developmental tasks (Havighurst, 1953). A developmental task is defined as "a task (or problem) that arises at or about a certain period in the life of the individual, successful achievement of which leads to his well-being, positive adjustment, and success with later tasks, while failure leads to unhappiness in the individual, disapproval by society, and difficulty with later tasks" (Havighurst, 1953, p. 2).

Tasks are said to arise from one or more of three basic sources: physical maturation, cultural pressures, and personal values and aspirations. Havighurst's basic hypothesis is that performance on developmental tasks at any given age is positively interrelated and that performance in a given task area at one age is positively related to subsequent performance in that area. Longitudinal research has by and large supported this hypothesis, although studies of the adolescent period have been more extensive than those which concern the early childhood years (Havighurst, 1956).

It is reasoned that certain developmental tasks are confronted by all children in the course of their development in western culture—some, in fact, represent cultural universals. These tasks are also tied to general

age periods and thus reflect a combination of maturational and cultural forces. Developmental tasks of infancy and early childhood (birth
to about age 6) are essentially biosocial in nature according to this system and include:[2]

> Learning to walk.
> Learning to take solid foods.
> Learning to talk.
> Learning to control the elimination of body wastes.
> Learning sex differences and sexual modesty.
> Achieving physiological stability.
> Forming simple concepts of social and physical reality.
> Learning to relate oneself emotionally to parents, siblings, and
> other people.
> Learning to distinguish right and wrong and developing a con-
> science.

Additional groupings of developmental tasks have been established
for middle childhood (ages 6 to 12) and adolescence. Among the former
relevant to this discussion are:

> Learning physical skills necessary for ordinary games.
> Building a positive attitude toward oneself as a developing person.
> Learning skills for effective social interaction.
> Learning an appropriate sex role.
> Developing fundamental skills in reading, writing, and calculating.
> Developing concepts necessary for everyday living (such as time,
> space, number, form, color, social roles).
> Developing conscience, morality, and a scale of values.
> Development toward personal independence.

Havighurst (1953) suggests that the developmental-task concept is
useful for thinking about educational objectives, providing clues for
curriculum development and the timing of educational activity, in-
vestigating children's problems, and evaluating their developmental
progress. In short, Havighurst conceives of education as society's effort
to assist children toward the achievement of certain of their developmental tasks. Obviously the family as a social unit, and the school as
society's educational instrument, must be involved cooperatively if these
outcomes are to be realized.

---

[2] These are broadly defined units and can be broken down into smaller, more specific
behaviors. Developmental task "mastery" is thought further to contribute to a child's
developing sense of self, including a basic attitude of trust and a sense of autonomy and
initiative.

To become operational, a developmental task system approach to education requires more detailed thinking than is indicated above. For example, criteria valid for judging "successful achievement" of any given development task must be worked out. Further, techniques for the measurement of these criteria are needed. Presumably, however, a criterion-reference approach, as first discussed in Chapter 4, would be fruitful (see, for example, Popham and Husek, 1969). The point is that the developmental task system has been derived from the study of child development and sociocultural phenomena with the best interests of all children in mind. Its use as a frame of reference requires but few value judgments. Most basically, one must only agree that to view oneself as "successful" on his own terms in the context of his social existence is a good thing. On the other hand, a critic might point out that many of these developmental tasks are based on a "middle-class" value system. Hence the issue of applying a uniform value system to all children is raised. It should be clear to the reader by now, however, that the issue of what values to embrace cannot be escaped. Ultimately, any decision regarding early childhood education involves a value judgment.

The reader is again encouraged to review the alternatives to early education discussed during the course of this book in terms of the developmental-task system. For example, the originators and executors of these alternatives do not place equal values on the learning of academic or social skills. For another, most approaches are apparently lacking in any systematic provision for the development of morality and values or sex role identification. Should more attention be paid to these aspects of children's total development (a philosophical question)? If so, why?

Psychological Constructs

There is still another way whereby psychology can contribute to educators' decision making regarding goals and analyses of early childhood education programs. It involves a selection of constructs from psychological research that are pertinent to school behavior and generally consistent with values stressed in the mainstream of our society. While many such constructs could be reviewed, only a sampling will be included for purposes of illustration.

Self-Concept The importance of children's self-concepts is discussed with great frequency by educators and psychologists.[3] Most generally,

[3] The reader is referred to the earlier discussion of this construct (Chapter 7) for appropriate references concerning the self-concept.

the self-concept is thought to represent an organized system of *expectancies* and *self-evaluative tendencies* (McCandless, 1967). Such expectancies may be reflected by an individual's subjective estimates concerning what he can or cannot do; self-evaluative tendencies may be manifested by the feelings one has about the quality of his behavior.

Child workers are generally concerned that children develop a positive, albeit realistic self-concept. Frequently this concern is grounded directly in self-theory. Protagonists of self-theory suggest that behavior is motivated primarily in terms of the maintenance, enhancement, and actualization of self.

The relevance of the self-concept to early education can easily be clarified. Psychologists generally agree that the self-concept is learned as the consequence of one's experiences with success and failure, evaluation by others whom one considers significant, and patterns of reward and punishment encountered during the course of socialization. Thus the nature of a child's early educational experience is reasoned to be especially important as it shapes his view of himself as a learner.

Sound as the above rationale may be, there has not been much systematic research into the effects of early education environments on children's self-concepts. Part of this problem is due to a lack of satisfactory means to measure the self-concepts of young children.[4] More positively, there are data from which one can infer that early experiences with learning tasks and significant adults (parents and teachers) do make a difference in self-concept development.

A set of data that may be taken as an example of the latter statement has been provided by Coopersmith (1968). This elaborate study of preadolescent boys represents an exploration into the antecedents of self-esteem.[5] Coopersmith found that self-esteem was linked with several factors, including parental behavior and school achievement. Specifically, two dimensions of parental behavior were associated with high self-esteem among children: acceptance and management style. The former dimension—acceptance—was indicated by parental expression of affection, concern for the children's problems, availability in the sense of providing clear, confident assistance to the child, and general rapport and congenial joint activities. Important management-style variables identified by Coopersmith were a structuring of the child's world of rules and parental demands, firmness and consistency in carry-

[4] Some progress is being made toward a solution of this problem. The interested reader should consult Engel and Raine (1963), Dreyer and Haupt (1966), Carpenter and Busse (1969), and Soares and Soares (1969).

[5] Self-esteem as defined here refers to a personal judgment of worthiness that is expressed in the attitudes an individual holds toward himself.

ing out such demands, and respect for the latitude of children's actions within defined limits. In addition, Coopersmith found that control techniques such as corporal punishment and the withdrawal of love were used much less frequently by parents of children with high esteem. These parents also were found to provide their children with more assistance in self-evaluation. Finally, Coopersmith discovered that parents of low-esteem children tended to place more importance on the punishment of "bad" behavior than the rewarding of "good" behavior. In view of these findings, Coopersmith (1968) argues that firmness, clear parental demands, and rule enforcement combined with affection and ample recognition of accomplishments assist children toward greater self-definition and serve to symbolize parental concern and attention.

No set of data should be accepted uncritically and Coopersmith's research does not permit the derivation of a cause-effect statement. However, similar patterns of parental behavior have elsewhere been associated with dimensions of competent behavior among preschoolers (Baumrind and Black, 1967). Further, there are ample data to demonstrate a positive relationship between self-esteem and school achievement (for example, Fink, 1962; Teiglund, 1966; Shaw and Alves, 1963; Coopersmith, 1968). Hence it seems reasonable to suggest that the self-concept is an important aspect of psychological development affected by various early experiences. It is further possible that the parent behavior variables identified in these studies will apply in some degree to teacher behavior. One might cautiously conclude that competence, under conditions of acceptance and respect as a person by others, breeds positive self-esteem, which, in turn, contributes to a child's success in dealing with his environment. In terms of the present discussion, the question is whether the advocates of a given approach to early childhood education have attended sufficiently to conditions that facilitate competent school behavior and conditions which define the emotional climate of an early education environment.

Locus of Control   A second, related construct that merits the attention of early childhood educators is termed *locus of control* (Battle and Rotter, 1963). This construct refers to the extent to which an individual perceives that a given reinforcement (consequence) is a direct result of his own behavior (therefore subject to his personal control) versus the extent to which reinforcement is perceived as being under the control of external forces independent of his instrumental behavior. In theory, it is one's perception of causality that results in expectancies concerning the source of reinforcements. If, across various situations, a child expects that reinforcement (or what happens to him generally) is directly contingent upon his own behavior or personal attributes, he is said to be operating from an *internal* locus of control. In contrast, if a child expects that reinforcement or treatment received from others is essentially unrelated to his own behavior (therefore subject to such "forces" as luck, chance, fate, or the arbitrary whims of others), he is thought to be operating from an *external* locus of control. According to theory, the internal-external distinction is not dichotomous; the important factors are the degree of internality-externality and the stability of one's control orientation across various situations.

Many data have accumulated to suggest that control orientation is a significant variable in relation to learning and motivation. For example, Rotter (1966) has concluded that an individual with a predominantly internal locus of control is more likely to (1) be alert to environmental events which provide useful information for future behavior, (2) take steps to improve upon his environmental circumstances, and (3) place a high value upon reinforcements which are contingent upon personal skill and achievement. Other researchers have discovered positive relationships between internality and lesser susceptibility to group pressures for conformity, a preference for circumstances under which greater control over outcomes can be exercised, a willingness to engage in self-corrective activity in order to solve problems, and persistence in situations where skill or personal prowess can contribute to successful performance (Crowne and Liverant, 1963; Julian, Lichtman, and Ryckman, 1968; Phares, Ritchie, and Davis, 1968; Lefcourt, 1966; Battle and Rotter, 1963).[6]

The literature about internal-external locus of control contains the strong suggestion that externality contributes to feelings of apathy, alienation, and helplessness. These feelings are thought generally to interfere with positive mental health and personal productivity. It therefore seems that attention to conditions which may facilitate the development of a realistic internal locus of control is warranted by those responsible for young children's welfare. This recommendation, however, is based on the further assumption that children's environments can be arranged so that they are, in fact, able to exert sufficient personal control over what happens to them. Surely a classroom can be so arranged by a teacher even if a child's home environment cannot.

The suggestion that classroom arrangements should be made to

[6] Most internal-external control research has involved adolescent and adult subjects. As such, these findings should not be automatically generalized to children. The position taken by this writer, however, is that the antecedents of locus of control can be traced to the preschool years.

facilitate personal control is especially appropriate in view of data gathered at the Fels Research Institute (for example, Crandall, Katkovsky, and Crandall, 1965). Fels research workers have developed a conceptual variation on the locus of control theme. Specifically, this variation involves the degree to which children believe that they control the reinforcements involved in intellectual-achievement situations and thus maintain self-responsibility for their successes and failures.[7] In contrast to externals, children high in intellectual-achievement responsibility are more likely to manifest stronger patterns of academic achievement (McGhee and Crandall, 1968) and report their parents as demonstrating less rejection and hostility, more positive involvement, and more consistent discipline (McGhee and Crandall, 1968; Davis and Phares, 1969). The latter finding has come from the recent study of parental antecedents of intellectual achievement responsibility. Additional research has led to the reasoned speculation that several parental behaviors are pertinent to children's development of such responsibility. Among these behaviors are parental reinforcement for children's verbalizations of internal (or external) thinking, the extent to which parents serve as models of internality, and the teaching of ideas concerning social and physical causality (Katkovsky, Crandall, and Good, 1967). Piaget-based experiences with causality may be particularly fruitful with regard to physical causality. The point, however, is that the aforementioned parent behaviors, plus a policy of contingent reinforcement, also seem plausibly to apply to teachers. If one's objective involves assisting children toward an internal frame of reference and toward accepting responsibility for their own actions, then systematic attention to antecedent conditions is desirable. Certainly this avenue of research offers many rich clues for psychologists and educators to pursue further.

Divergent Thinking Abilities Early childhood educators have traditionally paid lip service to the development or cultivation of children's creativity. Only occasionally, however, does one observe any specific delineation of behaviors that constitute creative expression or productivity. Many classroom activities described as "creative" are found when observed carefully to be convergent in nature; that is, they require children to meet uniform standards such as cutting patterns from manila paper or coloring pictures "by the numbers." Further, creative activities are often limited to art and music, with little attention given to creative thinking in areas such as science and social studies.

---

[7] Sex and social-class differences pervade this research to the extent that unqualified generalizations are not apparent. In the case of intellectual achievement responsibility research, for example, girls generally surpass boys in overall personal responsibility.

If educators are seriously concerned with the development of creativity among children, they may find helpful the work of psychologists who have attempted to identify the characteristics of creative behavior. A prime example is Guilford's (1967) study of certain intellectual processes or operations. One process that Guilford believes is fundamental to what we normally call creativity is termed *divergent production.* Divergent production is thought to involve a process by which one generates new information from given information, where the objective is a variety of ideas or problem solutions. This process stands in contrast to that which involves the production of one "right" or "acceptable" response to a question or problem (convergent production).

Divergent production, as presently measured, may be either verbal or figural. It could also involve the product of manipulative action performed on objects. But, according to Guilford, all divergent production abilities are characterized by certain unique properties, including fluency, originality, flexibility, and elaboration of thought. Fluency has been conceived in terms of the quantity or number of ideas produced by an individual in a given period of time, the completion of relationships, and facile sentence construction. Originality refers to degree of novelty, cleverness, or unusualness of a response or product. Flexibility refers to the ability to shift (1) between conceptual classes and within such classes at varying levels of abstraction and (2) between interpretations of or strategies for solving a given problem. Elaboration refers primarily to the production of a variety of implications or the specification of details for problem solution where only a general statement or situation exists.

A vast literature about creativity has gradually been developed. For the interested reader, examples of creative behavior, suggestions for the measurement of creativity, and statements of educational implications are available (for example, Gowan, Demos, and Torrance, 1967; Kagan, 1967; Taylor, 1964). This writer's objective is simply to introduce the notion that the development of divergent thinking abilities is an appropriate concern for early childhood educators. Attention to this facet of children's behavior may be seen to vary greatly among those whose early education strategies have been discussed in this book. This variation is seemingly a function of value judgments; empirical data have been presented to show that divergent production can be influenced by classroom conditions (Torrance, 1963, 1965). Among the important variables related to increased divergent production among children are providing children with (1) information concerning the characteristics of such production; (2) ample opportunity to engage in challenging problem-solving activities, (3) positive reinforcement, (4) a creative teacher-model, (5) a stimulus-rich learning environment, and (6) reduced pressures for conformity, both social and intellectual.

To conclude, psychological constructs such as the three described above may be of considerable help to educators who grapple with the problem of goals for early education. They may also serve as useful criteria for the evaluation of educational programs which are purported to be developmental in nature. Many other constructs could be presented.[8] The above three were selected for discussion on the basis of their relevance to the concerns of most teachers (and parents) and for purposes of illustration. It is suggested that a combination of the developmental task concept, the basic behavioral repertoire concept, and selected constructs of psychological development may provide a useful foundation upon which to base one's thinking about the objectives of early childhood education.

OTHER RELATED ISSUES: WHAT, HOW, WHEN, WHO, AND WHERE

Once the minimum goals of a program have been established, decisions to be made involve the *what* (content) and *how* (methodology) issues first discussed in Chapter 1. As we have seen, the content of many early education programs varies along such dimensions as specific concepts to be taught, materials to be used, and the degree of structure and sequencing imposed on content by teachers. For example, behavioral-analysis procedures do not necessarily include a given body of content, but they do involve a definite principle for sequencing material. Sequencing principles are also apparent in Montessori, in structural pedagogy for language development, and in Piaget-based curricula. In contrast, an emphasis upon sequencing is not always apparent in conventional programs, even when such programs are applied in a compensatory way. Perhaps the critical variable is whether a curriculum, including teaching procedures, is derived from developmental theory (as in the case of a Piaget-based approach) or an organized set of learning principles (as in behavior analysis). Another key variable concerns how content is organized for presentation. For example, structural pedagogy for language development includes a specification

[8] Examples of other promising constructs include achievement motivation (Heckhausen, 1967), cognitive style (Witkin and others, 1962) reflectivity-impulsivity (Kagan, 1966), and delay of gratification (Renner, 1964).

of content organized according to logic as practiced by adults. Whether children necessarily learn content best when so organized is a question perhaps most clearly raised in relation to British infant school practice.

As content varies along several dimensions, so does methodology. We have seen, for example, that didactics in early childhood education range from a preponderance of pattern drill exercises (structural pedagogy) to self-correctional materials (Montessori) to carefully arranged reinforcement contingencies (behavioral analysis). For this writer, it is noteworthy that children learn (manifest behavior changes) whatever teaching methods are used. At issue, however, are such concerns as economy of time (efficiency), retention, and transfer of learning. If our research findings are reasonably accurate, no one didactic package is uniformly "good" for all children at any one point in time. Thus, the degree of individual differentiation practiced within a given program should perhaps receive close attention by anyone evaluating that program. Also worthy of consideration is a determination (within any given program) of the extent to which progress toward an objective is a function of "maturation" or specific instructional experience. All the aforementioned variables—efficiency, retention, transfer, degree of individualization, and antecedent-consequent relationships—may be subjected to scrutiny through controlled research. We will return to the problem of research shortly.

The issue of timing educational experiences in ways appropriate to the developmental sequence (the *when* issue first introduced in Chapter 1) is perhaps the most ambiguous of all issues. With the exception of infant education practices, programs of organized experiences for children younger than three years of age are rare. Rationales for the selection of age 3 (and age 5 or 6 for beginning public school experiences) are not totally clear. It is possible that ethical and philosophical reasons are involved to a greater extent than are psychological ones; the reader is free to speculate on this matter. Research workers increasingly suggest that compensatory education delayed until age 4 or 5 may be "too late" for best results. Of course, there may exist better compensatory strategies that currently are practiced, but it also may be more profitable to think in terms of "preventative" rather than remedial education. No one has yet addressed the hazards of beginning educational efforts "too early" in an empirical fashion. There has been general resistance, however, to the notion of placing groups of children in educational settings prior to age 3. Resistance notwithstanding, the fact is that education, in its broadest sense, begins at birth. Our question concerns what forms of stimulation are most appropriate at what points in the developmental process; educational strategies based explicitly upon developmental theory probably come closest to answering this question.[9]

Still another issue first discussed in Chapter 1 concerns *who* will make a program for early childhood education operational. It is clear that the role of the teacher varies considerably according to which educational strategy is involved. A most obvious variable is the direct-indirect teacher behavior continuum exemplified by structural pedagogy and the Montessori Method respectively. Clearly, decisions regarding teacher role are dictated by one's preferred objectives, as are all other decisions related to procedures. Role considerations aside, several items pertaining to general teacher qualifications and specific program requirements deserve mention. For one, there seems to be widespread agreement that the success of any program, whether or not that program is articulated to the last detail, rests in the hands of the teacher (and, where applicable, her assistants). One appropriate concern, therefore, is what constitutes the effective or successful teacher. Theoretically, teaching effectiveness should be assessed in terms of how well children (learners) achieve the objectives of a program (assuming such objectives are valid and realistic). The acceptance of this criterion obviously requires systematic research into the kind and degree of behavior changes among the learner participants in a given program. Two general outcomes, by no means mutually exclusive, are perhaps most relevant: learner *competence,* in terms of cognitive and psychomotor skills (where applicable) and learner *sentiment,* including attitude development (Anderson, 1959).

A synthesis of research about teaching effectiveness across educational levels permits the inference that, in general terms, the most effective teachers (in terms of the criteria above) rate high in enthusiasm and communication skill (Evans, 1969). Similarly, other important variables include skill in (1) adapting teaching objectives, content, and method *in process* (in response to the reactions, learning problems, and needs of pupils) and (2) activating student interest and personal involvement. The latter two variables involve flexibility and motivational skill. Still other research workers have pointed to the importance of empathy and nurturance for teachers of young children (Hogan, 1969; O'Leary and Becker, 1969). One can argue that these qualities, together with the aforementioned characteristics—enthusiasm, communication skill,

---

[9] The views of David Weikart (1967) are appropriate in connection with this point. Weikart believes that the environmental experiences typically available to many children (for example, those identified as economically disadvantaged) are not adequate for successive normal development past the first year of postnatal life. He has strongly recommended that, for "preventative" purposes, we need more intensive education-based investigations into the two- or three-year period beyond age 1.

flexibility, and ability to involve children actively in the learning process—are desirable among all teachers involved in early childhood education. It is therefore incumbent upon those involved in the training and selection of teachers of young children to examine their procedures in relation to these attributes.[10]

Apart from general personal and technical skills, it is apparent that the successful enactment of programs discussed in this book depends upon various levels of specific knowledge and ability. The application of behavioral-analysis procedures, for example, involves advanced skills in contingency management and data-taking beyond those developed in most teacher education programs. A teacher in a Piaget-based program must, among other things, be thoroughly conversant with Piagetian theory and the *méthode-clinique*. A successful Montessori teacher must be an extraordinary observer of children and extraordinarily adept in the demonstration and arrangement of learning activities. The same holds for teachers in any program where a child-centered approach prevails. These skills are not likely to be developed apart from intensive training. This writer, for one, flatly rejects the contention so often heard in lay circles that, "Anyone can teach!" or the popular view that parenthood *per se* qualifies one as a teacher of young children. Clearly, the issues of pre-service and in-service training, the assessment of teaching effectiveness, and general professionalization are among the most critical we face. These issues are made more intense by those who support the trend toward the use of "paraprofessionals" and teacher aides for early childhood education (Schmitthausler, 1969). Finally, teachers can no longer afford to rationalize children's learning problems by blaming the poor home conditions of pupils or other conditions external to the classroom. Children's failures, when they occur, are more accurately teaching failures. Public support for the removal of conditions which contribute to teaching failures (for example, faulty teacher training procedures, inappropriate and insufficient learning materials, and tolerance of mediocre or incompetent school personnel) is sorely needed.

The issue raised in Chapter 1 regarding *where* early education programs are conducted is also difficult to resolve. Generally speaking, educational authorities have not dealt with this serious issue in explicit

---

[10] Recommendations concerning the preparation of nursery and kindergarten teachers have recently been made through the National Education Association's Commission on Teacher Education and Professional Standards (Haberman and Persky, 1969). One principal recommendation is that teachers of young children should be evaluated in terms of demonstrated competence and personal suitability as well as the usual criterion of academic preparation.

ways. Perhaps this is due to the traditional view that associates educa-tion with classroom activity. That is, many educators and parents assume (hopefully with good reason) that formal educational activities are best executed in special environments outside the home. It is likely, however, that efforts to extend compulsory education downward to in-clude children three years of age (or younger) will meet with widespread resistance throughout society. In this connection, it is interesting to note the influence of psychoanalytic concepts of personality on the literature of early childhood development. Among other things, early separation of children from their parents, particularly the mother, and "premature" group involvement are questioned by devotees of psychoanalysis.

Perhaps the area that involves the where issue most intensely con-cerns infant stimulation or education. It seems unlikely that American parents will be quick to approve of out-of-home educational activities for their infants, although it is possible that parent-executed stimulation programs will grow in popularity. A persistent question in this regard is, "Stimulation for what?" It may be that Cronbach's (1969) concept of an optimal maintenance environment can be applied effectively while special intervention programs remain largely an extra-home enterprise. Clearly, the where issue is intimately related to the problems of timing and content in early education; that is, where and when should what kinds of experiences be provided to young children?

To conclude, any consideration of strategies for early childhood education is incomplete without attention to the issues of what, when, how, who, and where. As we have seen, there are many variations in educational strategy within early childhood education. Yet every archi-tect of a curriculum for young children should be able to account for his underlying psycho-educational rationale. In short, the question of "why?" requires an answer for all four issues. Hopefully the answers to this ubiquitous "why?" question will be grounded firmly in valid theory and research.

RESEARCH

Ultimately the "proof" of any educational pudding is in the eating. In the present context we are concerned with the observable changes in children's behavior that result from our attempts to facilitate their development. Thus, in the opinion of this writer, empirical evidence becomes the final authority in deciding for (or against) a given program or technique. As we have seen, such authority is not easily achieved.

So many problems inhere in the research methodologies and measurement techniques currently applied to early childhood education that one wonders if a definitive statement about anything will ever be made.

An increased number of commentaries on the research or evaluation function in early childhood education has recently appeared. Glick (1968), for example, has warned us against several pitfalls, including a failure to differentiate between (1) a child's actual performance and his ability to perform, (2) children's achievement and the process or structure underlying such achievement, and (3) the potential positive *and* negative effects of early education (intervention) in terms of longer-term developmental change. Skager and Broadbent (1968) have expressed concern over the tendency for programs to be evaluated too narrowly, that is, where criteria sufficiently broad in scope are not applied or where an assessment strategy represents only the value system of the evaluator.[11] Similarly, Sroufe (1970) has stressed the notion that value judgments may subtly and negatively influence the objectivity necessary for a scientific interpretation of research.[12] He also decries the not so subtle tendency for researchers often to discuss correlational data as if they represented cause-effect relationships. A positive correlation between social class and intelligence, for example, cannot legitimately be interpreted in terms of an antecedent-consequent relationship. Finally, with respect to measurement problems, Sroufe (1970) is critical of the failure in many quarters to maintain the distinction between a construct and the procedure used to measure that construct: that is, a failure to qualify one's data in terms of the validity and reliability of the procedures utilized to gather those data. Thus, instead of speaking of the effects of intervention on intelligence (implying total adaptive capacity), it is more appropriate to speak of "intelligence" as measured by whatever instrument one has used. This sort of problem is built into any psychometric approach to the study of behavior and can be avoided in many respects by the measurement procedures unique to the experimental analysis of behavior (Chapter 5). Unfortunately, such procedures have not been used extensively in early childhood education research.

Although conceived within the context of Head Start research, Grotberg's (1969) analysis of research problems is among the most comprehensive and can be translated to early childhood education generally.

[11] This criticism is echoed in specific terms by Margolin (1969) who is critical of those who make an "artificial" distinction between intellectualism and exploratory work-play and of the widespread lack of attention to the study of aesthetic development in children.
[12] As an example, Sroufe (1970) refers to the value-based problems involved when lower-class black parents and children are observed and evaluated by middle-class white research workers.

In this analysis four particular research difficulties are brought to light: conceptual, methodological, logistical, and interpretational. According to Grotberg (1969), conceptual problems are frequently encountered during attempts to formulate clear questions that are amenable to research. For example, a legitimate intervention research question must be empirical. That is, it must be formulated in terms of "What are the effects?" as opposed to the philosophical "should" type of statement. For example, the question, "What are the effects of language programs X, Y, and Z upon the development of children's vocabulary and syntax?" is empirical. In contrast, the question, "Should language program X, Y, or Z be used with kindergarten-age children?" is not. One may be assisted toward an answer to the "should question" by first answering the former, empirical question. An answer to the empirical question depends, however, on the skill with which a researcher specifies precisely the components of each language program (antecedents) and his criteria for evaluating each program (consequents, or behavioral outcomes). Perhaps too frequently global programs (such as "kindergarten experience") have been "evaluated" with global measures (such as teachers' ratings of language development), and the results have limited, if any, value for the practitioner. Rarely are teacher-pupil interactions examined in method-comparison studies for the purpose of specifying precisely what teacher behaviors affect which pupil behaviors and vice versa. It is extremely important that such interaction be carefully charted in objective ways, because teacher role is clearly a critical variable in any approach to early childhood education. Further conceptual problems associated with most intervention research efforts include (1) the need for a distinction between immediate and long-term impact, (2) the relationship of target behavior changes to other responses in a child's development repertoire, and (3) the possibility that extra-program variables contribute in some undefined way to observed behavior changes.

Methodological problems run the gamut from sampling technique (means of selecting children for study) through limitations in measurement procedures to statistical analysis of data. For example, research projects frequently involve comparisons of extremely small numbers of children where background factors such as socioeconomic status and measured intelligence are insufficiently controlled. Valid measures are not plentiful, especially for purposes of measuring young children's affective characteristics. Frequently, one gains the impression that decisions regarding how data gathered from children will be analyzed are made after the data are in, rather than having been made in advance of one's study. A related problem is that statistical analyses may be made in violation of the fundamental assumptions about sampling upon which an analysis procedure is based. For example, many analyses which culminate in a statement concerning statistical significance depend upon the premise that one has selected a random sample of children for study. In practice, truly random samples are rare. This must be considered a serious limitation of early education research, particularly research that involves simultaneous comparisons of two or more programs.

A third set of problems, identified by Grotberg (1969) as logistical in nature, illustrates how events may impede and unduly complicate research progress. Some examples are the frequent loss of subjects (children) from a study due to illness or change in residence; the extensive time periods often mandatory for certain types of testing, interviewing, and observing; and the occasional inability or unwillingness of parents and teachers (or children) to "cooperate" in a given research program. In addition to the time problem, research is typically expensive in terms of materials, data analysis, and salaries of research workers. Unquestionably, logistical problems such as these have prevented otherwise promising research projects from getting off the ground.

Interpretational problems, a fourth class of problems discussed by Grotberg (1969), can most often be traced to differences among theoreticians regarding the nature and processes of child development and education, including compensatory education. We have seen, for example, how differently psychologists and educators who align themselves with cognitive-developmental theory, structural pedagogy, and behavioral analysis conceptualize research strategies and interpret research data. In addition, conflicting findings have resulted even when investigators employ similar techniques to study similar problems (such as language deficits) among similar groups of children. The sources of these conflicting data are generally difficult to pinpoint, and research workers' attempts to identify these sources often result in diverse speculation. As speculation is practiced, variations in theoretical and philosophical preferences occur. These variations tend to confuse many practitioners who are unfamiliar with the conceptual intricacies and abstractions characteristic of psychological theories. The complex interactions between instructional, content, and personal variables which frequently occur in method-comparison research create equally complex interpretational problems. We have seen examples of this type of problem in both Montessori-based and Piaget-based research, to name only two areas of study discussed in this book. Finally, a problem of interpretation is commonly associated with research designed to produce normative data: that is, a tendency to confuse what children can learn with what they have learned at a given point in time (Martin, 1965).

In summary, research in early childhood education involves a number of problems—conceptual, methodological, logistical, and interpretational. Comparative analyses of alternatives for early childhood education are therefore extremely complex. This complexity is perhaps increased by our tendency to reify a method or curriculum model because that method or model has a label (Banta, 1966). That is, most early education strategies are labeled, and because of this we often believe that the label refers to something unique—to components that differentiate one approach from another. Even if reification is deserved, there is the likelihood that components as described on paper may not be translated fully into actual practice. Thus, if one's purpose is a realistic analysis of any program, one must observe firsthand what is taught and how it is taught. Only through systematic observation are the distinguishing features of a given early education environment likely to be identified. A telling question is whether such features, even if unique, make a real difference in the educational development of children.

Attempts to "prove" the superiority of one approach over another will probably continue, although such attempts can easily be misguided. The traditional method-comparison type of research typically results only in data that reflect group averages. In other words, the "advantage" of one method over another is usually reported in terms of average gain for all the children in that group. In some cases the average gain may be of minor importance, given a broad perspective, even though it is statistically significant. For example, a comparison of two methods for reading instruction involving large numbers of children might result in an "advantage" for one group as measured by a reading achievement test. The test score advantage could be statistically significant yet only involve two or three points of difference, on the average, between the two groups. Such a finding could hardly be represented as a major breakthrough in the technique of reading instruction. Further, researchers who report data in terms of group averages rarely examine the extent to which a "treatment" may have increased (or decreased) the range of individual differences in classroom-based performance or whether a given method, while generally advantageous, has no positive effect on certain children within a given group. Thus, intra-group analyses are needed as well as more attention to combinations of experiences suitable for *individual children.*

The suggestion that educators should focus more sharply on the behavior of individual children can be related to the concept of gene-environment interaction (Caspari, 1968). That is, all aspects of behavioral development depend upon some combination of genetic and environmental factors. The implication of this concept for educational practice is, of course, that different children will respond differently to a given educational method. Thus, while one may find approaches that, in general, are better for more children than others, an optimal educational method for all children is not feasible, at least in principle. This, then, could be taken as further support for individualization in education. In terms of research, it is possible that Piaget's *méthode clinique* and behavior-analysis procedures, though vastly different in concept, can contribute in unique ways to the achievement of this goal.

THE GENERAL PROBLEM OF ETHICS

A final set of issues and problems to be discussed here is concerned with the ethics of curriculum variations (including goals) and research strategies in early childhood education. This set of issues and problems ranges from a distinction between education and indoctrination on the one hand to questions of authority for educational intervention on the other. For example, from what source does a teacher or research worker derive his authority to manipulate the social and intellectual lives of children (and, in many cases, of their parents)? What determines how far one has a right to go in terms of "moulding" a child's existence? Who actually makes the decisions concerning what, how, and to whom something will be done, allegedly in the "best interests" of children and society? It is not uncommon for objections to be voiced in various quarters regarding the hazards of experimentation and the ethical problem of imposing on children values that may conflict with those of their parents. The former argument is usually countered by the contention that not to perform reasoned experimentation which is dedicated to the pursuit of better ways to help children would be unethical. The latter problem, value conflict, has no easy solution. However, values taught to children are at least implicit in any statement of minimum goals for an early education program. This writer supports the view that open inquiry based on rational discourse and the objective study of children and society is the most promising route to follow for achieving solutions to such problems. Although as a guiding principle this view may contribute to sound decision making where ethics are concerned, it does not provide an answer to the broader immediate question: "What educational requirements can be applied to children in a society which purports to be democratic?" (Meacham and Wiesen, 1969).

The development of educational programs within a democratic

framework is particularly critical in relation to compensatory education. As mentioned in Chapter 3, forcible applications of standard middle-class values and virtues upon non–middle-class children is frequently considered as a breach of ethics. In other words, middle-class values of industriousness, skilled communicativeness, self-regulation, and social and cultural concern are generally held as the model for all children, regardless of social class, ethnic, or racial status. The point, however, is that if these values are not accepted as guidelines for educational development, what will substitute for them? As Cronbach (1969) states, "No one protesting against middle-classness has gone on to describe a possible, viable society in which large subsegments of society have radically different orientations and functions" (p. 341).

Perhaps those programs of education that emphasize the development of learning strategies and problem-solving skills are least likely to result in ethical problems. According to McCandless (1970), any way of life is usually more successfully pursued—provides the individual with a greater sense of competence and personal-social adjustment—if the individual is skilled at the problem-solving strategies that underlie that way of life. Thus, a specification and a cultivation of relevant problem-solving strategies are basic to any "good" education, compensatory or otherwise. A problem-solving orientation is also consistent with views expressed elsewhere: that the fundamental goal for early childhood education programs (especially compensatory programs) should be the development of children's conceptual learning ability and fluid thinking abilities (Cronbach, 1969). In this way, desirable school readiness and intrinsically valuable achievement may be facilitated.[13]

Perhaps a first step toward the resolution of ethical problems and value conflicts is for a teacher of children to be aware of his own values, how these values are expressed in behavior, and how they may influence the behavior of children. Such a step obviously requires a thoughtful self-analysis on the part of everyone involved in educational programs for early childhood. This notion is clearly reflected in the following excerpt:

> The educator at all levels must examine his own assumptions about human existence and determine, through careful analysis, whether his premises are based on reason or emotion, objectivity or conformity. Only after such a vital but painstaking self-examination by each educator will he be able to develop goals which are relevant to students and society alike; only then will he be devising curricula in a truly ethical manner. [M. L. Meacham and A. E. Wiesen, *Changing Classroom Behavior.* Scranton, Pa.: International Textbook Co., 1969, p. 112.]

[13] See Appendix B for a brief treatment of school readiness.

LOOKING AHEAD

At the time of this writing, the renaissance in early childhood education which began in the sixties is only beginning to be felt. All indications are that the momentum of this movement will continue to increase during the seventies. The situation is not unlike that which surrounds the proverbial wheel of fortune whose spinner remarks, "Round and round it goes! Where it stops, nobody knows!" It is clear, however, that many facets of contemporary early childhood education will continue to require the careful attention of professionals. Many of these facets have been discussed in this book in terms of major issues related to child development theory, curriculum development, and research. With respect to early childhood education generally there remains the problem of goals, both long- and short-term, and the basis for goal determination. Concerning compensatory education strategies, there is the unanswered question of how substantial the effects of early intervention on "learning capacity" can be. With increasing numbers of children attending "preschools," many of which are oriented to academic goals, there is the question of what transformations should occur in public school kindergarten-primary curricula across the country. Without improved education beyond the early childhood level, it is doubtful that early educational strategies will have lasting payoff, regardless of their quality. The community action idea associated originally with Project Head Start is bound to have a broader impact in years to come. Many new and exciting curriculum designs, both developmental (for example, Nedler, 1970) and ameliorative (for example, Karnes and others, 1970) merit broader implementation and study. Further, the newly formed Office of Child Development within the U.S. Department of Health, Education and Welfare, is likely to affect the thinking and activities of professionals in early childhood education, although its role is not precisely defined at the time of this writing. In this connection, however, it is significant that OCD has already initiated a "product conversion project" for day care services across the country. That is, during 1970, a major thrust will be made toward modifying or otherwise translating early education programs for action in day care centers. It is planned that operating manuals and other materials will be made available to day care personnel through OCD, with emphasis upon principles of effective day care practice and a pervasive educational orientation for day care personnel.

Still other new developments of interest to early childhood educators can be identified. For example, a concentrated effort is being made to design and implement on a broad scale special preschool programs for handicapped children (Harvey, 1969). Neither to be overlooked is the building movement in franchised day care centers and corporate-based preschools. Operations such as the Romper Room Schools and the Discovery Program (Whitney and Parker, 1970) give every indication of being catalysts for an educational-industrial complex. Also, beginning in 1969, an educational television program, *Sesame Street* (Children's Television Workshop, NET), was for the first time available for home viewing by preschool children. This 24-week program, complete with a series of packaged parent guides obtainable by mail, was focussed specifically upon children's general pre-academic skill development and the general education of parents. If continued, programs such as this could signal the implementation of an entirely new concept of mass education for young children who otherwise may not benefit from organized preschool experience. Any success that may be achieved through mass communication ventures will, of course, depend heavily upon the parents of preschoolers—a notion related to the still broader challenge of establishing more productive interaction between home and school, parents and teachers (Biber, 1969).

Perhaps what is most significant about the developments mentioned above is that they mark the development of new vistas in educational thought. Certainly new vistas are not easily reached. If genuine progress is to be realized, a number of ingredients are needed, including the creative problem-solving efforts of parents, teachers, and research workers who are united in their commitment to the total welfare of young children.

References

Anderson, R. "Learning in Discussion: A Résumé of the Authoritarian–Democratic Studies." *Harvard Educational Review,* 1959, 29, 201–215.

Banta, Thomas J. "Is There Really a Montessori Method?" Department of Psychology, University of Cincinnati, Cincinnati, 1966.

Battle, Esther, and Julian Rotter. "Children's Feelings of Personal Control as Related to Social Class and Ethnic Group." *Journal of Personality,* 1963, 31, 482–490.

Baumrind, Diane, and Allen E. Black. "Socialization Practices Associated with Dimensions of Competence in Preschool Boys and Girls." *Child Development,* 1967, 38, 291–328.

Biber, Barbara. *Challenges Ahead for Early Childhood Education.* Washington, D.C.: National Association for the Education of Young Children, 1969.

Black, Hugh C. "Pestalozzi and the Education of the Disadvantaged." *Educational Forum,* 1969, 33, 511–521.

Carpenter, T. R., and T. V. Busse. "Development of Self-concept in Negro and White Welfare Children." *Child Development,* 1969, 40, 935–939.

Caspari, Ernst W. "Genetic Endowment and Environment in the Determination of Human Behavior: Biological Viewpoint." *American Educational Research Journal,* 1968, 5, 43–55.

Coopersmith, Stanley. *The Antecedents of Self-Esteem.* San Francisco: Freeman, 1968.

Crandall, V. C., W. Katkovsky, and V. J. Crandall. "Children's Beliefs in Their Own Control of Reinforcement in Intellectual-academic Achievement Situations," *Child Development,* 1965, 36, 91–109.

Cronbach, Lee J. "Heredity, Environment, and Educational Policy." *Harvard Educational Review,* 1969, 39, 338–347.

Crowne, D. P., and S. Liverant. "Conformity under Varying Conditions of Personal Commitment." *Journal of Abnormal and Social Psychology,* 1963, 66, 547–555.

Davis, William, and E. Jerry Phares. "Parental Antecedents of Internal-external Control of Reinforcement." *Psychological Reports,* 1969, 24, 427–436.

Dreyer, A. S., and Dorothy Haupt. "Self-evaluation in Young Children." *Journal of Genetic Psychology,* 1966, 108, 185–197.

Elkind, David. "Piagetism and Psychometric Conceptions of Intelligence." *Harvard Educational Review,* 1969, 39, 319–337.

Engel, M., and W. J. Raine. "A Method for the Measurement of the Self-concept in Children of the Third Grade." *Journal of Genetic Psychology,* 1963, 102, 124–137.

Evans, Ellis D. "Student Activism and Teaching Effectiveness: Survival of the Fittest?" *Journal of College Student Personnel,* 1969 (March), 102–108.

Fink, Martin B. "Self-concept as It Relates to Academic Underachievement." *California Journal of Educational Research,* 1962, 13, 57–62.

Fowler, William. "The Effect of Early Stimulation: The Problem of Focus in Developmental Stimulation." *Merrill-Palmer Quarterly,* 1969 (April), 15, 157–170.

Furth, Edward J. *Constructing Evaluation Instruments.* New York: Longmans, & Co., 1958.

Getzels, Jacob W. "Preschool Education." *Teachers College Record,* 1966, 68, 219–228.

Glick, Joseph. "Some Problems in the Evaluation of Preschool Intervention Programs." In Robert Hess and Roberta Bear (Eds.), *Early Education,* Chicago: Aldine, 1968, 215–221.

Gowan, John C., George D. Demos, and E. Paul Torrance. *Creativity: Its Educational Implications.* New York: John Wiley, 1967.

Grossman, Bruce. "The Academic Grind at Age Three." *Educational Digest,* 1969, 34, 26–28.

Grotberg, Edith H. *Review of Research: 1965 to 1969.* Washington, D.C.: Project Head Start, Office of Economic Opportunity, 1969.

Guilford, J. P. "Factors That Aid and Hinder Creativity." *Teachers College Record,* 1962, 63, 380–392.

Guilford, J. P. *The Nature of Human Intelligence.* New York: McGraw-Hill, 1967.

Haberman, Martin, and Blanche Persky. *Preliminary Report of the Ad Hoc Joint Committee on the Preparation of Nursery and Kindergarten Teachers.* Washington, D.C.: National Education Association, 1969.

Harris, Beecher H., and Robert J. Fisher. "Distortions in the Kindergarten." *Young Children,* 1969, 24, 279–284.

Harvey, Jasper. *Staff Training of Exemplary Early Childhood Center for Handicapped Children.* Newsletter. Austin, Tex.: University of Texas Department of Special Education, 1969.

Havighurst, Robert J. *Human Development and Education.* New York: McKay, 1953.

Havighurst, Robert J. "Research on the Developmental Task Concept." *School Review,* 1956 (May), 215–223.

Heckhausen, Heinz. *The Anatomy of Achievement Motivation.* New York: Academic Press, 1967.

Hitt, William D. "Two Models of Man." *American Psychologist,* 1969, 24, 651–658.

Hogan, Robert. "Development of an Empathy Scale." *Journal of Consulting and Clinical Psychology,* 1969, 33, 307–316.

Julian, J. W., C. M. Lichtman, and R. M. Ryckman. "Internal-external Control and the Need to Control." *Journal of Social Psychology,* 1968, 76, 43–48.

Kagan, Jerome. "Modifiability of an Impulsive Tempo." *Journal of Educational Psychology,* 1966, 57, 359–365.

Kagan, Jerome (Ed.). *Creativity and Learning.* Boston: Beacon Press, 1967.

Karnes, Merle B., R. Reid Zehrbach, and J. A. Teska. "The Conceptualization of the Ameliorative Curriculum." Paper presented at a conference entitled "Conceptualizations of Preschool Curricula," City University of New York, 1970 (May 22–24).

Katkovsky, Walter, Virginia Crandall, and Suzanne Good. "Parental Antecedents in Children's Beliefs in Internal-external Control of Reinforcements in Intellectual Achievement Situations." *Child Development,* 1967, 38, 765–776.

Katz, Lillian. "Children and Teachers in Two Types of Head Start Classes." *Young Children,* 1969, 24, 342–349.

Kraft, Ivor. "Are We Overselling the Preschool Idea?" In Alvin E. Winder and David L. Angus (Eds.), *Adolescence: Contemporary Studies.* New York: American Book, 1968, 240–242.

Lefcourt, Herbert M. "Internal versus External Control of Reinforcement: A Review." *Psychological Bulletin,* 1966, 65, 206–220.

Margolin, Edythe. "Crucial Issues in Contemporary Early Childhood Education." *Childhood Education,* 1969, 45, 500–504.

Martin, John H. "Montessori After 50 Years." *Teachers College Record,* 1965, 67, 552–554.

McCandless, Boyd R. *Children: Behavior and Development* (2d ed.). New York: Holt, Rinehart and Winston, 1967.

McCandless, Boyd R. Personal correspondence, 1970 January 13.

McConnell, Freeman, Kathryn B. Horton, and Bertha R. Smith. "Language Development and Cultural Disadvantagement." *Exceptional Children,* 1969, 35, 597–606.

McGhee, Paul, and Virginia Crandall. "Belief in Internal-external Control of Reinforcements and Academic Performance." *Child Development,* 1968, 39, 91–102.

Meacham, M. L., and A. E. Wiesen. *Changing Classroom Behavior.* Scranton, Pa.: International Textbook, 1969, p. 112.

Nedler, Shari. "A Developmental Process Approach to Curriculum Design." Paper presented at a conference entitled, "Conceptualizations of Preschool Curricula," City University of New York, 1970 (May 22–24).

O'Leary, K. Daniel, and Wesley C. Becker. "The Effects of the Intensity of a Teacher's Reprimands on Children's Behavior." *Journal of School Psychology,* 1968–69, 7, No. 1, 8–11.

Phares, E. J., D. Elaine Ritchie, and W. L. Davis. "Internal-external Control and Reaction to Threat." *Journal of Personal and Social Psychology,* 1968, 10, 402–405.

Popham, W. James, and T. R. Husek. "Implications of Criterion-referenced Measurement." *Journal of Educational Measurement,* 1969, 6, 1–9.

Renner, K. E. "Delay of Reinforcement: A Historical View." *Psychological Bulletin,* 1964, 61, 341–361.

Rotter, Julian B. "Generalized Expectancies for Internal vs. External Control of Reinforcement." *Psychological Monographs,* 1966, 80 (I), No. 609, 28 pp.

Schmitthausler, C. M. "The Professionalization of Teaching in Early Childhood Education." *Journal of Teacher Education,* 1969, 20, 188–190.

Seifert, Kelvin. "Comparison of Verbal Interaction in Two Preschool Programs." *Young Children,* 1969, 24, 350–355.

Shaw, Merville, and Gerald Alves. "The Self-concept of Bright Academic Underachievers Continued." *Personnel and Guidance Journal,* 1963, 42, 401–403.

Skager, R. W., and L. A. Broadbent. *Cognitive Structures and Educational Evaluation.* Center for the Study of Evaluation of Instructional Programs. Berkeley: University of California Press, 1968.

Soares, A. T., and L. M. Soares. "Self-perception of Culturally Disadvantaged Children." *American Educational Research Journal,* 1969, 6, 31–45.

Solomon, Daniel. "Intellectual Achievement Responsibility in Negro and White Children." *Psychological Reports,* 1969, 24, 479–483.

Sroufe, L. Alan. "A Methodological and Philosophical Critique of Intervention-oriented Research." *Developmental Psychology,* 1970, 2, 140–145.

Staats, Arthur W. *Learning, Language, and Cognition.* New York: Holt, Rinehart and Winston, 1968.

Taylor, Calvin W. (Ed.). *Creativity: Progress and Potential.* New York: McGraw-Hill, 1964.

Teiglund, J. J. "Some Concomitants of Underachievement at the Elementary School Level." *Personnel and Guidance Journal,* 1966, 44, 950–955.

Torrance, E. Paul. *Education and the Creative Potential,* Minneapolis: University of Minnesota Press, 1963.

Torrance, E. Paul, *Rewarding Creative Behavior: Experiments in Classroom Creativity.* Englewood Cliffs: Prentice-Hall, 1965.

Ward, William C. "Creativity and Environmental Cues in Nursery School Children." *Developmental Psychology,* 1969, 1, 543–547.

Weikart, David P. "Preschool Programs: Preliminary Findings." *Journal of Special Education,* 1967, 1, 163–181.

Whitney, David C., and Ronald K. Parker. "A Systems Approach to Early Education: The Discovery Program." Paper presented at a conference entitled, "Conceptualizations of Preschool Curricula," City University of New York, 1970 (May 22–24).

Witkin, H. A., and others. *Psychological Differentiation.* New York: Wiley, 1962.

Appendix A

SOME FREQUENTLY USED TESTS IN EARLY CHILDHOOD EDUCATION RESEARCH

Appendix A contains brief descriptions of several tests or scales used in early education research which have been referred to in the course of this book. It is important that a consumer keep in mind the important criteria of validity and reliability when evaluating and selecting a test for use with children. Validity concerns the degree to which a test actually measures what it is intended to measure; reliability refers to the degree of consistency or accuracy of test results. There are different kinds of validity and reliability and a full discussion of them will not be attempted here; the important point to note is that generalizations concerning children's test performance are no better than the means by which their performance is measured. Any standard textbook on psychological or educational measurement may be consulted for elaborated discussions of test characteristics and acceptable testing standards.

Basic Concept Inventory (Chicago: Follett, 1968)

This test was designed by Seigfried Engelmann for use with children ages 3 to 9. Most basically it is a criterion-reference test for the Bereiter-Engelmann language program, although its use need not be limited to children who participate in this program. According to Engelmann, the *Basic Concept Inventory* measures five related classes of behavior. These include a child's ability to (1) follow basic instructions and understand key content words used in such instructions, (2) understand size, color, and relational concepts, (3) repeat statements and answer questions implied by them, (4) identify word-sound relationships and patterns, and (5) deal correctly with number statements. The BCI must be administered on a one-to-one basis. No statistical statements concerning validity or reliability are included in the test manual.

Cincinnati Autonomy Test Battery (Cincinnati University: Department of Psychology, 1966)

The CATB was designed to measure "self-directed behaviors that facilitate effective problem solving among children." Several relatively distinct aspects of self-regulating behavior pertinent to the development of problem-solving skills are reportedly measured by the CATB. These aspects include curiosity, exploratory behavior, persistence, resistance to distraction, impulse control, reflectivity, analytic perceptual processes, innovative behavior, and social competence. From a theoretical standpoint, the CATB represents an "eclectic" approach to child development theory; it is further based upon a diverse package of current research interests in developmental psychology. Language responses required of children for performance throughout the CATB are not stringent. Neither are the instructions given to children excessively verbal. Technical details and an overview of the rationale of the CATB are due to be published in 1970.[1]

Illinois Test of Psycholinguistic Processes, revised edition (Urbana: University of Illinois Press, 1970)

The ITPA purports to assess twelve aspects of psycholinguistic functioning in children ages 2 to 10. These twelve aspects, ranging from auditory and visual reception to visual sequential memory and sound blending, have been conceptualized in terms of three dimensions. First, children's auditory-vocal and visual-motor behaviors comprise abilities labeled *channels of communication.* Receptive, organizing, and expressive processes comprise the second major dimension, the *psycholinguistic processes.* The third dimension consists of two *levels of organization,* the automatic and the representational. Assessment by way of the ITPA leads to the charting of individual profiles, or intra-individual differences, in terms of these dimensions. Emphasis has been placed upon the identification of major psycholinguistic deficits or disabilities

[1] Banta, T. J. "Tests for the Evaluation of Early Childhood Education: The Cincinnati Autonomy Test Battery." In Jerome Hellmuth (Ed.), *Cognitive Studies,* Vol. 1. New York: Brunner-Mazel, 1970, pp. 424–490.

which may require remediation. The ITPA is administered individually. Special training is required for its use.

Metropolitan Readiness Tests (New York: Harcourt, 1965)

Six subtests comprise the Metropolitan battery: word meaning, listening comprehension, perceptual recognition of similarities, recognition of lower-case alphabet letters, number knowledge, and perceptual-motor control (copying). In combination these tests are intended to provide an assessment of children's development in skills that contribute to "readiness for first grade instruction." The Metropolitan battery is ordinarily given at the end of kindergarten or the beginning of first grade. Results may be used to classify pupils on a "readiness" continuum. Such a classification is presumed to be helpful for teachers who desire more efficient management of their instructional efforts. At least minimal skill in the use of writing instruments and paper is prerequisite for children to whom the Metropolitan is administered. However, no special training is needed by teachers for the administration and scoring of these tests. Norms are based upon a nationwide sample of beginning first-graders. In general, the reliability of these tests is high and their prediction validity is encouraging. The Metropolitan is among the most popular of batteries currently used in public school kindergartens and primary grades.

Peabody Picture Vocabulary Test (Minneapolis: American Guidance Service, 1959)

The PPVT is assumed to measure recognition (hearing) vocabulary by having a child identify correct pictorial representations (from among four alternatives) in a series as the examiner speaks a word corresponding to each picture. It was originally designed to predict school success, and results obtained from its use are often taken to estimate roughly a child's "verbal intelligence." Items are arranged from simple to complex. This test is suitable for use with children of preschool age and beyond and is easily administered. Further, the PPVT requires little in the way of special training for scoring and interpretation. In general, the reliability of this test is satisfactory, and scores derived from its use are correlated positively with a wide range of other measures of verbal behavior. Of studies performed to date relevant to the validity of the PPVT for predicting school success, it appears that the test is more effective with children beyond age 7 than with those of nursery and kindergarten age. Extensive use has been made of the PPVT for the study of mentally retarded children.

Preschool Inventory (Princeton, N.J.: Educational Testing Service, 1967)

The *Preschool Inventory* was designed in relation to Project Head Start. Its purpose is to assess achievement in areas regarded as necessary foundations for early school success. These areas have been labeled concept activation–sensory, concept activation–numerical, personal-social responsiveness, and associative vocabulary. The *Preschool Inventory* has been used as a rough diagnostic test, that is, to identify selected "cultural handicaps," and as a gross measure of the impact of Head Start experience on children. Limited norms are provided (based on the performance of children ages 2 to 6½ identified as products of "lower-" and "middle-class" backgrounds). Like so many preschool tests, this inventory must also be administered individually. The reliability of this test appears to meet acceptable standards, although no empirical statement of validity is reported in the test manual.

Stanford-Binet Intelligence Scale (New York: Houghton Mifflin, 1960)

The present version (1960) of this widely used test of general intelligence is a result of successive refinements of the original Binet Scales developed in France around 1905. As revised, the Stanford-Binet is composed of tasks which require a variety of responses from children, including the identification of common objects, hand-eye coordinations, word definition, practical judgments, arithmetic computations, sentence completion, analogy completion, and problem interpretation. As such, the S-B is based on the assumption that samples of verbal and sensory-motor behavior taken from a child of a given chronological age can serve as an indication of the quality or magnitude of that child's underlying mental ability. The S-B is suitable for use with children as young as age 2 and its norms (1960 revision) extend to age 18. The intelligence quotient derived from the use of this scale is strongly predictive of academic achievement, particularly during the elementary school years. Thus, many users conceive of the S-B primarily as a measure of scholastic aptitude. Impressive data in reference to the validity and reliability of this scale have accumulated over the many years of its use.

The S-B is an individual intelligence test and special training is required for its administration and scoring.

Torrance Tests of Creative Thinking (Princeton, N.J.: Personnel Press, 1966)

Two sections, verbal and figural tests, comprise this experimental, or research battery. The first section includes four measures of verbal behavior: flexibility, fluency, elaboration, and originality. The second section is based upon the same four criteria but requires instead responses that are essentially drawing or pictorial in nature. Conceptually, these tests are based upon Torrance's extensive research into the development of creativity (divergent production) among children, much of which is referenced in the present book. The verbal portion is best used with children beyond grade 3 because of the writing requirements involved. It can, however, be administered individually to children as young as age 5. The figural form of the tests is suitable for kindergarten children and beyond. Persons interested in using this battery should familiarize themselves completely with Torrance's major works, including criteria for scoring children's test responses. Reliability and validity data for this battery seem adequate for research purposes.

Recently Developed Measures Designed for Use with Young Children

The following instruments have recently been made available for research and/or school use. However, since these tests have not been generally utilized in studies reported in this book, content descriptions will not be provided here. Those readers concerned with the survey of young children's pre-academic development and early school achievement may find some of these instruments useful.[2]

> *Assessment of Children's Language Comprehension: Research Edition* (Palo Alto, Calif.: Consulting Psychologists Press, 1969)
>
> *Boehm Test of Basic Concepts* (New York: The Psychological Corporation, 1968)

---

[2] For the reader interested in an overview of the most commonly used "traditional" mental measures for very young children, the following reference has much to recommend it: L. H. Stott, and Rachell S. Ball. "Infant and Preschool Mental Tests: Review and Evaluation." *Monographs of the Society for Research in Child Development,* 1965, 30, Serial No. 101, 151 pp.

Cognitive Abilities Test (Grades K–4) (New York: Houghton Mifflin, 1968)

Cooperative Primary Tests (Princeton, N.J.: Educational Testing Service, 1967)

First Grade Screening Test (Minneapolis: American Guidance Service, 1966)

New York City Project Materials (Princeton, N.J.: Educational Testing Service, 1965)

Preprimary Profile (Chicago: Science Research Associates, 1966)

Preschool Attainment Record (Minneapolis: American Guidance Service, 1966)

Preschool Language Scale (Columbus, Ohio: Charles E. Merrill, 1969)

Stanford Early School Achievement Test (Level I) (New York: Harcourt, 1969)

Valett Developmental Survey of Basic Learning Abilities (Palo Alto, Calif.: Consulting Psychologists Press, 1966)

The Vane Kindergarten Test (Brandon, Vt.: Clinical Psychology Publishing Co., 1968)

Wechsler Preschool and Primary Scale of Intelligence (New York: The Psychological Corporation, 1967)

Wide Range Achievement Test (Wilmington, Del.: Guidance Associates, 1965)

Appendix B

SCHOOL READINESS

All the programs and strategies discussed in the book are directly or indirectly enmeshed in the issue of school readiness. Preschool programs are ultimately concerned with salutary developmental effects on children's health, socio-emotional, and intellectual status.

Kindergarten programs generally encompass a variety of "readiness-building" activities, although school readiness is actually a global concept. And, in practice, school readiness has traditionally been viewed as a function of chronological age. Evidence for this clearly comes from the use of chronological age by educators as a criterion for school entrance. Unfortunately, a concept of school readiness based upon chronological age may lead to several incorrect assumptions, including that children generally manifest similar maturation rates and share common experiences that prepare them for formal classroom work. But perhaps the most common problem associated with readiness is a tendency to confuse readiness with maturation. The latter term, as Ausubel (1959) indicates, is most legitimately reserved for changes that occur as a function of genetic influences or in the absence of specific practice experience. Hence, readiness is more accurately the broader concept of the two; it includes *both* a child's repertoire of motivational responses and learned skills and his constitutional status. Readiness for a particular activity, such as school tasks, is certainly an individual matter. It is precisely this idea that has led to a concern for readiness as *behavior* rather than as chronological age alone.

An intensive study of general school readiness based upon behavioral assessment (versus age-cataloguing) was conducted by Frances Ilg and Louise Ames of the Gesell Institute (Ilg and Ames, 1965). These workers believe that decisions concerning school entrance should be made with accurate knowledge of every child's *developmental level*—not just his age, his physical maturity, or even his measured intelligence alone. This belief is also extended to the notion of using developmental data to individualize instruction and as a basis for judging the child's "readiness" for promotion to higher levels of formal school experience (correct grade placement). One result of this line of investigation has been the construction of a developmental examination suitable for children ages 5 to 10. Specific components of the examination include:

1. *Initial Interview*—questions about age, birthdate, favorite activities, siblings (names and ages), and father's occupation.
2. *Pencil and Paper Tests*—writing name (or letters), address, numbers 1–20; copying six basic geometric forms and two three-dimensional forms; completing an Incomplete Man figure and giving his facial expression.
3. *Right and Left*—naming parts and sides of one's body, executing single and double commands, responding to a series of pictures of a pair of hands in which two fingers are touching (a verbal response is required, followed by a motor response).
4. *Form Tests*—matching geometric forms, a test of memory for forms or designs.
5. *Naming of Animals for 60 Seconds*—This item seeks to assess the tempo and organization of the child's thinking, his capacity to range, and the degree to which he sustains effort.
6. *Concluding Interview*—topics include home and play activities, both indoors and outdoors.
7. *Dental Examination*—assessment of teething rate, including both eruption and decay or fillings.

For supplementary use the Lowenfeld Mosaic Test is also used.

The interested reader may wish to consult Ilg and Ames (1965) for the scoring of this examination and the rationale behind each component. For the moment, however, the effectiveness of this approach for the prediction of school progress is of concern. Validating data submitted by the Gesell Institute include measurements from a longitudinal study of fifty-two children (Ames and Ilg, 1964). The examination was administered to these children at the time they entered kindergarten. On the basis of chronological age, all children were judged "ready" by school standards, although roughly half of the sample was judged "unready" or of "questionable readiness" on the basis of examination performance. The predictions made for the children at kindergarten entrance were then checked against school performance six years later. The correlation between sixth-grade school performance and readiness test performance for these children was .74, a strong positive relationship. By comparison, a correlation of only .54 was found between kindergarten IQ and sixth-grade performance. These results have been taken as evidence that better predictions of school success are possible by using the readiness battery than are likely using intelligence scales such as the Stanford-Binet. Moreover, Ilg and Ames found that all children initially judged "unready" at age 5 (17 percent of the original kindergarten group) were either in the lowest sixth-grade achievement group or had failed a grade and were operating in fifth-grade groups.

It is possible that school entry assessments more specific to academic skill development than the Gesell battery can increase prediction efficiency still further. For example, remarkably accurate predictions of early failure in reading and spelling achievement in grade 2 have resulted from a kindergarten readiness battery developed by Hirsch, Jansky, and Langford (1966). Regardless, Ilg and Ames have demonstrated the advantages of an approach to school readiness more specific than that which considers only general intelligence and/or chronological age. As a criterion, chronological age, together with instruments such as the Metropolitan Readiness Test, continues to dominate public school policies with respect to school entrance and class placement (Goslin, Epstein, and Hallock, 1965). Further, indications are that maximum use may not even be made of intelligence and reading readiness tests (Goslin, 1967). The limitation of such instruments may actually contribute to their own downfall. That is, if teachers do not find these instruments useful, the desirability of more relevant assessment techniques and teachers trained in how to use them is indicated.

One implication of the Gesell approach to school readiness is that if a child demonstrates insufficient readiness he should be held out of school until such time as more adequate readiness is exhibited.[1] Such a policy may not be acceptable to many educators, or to parents for that matter. Ausubel (1958, 1959), for example, believes that the solution to the problem is not the exclusion of a "less ready" child from school. Instead, he maintains that the problem is that of adjusting one's teaching methods and materials to a child's current level of functioning. In this case, a school program may assume responsibility for increasing

[1] Hopefully this strategy would not be motivated by a belief that "aging" will "cure" the readiness problem.

the readiness level of a child through an appropriate programming of experiences. This strategy will not obviate the need for a precise assessment of a child's behavior at the time of school entrance. The reader will recall that this emphasis upon entering behavior assessment to determine educational departure points is a matter of principle in precision teaching (see Chapter 5).

A synthesis of several authoritative statements about readiness indicates a set of questions useful for teachers concerned with this problem (Ausubel, 1958; Tyler, 1964; Gagné, 1965). This set of questions implies that educational readiness may be conceived, not in terms of school generally or of broad subject-matter areas, but in terms of specific requirements that vary with teaching methods and learning materials:

1. What, exactly, must the child know or be capable of in order to learn whatever it is I plan to teach in the manner I plan to teach it? (Task analysis)
2. To what degree does the child have at his command these prerequisite or subordinate skills and knowledge? (Assessment)
3. Is this child capable of attending sufficiently to this task so that he may master? (Motivation)
4. Can efficient learning be accomplished at this time? (Economy)

As Tyler (1964) has observed, the criterion of efficient accomplishment is significant for those who reject the notion that a child's "mere capacity" to perform at some ineffective level is sufficient justification to initiate formal instruction. Perhaps a more defensible position is to delay such instruction until the child can reap greater benefits.

As far as readiness for school entry is concerned, one must consider both the child's readiness—physical, socio-emotional, and intellectual—*and* what the school expects of children when they arrive (Brandt, 1970). It would seem that minimum guidelines for dealing with the readiness issue are precise assessment and flexibility in educational programming.

References

Ames, Louise B., and Frances L. Ilg. "Gesell Behavior Tests as Predictive of Later Grade Placement." *Perceptual and Motor Skills,* 1964, 19, 719–722.

Ausubel, David P. *Theory and Problems in Child Development.* New York: Grune and Stratton, 1958.

Ausubel, David P. "Viewpoints from Related Disciplines." *Teachers College Record,* 1959, 60, 245–254.

Brandt, Richard M. "The Readiness Issue Today." *The Record,* 1970, 71, 439–449.

Gagné, Robert. *The Conditions of Learning.* New York: Holt, Rinehart, and Winston, 1965.

Goslin, David. *Teachers and Testing.* New York: Russell Sage, 1967.

Goslin, David, Roberta Epstein, and Barbara Hallock. *The Use of Standardized Tests in Elementary Schools. Technical Report No. 2, The Social Consequences of Testing.* New York: Russell Sage, 1965.

Hirsch, K., J. J. Jansky, and W. S. Langford. *Predicting Reading Failure.* New York: Harper & Row, 1966.

Ilg, Frances L., and Louise B. Ames. *School Readiness,* New York: Harper & Row, 1965.

Jensen, Arthur R. *Understanding Readiness.* Urbana, Ill.: ERIC Clearinghouse on Early Childhood Education, 1969.

Tyler, Fred T. "Issues Related to Readiness to Learn." *Theories of Learning and Instruction.* 63rd NSSE Yearbook, Chicago: University of Chicago Press, 1964, 210–239.

Appendix C

A LISTING OF PRINCIPAL PREPRIMARY PROGRAMS FOR YOUNG CHILDREN

Following is a listing of many current preprimary and primary grade programs, most of which have been mentioned in this book. Included are the names and addresses of program authors or sponsors. Starred (*) entries indicate Project Follow Through Programs. While this list is far from inclusive, it does indicate most of the programs from which research data have been generated during the past several years. It should also be noted that most of these programs represent a strong cognitive-language development orientation, an orientation that is reflected throughout much of the present book.

Ameliorative Curriculum for Early Childhood Education
    Merle B. Karnes, Institute for Research on Exceptional Children, University of Illinois, Urbana, Illinois
*Autotelic-Discovery Approach to Early Childhood Education (Responsive Environment)
    Glen Nimnicht, Far West Laboratory for Educational Research and Development, Berkeley, California
*Bank Street Early Education Program
    Elizabeth C. Gilkeson, Bank Street College of Education, New York, New York
*Behavior Analysis: Research Approach to Early Education
    Don Bushell, Jr., University of Kansas, Lawrence, Kansas
Behavior Oriented Prescriptive Teaching Approach
    Walter L. Hodges, State College of Arkansas, Conway, Arkansas
*Cognitive-Developmental Curriculum for Young Children
    David P. Weikart, Eastern Michigan University, and Ypsilanti Public Schools, Ypsilanti, Michigan

*Community-Controlled Model for Early Education (Parent-Implemented Program)
    Anthony Ward, East Harlem Block Schools, New York, New York
*Continuing Growth Plan for Early Childhood Education
    David E. Armington, Education Development Center, Newton, Massachusetts
*Demonstration and Research Center for Early Education (DARCEE)
    Rosemary Giesy, George Peabody College, Nashville, Tennessee
Durham Education Improvement Program
    Robert L. Spaulding, Information Office, Mutual Plaza, Durham, North Carolina
*Florida Parent Education Model
    Ira J. Gordon, Institute for Development of Human Resources, College of Education, University of Florida, Gainesville, Florida
*Hampton Institute Nongraded Early Education Model
    Martha E. Dawson, Department of Elementary Education, Hampton Institute, Hampton, Virginia
*Home-School Partnership: A Motivational Approach
    Edward E. Johnson, Southern University, Baton Rouge, Louisiana
Institute of Developmental Studies Early Stimulation Program
    Martin Deutsch, 465 West End Avenue, New York, New York
*Instructional Games-Independent Learner Program
    Lassar G. Gotkin, Early Childhood Learning and Development Center, New Jersey State Department of Education, Newark, New Jersey
*Language Development-Bilingual Education Approach
    Elizabeth Ott, Southwest Educational Development Laboratory, Austin, Texas
*Learning To Learn Program for Early Childhood Education
    Herbert A. Sprigle, 1936 San Marco Blvd., Jacksonville, Florida
*Morgan Community School Model for Early Education
    John Cawthorne, Morgan Community School, Washington, D.C.
*Oral Language Approach to Cognitive Development (Cultural Linguistic Program
    Nancy L. Arnez, Center for Inner City Studies, Northeastern Illinois State College, Chicago, Illinois

Pennsylvania Preschool and Primary Education Project
   K. M. Kershner, State Departments of Education and Public
   Welfare, Harrisburg, Pennsylvania
Precision Teaching for Behavior Modification
   Norris Haring, Experimental Education Unit, University of
   Washington, Seattle, Washington
Preschool Language Remediation Project
   Carolyn Stern, Southwestern Regional Laboratory, 11300
   La Cienaga Blvd., Inglewood, California
*Primary Education Project and Individually Prescribed Instruction
   Lauren B. Resnick, Learning Research and Development
   Center, University of Pittsburgh, Pittsburgh, Pennsylvania
Project CHILD: Curriculum for Intellectual and Language Development
   Helen Robison, Teachers College, Columbia University, New
   York, New York
*Pupil-Parent-Teacher Model for Early Childhood Education
   South Central Region Education Laboratory, National Old
   Line Building, Little Rock, Arkansas
*Research and Development Center in Educational Stimulation
   (Georgia Follow-Through Model)
   Robert Aaron, University of Georgia, Athens, Georgia
*Systematic Use of Behavioral Principles in Early Education
   Wesley C. Becker and Seigfried Engelmann, University of
   Oregon, Eugene, Oregon
*Tucson Early Education Model
   Ronald W. Henderson, Early Childhood Education Laboratory, University of Arizona, Tucson, Arizona
University of Hawaii Preschool Language Curriculum
   Dorothy Adkins, College of Education, University of Hawaii,
   Honolulu
Verbal Behavior Laboratory
   S. M. Sapon, Fauver Hall, University of Rochester, Rochester,
   New York
*Virginia Union Model for Early Education
   Dorothy N. Cowling, Virginia Union University, Richmond,
   Virginia
Ypsilanti Early Education Program
   Constance Kamii, Ypsilanti Public Schools, Ypsilanti, Michigan

Index

355